D0699619

COBB

Would Have Caught It

Navin Field on opening day, 1930. (Courtesy of the Burton Historical Collection of the Detroit Public Library.)

COBB

Would Have Caught It

THE GOLDEN AGE
OF BASEBALL
IN DETROIT

Richard Bak

 WAYNE STATE UNIVERSITY PRESS   DETROIT

GREAT LAKES BOOKS

A complete listing of the books in this series can be found at the back of this volume.

PHILIP P. MASON, EDITOR
Walter P. Reuther Library, Wayne State University

DR. CHARLES K. HYDE, ASSOCIATE EDITOR
Department of History, Wayne State University

Library of Congress Cataloging-in-Publication Data

Bak, Richard, 1954–
Cobb would have caught it : the golden age of baseball in Detroit
/ Richard Bak.
p.   cm. —(Great Lakes books)
Includes index.
ISBN 0-8143-2355-3   (alk. paper). —ISBN 0-8143-2356-1
(pbk. : alk. paper)
1. Detroit Tigers (Baseball team)—History.   2. Baseball players—
Michigan—Detroit—Interviews.   3. Detroit (Mich.)—History—20th
century.   I. Title.   II. Series.
GV875.D6B35   1991
796.357'64'0977434—dc20   91–4156

Book design by Mary Krzewinski

For Mary, Hilary, and Rosemary

Contents

Contents

Introduction

Whenever I read about how technology is reshaping baseball as it enters a new century, I can't help thinking of George Uhle.

The stocky right-handed pitcher, whose story appears in this book, played for the Cleveland Indians and Detroit Tigers in the 1920s and 1930s. More than a half-century later, he remained a competitor with a heart of oak. This was evident on a July day in 1982 when I visited with the old ball player inside his suburban Cleveland home. Although George depended on oxygen tubes to battle the emphysema that would claim him nearly three years later, he graciously passed an afternoon recounting his days in the major leagues.

Blessed with an easy laugh and remarkable recall, George's wit and charm filled the room like a warm fire. His story telling was interrupted by occasional spells of coughing, but he would just excuse himself and, after taking a few moments to recuperate, move onto another tale. It was easy to see how such tenacity, coupled to talent, could product two hundred major-league wins and 393 career base hits. Although those are impressive totals for a pitcher in the pre-designated-hitter era, I can't help reflecting on how those numbers, not quite Hall of Fame credentials, might have been improved upon had he the benefit of today's technology.

Thanks to advances in sports medicine and physical conditioning, it's not unusual for a pitcher to remain effective—even overpowering—long past his thirty-seventh birthday, the age at which George Uhle retired in 1936. For example, high-speed shuttered cameras shooting up to a thousand frames per second can film a pitcher's motion from different angles. The video is then analyzed by a computer that prescribes exercises to build specific muscles. By contrast, George—whose work load created chronic arm problems so severe he more than once pitched a game underhanded— resorted to having his arm regularly stretched in a method borrowed from the Inquisition. His conditioning was limited to soaking a winter's worth of beer and sausage in the mineral baths of Hot Springs, Arkansas, before heading to spring training. The scientific knowledge that might have prolonged George Uhle's career simply didn't exist when he played. If it had, his right arm might have produced another forty or fifty victories and a ticket to Cooperstown. To his credit, the old ball player saw no need to complain. The man who had never even thought to keep the ball from his two hundredth career victory was truly happy, he stressed, just for the chance to play major-league ball when he did.

A simple love of a more primitive game emerges as the central theme of this book, which contains the autobiographies of George Uhle and sixteen of his contemporaries from Detroit's golden age of baseball. By any measure, the period from 1920 through the early post-World War II years remains the greatest in the long history of the Detroit Tigers Baseball Club. Between 1920 and 1950 the club won four pennants and two World Series, placed second seven times, and regularly fielded exciting, competitive teams. It only occasionally experienced a losing season and, until 1952, was the only major-league club never to finish last. Only the New York Yankees consistently drew larger crowds in the American League than the Tigers.

This was a time of exceptional talent. The Tigers' rosters between 1920 and 1950 were loaded with future Hall of Famers such as Ty Cobb, Harry Heilmann, and Heinie Manush, heavy-hitting outfielders who in one twenty-one-year stretch won seventeen batting titles between them. There also was the "G-Men" trio of Charlie Gehringer, Hank Greenberg, and Goose Goslin; fiery playing manager Mickey Cochrane; slick-fielding George Kell; and a host of others. Visiting teams regularly checked into Navin Field (and after 1938, Briggs Stadium) with lineups similarly filled with stars: Babe Ruth, Lou Gehrig, Al Simmons, Jimmie Foxx, Lefty Grove, Walter Johnson, George Sisler, Tris Speaker, Joe Sewell, Luke Appling, Ted Lyons, Bill Dickey, Ted Williams, Joe DiMaggio, and Bob Feller. World Series and All-Star Games produced brief appearances by

Dizzy and Daffy Dean and the "Gas House Gang" Cardinals, as well as other National League stars like Phil Cavaretta, Gabby Hartnett, Frank McCormick, and Arky Vaughan. With football and other professional sports in their infancies in the 1920s and 1930s, baseball attracted the best athletes and would continue to do so through the 1950s. The Darwinian nature of competition—there was a peak of 461 minor-league clubs in operation in 1949, or about twenty-three bush leaguers for every major leaguer—assured a caliber of play that has never been approached.

Personalities abounded. There was the mercurial Cobb, who put the hell in baseball during his twenty-two seasons in Detroit. Of more buoyant disposition were characters like Bob "Fats" Fothergill, a solid .300 hitter who just barely managed to hit more than his weight; Rudy York, the powerful Cherokee who was described as "part Indian, part first baseman" and led the league in both home runs and burned mattresses; and Gerald "Gee" Walker, a free spirit who pursued life in the same fashion he ran the bases—like a rogue elephant. The Tigers started radio broadcasts of its games in 1927 and telecasts in 1948, but the homogenization of American culture and behavior was still a generation or two away. Meanwhile, unaffected young men with outsized personalities and Runyonesque names like Stinky, Bobo, Flea, Chief, Schoolboy, Jo-Jo, Skeeter, and Dizzy continued to carry their grips from odd corners of the map to the cozy green cathedral at Trumbull and Michigan avenues, where the congregation cheered them with a religious fervor.

"You know, I played with the Senators for 12 years, the Browns for two, and the Tigers for four, and the best baseball town I ever played in and for was Detroit. The fans there were great," Goose Goslin, a popular outfielder of the 1930s, told Lawrence Ritter in his classic *The Glory of Their Times:*

> I *always* had a rooting section behind me in those left-field stands in Detroit. Mostly school kids, they'd have whole sections of the upper stands roped off for them. When I came up they'd all yell, "Yeah, Goose!" I loved it. We weren't allowed to throw balls into the stands, you know, but I'd always take four balls out with me, in my back pockets, when I went out for fielding practice. And just before I went back in, after I'd taken my throws, I'd sail them up to the kids.

Although organized baseball was first played in Detroit by amateur social clubs in the late 1850s, it took time for the town to warm

to the pro game. When Detroit's first professional baseball club began playing in 1881 at Recreation Park (a site now occupied by Harper Hospital), the city was a drowsy commercial center of 120,000
souls. The community went wild when the Detroits won the 1887
National League pennant and then defeated St. Louis of the American Association in a fifteen-game, cross-country play-off. But
within a year the cheers had turned into yawns, forcing the club to
fold after the 1888 season. A new franchise resurfaced in the Western League in 1894. This club, which by 1896 had been nicknamed
the "Tigers," became a charter member of the American League
when the Western League declared itself major in 1900. Games
were played at a rickety wooden park at Michigan and Trumbull.
Although the Tigers were the league's first powerhouse of the dead-
ball era, winning three straight pennants between 1907 and 1909,
attendance lagged. Not until after the advent of Sunday ball in
1910, the construction of a larger, modern concrete ballpark in
1912, and the introduction of a livelier ball in the 1920s was the
club able to take full advantage of the city's extraordinary population boom.

The 1920 census revealed Detroit to be the nation's fourth largest city—a noisy, sprawling, polytongued metropolis of nearly one
million people. By the twenties only Henry Ford was receiving
more local ink than Ty Cobb, quite an accomplishment in a city
that, thanks to the automobile, had more than its share of industrial, business, and civic heroes. Although three-quarters of the citizenry were immigrants or the children of immigrants, baseball
spoke a universal language. A factory hand recently arrived from
Sweden or Poland might know only a few phrases of broken En-
glish, but it was a good bet they included "hit the ball!" or "kill the
ump!" or even "yea, Goose!"

During this period professional baseball in Detroit completed
its evolution from a curiosity to a diversion to a municipal symbol
of almost spiritual significance. Even as fortunes waned during the
Great Depression, citizens found salvation in a winning team.
When Mickey Cochrane delivered a pair of pennants in the mid-
1930s, newspapers lionized the fiery playing manager as "the man
who made Detroit forget." By midcentury the game was so tightly
woven into the collective experiences of America that even a world
war wasn't reason enough to suspend it. As the city approached its
population peak of nearly two million during the postwar boom,
Detroiters jammed the ballpark in record numbers, including

twelve of the thirteen largest single-day crowds in club history between 1946 and 1950.

On the surface, it's easy to romance these years. While the rest of society was undergoing tremendous changes, baseball remained a bedrock of stability. Between 1903 and 1953, sixteen clubs played in eleven major-league cities without a single franchise shift; Detroit, Chicago, Cincinnati, and St. Louis were the western outposts. Technology was making inroads, with Cincinnati introducing night ball in 1935, but most games until World War II were played in the afternoon, under God's own lamp. (The ever iconclastic Tigers didn't install lights until 1948, the next-to-last major-league club to do so.) It was still an age of hand-operated scoreboards, train travel, and Fourth of July doubleheaders, a time when players spent most of their free hours hanging around hotel lobbies discussing yesterday's game and waiting for someone to drop a newspaper.

However, in a sinister way baseball resembled the smoking room in a private club. Franchises were not yet owned by faceless corporations, but by a handful of highly individualistic families and "sportsmen" tied together by mutual self-interest. It was inside this cozy environ that Tigers' owner Frank Navin operated.

Navin, a savvy, poker-faced accountant who gained control of the club in 1909, thought nothing of dropping several thousands of dollars in a single day at the racetrack. Yet when it came to contracts, he could nurse a nickel with the best of them. The reserve clause, which bound a player to one club as surely as leg irons, allowed owners to adopt a "take it or leave it" stance during difficult contract negotiations. In those days before free agency, a player who decided to "leave it" was ineligible to play until he came to terms or his club sold or traded him. In extreme cases, a dissident could be blacklisted from ever playing organized ball again.

On balance, Navin was a fair employer, one who could impulsively give a bonus for an outstanding performance or quietly take care of the affairs of a down-and-out former ball player. But no-trade, guaranteed, and multiple-year contracts were unheard of in Detroit, as elsewhere. A player had to prove himself year after year, which, if nothing else, guaranteed hard play up to the final pitch of the final game of the season. Baseball, after all, was a business, even if it was run more like a lemonade stand than General Motors. Charlie Gehringer remembers being docked three days' pay for attending his father's funeral in 1924, and Ed Mierkowicz recalls the day he went to see management about a raise. "Can you do anything else besides play baseball?" asked general manager Billy Evans. "You want to go work at Wyandotte Chemicals over there?" The young outfielder didn't want to work in a plant, but within a few years that's precisely what he was doing.

There may have been room in the game for novelties like one-armed outfielders and pinch-hitting midgets, but Navin and other owners honored a gentleman's agreement to bar bona fide Negro league stars like Oscar Charleston, Buck Leonard, and Josh Gibson from playing because of the color of their skins. The attitude of Walter O. Briggs, a silent partner who took over the Tigers upon Navin's death in 1935, was typical. Briggs had made his fortune manufacturing auto bodies. Although he employed more blacks in his sweatshops than any boss in Detroit other than Henry Ford, and although the city had one of the largest black populations in the north, Briggs insisted on a segregated club. Not until 1958—two years after the Briggs family had sold the club and eleven years after Jackie Robinson had broken the majors' color line with the Brooklyn Dodgers—did the Tigers finally bring up a black player. It was the next-to-last major-league club to do so. More than any other single factor, the refusal to develop black athletes spelled the end of the Tigers' golden age after the early 1950s.

*   *   *

With the thought that memories, unlike statistics, are a perishable commodity, I spent much of my free time between 1980 and 1990 recording the life stories of the forgotten men who, in their blousy knickers and pancake gloves, had once fueled a city's passion. With varying degrees of difficulty, I found nearly a score whose careers had fallen between 1920 and the early 1950s. There was no pattern to how life had treated them since their playing days. Some had stayed in the game as broadcasters or scouts; others had slipped into quiet anonymity as milkmen or machine repairmen.

The one constant were their generous gifts of time and reflection. I typically spent several hours inside the subject's home or place of business, taping our conversation and taking notes. In several instances I followed up with phone calls or correspondence to clarify a point or to pose questions I had originally failed to ask. I then edited the transcriptions, correcting errors of fact, eliminating redundancies and false starts, creating transitions where necessary, and rearranging passages to produce a smoother, more chronological narrative. At all times I strived to retain the flavor of the man's speech and the integrity of his character.

I decided from the start not to concentrate on just familiar names from Detroit's baseball past, but to collect as representative a cross section of former players as possible. Thus I not only talked with Hall of Famers like Charlie Gehringer and George Kell, I visited with unknowns like Bill Moore, Ed Mierkowicz, and George Lerchen, men who pursued their schoolboy dreams of big-league glory with the same dogged passion, if somewhat lesser skills, of their better-known counterparts. Along the way I discovered that the story of a man who spent a single afternoon in the major leagues can be as compelling as that of someone who stayed two decades. I also decided that, to put the past in perspective and give the reader a sense of time and place, it would be wise to preface the players' interviews with a short history of the parallel paths the city and professional baseball took from the end of World War I through the early 1950s. Included is a look at Detroit's all-but-forgotten black professional teams, particularly the Detroit Stars of the 1920s, who, owing to the Jim Crow practices of society then, had to play the game they loved in the cool shadow of anonymity. A result is a peak into the mind and soul of professional baseball as it was played in a dynamic, if racially polarized, city fifty, sixty, and even seventy years ago.

It's no secret that the summers since have not exactly been kind to fans who can remember that as recently as 1953, ball players still left their gloves on the field between innings. Many undoubtedly feel that as the game has matured, something more substantial than gloves has been left behind. The Briggs family's sale of the Tigers in 1956 to a syndicate headed by radio-television executive John E. Fetzer not only marked the end of an era in Detroit, it indicated the direction baseball was to take in the 1960s. To the distress of traditionalists, the game since has courted and accommodated the forces of television and advertising with the dignity of a drunk chasing a windblown dollar bill. The payoff—and backlash—have been spectacular. Television revenue has raised the average ball player's salary from $7,300 in 1939 to nearly $500,000 a half-century later.

However, in the process the one-eyed box also destroyed hundreds of minor-league clubs and ushered in an era of expansion, franchise shifts, player strikes, and owner lockouts. And as corporations have replaced individuals as club owners, tradition and competition have been diluted for the sake of entertainment and profit. "The trouble with baseball," Russell Baker moaned after club owners adopted artificial turf, the designated hitter, and divisional play in the 1960s and 1970s, "is that it grew up and became engineering." All of this has weakened the national pastime's perceived and real bonds to a simpler, more innocent past.

It was inevitable that the ball players I interviewed would address the popular hot-stove debate about whether baseball in their time was superior to today's. Their remarks for the most part were predictably caustic, but they were also at times surprisingly generous. Most of them remain bewildered by exploding scoreboards and love to grumble over multimillion-dollar, guaranteed contracts. But they also concede that getting around on a ninety-two-mile-an-hour fastball or stretching a double into a triple is no less difficult today than it was in 1929. Most reasonably assume that a modern player with the skills of an Alan Trammell or Lou Whitaker could have excelled in any era, just as "old-timers" with the tools and dedication of Ty Cobb or Hank Greenberg could dominate the modern game—and command today's fat salaries. And while all agree that expansion has watered down the caliber of play, many are understandably envious of the employment and pension opportunities today's expanded leagues provide even marginal ball players of questionable heart and talent. "I was born fifty years too early," lamented John Bogart, who labored a dozen years in the minor leagues before surrendering his dream of big-league glory.

For all the changes that have taken place since John Bogart and the other men in this book have hung up their spikes, it should be remembered that the Detroit Tigers is still one of baseball's most tradition-bound clubs. Pennants have been won and lost at the corner of Michigan and Trumbull for nearly a century now. Even the famous old-English D on the front of the uniform blouse has survived from the nineteenth century. The individual names and faces are forever changing, and the hot-stove league may now employ microwave ovens, but the game's basics are timeless. The grass, the sun, the ball, and the rituals continue on, building pitch upon pitch, inning upon inning, game upon game, season upon season, generation upon generation. Perhaps one day technology or some benevolent baseball god will resurrect George Uhle and a squad of his contemporaries and have them square off against a modern nine. Until that magical time, the safest thing that can be said about baseball in Detroit's golden age is not that the game was better or worse then but, as the following pages illustrate, that it was decidedly different.

PART ONE

SUMMERS

1

A Place in the Sun

One day in December 1913, a thousand men gathered inside the Pontchartrain Hotel in downtown Detroit to discuss the financing of a new and grand athletic facility to be built at the corner of Madison and John R. Although a first bond issue of $500,000 had earlier been subscribed, a second, larger issue of mortgage bonds needed to be sold before construction of the Detroit Athletic Club could begin.

Six hundred thousand dollars was needed, a considerable sum but small matter. In a single boisterous meeting the entire second issue was subscribed, as a thousand of the city's movers and shakers rocked the room with wave after wave of cheers.

Another landmark, Orchestra Hall, was built with similar gusto. In early 1919, world-famous pianist Ossip Gabrilowitsch refused the conductorship of the fledgling Detroit Symphony Orchestra unless a permanent home could be found for it by that autumn. Detroiters rolled up their sleeves. A building fund of $700,000 was collected and the site of the Westminster Presbyterian Church on Woodward Avenue bought. As the last wedding at the old church was held, workmen waited outside with picks and shovels, impatiently waiting to begin demolition.

An amazing four months and seventeen days later, a world-class concert hall with acoustics rivaling the best in Europe had been built. On opening night, when a full house of 2,018 Detroiters greeted Gabrilowitsch with a five-minute standing ovation, they could just as well have been applauding the sheer dynamism and unbridled optimism of the new century's golden city.

For this was Detroit as it roared past World War I and into the 1920s, a boomtown flush with enthusiasm, confidence, and money. Its evolution from a drowsy, well-ordered community by the river to a frenetic industrial anthill could be traced by the changing mottoes of its billboards and postcards, from the mellifluous "Detroit the Beautiful" and "Detroit, Where Life Is Worth Living" to the simple and direct "Dynamic Detroit." It was "a city of beauty, homes, action, and friendliness," recalled Josephine Fox Fink, whose family emigrated from New York in 1917. "There was electricity in the air and anticipation of what might come next."

Certainly Detroit was at the cutting edge of the decade that finally put to rest the slower-paced, agrarian nineteenth century. In 1896, the year Charles Brady King maneuvered the city's first automobile down Jefferson Avenue and the Western League "Tigers" moved their bats and balls to the site of an old hay market at the northwest corner of Michigan and Trumbull, Detroit's population stood at a comfortable 240,000. There were factories then, but even after Ransom E. Olds opened the city's first auto manufacturing plant in 1899 they were better known for producing stoves, cigars, shoes, pharmaceuticals, and refrigerated railroad cars. As for transportation, Detroiters used buggies, horses, electric streetcars, and good old-fashioned shoe leather in conducting their affairs. A city that many called the "Paris of the West" was ringed by a magnificent tree-lined boulevard of fashionable homes that was justifiably named Grand.

By 1920, however, the automobile had irreversibly changed the face of Detroit and the rest of the world. The city suddenly was the mecca of the new industrial age, thanks to visionaries like Henry Leland, the Dodge brothers, David Buick, Henry B. Joy, and Henry Ford (whose perfected mass-production techniques alone were responsible for putting an incredible fifteen million Model T's on the road by 1927). Immigrants, journalists, and luminaries from all fields were drawn to the city's cacophonous car factories, which were the wonder and symbol of modern times. Young men, fresh arrivals from amoeba-sized communities in Poland, Italy, Ireland,

and Sweden, were overwhelmed by the sheer size and din of Ford's Highland Park plant, which employed more than 68,000 workers in 1924, and the 1,115-acre Rouge Complex, the greatest industrial facility in the world, which by 1929 had more than 103,000 workers. A *Collier's* writer visiting the Highland Park plant wrote of its "interminable aisles, its whirling shafts and wheels, its forest of roof-supporting posts and flapping, flying leather belting, its endless rows of writhing machinery, its shrieking, hammering and clatter, its smell of oil, its autumn haze of smoke, its savage-looking foreign population—to my mind it expressed but one thing, and that thing was delirium."

Delirium, indeed. With more than 150,000 registered cars in the city in 1920—a figure that would climb to 500,000 by the end of the decade—traffic had all the organization of a dropped plate of

Automobiles and ball players—Detroit produced classic versions of both during the 1920s. Here, in front of the Richards-Oakland dealership on Milwaukee Avenue, future Hall of Famer Charlie Gehringer takes delivery of a spanking-new 1927 Oakland Six landau coupe, one of some 3.4 million cars to roll off the assembly line that year. In 1903, the year Gehringer was born on a farm outside Fowlerville, Michigan, there were only 11,235 cars built in the U.S. (Courtesy of John A. Conde.)

spaghetti. Cars competed for space with pedestrians, pushcarts, streetcars, horse-drawn wagons, bicyclists, and trains. No one had foreseen the automobile when most of the city's houses, factories, and office buildings were built in the nineteenth century. The subsequent lack of garages ("car barns"), parking lots, and paved roads meant that it was every man for himself, with right-of-way frequently awarded to the driver with the superior pugilistic skills. While the city hastily tore down buildings and widened streets in a desperate attempt to alleviate the madness, motorists continued to double- and triple-park on lawns, sidewalks, and in alleys. Traffic towers, a policeman stationed in each, were built at a handful of intersections, but motorists treated them more like racing pylons. And though Detroit recorded its first traffic fatality in 1902, not until World War I was the first traffic signal—a bicycle lamp attached to an iron pipe—installed at the corner of Woodward and Grand River.

Meanwhile, people continued to pour into Detroit. During the twenties city limits pushed out beyond Grand Boulevard, swallowing the satellite communities of Highland Park and Hamtramck in the process. Along the major spokes leading in and out of the city—Grand River, Michigan, Jefferson, and Woodward avenues—farms and vacant land gave way to subdivisions and industry. This massive urbanization was not peculiar to Detroit. The 1920 census revealed that for the first time there were more Americans living in urban areas than on farms. Although in 1920 there were still twice as many horses as there were cars, by the end of the decade that ratio, thanks to Detroit, had been reversed. When the city's last horse-drawn fire engine made its final run down Woodward Avenue in the spring of 1922, it symbolized a remarkable transformation that had in a quarter-century changed Detroit into the country's fourth-largest city, with more than one million people.

Despite considerable growing pains, Detroit was popping its vest buttons over its status as the world's foremost industrial city. Citizens seemed obsessed with being either the first, best, or largest in every endeavor. Newspapers wrote constantly of the world's greatest industrialist, Henry Ford; its greatest architect, Albert Kahn; and its greatest baseball player, Ty Cobb. The city even claimed a proprietary share of the greatest individual feat of the decade. When Charles Lindbergh crossed the Atlantic in 1927 in the *Spirit of St. Louis*, Detroiters were aware that the famous aviator had been born at 1120 West Forest Avenue and that at the time of his nonstop solo flight to Paris his mother was teaching at Cass Technical High School.

This quest to be best was an amalgam of civic-mindedness and mindlessness. Crowds cheered on sixteen couples participating in a ninety-six-hour dance marathon at the Majestic Institute in April 1923, then cheered even louder that Armistice Day when the J. L. Hudson Company unfurled the world's largest flag, a 90-by-123-foot banner that covered the front of its downtown store. Such energy was contagious and spread to new construction. In an eighteen-day stretch in 1927, for example, the Detroit Institute of Arts, Olympia Stadium, and City Airport all opened. A list of all new construction during the 1920s would include the General Motors Building, the Main Library, the Fisher Building, the Ambassador Bridge, the Fox Theatre, and the forty-seven-story Penobscot Building, the tallest of all the skyscrapers erected during the decade. "We have the biggest of nearly everything," boasted the 1925–26 edition of the *Detroit City Directory*, "the tallest building, the biggest electric sign, the longest bridge, the most money." Against this backdrop of tremendous population growth, unparalleled economic prosperity, and swelling civic pride, Detroit finally emerged as a major-league town in the years after World War I.

The Detroit Tigers had started play in the city's bicentennial year of 1901. As demonstrated by its quick succession of owners, the club in its early years was both a plaything and a losing business proposition. The original owner, Wayne County sheriff and hotel owner James Burns, sold the club to insurance agent Sam Angus in 1902. Two years later Angus sold it for fifty thousand dollars to Bill Yawkey, the playboy heir to a lumber fortune. Yawkey in turn sold a ten percent interest to the club's owlish bookkeeper, Frank Navin. Yawkey enjoyed being pals with the players and occasionally watched a game. But being a hands-on owner bored the young multimillionaire, who preferred the night life in New York to early mornings in Detroit. He turned over daily operations to Navin, then sold him the club outright in the fall of 1909.

Although he would later be considered a model citizen, at the time the thirty-eight-year-old Navin did not enjoy a savory reputation among the city's silk-stocking crowd. Bald, fat, and placid, Navin was an unrepentant gambler who was a fixture at local racetracks. His interest in the Tigers had been financed with the proceeds from an all-night poker game. Still, Navin was a shrewd businessman and a knowledgeable baseball man.

From the beginning Navin was constantly trying to improve Bennett Field. The park held only eighty-five hundred people, though overflow crowds could be accommodated by roping off the cavernous outfield. This was hardly necessary in the early years, for the club—located in the second-smallest city in the majors and fielding dull teams—failed to draw. It's almost certain that the franchise would have been sold and relocated had it not been for the almost simultaneous arrival of two independent events. Thanks to the automobile industry the city grew, and thanks to Ty Cobb the club became competitive. It was a fortuitous and winning combination. Equally significant, the ordinance banning Sunday ball was repealed in 1910, making Detroit one of only four major-league cities (Chicago, St. Louis, and Cincinnati were the others) to allow baseball to be played on the Sabbath. This gave many factory workers the opportunity to watch games on their only day off. Attendance quickly improved to the point that baseball men no longer regarded the Tigers as offering "big league baseball to bush league crowds."

Flush with the receipts from a winning team, Navin razed the shaky wooden park over the winter of 1911 and replaced it with a modern concrete and steel facility. The horseshoe-shaped grandstand and covered pavilions stretching down both foul lines had an official seating capacity of twenty-three thousand. For important games, thousands more could watch from temporary wooden "circus" bleachers erected beyond the outfield fences. Navin Field, which cost its namesake about $500,000 to build, was dedicated April 20, 1912, before a record crowd of 24,382.

Like most owners, Navin ran a lean ship. There was but a handful of employees, all of whom wore several hats. As president and owner, Navin still answered his own phone and took an occasional turn at the ticket counter. Making and saving a buck was of paramount importance, especially in an era practically devoid of the possibilities of outside income. Until 1927 there were no broadcast rights to sell, and the only available advertising space was on the outfield fences. With no other business interests, he couldn't offset losses by shifting money from one vest pocket to the other. Navin's niggardliness in negotiating annual player contracts was legendary, but understandable. Until his death in 1935, his personal and business fortunes were tied directly to the number of fans who walked through his turnstiles and the number of peanuts and hot dogs they consumed. But in this Frank Navin was lucky. Of the game's two biggest draws during his tenure, one was a tenant of his ball orchard and the other a regular guest.

Ty Cobb and Babe Ruth not only were rivals, they were polar opposites in their approach to the game and to life in general. Cobb, fastiduous in his training habits and a hated firebrand on and off the diamond, espoused the nineteenth-century's "scientific game" of skill, speed, and cunning, where runs were eked out through bunts, stolen bases, and creative strategy. However, the tempo of the national pastime was changed forever by the popular, carefree Ruth, whose gargantuan appetites and booming home runs made him the perfect metaphor of the brash, indulgent, freewheeling America of the Roaring Twenties.

Cobb had arrived in Detroit in 1905 as an eighteen-year-old rookie from Narrows, Georgia. "He came up from the south, you know, and he was still fighting the Civil War," teammate "Wahoo Sam" Crawford once said of the "Georgia Peach." Cobb's grandfather had been a Confederate general. But it was his father, a scholar and a state senator, that Cobb admired beyond all reason. And it was his father's accidental death at the hands of his mother, just weeks before Cobb was bought by the Tigers, that accounted for his incredible drive. "Don't come home a failure," the senior Cobb had warned his son when he left home to play ball. He didn't.

Ball players, umpires, grounds keepers, shoeblacks, butchers, waiters, even his own teammates—it didn't matter, Cobb battled them all. In 1912 he had even climbed into the stands to stomp on a cripple, earning him a suspension and precipitating a strike by teammates, who, even if they loathed him, understood that they needed his cruel brilliance in the lineup.

"The cruelty of Cobb's style fascinated the multitudes, but it also alienated them," Jimmy Cannon wrote after Cobb died, bitter and alone, in 1961. "He played in a climate of hostility, friendless by choice in a violent world he populated with enemies. . . . He was the strangest of all our national sports idols. But not even his disagreeable character could destroy the image of his greatness as a ballplayer. Ty Cobb was the best. That seemed to be all he wanted."

In 1907 Cobb had won his first of a record twelve (in thirteen years) batting titles, propelling the Tigers to the first of three consecutive pennants. That he performed poorly while the team lost all three World Series grated increasingly on Cobb's nerves as the summers rolled by and the chances of redeeming himself in another fall classic grew dimmer. In 1920 the Tigers collapsed completely,

Ty Cobb and Babe Ruth uneasily exchange small talk before a 1923 game at Navin Field. (Courtesy of the Burton Historical Collection of the Detroit Public Library.)

losing their first thirteen games and finishing seventh. Winning the pennant and World Series that year were the Cleveland Indians, managed by Cobb's close friend, center fielder Tris Speaker.

After the series Hughie Jennings resigned as the Tigers' manager. The popular, colorful Jennings had spent fourteen years at the helm, but his field judgment had been affected by age and alcoholism. Cobb also seriously considered retirement. Outside of winning a World Series, he had nothing left to prove on the field. And thanks to shrewd investments in General Motors and Coca-Cola, whose stock he had bought when both companies were still young, he was already the game's first millionaire.

Jennings recommended Cobb for his job. Cobb at first didn't want the responsibility, though he also didn't relish the idea of playing under Clarence "Pants" Rowland, Navin's alternative choice. Cobb considered Rowland, who had managed the Chicago White Sox to a world championship three years earlier, a fraud. This rabid dislike of Rowland, coupled to the challenge of matching Speaker's success as a player-manager, finally persuaded Cobb to accept the managerial job.

The new teacher officially took over the classroom at a series of ceremonies in Detroit on February 1, 1921. *Detroit News* sportswriter E. A. Batchelor, who had helped convince Cobb that he had all the necessary qualities to become an effective field general, later confessed that he may have been wrong about his man. Cobb "lacked the patience to make allowances for men who didn't think as fast as he did, nor had his mechanical ability to play ball. Like so many other great performers, he was impatient with stupidity, lack of ambition, and lack of what he considered normal baseball ability. The result was that he proved to be a poor teacher and that he never could get his team imbued with any real team spirit."

Cobb's hiring came on the heels of a far more important appointment. The previous September, eight members of the Chicago White Sox had been suspended for allegedly throwing the 1919 World Series. The allegations shocked the country. In an attempt to restore some much needed integrity to the game, federal judge Kenesaw Mountain Landis was appointed to the newly created position of commissioner of baseball, and until his death in 1944 he would devote himself to shining the game's badly tarnished image. But the man who would really be responsible for leading the national pastime through its greatest crisis and polishing it to an unprecedented luster was not the stone-faced judge named after a Civil War battlefield, but a muscular, moon-faced orphan from Baltimore named George Herman "Babe" Ruth.

Ruth, eight years younger than Cobb, had been a superlative pitcher for the Boston Red Sox from 1914 to 1919 before being sold to the Yankees for an unheard-of $125,000. The southpaw had won as many as twenty-four games in a season for Boston and all three of his World Series starts, in the process reeling off a record streak of 29 2/3 consecutive scoreless innings. (Cobb hit just .326 in forty-

six career at-bats against Ruth, with none of his fifteen hits going
for extra bases.)

But it was after being shifted to the Yankees' outfield that the
"Sultan of Swat" was to make his mark on baseball and American
culture. His fifty-four home runs in 1920, including ten against Detroit, was an astounding feat. To be sure, Ruth benefited from baseball owners' attempt to jazz up the game following the "Black Sox"
scandal. Spitballs and other trick pitches were phased out and
clean balls were regularly brought into play. A result was a leap in
the number of balls hit over the fence and a change in offensive
strategy. The dead-ball era was dead. Tape-measure blasts from the
affable, larger-than-life Ruth, not well-placed twenty-foot bunts
from the grim, surly Cobb, captured the public's mood and fancy
during the Roaring Twenties.

Theoretically, these changes aided all batters equally. But not
only did Ruth's home runs seem to soar higher and longer than any
other player's, his fifty-four round-trippers were more than any
other *team* hit that summer of 1920. Whether he was launching
another missile or fanning the breeze, Ruth's vicious uppercut
swings brought fans to their feet in every ballpark, especially Navin
Field. Record crowds overflowed the Detroit ballpark when New
York came to town that August. According to *Detroit News* sports
editor H. G. Salsinger, Ruth was given "the welcome due a conquer-
ing hero. He got the applause, the shrieking adoration of the multitudes, in Cobb's own city. Cobb, standing aside, could feel deeply
how fickle the adoration of the sports-loving public is. He saw before him a new king acclaimed." Navin Field would become the site
of a pair of historic blasts by Ruth. On June 8, 1926, he hit the longest home run of his career: a 626-foot blast off Lil Stoner that sailed
over the right-field wall. A paperboy stopped the rolling ball on
Brooklyn Street, two blocks from the park. And on July 13, 1934, he
walloped his seven-hundredth career home run off Tommy Bridges.

"Ruth saved baseball," said Billy Rogell, a Chicago orphan who
grew up worshiping Shoeless Joe Jackson from the bleachers. Like
the rest of the country, Rogell was devastated when his hero and the
other Black Sox were found to have spikes of clay. A few years later,
as a shortstop with the Red Sox and Tigers, Rogell had occasion to
experience Ruth's redemptive magic firsthand: "That's the only guy
who in my thinking was a super ball player. There was only one like
him. Listen, just walking out to the ballpark he'd have everybody

clapping like hell. Ever see them do that for any other ball player? Like hell."

It was clear to anyone within earshot of the diamond that Cobb harbored a deep resentment toward the man who was stealing his mantle as the greatest player ever. Cobb's taunting of Ruth over the years was systematic and vicious. On the field he regularly called him "nigger"—a dig at Ruth's broad nose and dark complexion—and would sniff the air as Ruth walked by: "Something stinks around here. Do I smell a polecat?" The gregarious but barely literate Ruth was never any good in a war of words, but as the sportswriters of the day were always only too happy to point out, he let his bat do his talking for him. In one of Cobb's first trips to New York as a manager, Ruth not only hit seven home runs in a five-game sweep of the Tigers, he started on the mound and got credit for one of the wins. He even struck out Cobb.

Such versatility had to gall Cobb. Throughout his six seasons at the helm, the Detroit staff typically had the fewest complete games and most relief appearances in the league—a reflection not only of the staff's ineptitude but of Cobb's impatience. It took little to prompt the playing manager to call time and begin the long walk in from the outfield to the mound, a practice that infuriated pitchers and exasperated umpires, especially because Cobb readily admitted that he knew next to nothing about pitching. Cobb even took a turn on the mound himself, picking up a save in 1925.

Teaching the science of hitting was a completely different story. The man who would retire with ninety batting and base-stealing records worked overtime imparting his knowledge of hitting. Not every pupil had the necessary talent to implement the old master's theories. One who did was a slow-footed first baseman from San Francisco named Harry "Slug" Heilmann, who hit only .291 from 1914 to 1920 for Jennings, but who whacked the ball at a .366 clip under Cobb's tutelage. Cobb moved Heilmann to right field, making room for newcomer Lu Blue, a slick-fielding, switch-hitting first sacker who checked into the majors in 1921 with his first of four .300-plus seasons under Cobb.

The lively ball made an impression that summer at Navin Field. In all, six regulars hit over .300, with the team as a whole batting a resounding .316, still the American League record. All three outfielders exceeded Bobby Veach's one-year-old club record of eleven home runs, with Cobb hitting twelve, Veach sixteen, and Heilmann

nineteen. Led by Heilmann's 139 runs batted in (RBI), the outfielders also became the first trio of Tigers to knock in more than a hundred runs in the same season.

Thanks to Cobb's instruction, Heilmann was developing into
the American League's most feared right-handed slugger. Outside
of Ruth—who with fifty-nine home runs, 171 RBI, and an .846 slugging average was enjoying what would be his greatest season—
Heilmann had the most explosive offensive season in the league,
finishing runner-up to Ruth in RBI and slugging and topping the
circuit in hits (237) and average (.394). Cobb, despite the added
pressure of managing, finished just behind Heilmann in the batting
race with a .389 average.

Accounting for some of this firepower was a season-long feud
that Cobb engineered between his fourth- and fifth-place hitters,
Veach and Heilmann. Cobb determined that the easygoing Veach, a

Babe Ruth is the center of attention at this Prohibition-era party,
held in 1925 in the basement of Detroit sportsman Alfred Tenge. To
the right of Ruth are Tigers Heinie Manush (number 12 in photo)
and Harry Heilmann (number 9), who is trying his best to shield his
well-known face from the camera.

simpleminded country boy from Kentucky who was well liked around the league, needed a boost to reach his full potential. Cobb convinced Heilmann that it was in the team's best interest to feed his friend Veach a steady diet of vitriol, creating a game-within-the-game of one-upmanship that resulted in banner seasons for both men. Unfortunately, Cobb left for Georgia after the season without explaining the gimmick to Veach, as he had promised. As a result, Veach remained enemies evermore with Heilmann, who from that point on despised Cobb with a quiet passion.

The following season Cobb again finished runner-up for the batting crown, this time to George Sisler of St. Louis. Cobb hit .401, aided by American League president Ban Johnson's ruling on a controversial scoring decision that gave him the base hit he needed to enjoy his third .400 season. More importantly, Cobb was able to goose the team into a third-place finish, the springboard to what Detroit fans were hoping would be a pennant-winning season in 1923. They were to be disappointed, however. Although Heilmann copped his second batting title with a .403 mark and George "Hooks" Dauss—still the club's all-time leader in wins (221) and losses (183)—enjoyed his last great season with twenty-one victories, the "Cobbmen" (as the writers had dubbed the team) finished a distant second to the Yankees, who won their third consecutive pennant in 1923.

At times Cobb grew exasperated with the antics of Dauss and Heilmann, who along with other rounders like Veach and Heinie Manush, occasionally reported for games hung over. Cobb would punish them by playing them anyway. One afternoon after a severe night on the town, Heilmann legged out a triple, his stomach rumbling and his eyes spinning like pinwheels. It's unclear whether he slid or simply fell into third base, but Slug then vomited all over the bag. No pinch runner was forthcoming.

For most Detroiters the purchase of illegal booze is what put the roar in the Roaring Twenties. "It was absolutely impossible to get a drink in Detroit," observed newspaperman Malcolm Bingay in his memoirs, "unless you walked at least 10 feet and told the busy bartender what you wanted in a voice loud enough for him to hear you above the uproar."

Bingay was hardly exaggerating. The government might as well have legislated against the sun rising in the morning as to try to enforce Prohibition in the city. Michigan's own prohibition act, effective May 1, 1918, was followed by the Eighteenth Amendment, national prohibition, on January 1, 1920. The law prohibited the manufacture or consumption of any beverage containing more than 0.5% alcohol. This closed down the city's 1,534 licensed saloons and forced breweries like Stroh's to make ginger ale and ice cream to survive. However, filling the vacuum were an estimated twenty-five thousand blind pigs, gin joints, and speakeasies, including one across the street from police headquarters that was well frequented by members of the department and press. Additionally, tens of thousands of private stills percolated peacefully in attics, basements, closets, and garages.

A sociable man, Heilmann enjoyed making the rounds of Detroit's after-hours joints, including Morey's, a restaurant at Michigan and Tarnow that served booze in its basement. John "Red" Cole played the sax at Morey's, a popular hangout for Ray Bernstein, one of the leaders of the Purple Gang. The gang of Jewish punks could be seen at Navin Field when they weren't busy smuggling shipments of Al Capone's favorite whiskey, Old Log Cabin, from Canada to Chicago. Avid sportsmen, they once celebrated a football victory by Michigan Agricultural College (later Michigan State University) by shooting their tommy guns out their car windows on the drive home from East Lansing. Cole remembered the Purples as "gentlemen bandits. Whenever Bernstein walked in the door, we'd start playing 'My Yiddish Mama.' We knew damn well that if we played that, he'd be good for a five-dollar tip."

And when the American League's batting champion walked through the door? "I'd announce, 'Ladies and gentlemen, Harry Heilmann has just come in. Let's give him a hand.' He'd kind of put his finger to his mouth and go ,'Shhh.'" Such precaution seems almost out of character for Heilmann, whose more celebrated exploits included driving his roadster down the steps of a basement speakeasy and up to its bar.

The 1924 season was as riotous as any speakeasy, with tensions between Cobb and Ruth reaching an inevitable climax on June 13 at Navin Field. That Friday afternoon the Tigers and Yankees squared off in a battle for first place. A series of brushback pitches finally ignited a half-hour free-for-all that involved players, policemen, and more than a thousand fans, some of whom uprooted seats and threw them onto the field. When the umpires were unable to clear the field, New York became the beneficiary of one of the few forfeits in league history.

At thirty-seven, the balding, round, and jowly Cobb had come

Harry Heilmann. "Slug" was a fixture in Detroit for nearly four decades, first as a heavy-hitting outfielder, then as a broadcaster. (Courtesy of the National Baseball Library, Cooperstown, New York.)

to resemble a true Georgia peach. Nonetheless, the chance to vindicate himself in one final World Series put a little extra steam in his stride. He played every game but the meaningless finale, banging out 211 hits and stealing twenty-three bases (including three thefts of home) on his scarred, tired legs. He threatened, he cajoled, he led by example, but it wasn't to be. The pitching failed and leadoff man Lu Blue missed the last quarter of the campaign with a knee injury. After bouncing in and out of first for much of the season, the Tigers faded to third, six games behind Washington. It was the closest the club would ever come to winning a pennant under Cobb, though Frank Navin was pleased. Over the winter he had added an upper deck to the main grandstand, increasing seating capacity from 23,000 to 29,000. Drawing from a swelling population base, attendance at Navin Field passed one million customers for the first time.

By the following season Cobb had grown weary of the increasing emphasis on the long ball. For all his faults, Cobb had never been a selfish player, as illustrated by his career-high twenty-seven sacrifice bunts in 1922, the year he was chasing the magical .400 mark and thus could've been forgiven for going strictly for base hits. (Sixty years later, Harmon Killebrew would enter the Hall of Fame after having not laid down a single sacrifice in twenty-two big-league seasons.) "I'll show you something today," Cobb told H. G. Salsinger before a game with the St. Louis Browns. "I'm going for home runs for the first time in my career." On May 5, 1925, Cobb unleashed one of the most astonishing displays of power hitting ever. He had six straight hits—including three home runs—and set a league record with sixteen total bases. The first two blasts landed in the right-field bleachers of Sportsman's Park and the third cleared them. The following day he smacked two more round-trippers, tying a major-league record of five home runs in two games. His point proven, Cobb then casually slipped back into his old habit of "nipping" at the ball, racking up a .378 average for the season.

For the second straight year the Tigers led the league in runs scored, and for the fourth time in five years, hit better than .300 as a team. Most of the sock came from an outfield that hit a combined .382. Veach's replacement, Absolom "Red" Wingo, bought from Toronto for fifty thousand dollars, enjoyed his only successful major-league season, hitting .370. And Heilmann captured another batting crown in one of the great stretch runs of all time. On Labor Day, Tris Speaker of Cleveland had a seemingly insurmountable fifty-point lead in the batting race. The aching Speaker played sparingly the rest of the way, which meant Heilmann would need a near-phenomenal finish to overhaul him. Slug went to work, and by the last day of the season he was just a point behind. While Speaker chose to sit out his last game, Heilmann had to contend with a season-ending doubleheader against the tough third-place Browns.

Nonetheless, Heilmann cracked out three hits in six trips in the first game. Between games, word came that Heilmann's performance had allowed him to squeeze by Speaker. There was no reason to jeopardize his third batting title by playing the second game. Teammates urged Heilmann to remove himself from the lineup.

"Not me," he said. "I'll win it fairly, or not at all. I'll be in there swinging." Heilmann then went three for three in the finale to finish at .393 for the year, four points ahead of Speaker.

Cobb's last season in Detroit was 1926. Although he surrendered his center field spot to Heinie Manush and played in only half the games, he was still earning his fifty-thousand-dollar salary, methodically driving in sixty-two runs (fourth best on the team) and striking out but twice in 233 at-bats. Manush, another natural hitter who benefited from Cobb's instruction, made his manager smile when he beat out Babe Ruth for the batting championship, .378 to .372, by collecting six hits in a season-ending doubleheader. The final edition of the Cobbmen had three of the circuit's top four hitters—Heilmann and Bob Fothergill both hit .367—but still finished sixth.

As expected, in October Detroit owner Frank Navin announced Cobb's retirement as player-manager. But a bombshell hit when, in November, Cleveland suddenly announced it was releasing Tris Speaker, who had just guided the Indians to a near-miss of the pennant. Something was amiss, but not until December did the baseball world learn the particulars of the biggest scandal since the Black Sox: former Detroit pitcher Hub "Dutch" Leonard had implicated Cobb and Speaker in helping fix a game between Cleveland and Detroit in 1919. Also named in Leonard's charges was Yale baseball coach Joe Wood, who played alongside Speaker in the Cleveland outfield in 1919.

Leonard had been a superb pitcher for years for the Red Sox and Tigers, but his reputation as a laggard and a complainer was tolerated only as long as he won ball games. When Cobb released the ailing pitcher midway through the 1925 season, then used his influence to waive him out of the league, Leonard swore revenge. The following summer, Leonard produced several letters that, though ambiguous, seemed to indicate that the three players had been involved in a wager of some sort.

Hoping to deal with the matter privately, league president Ban Johnson secretly bought the letters for twenty -two thousand dollars (the amount Leonard estimated he had lost in salary since being released) and persuaded the Detroit and Cleveland ball clubs to quietly release their managers after the season ended. Behind closed doors, Cobb and Speaker vehemently denied any wrongdoing, but they at first agreed to be silent to save the game and everyone involved embarrassment. However, the two stars soon changed their minds and secured legal counsel. Judge Landis was then made aware of the charges, which became public that winter.

Based on the damaging letters and Speaker's reputation as a gambler, and considering the open atmosphere of gambling and occasional game-fixing that permeated professional baseball at the turn of the century, it seems likely that some kind of impropriety did take place. The best evidence suggests that, though the game was not fixed, a bet was placed on its outcome. However, largely because Leonard refused to leave California to be interviewed by

Landis, the commissioner had little choice but to exonerate all three players. In January 1927 Landis restored Cobb and Speaker to their clubs' active rosters. Cobb subsequently signed with the Philadelphia Athletics, where he played two more seasons before retiring; Speaker went to Washington, then joined Cobb for one final season with the A's.

In the light of Cobb's strained relations with his players, Navin had already made up his mind to release Cobb long before the scandal broke. "Maybe I was not a managerial success," said Cobb upon leaving Detroit after twenty -two years, "but just as surely I was not a managerial failure." And although New York had copped four pennants to Detroit's none during his six years as manager, Cobb remained unconvinced of the Yankees' superiority. "In every other way but pitching," he said, "we spit in their eye."

George Moriarty, a hardnosed former teammate of Cobb's, replaced him at the helm in 1927. That spring, amid much fanfare, Cobb returned to Navin Field wearing the elephant insignia of the Philadelphia Athletics. Typically, he was under suspension at the time for "accidentally" bumping an umpire in Boston, but it was lifted the morning of his homecoming.

On May 10, 1927, an overflow crowd of thirty -five thousand packed Navin Field to celebrate Ty Cobb Day. Cobb responded to the warm welcome by belting a two-base hit into the right-field overflow his first time up. After he took his position in the bottom half of the inning, the game had to be held up for several minutes as he walked back and forth in front of the temporary bleachers, obliging dozens of autograph seekers. Perhaps Detroiters, dazed over the last year or so by the explosion of new technology—radios, talking movies, transatlantic phone calls, pioneering airplane feats of one stripe or another—were sensing the end of an era, a feeling reinforced two weeks later when Henry Ford announced that he was ceasing production of his beloved Tin Lizzy in favor of the more modern Model A. Because the Model T and T. Cobb had arrived together in the early days of the century, their names had grown to be synonymous with Detroit. In their time both populists had served the public well, but now they were just quaint reminders of a simpler, less frenzied past that, because of the rapidity of change, seemed more distant than it was.

Technology invaded the ballpark that summer with the first live radio broadcasts of home games. The games were aired on the *Detroit News'* WWJ, which in 1920 had become the world's first commercial radio station (though KDKA in Pittsburgh had been the first station to be issued call letters). It was KDKA that aired the first broadcast of a baseball game, a contest between Pittsburgh and Philadelphia, on August 5, 1921. By the middle of the decade many major news and sporting events were being broadcast live.

The ability to pluck faraway voices out of the air fascinated Detroiters, who in April 1922 packed the fourth floor of the General Motors Building to attend the country's largest radio trade show yet. "Ninety days ago . . . radiophony had received but scant attention," the *Detroit Free Press* observed at the time, "but now everybody is interested, far more so than they were years ago in the automobile and earlier in the bicycle, because the auto and bicycle cost real money, and a radio set, complete including installation by a so-called expert, may be had for him $20 to $30." By then there were 120 companies in the city manufacturing radio sets, parts, or cabinets to put the sets in. The sale of radio equipment nationally jumped from $60 million that year to nearly $1 billion in 1929.

Baseball owners would remain ambivalent about the new phenomenon up through World War II. Many feared "giving the game away" would hurt attendance, while others argued broadcasting would introduce the game to new fans. Their response ranged from Chicago Cubs owner Phil Wrigley, who in 1925 allowed all area radio stations to broadcast all Cubs games free, to the bosses of the three New York clubs (the Yankees, Giants, and Dodgers), who banned all radio, including telegraphic re-creations, from 1932 to 1938. Navin's decision to finally open his games to radio in 1927 was undoubtedly influenced by the change of heart of doubters like University of Michigan football coach Fielding Yost, who in the mid-1920s discovered radio enhanced rather than hurt attendance, and the undisclosed amount of money WWJ paid the Tigers for broadcast rights.

The man behind the microphone for that first Tiger broadcast was a droll, bird-faced thirty-nine-year-old native of Tyrone, Pennsylvania, named Edwin "Ty" Tyson. He quickly became Detroit's first media "star," though no one thought in such terms then. To a generation of Detroiters he was simply the familiar voice that in those mysterious but wonderful early years of radio magically brought the immediacy of a distant ball game into their kitchens and living rooms. His popularity was such that, when Judge Landis's ruling barring "partisan" hometown announcers meant Tyson would not be able to broadcast the 1934 Detroit–St. Louis World

Series, a staggering 600,000 fans petitioned the commissioner to change his mind. He did.

"His appeal was that he did a straightforward report of the ball game," recalled Fran Harris, who joined the station as a copywriter in 1930. "He didn't embellish a great deal, but just described what was going on. And he was known on occasion, when there wasn't anything going on, to say nothing. There'd be empty air."

Tyson handled the play-by-play until 1942. During that time only home games were broadcast, and, in the early years of the depression, not even all of those. Because of Navin's fear that radio would give financially strapped fans a reason to stay home from Navin Field, no Sunday games were broadcast from 1930 to 1932, a policy that was expanded to include all weekend games in 1933.

To save the expense of sending a radio crew to another city, all the Tigers' away games through the 1940s were reconstructed broadcasts. A telegraph operator in Boston's Fenway Park, for ex-

Ty Tyson at the mike of the first radio broadcast of a baseball game in Detroit, April 20, 1927. (Copyright © 1927 by the *Detroit News*. Used with permission.)

ample, would bang out a pitch-by-pitch description of the game in Morse code and send it to the WWJ studio in the Detroit News Building. There another operator typed out the dispatches and handed them to Tyson, who had to use every ounce of imagination to flesh out the terse game accounts (strike . . . foul ball . . . Gehringer triples to right) into a palatable reconstruction ("Here's the two-strike pitch by MacFayden . . . Gehringer hits it to right center . . . it's between the outfielders . . . Gehringer races around second, heading for third . . . here's the throw by Rothrock . . . he slides . . . he's in there safely with a three-base hit."). Listeners weren't fooled by reconstructions, nor with the distinctive tapping of the telegraph key often audible in the background, were they expected to be. Reconstructed ball games were no different from the other primitive dramas that filled the airwaves and depended on that great theater of the mind to make fantasy come alive.

Providing much of the excitement that first radio summer was Harry Heilmann, who was destined to become a fixture behind the mike himself. In 1927 Slug became the third Tiger in a row to win the batting title on the last day of the season, going seven for eight in a doubleheader against Cleveland to edge Al Simmons of Philadelphia. Heilmann's .398 mark not only gave him his fourth and final batting crown, it capped the club's amazing string of seventeen batting champions in twenty-one seasons. Spoiled Tiger fans would have to wait a full decade for another.

Moriarty was fired after the 1928 season and returned to umpiring. Stanley "Bucky" Harris, the acclaimed "Boy Wonder" who had guided Washington to pennants in 1924–25, was brought on board to restore the Bengals' roar. What were to follow instead were five straight second-division finishes, the yawns occasionally stifled by the play of fan favorites like Heilmann, Dale Alexander, Bob Fothergill, Earl Whitehill, and Charlie Gehringer.

Harris's 1929 squad was the first major-league team ever to lead the league in runs scored (926) and runs given up (928). That year the Tigers also led the circuit in batting, slugging, doubles, and triples; had the stolen base champion in Gehringer, a .339 hitter who also led in doubles (45), triples (19) and runs scored (131); and featured a pair of sensational rookie performances by left fielder Roy Johnson and first baseman Dale Alexander, who tied each other for the league lead in hits with 215. Despite all this firepower, the team finished a distant sixth.

Alexander, in particular, symbolized the kind of statistically schizophrenic season Navin Field fans had come to expect. The man they called "Moose," a six-foot-three, 210-pound offensive machine from Greenville, Tennessee, broke into the bigs with a club-record twenty-five home runs (and a club-record sixty-three strikeouts). The right-hander batted .343, was third in the league with 137 RBI, and second with 363 total bases (just four shy of Cobb's 1911 team mark). If Moose could have been transported forty years into the future, he might have become the game's premier designated hitter. Alas, he had to play the field—apparently with a hatchet, for he led all first sackers in errors his first two seasons.

Alexander's defensive liabilities could be tolerated, as long as the big country boy was putting milk into the pail. However, after his home run production dropped dramatically from twenty in 1930 to just three in 1931 (he still hit .325 with forty-seven doubles that season), Alexander was shipped to the Red Sox early in 1932. Hitting but .250 at the time, he rebounded to hit .372 in Boston, becoming the first man to win a batting title playing for two teams in the same season. By 1934 Moose was back in the minors for good, but his .331 average with Detroit remains the club's fourth highest of all time.

While Alexander's trade was expected, Heilmann's was not. Slug had a good season in '29, leading the team with a .344 average and driving home 120 runs. But he turned thirty-five during the season and was beginning to suffer from arthritis, a condition that would end his career two years later. More significantly, he couldn't get along with Harris, who suspended him once. The result: Heilmann was sold to Cincinnati at the end of the '29 season. The move outraged Tiger fans but probably pleased Heilmann, who recognized Cincinnati as a good beer town.

Another man who demanded little more out of life than a juicy steak, a pitcher of beer, and a good smoke after the game was Bob "Fats" Fothergill, who was moored like a zeppelin to left field for much of the twenties. "Hey, Bob," fans yelled, "when does the balloon take off?" The fun-loving and surprisingly agile Fothergill was a notorious right-handed pull hitter who hit better than .353 four of five seasons between 1925 and 1929. By 1930 he was covering more ground than ever in the outfield, but that was because his size had ballooned to frightful proportions. That summer Fats was waived to the White Sox, leaving behind a sparkling .337 lifetime average that remains the club's third highest behind Cobb (.369) and Heilmann (.342).

Earl Whitehill was a minor celebrity in Detroit from 1923 to 1932, by dint of his marriage to Violet Oliver, an ex-Broadway chorine and former Miss California who also was the dark-haired beauty on the California raisin box. Hard, aloof, and drop-dead handsome, the dashing lefty from Cedar Rapids, Iowa, could be temperamental, once running Cobb himself off the mound and another time heaving an umpire's whisk broom over the stands to protest a call. Whitehill was a premier pitcher for more than a decade, methodically stacking up thirteen consecutive seasons of double-digit wins, the first nine with Detroit. After the 1932 season he was traded to Washington, where he immediately won twenty-two games and shut out the Giants in his sole World Series start. He won 218 games in his seventeen-year career, 133 with Detroit.

Perhaps the most popular Tiger of them all was Gehringer, a quiet, uncomplaining sort who embodied Thoreau's dictum to "live your life, do your work, and then take your hat." His "Mechanical Man" moniker did him a disservice. Gracious, shy, and immensely talented, Gehringer had a gentle nature and keen wit that made him a favorite of fans, players, and umpires around the league. It didn't hurt that he was also the best all-around second baseman since Eddie Collins. A strong Catholic who attended mass every morning, even when on the road, Gehringer postponed marriage for years to care for his mother, Teresa, in their northwest Detroit home.

"Charlie was devoted to his mother," recalled Edgar Hayes, who covered sports for the *Detroit Times* from 1927 to 1960. "She used to attend a lot of the games or stay at home and listen to the game on the radio. Whenever Charlie had a bad day and he came home, she'd be rocking on the back porch and say, 'What's the matter, aren't you trying anymore?' "

That question might have been asked of the entire team, which by the early thirties was as listless as a sailboat on a calm sea. Sluggers used to seemingly roll off the assembly line in Detroit. But now Fats, Moose, and Slug had been replaced by pedestrian hitters such as outfielders Roy Johnson, John Stone, and Liz Funk and first sacker Harry "Stinky" Davis (he liked cigars) in the traditional power positions. A batch of young players from a strong Beaumont farm team, including outfielder Pete Fox, pitcher Lynwood

"Schoolboy" Rowe, and first baseman Hank Greenberg, provided a glimpse of the future in 1933.

Certainly anything would be better than the present, reasoned the natives. The Tigers finished a lackluster fifth in 1933, and Harris didn't even bother to stick around for the final act, resigning with a week still to go in the season. "We want Tigers," declared a *Free Press* editorial, "not tame kittens."

Detroit's top pitcher of the twenties, Earl Whitehill. (Courtesy of the Burton Historical Collection of the Detroit Public Library.)

2

The New Deal Tigers

By 1933, distracted Detroiters had more important matters on their minds than baseball. Two weeks after Harry Heilmann had been sold to Cincinnati in October 1929, a bigger shock had hit the city. The stock market nosedived, and the freewheeling days of the twenties skidded to a disastrous halt. By the following year car production had been halved, and by 1932 about forty percent of the city's work force was idle. The optimism and gaiety of the Roaring Twenties suddenly seemed like ancient history to a populace mired in massive depression, economic and otherwise.

These were long years of tears, anger, and confusion, especially in Detroit, as ordinary people tried to come to grips with the most terrible economic depression in the country's history. Almost overnight, factories closed, small businesses went bankrupt, and public welfare and private relief agencies were overwhelmed with desperate, bewildered people. "I have never confronted such misery as on the zero day of my arrival in Detroit," social worker Helen Hall wrote in 1930:

> After breakfast . . . we set out for the Department of Public Welfare. There we came upon muffled men and women at the entrance. They crowded the lower corridors and we had to push by.

They were on the stairs and filled the upper halls, standing, waiting their turn. I wanted to look at them and see what type of men
and women they really were, but I was ashamed to look. I felt suddenly conscious of the fur lining of my coat and the good breakfast
I had eaten. Perhaps it was the bitter cold I had come in from that
gave me the impression that they were congealed into one discon-
solate lump.

It used to be that a man who wanted to work needed only to go
to the employment office at Timken Axle or Dodge Main and apply.
This was the American creed and it kept people pouring into Detroit through the twenties. But now wanting to work was not
enough, and the average breadwinner blamed himself for his job-
lessness and his family's predicament. "It seems to me I have lost
all my ability as a responsible man," an unemployed worker who
refused welfare wrote Mayor Frank Murphy. "It seems to me I have
some short comings some where [sic]."

Men who only wanted to work were fired upon and killed when
they demonstrated in front of the Rouge plant on March 7, 1932.
Fifteen thousand people crowded into downtown for the funeral
march and talked angrily of communism. That fall, President Herbert Hoover, running for reelection against Franklin D. Roosevelt,
made a campaign stop in Detroit. "Never can I forget that experience," wrote an observer. "We drove to a hall where he was to make
a speech through miles and miles of silent men and women gathered along the streets." The city's banks closed the following February for an extended "holiday," panicking depositors; when they
reopened, municipal workers were paid in scrip. By then dispirited
Detroiters understood little and cared less about the economic
forces that had brought on the Great Depression—about overspe-
culation in the stock market, the loss of foreign markets, and the
slump in agricultural purchasing power. All they knew was that life
had unraveled like a cheap suit.

Baseball felt the pinch along with the rest of the country. In
1930, thanks to a juiced-up ball that created a summer of unparalleled offense (eleven of sixteen teams hit .300 or better), major-
league attendance exceeded 10.1 million, the highest figure of any
season between 1901 and 1945. But hard times soon stilled the
turnstiles. In 1932, the worst year of the depression—some 15 million Americans were out of work—major-league attendance
dropped to 8.1 million. The following year it fell to 6.3 million. Despite such gimmicks as regularly scheduled doubleheaders (they

had been played before only for make-up games) and pregame milking contests and footraces, attendance dropped from more than eight thousand per game in 1930 to less than five thousand in 1933.

The Tigers didn't even do that well, with but 321,000 fans—a little more than 4,100 a game—paying to watch the fifth-place team that summer. Navin, who had lost a considerable amount of his fortune when the stock market crashed, was not only feeling the effects of a ball club that was as moribund as the economy, he had to deal with a dwindling population base: between 1930 and 1932, Detroit lost a whopping nine percent of its population, as single men and entire families drifted away in search of work. After the 1933 World Series between the Senators and Giants produced the lowest players' shares since 1922, American League president Will Harridge told Navin and other league owners to cut overhead and salaries. By then, however, the average player's salary had already been sliced from a predepression high of seventy-five hundred dollars in 1929 to just six thousand dollars in 1933.

On the Tigers' payroll during these lean years was a speedy, light-hitting infielder named George "Heinie" Schuble, who was bought from the Cardinals in the fall of 1928 for thirty -five thousand dollars. "I joined Detroit in 1929," remembered Schuble, who lives in his hometown of Houston. "That's when everybody lost everything. I didn't make enough money to lose."

Schuble made forty-five hundred dollars as the Tigers' starting shortstop in '29, then was shipped to Beaumont for two seasons before returning to Detroit as the starting third baseman in 1932. "I took salary cuts three straight years," said Schuble, a married man who worked part-time for the post office in the off-season to make ends meet. "They could get away with stuff then." It would take another three seasons in the bigs before he got back to his original salary. Still, at a time when some hungry Detroiters resorted to stealing dog biscuits from the city dog pound, Schuble had to consider himself a lucky man. Some ball players were making as little as two thousand dollars in 1933, and even a promising slugger like Hank Greenberg made all of fifty-five hundred dollars that year.

In retrospect, there was one positive effect of the depression. It forced Philadelphia A's owner Connie Mack to sell his best players to survive, bringing to Detroit the man who, outside Ty Cobb, remains the greatest competitor ever to wear a Tiger uniform.

Gordon Stanley "Mickey" Cochrane was in the prime of a career that was already earning him recognition as the finest all-around catcher in the game's history. A five-foot-nine, 170-pound dynamo from Bridgewater, Massachusetts, Cochrane had been a football standout at Boston University, where he earned a degree in business administration, dabbled in music and the theater, and enjoyed reading Kipling. The one activity he didn't enjoy was catching—he fancied himself an outfielder—but his first minor-league manager set him straight. "I got outfielders," he said. "You catch—or it's off the payroll."

The most important thing Cochrane caught was the eye of Connie Mack, who reportedly bought the entire Portland team of the

The Tigers' two greatest competitors of the age, Ty Cobb and Mickey Cochrane, grip and grin for the cameras at Navin Field in September 1934. (Courtesy of the Burton Historical Collection of the Detroit Public Library.)

Pacific Coast League to obtain his rights. In one of those odd twists of baseball history, Cochrane and another notorious firebrand, Robert "Lefty" Grove, broke into the majors in the same game with the Philadelphia Athletics in 1925. The battery formed the backbone of the A's three pennant-winners and two world championship teams, with Cochrane voted the league's most valuable player in 1928.

"Greatest catcher of them all, Cochrane was," Grove told writer Donald Honig a half-century later. "Great ballplayer, all around. Good hitter, good runner, good arm, smart. Hardly ever shook him off. If Mickey was living today, he'd tell you I only shook him off about five or six times all the years he caught me. Funny, before I'd even look at him, I had in my mind what I was going to pitch, and I'd look up and there'd be Mickey's signal, just what I was thinking. Like he was reading my mind. That's the kind of catcher he was."

In the fall of 1933, the thirty-year-old backstop was coming off a typically productive season with the A's: a .322 batting average (including a .500 mark against the Tigers), 104 runs scored, 106 walks, 15 home runs, and a league-leading .459 on-base percentage. Because he was a good hit-and-run man who rarely struck out, Cochrane typically batted second or third in the lineup. He was regarded as the game's top defensive catcher, his mobility and glove work (he perfected the technique of catching one-handed) described as that of a "shortstop in shin guards." In the fire sale that Connie Mack would conduct for most of the thirties, a price tag of $100,000 was attached to the prize catcher.

Navin coveted Cochrane as a player-manager, but he was not his first choice that winter. Babe Ruth was. The fading Ruth, who was taking a pay cut from $52,000 to $35,000 for the '34 season, would undoubtedly have been a draw in Detroit. With the Yankees' permission, Navin got hold of him on the phone and asked him to Detroit for a conference. "But I'm just catching a train for San Francisco to take a boat to Honolulu," the thirty-eight-year-old slugger said. "I got some exhibition games to play in Hawaii. Can't it wait?"

It couldn't. After an exchange of correspondence proved fruitless, Navin settled on Cochrane. Navin went to see his partner, Walter O. Briggs, about the price. "That's all right with me," said Briggs. "If he's a success here, he may be a bargain at that price. I'll furnish the money. Go and get him." A young catcher, John Pasek, was thrown in to complete the deal. At the league's annual meeting in

December, a tearful Connie Mack announced that Mickey Cochrane was now a Tiger.

Two days later, Navin swung a second deal, this time swapping outfielders with Washington. He traded John Stone, a free-swinging .300 hitter who had compiled a thirty-four-game hitting streak in 1930, even-up for thirty-three-year-old Leon "Goose" Goslin, a New Jersey farm boy noted for his blistering hitting and a proboscis the size of a shade tree. The temperamental Goose was feuding with Washington's front office at the time, which made the trade that much easier to pull off.

How important were the additions of Cochrane and Goslin? Consider this: between 1921 and 1939, the only teams to beat out the Yankees for the pennant had either Goslin (1924–25 and 1933 Washington), Cochrane (1929–31 Philadelphia), or both (1934–35 Detroit) in their lineup. Although most observers considered the two left-handed-hitting veterans important acquisitions, few at the time were bold enough to predict that they would immediately produce a pennant in Detroit. There were the questions of the lead-footed Goslin's minimal defensive skills and Cochrane's untested managerial ability.

"We all knew Cochrane was a great catcher," recalled Edgar Hayes of the *Detroit Times*. "But nobody knew what kind of a manager he'd be. Remember, he had never managed in Philadelphia." The result? "Well," said Hayes, "he turned the town on its ear."

Because of Cochrane, 1934 belongs in that select circle of summers—1968 is another—when a mere game was somehow lifted to a higher plane of communal meaning. "To Detroit, Mickey Cochrane was a hero—a towering one." An anonymous *Free Press* editorial writer, perhaps remembering his youth spent in the bleachers cheering on Goose, Schoolie, and the boys, reflected upon Cochrane's death in 1962:

> Had he come to it at another time he might be remembered as a colorful, fiery playing manager who led the Tigers to two pennants and a World Series win—and nothing more.
>
> But there was an alchemy of era and man. To a depression ridden Detroit, Cochrane's baseball leadership brought an interest, an enthusiasm, an elan that somehow kept hearts high and grins going despite life's daily disappointments.
>
> It has been said that Mickey Cochrane licked the depression in Detroit. That's overstating it, naturally. But the man had a

magic about him that made it easier for Detroit to ride out those early 30s.

With the Tigers under Cochrane, Detroit talked, thought and lived baseball, and in so doing was at least partly able to forget its travail.

Cochrane's greatest asset—and ultimately the cause of his downfall—was an unmatched intensity. He set a tremendous personal pace on the field. You had only to watch him return the ball to the pitcher. There were no lollipop lobs from the scowling, jug-eared catcher the papers dubbed "Black Mike." He fired it hard and true, a clothesline back to the mound that you could hang the accompanying expletive on. The message was clear: if you weren't in the game, you might suddenly find yourself out of it.

Despite his temper, Cochrane was by all accounts a fair man and a good teacher. Even a veteran like Ray Hayworth, a fine defensive catcher who had set a major-league record with 439 consecutive errorless chances the year before, was able to learn a thing or two from the new manager.

"Mickey was in his prime," recalled Hayworth, who accepted his demotion to second fiddle without a whimper. "I knew that when he was at Philadelphia he was the premier catcher in the game. Mickey taught me things, like getting rid of the ball faster on throws, and pulling low balls up and high pitches down." Cochrane platooned the righthanded-hitting Hayworth against lefties. The move paid off, not only in offense (the arrangement allowed Hayworth to hit well over his lifetime average), but in morale.

"I always said I'd rather be a backup on a championship team," said Hayworth, "than starting for a last-place club."

Hayworth would get his wish, thanks to a commodity that had been all but forgotten by Detroit fans: pitching. The mound staff Cochrane inherited included old hands like Fred "Firpo" Marberry, who had been the game's first true relief specialist while with Washington in the twenties. Marberry had won sixteen games as a starter for Bucky Harris in 1933 and would win fifteen more during Cochrane's first season. But the nucleus of the staff was a trio of talented youngsters—Tommy Bridges, Eldon Auker, and Schoolboy Rowe—that, thanks to Cochrane's guidance, would give the Tigers as good a starting rotation as any in the game over the next three seasons.

At twenty-seven, the right-handed Bridges was coming off consecutive 14–12 seasons under Harris. The son of a small-town doctor in Tennessee, the quiet, slightly built Bridges had the best curveball in baseball. He had already thrown three one-hitters in his short career, including a controversial near-miss of a perfect game on August 5, 1932. On that day Bridges had retired the first twenty-six Washington Senators to face him. All that prevented him from becoming the sixth major-league pitcher to hurl a perfect game was Senator pitcher Bob Burke.

At this point the Tigers were ahead 13–0, but Washington manager Walter Johnson inserted a pinch hitter, Dave Harris. Harris slapped Bridges's first pitch to left field for a single, and the bid for immortality went up in smoke. The expressionless Bridges then retired the next batter to sew up the victory. Johnson caught hell for not letting his pitcher bat for himself, considering the hopelessness of his cause. Bridges, however, was not one of the critics. "I didn't want the perfect game to be given me on a platter," he said. "I wanted it with the opposition doing its best. And that's all there is to it."

Bridges blossomed under Cochrane, winning twenty-two games in 1934, twenty-one in 1935, and a league-high twenty-three in 1936. The last two years he also led in strikeouts. Bridges won 194 games for the Tigers between 1930 and 1946, as well as four of five decisions in World Series play.

Auker, twenty-three, was the right-handed complement to lefty reliever Elon "Chief" Hogsett, the Tigers' other submarining pitcher. "Boy, is Ruth mad at you," a New York coach told Auker during his rookie season of 1933. "The Babe says he's been struck out by many pitchers, but this is the first time by a girl."

Had Ruth been better aware of Auker's background, he might have held his tongue. Auker had made All-Conference in three sports at Kansas State University, where he had studied pre-med. He graduated in June 1932 "and things were kind of rough then for jobs," recalled Auker, who lives today in Vero Beach, Florida.

"I played halfback in football, and I was offered a contract by the Chicago Bears. I was going to play baseball in summer and football in the fall, but Navin said no. I liked football better, but I chose baseball because the season was already underway and I could make four hundred fifty dollars a month."

After suffering a separated shoulder playing football, Auker had experimented with throwing the ball in a submarine motion. Not only was this baffling to most hitters, at its most extreme it resulted in pebbles flying toward the plate along with the ball. At Auker's first minor-league stop, his manager suggested he try his unusual delivery in an actual game. "The first-place team came to town, and I beat them, 1–0. I gave up two hits and struck out twelve. From then on I pitched that way until it seemed the natural way to throw." Auker's underhand sinker made him a consistent winner. He posted a 15–7 record in 1934 and an 18–7 mark in 1935. He followed up these numbers with seasons of thirteen, seventeen, and eleven wins before being traded to the Red Sox after the 1938 season.

An even better all-around athlete was Schoolboy Rowe, a six-foot-four, 210-pound right-hander who had grown up in the oil boomtown of Eldorado, Arkansas. Espousing a diet that included plenty of spinach and red steaks, Rowe excelled in every sport he tried—football, basketball, track and field, boxing, golf, even target shooting. But it was in throwing and hitting a baseball that Rowe made his mark. In his first professional season, 1932, he won nineteen games and hit ten home runs for Beaumont in the Texas League. The following season he shut out the White Sox in his first major-league start. He seemed to be on his way to a big year until, in an early-season game against Philadelphia, he injured his shoulder fielding a bunt laid down, ironically enough, by Cochrane. Rowe, who would be affected by occasional lapses of self-confidence throughout his career, openly fretted. However, in the off-season a doctor performed wonders on his sore arm, and starting in spring training, Cochrane applied regular doses of confidence to the twenty-four-year-old's fragile psyche.

Outside Cochrane, no one captured Detroiters' imagination in 1934 more than Rowe. Starting, relieving, pinch-hitting—Rowe won games with his arm and his bat. On June 6, he pitched the Tigers into first place for the first time since August 12, 1924, with a 2–1 win over Cleveland. "This Is Exciting" read a headline in the *Detroit News,* as Navin Field experienced the first overflow crowds since the depression started. The unpretentious Schoolboy, who won twenty-four games, including a record-tying sixteen in a row, and hit .303 with a couple of home runs, reveled in all the attention. A common postgame sight was that of the towering star pitcher, "as inconspicuous as a giraffe," signing autographs and chatting with the legions of young fans trailing after him down Michigan Avenue.

Rowe's performance was just one of many that made 1934 so memorable. The public fascination with gangsters—that summer saw the demise of John Dillinger, Charles "Pretty Boy" Floyd, and Bonnie Parker and Clyde Barrow—inspired the press to dub the

Thanks to trick photography, Schoolboy Rowe is sitting on top of the baseball world in 1934, the year he won twenty-four games. Rowe, who would win 158 games in a fifteen-year career with the Tigers and Phillies, got his nickname as a youngster when he outpitched the coach of his church league team in a semipro game. The headline in the next morning's newspaper read "Schoolboy Beats Teacher." (Courtesy of the Burton Historical Collection of the Detroit Public Library.)

Tigers' heavy-hitting trio of Gehringer, Greenberg, and Goslin the "G-Men." Goslin hit .305 with 100 RBI, and Gehringer hit .356 (second only to Lou Gehrig), drove in 127 runs, and led the circuit in hits (214) and runs (134). Greenberg's ninety-three strikeouts broke his own team record, but that was compensated by a .339 average, 139 RBI, and twenty-six home runs, the last erasing Moose Alexander's team mark.

Greenberg, with sixty-three, and Gehringer with sixty, also finished 1–2 in the league in doubles. With shortstop Billy Rogell and third baseman Marv Owen, they put together the finest single season of any infield in history. Not only did they drive in a collective

462 runs (the all-time high), they set another major-league mark by missing but one game between them all year. Talk about punching the time clock! Ironically, it was Greenberg—a man with a legendary work ethic—who kept his lunch pail home that one time, an occasion that quickly became a part of the city's lore.

Greenberg had grown up in the Bronx, New York, the tall, awkward son of Romanian immigrants. It was purely through endless hours of practice that he was able to mold himself into a ball player. As a rookie, his fielding had been likened to that of an elephant trying to pick up marbles with his toes, but in time he made himself into a more-than-adequate defensive player. Even after he became one of baseball's top sluggers, he could be found in an empty ballpark hours before a game, paying local sandlotters out of his pocket to pitch batting practice and shag fly balls.

In only his second big-league season, the twenty-three-year-old Greenberg was already being heralded in some Jewish periodicals as "the Jewish Babe Ruth." Greenberg was never particularly religious, but he did feel a responsibility to observe his faith's two most important holidays—Rosh Hashanah, the Jewish New Year, and Yom Kippur, the Day of Atonement. In 1934 both holidays came in the heat of a pennant race. Whether Greenberg should play on those days quickly became a national issue.

The question was finally put before Detroit's leading rabbi, Rabbi Leo Franklin. The rabbi, possibly a baseball fan himself, consulted the Talmud and declared that Hank could play on Rosh Hashanah, for that was a happy occasion, one that could be celebrated with play. So, on September 10, the *Detroit Free Press* ran a front-page headline—"Happy New Year, Hank"—in Yiddish, and baseball's greatest Jewish star celebrated in storybook fashion with a pair of home runs to beat Boston, 2–1.

Unfortunately for Greenberg, who lived at the downtown Leland Hotel, his phone rang off the hook after the game. Parishioners, several rabbis, and his parents in New York had been upset with his decision to play. So when Yom Kippur arrived ten days later, Greenberg made it his personal day of atonement. At 10:30 A.M. , the time he would usually be taking batting practice at Navin Field, he entered the local synagogue for prayer. The rabbi was praying when, suddenly, "everything seemed to stop," Greenberg later recalled. "The rabbi looked up; he didn't know what was going on. And suddenly everybody was applauding. I was embarrassed; I didn't know what to do. It was a tremendous ovation for a kid who was only 23 years old, and in a synagogue, no less!" Edgar Guest, the nationally syndicated poet of the *Free Press*, was moved to write a poem that over the years has become a classic of sorts. Its last lines read: "We shall miss him on the infield and we shall miss him at the bat / But he's true to his religion—and I honor him for that!"

As Yiddish headlines and syndicated poetry illustrate, local media coverage of baseball clearly turned a corner with the '34 Tigers. Before then, even important regular season games had rarely warranted more than a reporter or two from each daily. Photographers were generally thought too precious a commodity to waste at a ball game. Now the *Free Press* alone was sending eight reporters to cover each contest. And that didn't include its pseudonymous baseball expert, a long-bearded sage named "Iffy the Dopester."

The Tigers' success in the mid-1930s brought even casual fans out to Navin Field. Here Edsel and Henry Ford chat with Mickey Cochrane.

Iffy was the creation and alter ego of *Free Press* editor Malcolm Bingay, who had covered the Tigers' 1907–8–9 pennant winners as a *Detroit News* reporter. Every sports section at that time ran a schedule of the day's games, accompanied by standings that showed a team's record "if they win" and "if they lose," hence Iffy's moniker. Iffy's columns were an irreverent blend of commentary and nostalgia, filled with colorful tales of Tigers past and present. *Free Press* artist Floyd S. Nixon drew the white-whiskered old coot, whose memory, Iffy reminded readers, stretched all the way to Abner Doubleday, the dubious creator of baseball. It was a perfect forum for the fifty-year-old Bingay, a noted raconteur and drinker who was equally at home in salon or saloon.

Iffy and the Tigers proved a winning combination. The depression had killed one Detroit paper, the *Mirror*, and cut into the circulation of the surviving dailies. The circulation of the three-cent *Free Press* alone had dropped more than twenty-three percent, from a high of 245,898 in September 1929 to 188,408 by September 1933. However, the revived interest in the Tigers, coupled with a recovering economy, worked wonders. The coverage of late-breaking news always suffered in an evening-newspaper town like Detroit, but now citizens were more interested in reading about what had happened at that afternoon's game at Navin Field. Capitalizing on this, the *Free Press* moved up the press time of its first edition from 8:07 P.M. to 7:22 P.M. and increased the number of copies run off before midnight. By 1935 the paper had increased its press run to 280,000 copies, of which 164,000 were printed before midnight. Not until the early 1950s, with the growth in night baseball and other late-starting sports, did the *Free Press* shift its emphasis to its morning edition.

"There was a great amount of competition between the *Times*, the *News*, and the *Free Press* then," recalled sportswriter Edgar Hayes. "There were more street sales than today. The Tigers would

Malcolm Bingay, editor of the *Detroit Free Press*, was so enamored of the Tigers he created the character of Iffy the Dopester in the closing weeks of the 1934 pennant race. *Free Press* artist Floyd S. Nixon was responsible for drawing Iffy and his distinctive flowing beard. Iffy fan clubs sprouted up around the city. Though most Detroiters suspected Bingay was the real Iffy, he didn't officially 'fess up until a *Saturday Evening Post* article in 1939. (Courtesy of the Burton Historical Collection of the Detroit Public Library.)

Iffing on All Eight

start playing at three o'clock, and the game would be over by five o'clock, so we'd try to get a paper on the street to catch the crowd going home. All dailies were primarily evening newspapers, but we had dozens of editions. The first one was at 7:30 A.M. The last, which was a super redline edition at 6:00 or 6:30 P.M., would hopefully have the box scores of all the afternoon games. In the press box at Navin Field there were three writers and three telegraphers, a pair from each paper. The story had to get out. The telegraphers would send out the play-by-play as the game was in progress, so each new edition carried an update. It was hectic."

Not to be outdone, late in the season the *Detroit News* flew in Schoolboy Rowe's sweetheart from Arkansas. Earlier, when Eddie Cantor had had the Tiger pitcher utter a few lines on his radio show, Schoolboy innocently whispered, "How'm I doin', Edna?" into the microphone. That line not only became a standard cry from opponents' dugouts whenever Schoolie pitched, it prompted the obvious question, Who is Edna? Detroiters soon found out, as the paper plucked Edna Mary Skinner out of quiet Eldorado and deposited the pretty and slightly bewildered brunette into baseball-mad Detroit. The *News* had Edna write about anything she wanted— cooking, baseball, whatever—and sat back and watched circulation climb. This was pure hokem, but the paper believed it was justified. After all, what was a pennant race without a good love story? And Schoolboy and Edna *did* get married after the World Series.

The *News* already had the most knowledgeable and respected baseball writer in town in Henry George Salsinger, who was the paper's sports editor from 1907 to 1958. "Sal," as his friends knew him, was a warm, dignified man of culture given to black cigars. His close-cropped hair and aloof manner made him even more formidable in the eyes of the ball players he wrote about. His column, "The Umpire," was perfectly titled, for the Springfield, Ohio, native always called them as he saw them. And like many writers, Salsinger was a confidant of players and management, one whose opinion was sought on such matters of importance as trades, lodging, and who to see about some bootleg liquor. It was almost even money that a Tiger would first discover that he'd been traded, not from a telegram from the front office, but from a phone call from a favorite sportswriter.

Over the years, Detroit's high priest of sportswriting was joined in the press box by such respected colleagues as Sam Greene of the *News*, Bud Shaver of the *Times*, and Harry Bullion and Charlie

Ward of the *Free Press*. Despite the city's long tradition of compe-
tent sports journalism (the Baseball Writers Association was
founded at the Pontchartrain Hotel in 1908), it never produced the
school of "literary" sportswriters that New York and Chicago did.
Salsinger, in particular, was handicapped by the lack of a national
syndicate or the wire service outlets more famous wordsmiths like
Ring Lardner, Hugh Fullerton, Damon Runyon, and Grantland Rice
enjoyed. Nonetheless, in 1969 Salsinger would become the first of
the so-called regional selections to be inducted into the sportswriters wing of the Baseball Hall of Fame.

This was a decidedly less sophisticated era in sportswriting.
The experiences of a pair of Edgars—Edgar Hayes of the *Times* and
W. W. (Eddie) Edgar of the *Free Press*, both hired in 1924—give a
taste of newspapering then.

Before leaving Pennsylvania for Detroit, Eddie Edgar had been
the one-person sports staff of the *Allentown Record,* a position he
thought deserved a spot to park his Remington typewriter. "When I
asked for my own office," Edgar told Neal Shine of the *Free Press*
many years later, "they took out the tub and the toilet in the upstairs
bathroom and moved me in."

Edgar got even less respect when he reported to work at the *Free
Press.* He arrived just as the paper's short-fused sports editor, Harry
Bullion, was throwing his phone out the window. "Then he asked
me what my initials, W. W., stood for," recounted Edgar. "I told him
it was Wilson William and he said, 'not here it isn't.' He said he
wasn't going to have anybody on his sports staff with a sissy name
like that."

After some deliberation, the staff gave him the name "Eddie"
and then ridiculed him for wearing a medal representing twenty
years' perfect attendance in Sunday school. He spent the rest of his
first night ducking Bullion, who threw his phone out the window
two more times, then was tossed out of a restaurant after a fellow
reporter caused some sort of commotion. Edgar later accompanied
Bullion to a blind pig where, in a fit of rage over losing a game of
Indian dice, the editor wound up and fired the dice cup. It hit Edgar
square in the mouth and split his lip. Despite all this, Eddie Edgar
stayed with the *Free Press* until 1948.

Edgar Hayes was born in 1907 in Corktown, the Irish neighborhood surrounding the ballpark, and grew up rooting for the Tigers.
"I was maybe the worst baseball player that ever went out for a
team," he confessed, "so I took to hanging around the downtown

offices of the *Detroit Times*. Finally, Henry Montgomery, the *Times's* editor, said, 'This guy's hanging around so much, put him to work!' I was seventeen and going to high school at the time, so they made me a high school correspondent."

Three years later, Hayes dropped out of the University of Detroit to accept a full-time position for $25 a week, plus an extra $6.40 for working Sundays. "There was no such thing as a journalism class then. You didn't even have to be a high school graduate. In those days, I'd say eighty percent of the newsmen couldn't pass the psychological tests they give reporters now. We had one photographer on the staff who got his start when he was a cab driver hustling plates back and forth. One day he said, 'Why don't you hire me in there?' They did, and he became a pretty good photographer."

Sportswriters and athletes were always tripping over one another in speakeasies and at racetracks, so reporters like Hayes and Edgar heard and saw plenty. They knew about that night in Detroit when Babe Ruth ducked into an empty cab to avoid being shot by an angry gun-toting man (probably a jealous husband), or the time Ty Cobb slapped a black maid in a downtown hotel. These never made the sports pages. The fact that a pitcher missed a turn on the mound because he was out the night before with a woman not his wife was always conveniently overlooked.

"You didn't step on toes then," admitted Hayes. "The theory was, you're a guest in the clubhouse, so you didn't repeat what you saw or heard in there. Formal interviews were okay, but what happened in the clubhouse stayed there. The same when you saw an athlete around town. There are all kinds of stories I could tell you concerning big names that will never see the light of day, and that's an attitude most writers had then."

Reporters, in the main, subscribed to the gee-whiz theory of sportswriting, which at its most extreme was a mix of cheerleading and classical allusions. The rhapsodic recounting of that day's game could turn a dusty baseball diamond into the blood-soaked Plains of Abraham, complete with melodramatic (and usually fabricated) quotes from the combatants.

"Actually, for a long time the writer wouldn't even bother going into the dressing room," said Hayes. "He'd write what he saw, his feelings of the ball game. He didn't give a damn what the athletes thought. Harry Salsinger of the *News* was sports editor for a long time, and I don't think I ever saw him in the dressing room. Long columns of quotes? Make 'em up. Before tape recorders, it was a common practice. It was your literary license. I did it, sure. You could make an illiterate pitcher right off the farm sound like a Rhodes scholar. You would never write anything that made the guy look bad, but if you could reasonably expect that person to say something like that, you could invent whole conversations. The players accepted it. Hell, they *expected* it."

Pouring fuel on the media frenzy was radio station WXYZ, which began airing Tiger games that year over its Michigan Radio Network. WXYZ, inside the Maccabees Building next to the Main Library on Woodward Avenue, was developing into the country's foremost creator of original programming, with such popular shows as "The Lone Ranger," "Warner Lester, Manhunter," "The Green Hornet," and "Sergeant Preston of the Yukon" originating from its studios during the thirties. Frank Navin had at first resisted the station's overtures, arguing that WWJ had enjoyed exclusive broadcast rights since 1927. However, when WXYZ offered twenty-five thousand dollars for the rights to feed ball games, by telephone lines, to affiliates in Battle Creek, Kalamazoo, Flint, Bay City, and Jackson, Navin, who was coming off a financially dismal 1933 season, relented. Not only was the money needed to pay off his spring-training debts, the network would introduce his product to hundreds of thousands of outstate fans.

Hired to announce the games for fifty dollars a week was an old favorite, Harry Heilmann, who had been working as an under sheriff since retiring from the Cincinnati Reds. Though never a polished speaker, Heilmann's easy, authoritative voice would become a fixture of Michigan summers over the next two decades.

For Heilmann was something that his competitor on WWJ, Ty Tyson, could never be, and that was the link connecting Tigers past and present. Slug's specialty was story telling, an art he put to use during rain delays, pitching changes, and whenever the mood struck him. Self-effacing almost to a fault, Heilmann never described his considerable accomplishments. Instead, tugging on his ever present cigarette, he would draw from a bottomless well of anecdotes about his teammates from the twenties.

Like most announcers, Heilmann had his pet lines. An early sponsor was the Socony-Vacuum Company, makers of an insect spray called Bugaboo. "There's a fly ball to left," Heilmann would say. "Goslin drifts under it and . . . Bugaboo! Another fly is dead!" Another pet phrase was "Trouble! Trouble!" which he used whenever a Tiger hit a fly ball that looked like it had a chance of leaving the ballpark. Prolonging the suspense almost did in a butcher named Otto Schwarzhauser, who wrote to Heilmann complaining that he nearly cut off his thumb while listening to a broadcast. Heilmann read the letter on the air, then later in the broadcast exclaimed as a Tiger hit a home run: "Trouble! Trouble! Look out, Mr. Schwarzhauser!"

But Ol' Slug's most memorable line, used sparingly but effectively, came after an outstanding play had produced a crescendo of appreciative cheers and applause. During such moments Heilmann would simply stop speaking and turn the microphone toward the murmurous crowd. "Listen," he would quietly say, "to the voice of baseball. . . ."

All this attention on a group of ball players was a welcome diversion from the grimmer realities of daily life. "Golly, the club was a shot in the arm to the city," recalled Eldon Auker, a trace of wonder still in his voice. At a time when the average auto worker was making seventy-six cents an hour (when he worked), a fan could get into Navin Field for as little as fifty cents for a bleacher seat; the more affluent paid $3.50 for a box seat. In either case, hot dogs, pop, and ice cream each cost a dime. A trolley ride to the ballpark was a nickel (seven cents with a transfer); if you drove, a uniformed attendant would park your car at the Sports Parking Lot at Cherry and Trumbull for a quarter. With the city slowly regaining its economic legs under another inspirational leader, Franklin Roosevelt, and the Tigers stalking their first pennant in a quarter of a century, Detroiters were more than ready to cut loose and have some fun cheering for the home team. Attendance at Navin Field nearly tripled to a league-high 919,000 in 1934; the following season it would surpass 1 million, the best in the majors.*

With 101 victories, the '34 Tigers finished seven games ahead of the Yankees, who were hampered by center fielder Earle Combs's broken collarbone and an aging Babe Ruth stumbling through his final season in pinstripes. Detroit led the league in batting (.300),

---

*In the 1932 presidential election Detroiters had voted Democratic for the first time in a half-century. Franklin Roosevelt, who over the next two years helped put the country back on its feet with a flurry of bold, experimental, and oft-criticized social legislation and public works programs, certainly spoke the language of the average hardworking bleacherite. "I have no expectation of making a hit every time I come to bat," he said. "What I seek is the highest possible batting average."

runs (958), and—shades of Ty Cobb—stolen bases, as outfielders Gerald "Gee" Walker, Jo-Jo White, and Pete Fox each stole more than twenty.

Jo-Jo, who got his nickname because of the way he pronounced his home state, Georgia, was considerably quicker than his drawl. He was one of the best base runners in baseball and usually batted leadoff. His direct opposite on the base paths was his good friend, Walker, a Mississippian, whose wild and crazy ways exasperated more serious-minded players like Gehringer and Cochrane.

Walker was a talented but uneven sort who could hit for power and average. He also was a solid stolen-base threat, finishing runner-up in that category in 1932 and 1933. "The people in Detroit loved Gerry," said White. "I remember one time he misplayed a ball in the outfield and the crowd got all over him. The next inning he hit a double, and as he was standing on second base, he turned around and gave the crowd the finger. Everybody started cheering." Bucky Harris had tolerated Walker's shenanigans, which included playing an inning in the rain in his bare feet, but Cochrane wasn't having any. He suspended Walker midway through the 1934 season and used him sparingly thereafter.

Cochrane's own stats (129 games, .320 average) paled alongside those of Triple Crown winner Lou Gehrig. However, it was Black Mike who was named Most Valuable Player by the sportswriters around the league, who recognized that the field manager's value transcended mere numbers. Some even hailed him as a "miracle man," though Iffy the Dopester pooh-poohed that.

"He is about as mystical as a keg of nails," observed Iffy. "He is merely doing that which every old-time student of baseball thoroughly understands. He is fighting like 'll and inspiring his teammates to do the same, because they recognize his common sense as a leader."

The Tigers' opponent in the World Series was the St. Louis Cardinals, who had put on a tremendous stretch run to nose out the New York Giants. The Cardinals were led by their buffoonish but immensely talented pitcher, Jay Hanna "Dizzy" Dean, whose thirtieth win had clinched the pennant on the last day of the season. Despite the presence of Dean and such certified characters as shortstop Leo Durocher and pitcher Dazzy Vance, the Cardinals were not nearly as wacky as legend has made them out to be. Dizzy's younger brother, Paul, nicknamed "Daffy," was a mild type who quietly racked up nineteen wins that summer, and left fielder Joe

Medwick's grim, mean-spirited style belied his "Ducky" moniker. The team was not dubbed the "Gas House Gang" until the following season. Still, there was a fierce, free-spirited edge to their play, epitomized by players such as third baseman John "Pepper" Martin, who openly confessed that he played the hot corner and stole all those bases with nothing on beneath his knickers.

The matchup between Detroit and St. Louis was so appealing that Henry Ford paid a record hundred thousand dollars to commercially sponsor the broadcast. The Tigers were slight favorites, but Dizzy's antics and braggadocio amused spectators, inspired his teammates, and ultimately intimidated the Detroit club. In the series opener, a Navin Field crowd of 42,505 watched glumly as Dean clowned and pitched his team to an easy 8–3 victory. The Detroit infield fell apart with five errors, and Dean openly taunted Greenberg, who was singled out for special abuse by the St. Louis bench throughout the series.

In the eighth inning of that opening game, player-manager Frankie Frisch had to trot in from second base to admonish Dean. "Damn it, Jerome, quit fooling around or I'll yank your butt out of there," said Frisch. "Keep the ball down."

"Oh, Frankie," replied Dean in his Ozark twang, "you ain't a-gonna take out ol' Diz. All these good folks would think you was crazy. I'm just a-figurin' that Moe can't hit my high hard one." Greenberg proved Dean wrong, depositing his next fastball deep into the temporary seats in left. As Greenberg circled the bases, Dean tried calming Frisch down. "Don't get excited, Frank, 'cause it won't happen again. 'Sides, you're right. Moe can hit the dog shit out of a high fast one."

Cochrane had held out his ace for game two, and Schoolboy Rowe responded with a strong twelve-inning performance. With the Tigers trailing 2–1 in the bottom of the ninth, Gee Walker pinch-hit for his buddy, Jo-Jo White, and lined a single to tie the game. Representing the winning run, Walker was then characteristically picked off base. But Goslin's RBI single in the twelfth redeemed Walker and knotted the series. At one point Rowe retired twenty-two Cardinals in a row, a record not broken until Don Larsen's perfect game in 1956.

The next three games were in St. Louis. Paul Dean bested Tommy Bridges in game three, 4–1, but Eldon Auker went all the way in a 10–4 victory the following afternoon. Although he wasn't pitching, Dizzy Dean again managed to capture center stage, rush-

Detroit's first pennant in twenty-five years prompted the
J. L. Hudson Company to hang a seven-story banner on
the face of its downtown store. (Courtesy of Manning
Brothers, Photographers.)

ing onto the field as a pinch runner for slow-footed Spud Davis
during a fourth-inning rally before Frisch knew what was going
on. Frisch's worst fears were realized moments later, when Billy
Rogell fired the ball directly into Dean's forehead on a double
play grounder. The ball caromed into the outfield, allowing the tying run to score, but Dean had to be carried off the field on a
stretcher. While the Tigers scored six late-inning runs to salt away
the game, Dean was being examined at a hospital. X rays of Diz's
skull "showed nothing," reported the newspapers, which surprised no one.

Dean took his regular turn in game five, and Bridges outdueled him, 3–1. With the series returning to Detroit and Rowe pitching, Tiger fans were certain the peanut was in the bag.

It wasn't to be, however, as the Redbirds forced a seventh game with a 4–3 victory before a packed house of 44,551 Navin Field fans. Rowe went the distance, but faltered against the eighth- and ninth-place hitters. Weak-hitting Leo Durocher smacked three hits, while Paul Dean aided his cause with a seventh-inning single that scored Durocher with the winning run. This was after the Tigers had rallied in the bottom of the sixth to tie the game at three runs apiece. The biggest controversy of the series up to that point occurred during the rally, as an obviously bad call at third base probably prevented the Tigers from enjoying a bigger inning than they did. As it was, Rowe, batting for himself with two outs in the ninth, brought the crowd to its feet with a long fly to deep center that, symbolically, fell just short of paydirt.

The Detroit clubhouse, primed for a celebration, suddenly had an air of dread. The Tigers knew they would have to face Dizzy Dean in the decisive seventh game, and though everyone else on both teams tried their best to disguise their butterflies, Dizzy reveled in the pressure. Before the game he grabbed a tiger rug from baseball clown Al Schacht and paraded around the field, announcing, "I got that tiger skin already." Spotting Eldon Auker, Cochrane's choice as starter, warming up, Dean chided, "Hey, podnah, you don't expect to get anybody out with *that* shit, do you?"

The unflustered Auker matched goose eggs with Dean, who was pitching on a single day's rest, until the third inning, when Dizzy took matters into his own hands. With one out, he drove an Auker pitch into left. Seeing Goslin strolling in to field the ball, Dean immediately took off for second, sliding in safely with a double as amazed Tiger infielders stood dumbly in their tracks.

From little acorns grow giant oaks. The next batter, Martin, hit a slow roller to Greenberg that could easily have been a force-out at second, had Dean been on first. Instead, Greenberg, fielding the ball to his right, had to throw cross-body to first, and just missed getting Martin. Jack Rothrock walked, bringing up Frisch. At thirty-seven, and playing in his fiftieth World Series game, Frisch still was nervous enough that he wet his pants before each contest. The only one in on Frisch's secret was the equipment manager, who kept a dry jockstrap ready in the clubhouse.

Auker worked the count full on Frisch, who fouled off several pitches before ending the drama with a line drive over Greenberg's outstretched glove and into the right-field corner. Three runs scored, and before the inning was over St. Louis had scored four more times for a 7–0 lead, with the all-purpose Dean adding his record second hit of the frame. Dean responded to the growing chorus of boos with several handsprings, a tip of the cap, and a deep bow.

The lead grew to an insurmountable 8–0 after Joe Medwick bounced a long drive off the right-center -field bleachers in the sixth inning, scoring Martin. Roaring like a freight train around second, and not knowing whether a play was going to be made on him at third, Medwick slid hard into Marv Owen. Lying in the swirling dirt, Medwick exchanged words with the frustrated Owen, who turned away from Medwick's offer to shake hands. The restless crowd booed lustily.

Medwick then scored on Rip Collins's base hit, inciting the nearly forty-one thousand fans even further. When Medwick took the field in the bottom of the inning, he was pelted with a barrage of garbage from the howling, jeering fans jammed into the temporary bleachers in left field. Oranges, bottles, rolled-up scorecards, hard-boiled eggs, apple cores, and half-eaten sandwiches rained down on Medwick, who retreated long enough for the ground crew to clean up the mess. The situation was hopeless, though, as the supply of venom and ammunition (an enterprising vendor on Cherry Street continued to toss fruit up to the bleacherites) directed toward Medwick proved endless. After three delays totaling about twenty minutes, Commissioner Landis called Medwick, Owen, Frisch, and the umpires to his private box. Satisfied that the game was out of reach, Landis ordered Medwick out of the game.

"Why should I take him out?" complained Frisch.

"Because I say so," demanded Landis. "We want to go on with this game, and it wouldn't look so good if a World Series game had to be forfeited. So get it over with." Thus ended the "Battle of Produce Row," the lone victory in an otherwise abysmal 11–0 loss.

The demoralized Tigers started off slowly in 1935, languishing in sixth place in late May. By late July, however, they had overhauled the Yankees for the top spot and were never headed. Gehringer hit .330, Pete Fox .321, and Cochrane .319 as the Tigers once again led the circuit in batting (.290) and runs scored (919). Supplementing Bridges's twenty-one wins was Schoolboy Rowe, who won nineteen games and hit .312 to boot.

However, the lion's share of the credit had to go to Greenberg.
Although he had hit .321 and led both teams in slugging and RBI in
the '34 World Series, Greenberg was criticized by many over the
winter for having had a poor postseason. He had struck out nine
times, many in clutch situations, and he admitted that he had let
the Cardinals get his goat. He had lost his composure completely in
his final at-bat in the seventh-game wipeout, striking out on a Dizzy
Dean fastball that was a good foot over his head. Nonetheless, Navin
had rewarded Greenberg by tripling his salary to fifteen thousand
dollars, and the first sacker went about proving that he was worth
every cent. In 1935 he led the league in home runs (36), RBI (170,
including an astounding 103 by the All-Star break), and total bases
(389), all new club records. He also finished second in doubles and
slugging. Greenberg was voted the league's Most Valuable Player as
the Tigers copped their second straight pennant with ninety-three
wins, finishing three games ahead of New York.

An untold story of that summer concerned Greenberg's special older-brother relationship with batboy Joe Roggin, who had
changed his name from Roginski in an attempt to disguise his Polish ancestry. This was nothing new in an era when ball players and
factory workers alike thought they could get a leg up on prejudice
by anglicizing their names. The major leagues in the first half of this
century were filled with players like Aloysius Syzmanski, who
made it into the Hall of Fame as Al Simmons, and Detroit sandlotter Casimir Kwietniewski, who became Cass Michaels after being signed by the White Sox.

As Greenberg learned to his dismay, a player's ethnicity was a
prime target of abuse from bench jockeys. Jockeying was a vicious,
profane, but time-honored carryover from a more primitive game.
Some players hung on in the majors simply by their ability to get
under an opponent's skin. "I remember when Jimmy Dykes managed the White Sox," recalled Billy Rogell. "He'd yell out to Hank,
'How can you get along with those Catholics and you being a hebe?
Three Catholics and a hebe on the infield, how do you expect us to
beat ya?' We didn't like it either. But you know, that was baseball."

Ball players are nothing if not superstitious, and the Tigers of
the thirties were no exception. Goose Goslin, for example, always

Hank Greenberg and mascot Joe Roggin in 1935. (Courtesy of the Detroit
Tigers.)

wanted his bat delivered to him in the batter's box, and Schoolboy
Rowe never picked up a glove with his right hand. So when word
reached the club that a local sandlot team had won four straight
amateur titles with little Joe Roginski as its mascot, Alex Okray, the
equally superstitious clubhouse manager of the Tigers, brought him
into the fold.

Greenberg took the thirteen-year-old batboy, who grew up on
the city's near west side, under his wing. The youngster "was afraid
of being Polish," recalled his son Michael, today a policeman in
Florida. "He thought if the club found out he was Polish, he
wouldn't be around long. He wanted to fit in, so that's why he
changed his name. He thought Roggin sounded Irish. My mom
thought he was Irish. When they were dating he wouldn't take her
home because his parents spoke Polish."

Greenberg would occasionally take Joe on road trips and visit
the modest Roginski home on Wesson Avenue. "Hank would come
over and have a bowl of *czarnina*, duck blood soup," recalled Joe's
brother, Stanley. "Word would get out and a half-hour later there
was five hundred kids gathering outside." As Greenberg pursued
his first home run crown, he developed a routine of always warming up before games by playing catch with his "good luck charm."
And after he clouted one into the seats, he insisted that Roggin be
the first to greet him at home plate.

The ritual continued into the World Series that year between
the Tigers and Chicago Cubs. The series was especially vicious,
with both benches keeping up a steady stream of profanity. "Throw
him a pork chop, he'll never hit it," was one of the milder insults
directed at Greenberg, who went hitless as the Cubs won the opener
in Detroit, 3–0. At one point umpire (and ex-Tiger manager) George
Moriarty stopped the game to trade insults with the Chicago bench.
Judge Landis wound up fining several Cubs *and* Moriarty, who for
the rest of the series saw fit to call several close plays Detroit's way.

The Tigers knocked out Chicago starter Charlie Root in the first
inning of the second game, scoring four runs before he could get a
man out. The last two runs scored on Greenberg's home run into the
left-field stands; as always, Joe Roggin was standing at home plate,
waiting to shake his hand first.

This time, though, Greenberg's good-luck charm failed him.
Late in the game, trying to score on a Pete Fox single, he collided
with Cubs catcher Gabby Hartnett, who fell on Greenberg's left

wrist. Greenberg finished playing in the 8–3 victory, but on the train ride to Chicago it had swollen so badly it was clear that the Tigers' top gun was out for the series.

Marv Owen moved to first base, and light-hitting Herman "Flea" Clifton took over Owen's spot at third. Clifton and Owen would wind up with one single between them in thirty-seven series at-bats, but destiny—for once—would prove to be with Detroit. In game three at Wrigley Field, the Tigers fought back from a three-run deficit and ultimately pulled out a 6–5 win when Jo-Jo White's single scored Owen with two outs in the eleventh inning.

The next day, Alvin "General" Crowder, whom the Tigers had picked up late in the 1934 season, twirled a masterful five-hitter. Crowder, who had won sixteen games in 1935, gave up a solo home run to Hartnett in the second inning, then scored the tying run the following inning on a Gehringer double. The game remained deadlocked until the sixth, when Clifton put on the afterburners and reached second base after Augie Galan dropped his fly ball in left. The speedy Clifton then scored what proved to be the winning run when shortstop Billy Jurges misplayed Crowder's grounder.

The 2–1 victory meant Chicago would have to sweep the final three games to win the series. They made it one-third of the way back with a 3–1 win in game five, as Chuck Klein hit a two-run homer off loser Schoolboy Rowe. That brought the series back to Navin Field with Detroit needing only one win in the final two games—the exact situation it was in the year before with St. Louis.

This time the outcome was different. Tommy Bridges went up against the Cubs' Larry French, who held onto a precarious 3–2 lead entering the bottom of the sixth. With two out, Rogell hit a ground-rule double to left. This brought up Owen, who lined his only hit of the series to tie the game. The game remained tied going into the ninth, with the suspense and crowd noise building to an almost unbearable climax. Then Chicago third baseman Stan Hack led off the top of the inning with a long triple over Gee Walker's head in center, and suddenly it was as if 48,420 fans had been struck dumb all at once.

Operating in a park that, outside some odd shouts from National League fans, was eerily quiet, Bridges went to work on the next three batters. With only a fly ball or the right kind of grounder needed to score Hack, Bridges then proceeded to strike out Jurges. *One out.* He induced French to tap weakly to the mound, Hack holding third. *Two out.* Then the ever dangerous Galan flied harm-lessly to Goslin for the third out, ending one of the great clutch-pitching performances in club history.

Clifton struck out to start the bottom half of the ninth, but then Cochrane lined a single off second baseman Billy Herman's glove. Gehringer ripped a grounder to first baseman Phil Cavarretta, who made the play as Cochrane took second. Up to the plate strode Gos-lin, who hadn't got the ball out of the infield in four previous at-bats against French. But with two outs, the score tied, and a cham-pionship hanging in the balance, he was confidence personified.

"If they pitch that ball over this plate," Goslin told the umpire, "you can go take that monkey suit off." True to his word, Goslin then slapped a French pitch toward right field. It floated like a soap bubble over Billy Herman's outstretched glove before plopping onto the grass in short right field. Cochrane, off with the crack of the bat, raced around third and roared home, stomping his spikes several times on the plate to seal Detroit's first-ever World Series win.

Goose's single set off the greatest spontaneous celebration in the city's long history. With a jungle-throated roar, the crowd surged onto the field, mobbing Cochrane and company and carrying Goose into the clubhouse on its shoulders. One of the celebrants was seventeen-year-old Betty Martin, who had skipped classes at Southeastern High School to stand in line to buy a bleacher seat. "And who did I run into but my mother, who was playing hooky from her job at Universal Cooler," she recalled. A year earlier the schoolgirl had sat in the left-field bleachers and watched approv-ingly as fruit sailed over her head in the general direction of that villain, Joe Medwick. Now she joined the army of Detroit fans who stood in the shadows of a cool autumn afternoon, backslapping each other and yelling themselves hoarse.

Outside the ballpark, the din couldn't have been any greater if President Roosevelt himself had suddenly gone on the radio and announced that the depression was immediately, officially, and ir-revocably over. People banged on pots and pans, tooted car horns, and snake-danced through Grand Circus Park and Cadillac Square. Over-zealous fans fired machine guns from office windows, and someone snuck into the tower atop City Hall and rigged the clock to clang every sixty seconds. Traffic on Woodward Avenue and all the other major thoroughfares was hopelessly stalled as revelers flocked downtown. Betty Martin joined the throng of friends and

Fans finally file out of Navin Field on October 7, 1935, after yelling themselves hoarse over the Tigers' first world championship. (Copyright © 1935 by the *Detroit News*. Used with permission.)

strangers who made their way through the clogged, boisterous streets. She stopped at a beer hall on Second Avenue, just one of the many drinking joints that stayed open until the following morning. "There was confetti and ticker tape all over the cars, the buildings, everywhere," said Martin, who took home a long strip and carefully wrote on it the score of the game and the names of some of the members of that unforgettable team: Tommy Bridges, Goose Goslin, Charlie Gehringer, Billy Rogell, Marv Owen, Hank Greenberg, Gee Walker—"and of course, Mickey Cochrane, who was everybody's hero."

Of course, Mickey Cochrane. Roosevelt's New Deal legislation had rejuvenated industry, helped spur employment, and made Detroit a Democratic town for the first time since the nineteenth century. The administration had even repealed Prohibition, which meant that on the opening day of the 1934 season Navin Field customers could buy beer for the first time in sixteen years. But if a general election had been held in the fall of 1935, the man with the monocle and tilted cigarette holder would have finished a poor second to the man in shin guards and chest protector.

"I better not make Mickey Cochrane too wonderful," joked Frank Navin at a victory celebration. "I've got to sign him for next year." Tragically, Navin did not savor his long-awaited world championship for long. Just five weeks after Goslin's historic single, the Tigers' sixty-four-year-old owner died of a heart attack while horseback riding at the Detroit Riding and Hunt Club. Taking over the reins was Walter O. Briggs, the millionaire industrialist who would guide the club through the second half of its golden age.

Briggs was one of the many young men of vision and industry who had made their fortune during those heady turn-of-the-century days in Detroit. As a teenager he had worked for the Michigan Central Railroad as a five-dollar-a-week car checker. Later he joined the B. F. Everitt Company, a trim and painting shop owned by a childhood friend. Everitt sold the firm to Briggs in 1909. The reorganized Briggs Manufacturing Company caught the auto boom at its crest and went on one long, uninterrupted ride, making bodies and tops for automakers like Ford, Chrysler, Chalmers, Hudson, and Packard. Briggs quickly became the largest auto-body manufacturing company in the country, at its peak employing more than forty thousand workers at sixteen plants, including nine in Detroit.

Briggs and fellow industrialist John Kelsey had each bought a quarter-share interest in the Tigers in 1920. Seven years later, Briggs bought Kelsey's share from his estate. Now, in 1935, he became sole owner when Navin's widow decided to sell. One of the first things he did upon taking over the club was appoint Cochrane vice president. This meant that besides catching and managing full-time, he would now be responsible for running the whole show. Briggs paid Cochrane $45,000—a lot of money at a time when a top shortstop like Billy Rogell was making a comfortable $13,500. But the pressure of handling three jobs would soon exact a toll no salary could compensate.

The Tigers' World Series win was just one of several championships Detroiters had celebrated by the time the team came north from spring training in 1936. The football Lions and hockey Red Wings had also won their first titles in the intervening months, and fighter Joe Louis was poised to capture the heavyweight crown. And in balloting to determine the first class of immortals to be inducted into baseball's newly created Hall of Fame, Ty Cobb had garnered more votes than anyone, including Babe Ruth. With natives winning laurels in bowling, track, golf, swimming, and a slew of other amateur and professional sports, Detroit was attracting national attention as "the City of Champions." That label seemed especially secure after Cochrane persuaded Briggs to buy hard-hitting Al Simmons from the White Sox for seventy-five thousand dollars. A third-straight pennant seemed certain.

Instead of another dream season, however, the summer of 1936 quickly turned into one long, unremitting nightmare. Twelve games into the season, Greenberg's left wrist was reinjured after a collision with Washington's Jake Powell and he was forced to sit out the season. Cochrane acquired the Browns' Jack Burns, but he fell miserably short of replacing Greenberg's punch. In July, General Crowder, plagued by stomach ailments, retired. The rest of the pitching staff was inconsistent. Bridges wound up winning twenty-three games and Rowe nineteen, but Cochrane found himself increasingly questioning Schoolboy's dedication. Meanwhile, the hard-headed Simmons didn't take kindly to Cochrane's criticism and was sent packing to Washington after the season ended.

As catcher, manager, and vice president, Cochrane's woes were threefold. The pressure, aggravated by a succession of minor but painful injuries, finally did him in. In June he suffered a nervous breakdown in Boston and was sent home to Henry Ford Hospital, where he spent ten days under treatment. Then on June 21 he boarded the *Detroit News*'s "Early Bird" airplane and flew to a friend's ranch in Wyoming for an extended vacation. In all, Cochrane relinquished control of the team to coach Del Baker for two months. By the time he returned to the bench the Yankees, under rookie sensation Joe DiMaggio, were running away with the pennant. The Tigers had four 100-RBI men in Gehringer, Goslin, Owen, and Simmons. Gehringer hit .354 with a league-leading sixty doubles, while Gee Walker was right behind him in both departments with a .353 average and fifty-five two-base hits. But the Tigers barely finished second by percentage points over Chicago.

It went from bad to worse in 1937. Rowe reported to camp out of shape and was suspended; he would win a single game that summer. Goslin had slowed to a walk and was replaced by Walker in left. And on May 25 at Yankee Stadium, Cochrane had his playing career—and nearly his life—ended by a Bump Hadley fastball.

In the fifth inning Cochrane, who had hit an inside-the-park home run to tie the game his previous at-bat, was leaning in on a 3–

After recovering from a nervous breakdown, Mickey Cochrane rejoins the team in Yankee Stadium on July 15, 1936. Goose Goslin shakes hands with Cochrane as Jack Burns (far left) and Billy Rogell look on.

1 pitch when he lost sight of the ball. Hadley's high fastball crashed into his left temple with "a moist, sickening sound," recalled an observer. Cochrane was carried off the field and taken to St. Elizabeth's Hospital, where doctors discovered that he had suffered a fractured skull, a cracked right sinus, and a mild cerebral concussion. Their greatest fear was that meningitis might set in through one of the fractures. For several days Cochrane was in critical condition, though he remained conscious. His wife rushed from Detroit to his bedside, and he confided to her that he never expected to catch again. "After what happened last year, and this," a weary Mary Cochrane told the reporters keeping vigil, "well, I guess Mike just fights too hard."

After two weeks Cochrane was moved to Henry Ford Hospital, where he was inundated with several thousand letters, postcards, and bouquets from Detroit fans. He slowly regained his strength as Del Baker once again filled in. The '37 Tigers were almost a carbon copy of the '36 edition, finishing a distant second to New York. Once again they were short on pitching, but with a murderous offense. In one afternoon alone the team scored thirty-six runs in a doubleheader sweep of the Browns. Four Tigers—Gehringer, Greenberg, Fox, and Walker—each racked up two hundred hits, tying a major-league record, as the team led the circuit in batting with a .292 mark. Although he became the first Tiger to break the century mark in strikeouts, Greenberg had what he later considered his greatest season, bettering his own team records in home runs (40), total bases (397), and RBI (183, one short of Lou Gehrig's league mark). And at age thirty-four, Gehringer became the oldest first-time batting champion ever with a .371 average. Despite banner seasons from the Yankees' DiMaggio, Gehrig, and Bill Dickey, Gehringer became the third Tiger in four seasons to be voted the league's Most Valuable Player, which many surprised fans took as a belated tribute to his many years of consistently brilliant play.

Cochrane resumed managerial control on July 25, just in time to witness one of the great home run–hitting exhibitions of all time. Rudy York replaced Cochrane behind the plate and, in his first full season, immediately wreaked havoc on American League pitching, clubbing a major-league record eighteen home runs during August. York, who turned twenty-four during the month, was a fierce-looking presence with a bat in his hand: six-foot-one, 210 pounds, with a long scar—the result of being struck in the face with an ax when he was nine—creasing his left cheek. The powerful right-hander clouted thirty-five round-trippers and had 103 RBI in only 104 games in 1937. York was to maintain that kind of run production for the rest of his thirteen-year career, retiring in 1948 with 277 home runs and 1,152 RBI.

Those numbers might have been more imposing had York been given a permanent position and had he taken better care of himself. York would spend his first several seasons bouncing between first base, third base, catcher, and the outfield. Writers loved to describe the Cherokee as "part Indian, part first baseman," but the truth of the matter was York was a better-than-adequate fielder, albeit one who could create high drama out of a simple pop fly. As a Tiger first baseman he would set a league record in 1943 for assists, and the following year establish a major-league record for double plays.

York had grown up dirt-poor in Georgia and was forced to quit school in the third grade to work in a mill. Consequently, he squeezed the good life as hard as he could when it finally came his way. He later estimated that he'd made—and spent—$250,000 in his career, with most of that going for booze, women, and a new car every year. "But son, leave that liquor alone," the five-time All-Star later warned in a magazine piece. "I can tell you it never helped anybody, and if I had to do it over again that's one thing I'd use a lot less. I'd have had a couple more years of baseball left in me if I'd stayed away from it."

As 1937 wound down, the euphoria that had surrounded both the coming of Mickey Cochrane and the New Deal gave way to the malaise of a sick economy, the tumult of labor unrest, and the dread of impending war in Europe and Asia. Sit-down strikes became the vogue as workers took advantage of a Supreme Court decision giv-

The irrepressible Gee Walker. In a fifteen-year career he hit .294 with 124 home runs and 223 stolen bases, but his real contribution was his unabashed enthusiasm.

ing them the right to organize on the job for better pay and working conditions. Violent clashes characterized the organization attempts of auto plants, cigar factories, and even department stores. Meanwhile, the Roosevelt administration cut back drastically on federal work programs, and an unintended result was a collapse of the recovery. Between 1937 and 1938, auto production fell forty-eight percent. By March 1938, 310,000 of Detroit's 760,000 workers were unemployed.*

That spring, Cochrane added to the upheaval by trading the team's most popular player of the thirties, Gee Walker, to the White Sox for pitcher Vern Kennedy, outfielder Fred "Dixie" Walker, and infielder Tony Piet. Joining Gee on the Chicago-bound train were Marv Owen and a promising Detroit-area catcher, Mike Tresh. Detroiters were helpless to do anything about most outrages—the Germans in Austria, the Italians in Abyssinia, the Japanese in China— but Gee Walker in Comiskey Park was something they could take to the streets over. The front office was hammered by a flood of angry phone calls and letters, while tens of thousands of signatures were scrawled across petitions calling for the trade to be rescinded and threatening a boycott of the club if it wasn't.

"I hated to let Walker go," responded Cochrane, who explained that some sacrifices were necessary to make the club a contender again. "If this business does not turn out to benefit the Tigers," he said prophetically, "I'll take the rap."

On April 22, 1938, the Walker-less Tigers participated in

---

*The day after Cochrane was beaned in Yankee Stadium, Richard Frankensteen, Walter Reuther, and other organizers from the fledgling United Auto Workers were violently beaten while distributing leaflets outside the Ford Rouge plant in Dearborn. Administering the beating were goons from Ford's service department, headed by Henry Ford's hatchet man, Harry Bennett. The famous photographs of "the battle of the overpass" more than eclipsed news of the gravely injured Cochrane on Detroit's front pages; it turned public opinion against Ford and helped solidify organized labor's rise in what had once been a notoriously open-shop town.

Ironically, Bennett and Cochrane were close friends; it was at Bennett's Wyoming ranch that Cochrane had recuperated after his nervous breakdown in 1936. The rough-hewn Bennett liked to surround himself with boxers, college football players, and other athletes, many of whom, such as Jo-Jo White and Bob Fothergill, worked off-seasons in the service department. Identified in the photographs of the beating was Eddie Cicotte, a native Detroiter and ex-big league pitcher who had been one of the eight Black Sox banned from organized ball for allegedly throwing the 1919 World Series.

dedication ceremonies of renovated Navin Field, which was officially christened Briggs Stadium. Walter Briggs had spent well over a million depression dollars between 1936 and 1938 to expand the park to its present configurations. The first- and third-base pavilions were replaced by a double-decked grandstand in left and right field and a two-story bleacher section was constructed in center field. The improvements made it the first playing field in the majors to be completely enclosed and double-decked. The most modern sports arena of the day, it quickly became home to championship boxing matches, concerts, and, starting that fall, the football Lions.

Although the park's official seating capacity of fifty-three thousand was second only to Yankee Stadium, Briggs Stadium was more a monument to its namesake's ego than to his greed. Briggs was a true sportsman, someone who viewed the game through the eyes of a fan, not an accountant. After all, the Tiger boss had at first bought

The center-field bleachers under construction in February 1938. After taking over as owner, Walter O. Briggs expanded Navin Field between 1936 and 1938, then named the stadium after himself. (Courtesy of the Detroit Tigers.)

into the club in 1920 as a way of staying close to a game that he had enjoyed watching since the turn of the century. As Frank Navin's silent partner, he had delighted in buying players suits of clothes for winning an important series. And it was his money that had brought Mickey Cochrane to Detroit. Though Briggs wasn't in the baseball business to lose money, as sole owner he never took a dollar in salary and readily plowed profits back into the club. He made his fans comfortable, paid his managers and players well, and could always be found in his special box seat at Briggs Stadium, smoking long, thin cigars and shaking his fist at calls that went against the home team. More than anything, he wanted a championship banner of his own to hang on the center-field flagpole. By 1938 the sixty-one-year-old industrialist was growing impatient pursuing that dream, even with the man who had produced a world title for Frank Navin three years earlier.

For as a bench manager, Cochrane was badly miscast. He was fidgety, irritable, and prone to second-guessing his teammates. Always high-strung, and still suffering from the effects of his nervous breakdown and near-fatal beaning, he could no longer direct events or blow off steam on the field. He was under tremendous pressure. The deal with the White Sox failed to pay dividends, as Vern Kennedy won his first nine games with Detroit, then won only three more times after early June. There also were several arguments with Briggs's son, club secretary Walter "Spike" Briggs, Jr., as well as disciplinary problems with Cletus "Boots" Poffenberger, a wayward pitcher who had caused Cochrane nothing but grief since joining the team the previous summer.

The end came on August 6. The Tigers were in fifth place, three games under .500. After being creamed that afternoon by the Boston Red Sox, Cochrane had his usual postgame conference with Briggs. "Well, what is the alibi for today?" demanded Briggs.

"To tell you the plain truth, Mr. Briggs, you haven't got the players to win," Cochrane responded.

"That's not what you said in the spring," said Briggs. "Maybe it isn't the players. Maybe you are the cause and it would help matters if you quit." Assured that he would be paid the balance of his thirty-six-thousand-dollar salary for the season, Cochrane did just that.

Public sympathy was with the star-crossed catcher. "Mickey did more for baseball in four years here than Briggs can do in a lifetime," said Cochrane's old batterymate, Lefty Grove, in town as a member of the Red Sox. "Just look at the stadium—that's the stadium that Mickey Cochrane built." Cochrane, extremely distraught, tried to leave Detroit quickly and quietly. Instead, thousands of disbelieving Detroiters flocked to City Airport to see him off. The impromptu outpouring of affection left Cochrane speechless, but not his fans. As Cochrane boarded his plane for Chicago, one cried and draped his arm around his shoulder. "We'll never forget what you did here," he said.

Under new manager Del Baker the team played .649 ball the rest of the way to finish fourth. Most of the credit belonged to York and Greenberg, the majors' most potent home run duo. York hit thirty-three home runs, including four grand slams, and drove in 127 runs. Meanwhile, Greenberg captured the country's attention by chasing Babe Ruth's 1927 single-season record of sixty round-trippers. On September 26 he blasted his fifty-seventh and fifty-eighth home runs at home in a doubleheader sweep of the Browns, leaving him with five games in which to catch the Babe.

That final week of September 1938 saw Adolf Hitler bully France and Britain into signing the Munich Pact, which effectively surrendered Czechoslovakia to the Nazis. Meanwhile, the persecution of Jews continued unabated; within a month, some thirty thousand would be rounded up and sent to concentration camps. Locally, German Bund rallies and the inflammatory rhetoric of Royal Oak's nationally known "Radio Priest," Father Charles E. Coughlin, excited anti-Semetic sentiment. In this climate, athletics took on a new importance as a vicarious form of political expression. Just three months earlier, on June 22, Detroit's Joe Louis had destroyed German challenger Max Schmeling in a heavyweight fight fraught with symbolism.* Now Hank Greenberg was being asked to be a standard bearer for Jews everywhere.

"Sure, there was added pressure being Jewish," he later recalled.

---

*Louis, who had captured the heavyweight crown from Jim Braddock exactly one year earlier, avenged his sole professional defeat by knocking out Schmeling in two minutes and four seconds of the first round. To the millions of Americans huddled around radios, it was a symbolic defeat of Naziism and racism. Detroiters in the black entertainment district of Paradise Valley took to the streets and sidewalks immediately afterward, laughing, dancing, and sharing drinks into the wee hours of the morning. Above the tumult waved a homemade banner: "Joe Louis knocked out Hitler."

How the hell could you get up to home plate every day and have
some son of a bitch call you a Jew bastard and a kike and a sheenie
and get on your ass without feeling the pressure. If the ballplayers
weren't doing it, the fans were. I used to get frustrated as hell.
Sometimes I wanted to go up in the stands and beat the shit out of
them.

Being Jewish did carry with it a certain responsibility. After all,
I was representing a couple of million Jews among a hundred million gentiles. . . . I didn't pay much attention to Hitler at first or
any of the political going-ons at the time. I was too stupid to read
the front pages, and I just went ahead and played. Of course, as
time went by, I came to feel that if I, as a Jew, hit a home run, I was
hitting one against Hitler.

Legend has it that anti-Semitism prevented Greenberg from
achieving the record, but Greenberg always maintained that just
about everyone in baseball—except, understandably, opposing
pitchers—was pulling for him. St. Louis first baseman George
McQuinn deliberately dropped a pop fly to give Greenberg another
swing, and umpire Bill McGowan called Greenberg safe at the
plate on his fifty-seventh home run—an inside-the-park job—even
though he was out by ten feet.

Greenberg went into the final day of the season still needing
two home runs to tie the record. On an overcast Sunday in Cleveland's cavernous Municipal Stadium, he faced the Indians'
nineteen-year-old fireballer, Bob Feller, in the first game of a
doubleheader. Movie cameras had been set up to record Greenberg's
historic blasts, but what they captured instead was a new single-
game strikeout record as Feller fanned eighteen Tigers, including
Greenberg twice.

In game two Greenberg collected three singles and a walk off
rookie pitcher Johnny Humphries. Despite the enveloping darkness, umpire George Moriarty kept the game going well past the
point where play should have been suspended. After seven innings,
Moriarty finally called the game. "I'm sorry, Hank," he said. "But
this is as far as I can go."

"That's all right, George," responded Greenberg. "This is as far
as I can go, too."

Despite a winning record, the Tigers placed fifth the following
season, 1939. Greenberg "slumped" to thirty-three home runs, finishing just two behind leader Jimmie Foxx of Boston. That summer
the theme at the ballpark was out with the old, in with the new. On

May 2, on the Yankees' first trip to Detroit, an ailing Lou Gehrig finally took himself out of the lineup after 2,130 consecutive games in pinstripes; two days later, Boston rookie Ted Williams became the first man ever to hit a fair ball completely out of Briggs Stadium.

After Cochrane's dismissal farm-club director Jack Zeller had been promoted to general manager, and he busied himself in securing a mix of prospects and veterans. By 1939 only six members of the '35 championship team remained. The rookie crop included pitcher Paul "Dizzy" Trout, whose fastball was as erratic and overpowering as his personality, and Detroit natives Barney McCosky and Hal Newhouser. Center fielder McCosky was an immediate sensation, batting .311 and putting some much needed speed into the lineup. The eighteen-year-old Newhouser had worked his way up from Class D to the big leagues in one season, but the Tigers would have to wait several seasons for the hot-headed lefty to abandon his bush-league temperament.

Other new faces included the dependable Mike "Pinky" Higgins, acquired from the Red Sox, who would solve the Tigers' third base problem for the next six seasons, and the garrulous, grizzled, always-available-for-a-good-time Norman Louis "Buck" Newsom, who preferred to call himself "ol' Bobo."

Writers have invariably described Newsom as "well traveled," which is to say that the portly rubber-armed pitcher, who broke in with Brooklyn in 1929, managed to wear out his welcome in more cities than any man who ever played the game. Washington alone traded him four times; the fifth time they merely released him. When the Tigers traded for the thirty-one-year-old righthander in May 1939, they became his seventh employer in ten years. Newsom would spend three memorable seasons in Detroit, which amounted to a mere layover. Down the road were stays of varying lengths with Washington, St. Louis, Philadelphia, all three New York clubs, as well as a handful of minor-league teams. Wherever there was an opening on a pitching staff, Newsom kept showing up like a bad penny. All told, Newsom would win 211 games and lose 222 in a twenty-year major-league career that finally came to a halt in 1953—not for lack of ability, one suspects, but because ol' Bobo's trunk had simply run out of space to slap a travel sticker on.

Jack Zeller could work out a trade for the Browns' twenty-game winner because Newson, characteristically, was in trouble after a shouting session with his manager on May 11. Two days later, the Tigers were in St. Louis for a series. After a marathon bargaining session at Sportsman's Park, during which Newsom beat the Tigers for his third victory, Zeller and St. Louis general manager Bill DeWitt announced one of the biggest player swaps ever, involving six Tigers and four Browns. The principal was Newsom, who went on to win seventeen games in a Detroit uniform, giving him twenty for the season.

The trade was a coup for Zeller, who that December swapped promising infielder Benny McCoy and a pitcher to the Athletics for outfielder Wally Moses. Tiger fans were imagining that Moses, a proven .300 hitter, could help bring the team back to the promised land when suddenly, on January 14, 1940, Judge Landis handed down a decision that threatened to destroy the club's competitiveness for years to come.

The Detroit club was charged with fake transfers of contracts, gentleman's agreements, and other irregularities involving players on a dozen minor-league teams. Zeller had tried to skirt the rules

Manager Del Baker congratulates Schoolboy Rowe, who has just pitched Detroit into first place with a 6–3 win over the Yankees late in the 1940 season. Joining in the clubhouse celebration are Bobo Newsom (far left), catcher Billy Sullivan, and third baseman Pinky Higgins (who already has a victory smoke in his hand). (Courtesy of the Detroit Tigers.)

governing the number of times a player could be optioned out by "hiding" them on teams that supposedly had no connections with the Tigers. Zeller took full responsibility for his actions. Walter Briggs, who had no knowledge of the machinations, forgave his general manager. But the penalty was steep. Ninety-one players were declared free agents, allowed to sign with any club they wished. This included McCoy, which nullified the Moses trade. Fifteen other players were paid grievance pay totaling $47,250. The biggest losses were McCoy, who sold his services to the Athletics for $45,000, and former Detroit sandlotter Roy Cullenbine, an outfielder who signed with Brooklyn for $25,000.

Given this turmoil, and the fact that the Yankees were coming off their fourth consecutive World Series win, most observers picked the aging Tigers to finish fourth or fifth. But improbability is the very essence of sport, something the baseball world had to acknowledge after the Tigers captured the 1940 pennant by a game over Cleveland and two over New York.

That spring, Del Baker shook up the lineup. Billy Rogell was sent packing to the Cubs and Dick Bartell, a veteran National Leaguer, was brought in to play shortstop. Bruce Campbell was acquired from Cleveland and alternated with Pete Fox in right field. George "Birdie" Tebbetts, a fine defensive catcher, had pushed Rudy York to the bench. To make room for York's potent bat, Greenberg was asked by Zeller to move from first base to left field. High Henry, by now an accomplished negotiator, said he would—for an extra ten thousand dollars. Zeller acquiesced, and Greenberg responded with his second Most Valuable Player season. He led the league with 41 home runs, 50 doubles, 150 RBI, and 384 total bases. York, who belted 33 round-trippers, was right behind with 46 doubles, 134 RBI, and 343 total bases. Barney McCosky hit .340 and topped the lists with 200 hits and 19 triples, while thirty-seven-year-old Charlie Gehringer creaked his way to his last .300 season.

Although the power-laden Tigers led the circuit in scoring and hitting, their pitching provided the razor-thin margin of victory. Schoolboy Rowe, who had spent 1938 in the Texas League straightening out his head and arm, made up for a disappointing 1939 season with a 16–3 mark. Old pro Tommy Bridges chipped in with a dozen wins, and Al Benton, a strapping Oklahoman who had been rescued from the Athletics' scrap heap in 1938, was converted from a spot starter to a relief specialist. He finished with seventeen saves, easily the best in the league.

But leading the parade was ol' Bobo, who lost his first start and then reeled off thirteen straight wins before losing again. Although he missed three weeks of the campaign with a broken thumb, he finished second to Cleveland's Bob Feller in victories and earned-run average. In the last week of the season he won both ends of a doubleheader with the White Sox. He pitched the final two innings in relief in a 10–9 Tiger win, giving him his third straight twenty-win season. Then he took his regular turn in the nightcap, going the full nine in a 3–2 triumph that produced his final 21–5 record.

Newsom's iron-man performance all but wrapped up the pennant. The season came down to a final three-game series at Cleveland. The Indians, two games out in the standings, needed a sweep to capture the flag. The Tigers needed a single win to clinch. As expected, Cleveland sent twenty-seven-game-winner Feller to the mound. Del Baker, willing to concede the first game so that his aces—Newsom, Rowe, and Bridges—would be fully rested for the final two contests, countered with an unknown just up from Buffalo, thirty-year-old right-hander Floyd Giebell. Everyone in the park blinked their eyes and scanned their scorecards. Floyd *who?*

The odd duel was a perfect cap to a strange season. In June Cleveland players, chafing under manager Ossie Vitt, had petitioned management to fire him. That had given the Indians their unfortunate "cry babies" sobriquet, which followed them around the league. In their last series in Detroit, upper-deck fans had dangled baby bottles on strings in front of the Indians' dugout. Now, as Feller and Giebell swapped goose eggs, Indian fans peppered their guests with obscenities and trash. Birdie Tebbetts, minding his own business in the bullpen, was knocked out when someone in the upper deck dropped a basket of empty beer bottles and garbage on him. That proved to be Cleveland's sole victory, as Rudy York hit a two-run homer in the fourth and Giebell blanked the Indians on six hits, 2–0. The jubilant Tigers carried Floyd Who off the field on their shoulders, unaware that this would be the last game he would ever win in the majors.

Despite compiling the lowest winning percentage of any pennant winner in league history, the Tigers were slight favorites to beat the Cincinnati Reds, who were appearing in their second straight World Series. The Reds, who had been swept by the Yankees the previous October, sent twenty-one-game-winner Paul Derringer to the mound in the opener October 2 at Crosley Field. This time, Del Baker's pitching choice was no surprise.

"Who else but me would start?" said Bobo Newsom, who scattered eight hits in a 7–2 Tiger triumph. A five-run second inning chased Derringer, and Bruce Campbell's two-run home run clinched the win. In the stands that sunny afternoon was Bobo's father, Henry Quillen Buffkin Newsom. Along with other family members, the frail sixty-eight-year-old retired farmer had traveled from Hartsville, South Carolina, to cheer on his son in his first World Series. "I feel great over this one," Newsom said after the game, "because my father was out there watching me."

Joy unexpectedly turned to sorrow the following day, however, when Newsom's father collapsed and died of a heart attack inside his Cincinnati hotel room. While the sobbing Newsom attended the simple funeral services, the Reds evened the series with a 5–3 win over Schoolboy Rowe. As the series moved to Detroit for the next three games, Newsom announced that he would take his regular turn in the rotation.

Tommy Bridges and Jim Turner locked horns in the third game, which remained tied at a run apiece going into the bottom of the seventh. Greenberg opened the inning with a single, and then York launched a home run into the lower left-field seats. Bruce Campbell followed with a single, and then Pinky Higgins lifted a pitch into the upper deck in left. The blitzkrieg put the Tigers in command of a game they went on to win, 7–4.

Derringer faced Dizzy Trout in the fourth game. Derringer had lost four straight series starts over two years, and he was considered a soft touch. Instead of starting his ace, Newsom, Baker gambled on Trout—who had compiled an unimpressive 3–7 record that summer—giving the Tigers a strong outing and a nearly insurmountable three-games-to-one series edge. The gamble fizzled. Trout was driven off the mound in the third inning, while Derringer went the distance in a 5–2 Cincinnati triumph.

That brought up game five. That summer the success of Bobo and company had swelled attendance at Briggs Stadium to a record 1,112,693 customers. On the afternoon of October 6, another 55,189 fans—the second-largest crowd in Tiger history to that point—packed the ballpark to watch Bobo Newsom try to win a game he had dedicated to his father.

The Tigers jumped all over Junior Thompson and a succession of Cincinnati pitchers. In the third inning McCosky and Gehringer singled. This set the table for Greenberg, who walloped a Thompson pitch deep into the upper deck in left. That made 3–0. With a grim-faced Newsom surrendering just three singles, the Tigers coasted to an 8–0 victory. Afterward, reporters and photographers surrounded Newsom in the clubhouse. "I don't think anybody could have beaten me today," he said. "It was the game I wanted to win most."

Rowe was given the task of closing out the series back in Cincinnati, and the Schoolboy flunked his assignment—miserably. He pitched to only five batters, four of whom collected hits and two of whom scored. Those were all the runs Bucky Walters needed in a 5–0 whitewashing. Rowe's sorry performance closed out his undistinguished postseason career with Detroit, which included five losses in seven series decisions.

Baker had no choice but to bring back Newsom for the deciding seventh game. As in the opener, his opponent would be Derringer. The Tigers reached Derringer for an unearned run in the top of the third on third baseman Billy Werber's wild throw. Meanwhile, Newsom continued to mow down the Reds, nursing the one-run lead through the first six innings. It looked like he would become the first pitcher since 1920 to win three games in a World Series. In the bottom of the seventh, however, first baseman Frank Mc-Cormick led off with a double. Left fielder Jimmy Ripple then smacked a drive off the right-field screen. Shortstop Dick Bartell had a very real chance of nailing the lumbering McCormick at the plate, but for some reason—indecision, crowd noise—he held onto the relay throw as McCormick scored. A sacrifice bunt and a long fly to center then brought in Ripple with what proved to be the winning run in a 2–1 Cincinnati victory.

It was a bitter loss for the Tigers organization. For the second time in seven Octobers, the club had dropped a World Series in which it had led three games to two. "I feel terrible," Newsom told a reporter. "I really wanted this one."

The reporter thought he understood. "For your dad?" he offered.

"Naw," admitted Newsom. "I wanted this one for Bobo."

3

Black Diamonds

In contrast with Tiger stars such as Hank Greenberg, whose likeness could be spotted everywhere from the sports pages to billboard ads endorsing Wheaties, Norman "Turkey" Stearnes was the greatest baseball player that Detroit *never saw.*

During the 1920s, inside the emerald confines of old Mack Park on the city's near east side, Stearnes regularly thrilled crowds with feats of batting and fielding brilliance that, had he been born a white man, would have won the wiry outfielder fame, money, and a starring role with the Tigers or any other major-league team. Instead, Stearnes's style and accomplishments merely made him the most conspicuous member of the Detroit Stars, a charter entry in the Negro National League and the city's first and foremost black professional baseball team.

"He was one of the darlings of the crowd," a fan remembeed years later. "Some chick would cry out, 'Hit that ball, Turkey Breast! Hit it, baby!' When Turkey swung and missed, it would set up a Pentecostal wind in Mack Park."

More often than not, though, Turkey would connect. Parlaying powerful shoulders with a memorable batting stance—chest puffed out, the toe of his right foot pointed skyward—the lefthanded-hitting Stearnes swatted a truckload of home runs. In 1923, his first season with the Stars, he hit a league-leading seventeen home runs in just sixty Negro league games. Including exhibitions, he hit more than fifty the following season, after which he "just quit counting." He hit the ball far, too: one round-tripper carried 470 feet out of Mack Park, and another blast in St. Louis soared an estimated 500 feet.

Although game accounts are incomplete, surviving score sheets reveal that Stearnes compiled a lifetime batting average of .359 in Negro league play and led the circuit in home runs six times, including his first three seasons with Detroit. In 1930, while across town the Tigers were floundering in fifth place, Stearnes almost single-handedly propelled the Detroit Stars into a play off with the St. Louis Stars for the Negro National League pennant. Although Detroit lost in seven games, Stearnes put on a one-man show, cracking out five hits in the second game alone. The excitement and level of play at times approached that of the major leagues' World Series. But in the *Sporting News*, long the self-proclaimed "bible of baseball," there was not a single mention of the heroics of Turkey Stearnes and his black contemporaries. It was almost as though black baseball didn't exist—which, in a very real sense, it didn't.

Invisible men. That is how baseball historians describe this legion of black athletes, many blessed with extraordinary talent, who toiled in obscurity in baseball's gulag during the first half of this century, their deeds and faces absent from the sports pages and bubble gum cards of white America. For these men, denied a chance at the major leagues and all that it represented in achievement, recognition, and security, the notion of the national pastime in a segregated society proved to be a myth.

"I'd go out on the street," lamented Ray Dandridge, a superb third baseman who broke in with the Detroit Stars in 1933, "and the kids didn't know a thing about our Negro baseball."

Stearnes and Dandridge were only two of the many black diamonds that sparkled during the heyday of black baseball, a period measured roughly from the formation of the Negro National League in 1920 to 1947, when Jackie Robinson finally shattered the major leagues' color barrier as a member of the Brooklyn Dodgers. Robinson's success led to a lemming-like rush for similarly gifted black athletes. By the end of the fifties the Negro leagues were all but extinct, robbed of their finest talent by the same league it had hoped for so long to integrate. It was a bitter and ironic ending to a game that had flowered into a black cultural institution of the highest order.

On February 13, 1920, a group of black men met in a Kansas City YMCA and put up five hundred dollars each toward the formation of the Negro National League. Before that, all-black teams had existed in Detroit and elsewhere on an independent, semipro basis, barnstorming through the countryside and playing games whenever an opponent and ball field could be found. The most notable of these early black teams in Michigan was the Page Fence Giants, sponsored from 1894 to 1898 by the Page Wire Fence Company of Adrian. Playing against white sandlot teams throughout rural Michigan, the Giants at one point reeled off eighty-two consecutive victories. The team finished the 1895 season with a flourish, defeating a squad of handpicked white professionals, 18–3, in an exhibition game in Detroit.

The Negro National League, however, represented the first successful attempt to organize black teams along the lines of the white major leagues. Andrew "Rube" Foster, the league's chief organizer and president (and today known as "the father of Negro baseball"), correctly foresaw a burgeoning market for his league in the country's emerging northern ghettos: New York's Harlem, Chicago's South Side, and Detroit's Black Bottom, among others. Franchises came and went, owing to shaky finances, but before Foster's league folded during the Great Depression, its teams were playing before weekend crowds of four thousand or more and its top stars were drawing salaries of several hundred dollars a month.

The Detroit Stars were formed in 1919 as a charter member of the Negro National League, which began play the following year. John T. "Tenny" Blount, the policy king of Detroit's black community, headed the Stars' operation. The club rented Mack Park, located at Mack and Fairview and owned by a popular pants store owner named John Roesink, for league games and exhibitions.

Foster stocked the Stars with many of the players from his Chicago American Giants, including Bill Holland, a righthanded pitcher who led the league in victories in 1920 and 1922; shortstop Orville Riggins, a consistent .300 hitter who played from 1920 to 1926; and Pete Hill, a line-drive-hitting lefty generally acknowledged as the first great outfielder in black baseball history.

The 1920s were the zenith of black baseball in Detroit. The Stars proved one of the most stable of the league's franchises and played winning and exciting ball. Although they managed to make

The 1920 Detroit Stars, a charter member of the Negro National League. Catcher Bruce Petway is third from left in the top row; owner Tenny Blount is seated in the center. (Courtesy of the National Baseball Library, Cooperstown, New York.)

it into the play-offs but once, in talent they were just a notch below perennial powerhouses such as the Chicago American Giants, Kansas City Monarchs, and St. Louis Stars.

The club's playing manager was Bruce "Buddy" Petway, another Chicago transferee considered by many the first great catcher in black baseball history. Petway, who played with the Stars from 1919 to 1925, gained a measure of fame in a series of exhibition games played in Cuba in 1910 against the Detroit Tigers. Besides hitting .390 against the defending three-time American League champs, Petway repeatedly gunned down Ty Cobb trying to steal bases.

The enigmatic Edgar Wesley was the Stars' slugging first sacker from 1919 to 1927. As with so many of the black stars of the era, little is known of Wesley, who led the Negro National League in home runs with eleven in 1920 and with seventeen in 1923 before jumping to the Harrisburg (Pennsylvania) Giants in the rival Eastern Colored League in 1924. Returning to Detroit, Wesley batted a league-high .416 in 1925 and tied Stearnes for the home run title with eighteen. Other name players on the Stars' roster during the twenties included second baseman Bingo DeMoss, a smooth-fielding singles hitter who usually batted second in the lineup; and mound ace Andy "Lefty" Cooper, a six-foot-one workhorse from Waco, Texas. Cooper compiled a .662 winning percentage (92 wins, 47 losses) during his nine seasons with the Stars, at various times leading the league in victories, saves, shutouts, appearances, and innings pitched.

However, the brightest Star of all was Turkey Stearnes, a 168-pound center fielder, who Leroy "Satchel" Paige once described "as good as anybody who ever played baseball." Stearnes was born in 1901 in Nashville, Tennessee, and came up north to work for the Briggs Manufacturing Company in March 1923. Although Briggs operated some of the most notorious sweatshops in the city, the cyclical nature of the work and a high turnover rate were to the advantage of seasonal employees such as ball players. "We worked in the paint shop in the winter and played ball in the summer," Stearnes later recalled. "All that gang, about nineteen of us, with the secretary and manager and all, about twenty-two or twenty-three of us."

Stearnes, who earned his nickname by the way he flapped his arms as he ran the bases, played through the 1931 season with Detroit. In his rookie season of 1923 he hit .365 and topped the Negro National League in home runs (17) and triples (15). The following season he hit .358 and again led in home runs (10) and triples (12). He added batting averages of .375 in 1926, .378 in 1929, and a league-high .430 in 1935, by which time he was playing with the Chicago American Giants. Stories of Stearnes's hitting prowess reached Hank Greenberg, who years later asked black Hall-of-Famer James "Cool Papa" Bell if they were true. "That man could hit the ball as far as anybody," said Bell, "but they don't say too much about him. If they don't put him in the Hall of Fame, they shouldn't put anybody in."

The Stars were supported by a black community that had grown from fifty-seven hundred in 1910 to more than forty-one thousand a decade later. Most of the city's black citizens were squeezed into dilapidated housing inside a sixty-square-block neighborhood on the near east side known as Black Bottom. The neighborhood's boundaries roughly were East Grand Boulevard on the north, Russell on the east, Jefferson on the south, and John R on the west. There were pockets of Italians, Germans, and Greeks sprinkled throughout, but generally speaking, the only whites walking the sidewalks were landlords, insurance salesmen, and cops. Auto plants provided work for the steady influx of blacks from the Deep South, while the Stars afforded black workers and their families one of the few recreational activities in a segregated city.

John Glover, a photographer whose family migrated to Detroit from Alabama in 1919 when he was seven years old, remembered Mack Park in the twenties. "At that time, Mack Park was considered way out of town," he said. "We used to take the Mack streetcar down, and if you were the least athletically inclined you could hop off the car before the conductor came through and collected fares. I don't know how many the park officially held, maybe three or four thousand. But it was always filled when I was there. You even had a few whites in the crowd."

Years later, black businessman and *Detroit News* columnist Lawrence Carter remembered some of the excitement surrounding the only black professional athletes in Detroit. "On Sundays," recalled Carter, "Mack Park would be jam-packed to watch the Stars play the Kansas City Monarchs with their peerless pitcher Bullet Rogan, the Pittsburgh Homestead Grays with the legendary home run hitter Oscar Charleston, or maybe the Cuban All-Stars. . . . Across Gratiot at St. Antoine near Beacon was 'Brosher the Biscuit King' . . . a fervent booster of the Detroit Stars. When they won, Brosher, a stompin'-down good piano player, would celebrate with music and eats. It was a great time."

Turkey Stearnes, an odd bird in more than name, didn't participate in such postgame activities. Teammates remember him as a loner, a no-nonsense type who didn't drink or run around. Though pleasant when spoken to, he wouldn't allow anyone to borrow his bat or glove. He also had the disconcerting habit of talking to his bat after making an out: "They say I can't hit. Why can't I hit?"

John Glover has a special recollection of Stearnes, who one afternoon spied Glover and two friends trying to sneak into the park through a hole in the center-field fence. "Turkey was playing center field," said Glover. "He called time and stopped the game to personally escort us out the same hole in the fence, all the while saying some uncomplimentary things about me."

Blacks were allowed into Navin Field to cheer for the Tigers, but

Norman "Turkey" Stearnes:
"the greatest baseball player
that Detroit never saw."

few dared dream of one day playing for them. Even Mayor Coleman Young, who as a youth growing up in Black Bottom thrilled to the Tigers' radio broadcasts, admitted as much to reporters while attending the Tigers' spring training one year. "We were more likely to dream about playing for the Homestead Grays," said Young.

It would take eighty-four years after slavery was abolished before the majors would issue their own emancipation proclamation. At the heart of this bigotry was the myth of white supremacy—the assumption that, Jim Crow aside, black athletes could not compete with their white counterparts. That assumption was a constant sore point with all Negro leaguers, and one that crumbled in the face of evidence.

Ray Sheppard came to the Stars on July 4, 1924, after his previous club, the Indianapolis ABCs, folded because of financial problems. In his first at-bat for Detroit, he smashed a pinch-hit, game-winning home run—a harbinger of an outstanding career that was never allowed to go further than the Negro leagues.

"If we'd only been given the opportunity, a lot of us would have made the majors," said Sheppard, a retired Galveston, Texas, schoolteacher. "This isn't bragging, but over ten years I hit .300 or better each year. And the proof that our players were equal to, if not better than, the major leaguers was apparent whenever white all-star teams would play black all-star teams in exhibition games when both of their seasons were over."

Negro league clubs typically played between sixty and eighty "official" league games against one another in a season that ran from early May through early September. They also filled in their schedules with as many exhibition matches as possible. "Saturday, Sunday, Monday, Tuesday we'd play league games against Chicago, Kansas City, and them," Stearnes told baseball historian John B. Holway many years later. "Wednesday and Thursday we'd play exhibition games with the white kids. We used to work Canada, all those places, the little leagues they got over there. Sometimes we'd go three hundred miles. Everybody thought they could beat us, until they found out."

The most exciting exhibitions were those played against white major-league teams. These typically were played in the autumn, after the regular season had ended. The Stars and the St. Louis Browns squared off in a three-day series in October 1923. Six thousand fans packed Mack Park to watch the Stars win the first two games. "Some folks said it couldn't be done," wrote the *Detroit Times* after the lightly regarded Stars, thanks to a ninth-inning home run by Ed Wesley, overcame a six-run deficit to win game one, "but now they are really convinced."

The Tigers, who had played a three-game exhibition series against the St. Louis Giants the previous fall, were already convinced. The Tigers did without the services of Cobb, who—perhaps still smarting from that exhibition in Cuba—refused to share a diamond with blacks. Even without Cobb, the Detroit lineup included Lu Blue, Bobby Veach, Fred Haney, and three other .300 hitters. No matter. The Tigers were almost single-handedly turned into pussycats by the Giants' barrel-chested center fielder, Oscar Charleston, whose power hitting and aggressive base running gave the Giants victories in the first two games. Some observers started calling Charleston "the black Ty Cobb," though Negro leaguers were more apt to consider Cobb "the white Oscar Charleston."

To avoid further embarrassment, Commissioner Landis soon banned individual clubs from scheduling such exhibitions, though white all-star teams continued to face Negro leaguers regularly during barnstorming tours. Though records of these contests are incomplete, it's estimated that black teams won sixty percent of their games against white teams. Stearnes hit .313 and four home runs in the fourteen known games he played against major leaguers.

The Stars played several games at Hamtramck Stadium, a park

built by John Roesink at Van and Joseph Campau in Hamtramck. There, on June 27, 1930, the Stars became the first Detroit team to play a professional baseball game under the lights. The visiting Kansas City Monarchs provided the lights, which consisted of six towers with giant reflectors. Additional lights were positioned on the grandstand roof. Many of the bulbs didn't work, but illumination proved adequate for both grounders and fly balls. The only problem was when a photographer's flashbulb blinded the Stars' first baseman, allowing a throw to get past him. Pitcher Andy Cooper laughed at the sight of his teammate scrambling after the ball, but the Monarchs—thanks to "Goo Goo" Williams's three home runs over the left-field fence—had the final laugh, winning 17–4.

Despite gimmicks like night ball, the Great Depression dealt a severe blow to the Negro National League. Some of the better capitalized clubs staggered through the thirties before emerging stronger than ever in the forties. Other clubs, such as the Detroit Stars, went down for the count. With unemployment among Detroit blacks estimated at eighty percent during the dog days of the depression, the black community was hard pressed to support a family, much less a ball team.

After the Negro National League's collapse after the 1931 season, Cumberland "Cum" Posey, owner of the independent Homestead Grays, established the new East–West League. Posey installed a team in Detroit called the Wolves, which despite its winning ways failed to attract any fan support. In an unusual attempt to survive, the Wolves combined with the Grays in June 1932, but by July 1 the league went under.

The following year the reorganized Negro National League started play with six teams, including the Indianapolis ABCs. The ABCs moved to Detroit in late May, where they became the Detroit Stars. Long-time Negro leaguer "Candy Jim" Taylor was manager of the club, which in the spring of 1933 played an exhibition game in Richmond, Virginia, against the Paramount All-Stars. Playing shortstop for Paramount was a young man named Ray Dandridge. Dandridge was as bowlegged as a pair of apostrophes, but his fielding and hitting prowess earned exclamation marks from all who watched him play. After the game Taylor asked Dandridge if he'd like to accompany the team to Detroit.

"Man," asked Dandridge, "where is Detroit?"

The nineteen-year-old Dandridge, who really didn't want to

leave home for the great unknown, soon found out. Taylor bribed Dandridge's dad into persuading his son to give it a try. The following morning the young man was on the Stars' rickety bus, heading north. However, the fat days of the twenties were long gone. Instead of salaries, players had to depend on passing the hat at games and splitting the meager receipts. The club failed to finish its second-half schedule and Candy Jim had to pawn the team bus to pay Dandridge's way back home.

Detroit remained without a professional black team until a brand-new version of the Detroit Stars reappeared briefly in 1937 as a member of the Negro American League. The team, which folded after one summer, had twenty-five-year-old Charles "Red" House as its third baseman.

Approaching eighty, House maintains the misshapen hands and gentle demeanor peculiar to so many boxers. Growing up in the Rivard-Hastings section of Black Bottom, House exhibited skill in both boxing and baseball. He was the 1932 Golden Gloves middleweight champion, as well as an infielder on several Detroit-based semipro teams. "I loved both sports," said House, flipping through a scrapbook in the dining room of his River Rouge home. "But baseball was a little better because they didn't hit you back."

Before he joined the Stars, House barnstormed with several teams during the depression, including an outfit called the Zulu Giants. "That was in 1933–34," he recalled. "We got all the best players that weren't working and booked games every day from here to the West Coast. Phoenix, Butte, Seattle, Oakland, you name it. We wore straw skirts and painted our faces. Yea, that's right. How do you think we drew crowds? Especially whites. They were crazy about it."

Embarrassing? "I felt okay," replied House, with the conviction of a practical man. "I made four or five dollars a game." House made three hundred dollars a month playing with the 1937 Stars, "which was real good money, I'm tellin' ya."*

---

*One of House's close friends, Joe Barrow, grew up on Catherine Street in Black Bottom, naively dreaming of someday playing for his beloved Tigers. It wasn't until after Barrow changed his name to Joe Louis and became boxing's heavyweight champion that he was able to realize a watered-down version of his dream. Organizing twenty-two unemployed friends into the Brown Bomber Softball Team, and playing first base himself, Louis sank thirty thousand dollars into a cross-country tour that eventually collapsed on the West Coast.

The absence of a black professional team created a void that was filled by a variety of semipro nines. The best-known was the Detroit Cubs, which had an outstanding catcher-manager named Barney Jenkins. While most of the city was watching Mickey Cochrane lead the Tigers to pennants in 1934 and 1935, Black Mike's black counterpart was exciting the north side of town with his hitting and field leadership.

Like many semipro teams of the time, the Cubs started out as a loosely organized group of young men tied together by a common neighborhood or employer and their love of the game. "Back then one street would form a team and play the others," recalled Otis Johnson, who was a charter member of the Cubs in 1928 as a fifteen-year-old center fielder. Like most of his teammates, he worked weekdays at the Ford Rouge plant. "We'd play Saturdays and Sundays, raking and scraping a field where we could. We got organized from there."

Although they occasionally barnstormed against teams in Grand Rapids, Bad Axe, and Ontario, Canada, the Cubs typically played weekend games at Dequindre Park at Modern and Dequindre, where the Vlasic pickle works later stood. Fred Williams grew up down the street from the ball field.

"I can see it in my mind so clear," he recalled. "You'd go there on Sunday and see at least a doubleheader. Cost maybe a buck to get in. It was mostly black crowds, because in those days the whites would go to Navin Field to watch the Tigers. That park would always be full, too. The park would hold a few thousand. It had those old wooden bleachers. Nothing fancy.

"One of the teams would be the local guys, who couldn't travel because they had to raise families or there wasn't enough money in it to make a living. There was no fighting or anything like that at those games. It was like a big family picnic. You had people walking around with coolers, selling hot dogs, beer, pop, ice cream. A lot of people would bring a shoe box, lined with wax paper and filled with fried chicken and biscuits. Oh, that was quite an era."*

---

*No description of this era would be complete without a mention of policeman Henderson "Ben" Turpin, an urban legend of the first order. "When you get to talking about Ben Turpin," warns Fred Williams, "you get to thinking the man was eight feet tall." A swaggering bull of a man who strapped a pair of pearl-handled revolvers around his considerable waist, Turpin patrolled the sidewalks of Black Bottom with

The 1940s witnessed both the high point and swan song of the Negro leagues. After Gus Greenlee, Pittsburgh's most prominent black gangster, had underwritten the Negro National League's comeback in 1933, a rival black league, the Negro American League, started operations in 1937. Together the two leagues staged special events such as the Negro World Series and the East-West Classic all-star game. With the black population of northern cities increasing dramatically in the forties, largely because of defense plant work (the number of Detroit blacks doubled from 149,000 to 300,000 during the decade), crowds of tens of thousands were commonplace. The 1943 East-West Classic attracted 51,723 fans to Comiskey Park in Chicago. Turnstile counts like these caught the attention of major-league owners, who also were under pressure from labor unions to integrate the game.

In 1946, Branch Rickey, a University of Michigan graduate and president of the Brooklyn Dodgers, took the first big step toward ending the major leagues' color bar. He signed Jackie Robinson, a standout for the Kansas City Monarchs in the Negro National League, to a contract with the Dodgers' top farm club in Montreal.

Robinson's signing understandably caused a ripple of excitement in Detroit's black community. John R. Williams, a black sports promoter, arranged buses for five hundred blacks to witness Robinson's first game in Toronto. On another occasion, when a scheduled train trip to Montreal sponsored by the Frederick Douglass Non-Partisan Civic League of Detroit was suddenly canceled, half of the three hundred disappointed fans still made it on their own to the Montreal ballpark. Robinson responded by banging out the game-winning hit.

----

head-splitting efficiency, at various times punching out Coleman Young's father, gunning down a member of the Purple Gang, and straightening out a young Joe Louis.

He also was a baseball fanatic who in the late 1930s formed a team out of young men from Black Bottom. Wearing uniforms sporting the initials "T. A. C." for "Turpin's Athletic Club," they competed on weekends against local church and semipro teams, including the Cubs, as well as occasional barnstorming professionals. One suspects that most close calls on the diamond went Turpin's way, for he wore his pearl-handled revolvers while managing, or squirreled them away in the catcher's equipment when playing. According to local legend, once Turpin took his team to Chicago, where they were routed by a superior ball club. Incensed, Turpin abandoned his players in a hotel without money or transportation home while he drove the team bus in the countryside in search of better talent.

Robinson made it to the big time the following season, leading the Dodgers into the 1947 World Series and winning Rookie of the Year laurels. That summer Cleveland fielded the American League's first black, outfielder Larry Doby. As expected, Doby's presence inspired bitter bench jockeying and a flurry of brushback pitches, including a pair of heated incidents with the Tigers' Dizzy Trout.

Most Tigers in the late forties and early fifties were noncommital about playing against blacks; if they didn't welcome them with open arms, neither did they greet them with closed fists. Some exhibited considerable class. Rudy York, a native of Cartersville, Georgia, said of Robinson, "I wish him all the luck in the world and hope he makes good." Hank Greenberg, himself no stranger to prejudice, was openly supportive of Robinson as he was finishing his career with the Pittsburgh Pirates. Robinson's courage in the face of racial slurs, unfriendly teammates, and threats on his life has been well documented elsewhere. Suffice it to say his example paved the way for scores of blacks during the fifties, with major-league clubs buying the finest players off Negro league rosters at bargain-basement prices.

By 1958, every major-league club except Boston and Detroit was integrated. The Tigers' all-alabaster lineup was especially irritating to Wendall Smith, a native Detroiter who had gone on to national prominence as a sportswriter for the *Pittsburgh Courier*, the country's leading black weekly. In 1933, Smith had pitched his American Legion team to a 1–0 play-off victory in front of a Tiger scout, who then signed Smith's white catcher and the losing pitcher to contracts. "I wish I could sign you, too, kid," said the scout. "But I can't." With the sports page his pulpit, Smith became an unflagging crusader for baseball's integration. He never quit criticizing Tiger owner Walter O. Briggs, describing him as "oh, so very prejudiced. He's the major league combination of Simon Legree and Adolf Hitler."

Tigers management responded to all critics with the same refrain: they would integrate the team when they had a black player of major-league caliber. But those close to the team knew this to be an empty promise. "The saying around the press box was 'no jiggs with Briggs,'" recalled sportswriter Edgar Hayes. "Despite the fact that the winning teams in both leagues were those that were signing the good black players, he was dead-set against having blacks play for him." The club did not even bother recruiting blacks for its farm system until after Briggs died in 1952 and the club was sold.

Industrialist Walter O. Briggs, owner of the Detroit Tigers from
1935 to 1952. One sportswriter remembered him as "oh so
prejudiced." (Courtesy of the Burton Historical Collection of the
Detroit Public Library.)

By 1958, the city's black population had edged past 450,000.
Even though the new owners claimed to have spent seventy-five
thousand dollars on developing seventeen black players, most lan-
guished in the lower minor leagues. That April an ad hoc civil
rights group, the Briggs Stadium Boycott Commission, threatened a
boycott of Tiger games if the club didn't integrate—fast. On June 6,
1958, the Detroit Tigers finally entered the twentieth century, calling up a black infielder, Ozzie Virgil, from their Charleston farm
club.

By then the dismantling of the Negro leagues was nearly complete. The Negro National League shut down in 1948, though the

Negro American League was able to limp through the early sixties. The last several years it fielded but four clubs, including a revived version of the Detroit Stars that in the late fifties had off-season basketball players Nat "Sweetwater" Clifton of the Detroit Pistons playing first base and Reece "Goose" Tatum of the Harlem Globetrotters in right field.

"We could've still survived, if only the majors had the desire to help the black leagues," contends Ted Rasberry, a Grand Rapids promoter who bought the Stars in 1953. "We operated on a lot less money than their minor leagues. Instead, it was like sucking blood. They'd pay you a little money for players—nothing much, just enough to operate on. And we folded. They just took all the drawing power away from the Negro leagues."

The major leagues' desegregation came too late for Negro leaguers such as Ray Dandridge who were past their prime when the color bar was lifted. After leaving the Detroit Stars in 1933, Dandridge went on to forge an outstanding career with the black Newark Dodgers, as well as with teams in Cuba and Mexico. Cum Posey, perhaps the leading authority on black baseball as played in the first half of this century, named Dandridge as his all-time third baseman.

Lying about his age, Dandridge was finally signed to a minor-league contract by the New York Giants in 1949. He played several seasons with the Triple-A Minneapolis Millers, helping to develop a young outfielder named Willie Mays and waiting for a call that never came. Dandridge finally retired from baseball at age forty-two, finishing up with a team in Bismarck, North Dakota. Years later he ran into Giants owner Horace Stoneham. "Gee," asked Dandridge, "couldn't you at least have brought me up even for one week, just so I could say I've actually put my foot in a major league park?" Some consolation came in 1987, when Ray Dandridge was elected to the Hall of Fame. It was a belated form of recognition that many of his equally worthy contemporaries, including Turkey Stearnes, were never able to enjoy.

Stearnes's last season was 1942. By then he had found a wife, a job in Ford's foundry, and a small, neat house on the east side of Detroit. According to his wife, Nettie, he never expressed any bitterness over the major leagues' failure to integrate earlier. "I never heard him say anything about it," she said. "He was a quiet man, but I guess he felt good that avenues were being opened up for our race."

To the very end, Stearnes attended almost all of the Tigers' home games, even when they carried past midnight and he had to get up early the next morning and go to work. He died in 1979. One can only speculate on how often the action on the grass drew an old man in the bleachers back in time, back to innings and afternoons spent on dusty diamonds, when perhaps the finest ball player in all Detroit was a young black man by the name of Norman "Turkey" Stearnes.

4

War and Peace

Pearl Harbor Sunday was still seven months away when the big bomb was dropped on Detroit in the spring of 1941.

Hank Greenberg was drafted.

Baseball fans everywhere were incredulous. True, Greenberg had been one of the 16 million men between the ages of twenty-one and thirty-five who had dutifully registered with their draft boards the previous fall. But until now no major leaguer of distinction had been called up for active duty. How could the Tigers defend their American League pennant, Detroit fans argued, if the premier slugger in the game was forced to practice his home run trot in combat boots? The country wasn't even at war yet. And besides, Hank had flat feet.

All this was to no avail. Greenberg himself did no complaining, making the transition from $55,000-a-year star to $21-a-month private with characteristic grace and class. "I don't want any special treatment," he said. On May 6 he hammered his first two home runs of the season to beat the Yankees, then reported the next day for duty at Camp Custer in Battle Creek. Five thousand soldiers from the Fifth Division turned out to greet him. The only other chance to cheer Hammerin' Hank again in 1941 occurred weeks after the sea-

Hank Greenberg, obviously the apple of one fan's eye in this prewar
photo, would make a triumphant return to center stage after four years
in the army. (Copyright © 1940 by the *Detroit News*. Used with
permission.)

son ended, when newly promoted Sergeant Greenberg rode atop a
tank in an Armistice Day parade through downtown Detroit.*

Without Greenberg the Tigers slumped badly, finishing fifth,
twenty-six games behind the Yankees. Walter Briggs had rewarded
Bobo Newsom for his fine 1940 performance with a contract for
thirty-five thousand dollars, the most ever paid a major-league
pitcher. Newsom responded by losing a league-high twenty games.
Attendance plunged by 400,000. One of the few bright spots in an
otherwise dismal season occurred July 8, as Detroit hosted the annual All-Star Game for the first time. In the most dramatic All-Star
contest yet, Ted Williams came to bat with two outs in the bottom of
the ninth and smacked a three-run homer to sink the National
League, 7–5.

Because of his age, Greenberg was discharged December 5,
1941, a month short of his thirty-first birthday. Two days later, the
Japanese sucker-punched the U.S. fleet docked at Pearl Harbor in
Hawaii. America suddenly found itself in a shooting war, one in
which everybody—ball players included—would be expected to
do their part. Without blinking, Greenberg reenlisted, eventually
obtaining a commission and serving in the China-Burma-India theater of operations.

The government had issued a "work or fight" order during
World War I, curtailing baseball activities as nonessential, and club
owners wondered if the game would shut down for this one. Not to
worry, responded President Roosevelt: "I honestly feel that it would
be best for the country to keep baseball going. . . . These players are
a definite recreational asset to at least 20 million of their fellow citizens—and that in my judgement is thoroughly worthwhile."

"Recreational asset" was a generous assessment of the first wartime edition of the Tigers, which stumbled home fifth in 1942.

---

*Private Greenberg at first resisted all attempts to play baseball during his limited
free time at Camp Custer. However, in June a special request was made by Abe Bernstein, an acquaintance and one of the three baseball-loving Bernstein brothers of
Purple Gang fame. Would Hank play in an upcoming contest at the state prison in
Jackson? It would mean so much to brother Joe, a big fan who was serving a life
sentence for murder. Wearing a prison uniform, Greenberg played for the inmates'
team. As prisoners rode the umpire—a fellow inmate—with cries of "You thief! You
crook!" Greenberg had a perfect day at the plate, including a home run that sailed
clear over the prison wall. "No one had ever done that before," said Greenberg. "And
of course all the inmates were hollering, 'I'll get it! I'll get it!'"

Briggs wanted to slash Newsom's salary by twenty thousand dollars. When Ol' Bobo stayed home from spring training in protest, Briggs sold him to Washington. A little later Rowe was sold to the Phillies, writing finis to the Schoolboy's erratic nine-year career with Detroit. And thirty-nine-year-old Charlie Gehringer played out his last season as a pinch hitter and coach before joining the navy. For the first time since 1905, no regular hit .300, though that could be attributed in part to the rubber shortage that forced the majors to adopt a synthetic baseball for the duration. With a lackluster squad and many of the old favorites gone, attendance plunged another 100,000 customers to just 580,000, the lowest in a decade. At the end of the season, manager Del Baker was fired. He was replaced by Steve O'Neill, an ex-Cleveland skipper who was managing the Tigers' farm club in Buffalo.

Bataan . . . Guadalcanal . . . Bizerte . . . Anzio . . . With Americans fighting and dying in places that most people back home could barely pronounce, much less locate on a map, baseball tried to help out in any way it could. Members of the Tigers' front office joined officials of all major-league clubs in setting aside ten percent of their salaries to buy war bonds. Clubs also donated the receipts from many selected games to war-related charities and bonds and regularly sent new equipment to service teams. Spectators were urged to return any foul ball hit into the seats for delivery to overseas troops; the Tigers offered a twenty-five-cent war stamp for every ball turned in. Broadcasters such as Harry Heilmann were not allowed to mention weather conditions, even during rain delays, for fear of aiding potential enemy bombing attacks, and "The Star-Spangled Banner," previously performed only on special occasions, became a staple of every ball game.

Gas rationing meant ball players had to carpool to the ballpark and train close to home. The Tigers trained in Evansville, Indiana, which in February was considerably less balmy than the Lakeland, Florida, site they had used since 1934. One spring, when travel restrictions forced the team to cancel its exhibition schedule, general manager Jack Zeller suggested O'Neill could lead the team in walking to the White Sox camp in Terre Haute, Indiana, for a game. It would be great exercise, as well as a commendable contribution to the war effort. Besides, Terre Haute was only 112 miles away.

"Have them carry their uniforms and bats on their backs," Zeller told O'Neill. "There are a few million boys who aren't athletes and are walking 10 to 20 miles a day and they're carrying something heavier than uniforms and bats. You could take five or six days to get there, stopping along the way."

Patriotism was one thing, reasoned O'Neill, foolishness quite another. "If they walk," he responded, "they'll have to go without the manager."

The Tigers finished fifth for the third straight season in 1943 despite several fine individual performances. Dizzy Trout won a league-high twenty games, and Rudy York overcame a slow start to lead the circuit in home runs (34), RBI (118), slugging, and total bases. In the outfield, Roger "Doc" Cramer, acquired from Washington the previous season, and bonus baby Dick Wakefield were two of only four American Leaguers to top the .300 mark. Wakefield, a University of Michigan star who was given an astounding $52,000 (and a car) to sign with the Tigers in 1941, had the only outstanding full season of his career. The twenty-two-year-old left fielder lost the batting title to Chicago's Luke Appling in the final week, but he still hit .316 and led all hitters with two hundred hits and thirty-eight doubles.

No success on the diamond could compare with the industrial miracle taking place in Detroit's factories, which had been retooled after Pearl Harbor. The production of civilian passenger cars had been halted in February 1942, and now bombers, trucks, and other equipment essential to fighting a global war rolled off the assembly lines. National publications marveled over the "Arsenal of Democracy," which was supplying the bulk of American war material. "Just as Detroit was the symbol of America in peace," wrote a *Forbes* reporter in 1942, "so it is the symbol of America at war. Other towns make arms, as other towns make automobiles, but whether we win this war depends in great measure on Detroit."

Detroit-area plants were awarded nearly $12 billion in defense contracts during the first two years of the war alone, including Briggs, which switched from making car bodies to tanks. During this time an estimated 350,000 people moved into the city to take advantage of the booming defense work. Many of them were Appalachian whites, who settled on the city's near west side, and southern blacks, who were shoehorned into the squalid, overcrowded east-side ghetto known as Black Bottom. Despite the spirit of wartime solidarity, racial rifts quickly developed. Ugly incidents accompanied attempts to move blacks into the new Sojourner Truth housing project in a northeast neighborhood, and employees at the Packard plant went on strike to protest "mixing white and black workers" on the shop floor. As friction between the races increased, it was almost inevitable that there would be an explosion of some type.

It occurred June 20, 1943, on Belle Isle, always a popular spot on muggy Sunday afternoons. As usual, tens of thousands of Detroiters, black and white, spent the afternoon picnicking, swimming, and listening to the play-by-play of the Tigers' doubleheader with St. Louis at Briggs Stadium. As dusk fell and Detroiters started to make their way home from the island, a series of fights between white sailors and black youths broke out on the bridge leading to the mainland. The battle spilled over to the Brodhead Naval Armory on Jefferson Avenue. Rumors flew through Paradise Valley, a black neighborhood and entertainment district, that a black woman and her baby had been thrown off the bridge. Similar rumors had a

Barney McCosky swaps hats with his brother Al before a 1942 game at Briggs Stadium. The Tigers' center fielder joined his brother in the navy after the season. Barney made it through the war safely, but Al was killed in a training accident on Grosse Ile.

white woman being raped by a black man. By daybreak Monday, rioters of both races were taking turns attacking and beating one another in an orgy of hate. Cars were overturned and torched; stores broken into and looted; people pulled off Woodward Avenue street-cars and clubbed.

Five thousand army troops began moving into the city Monday night and, at bayonet point, swept through the downtown area and quickly restored order. The Tigers, who were off that day, canceled Tuesday's game with Cleveland because of the violence. Doc Cramer, staying at the Leland Hotel at the time, ignored club warnings to stay put. He and umpire Cal Hubbard approached the barricades along John R and Brush streets, where police were exchanging heavy fire with snipers holed up inside the Frazer Hotel.

"This sharpshooter had his rifle right on top of a car," recalled Cramer. "He said, 'Let him shoot so we can see where he's at. He'll raise up to shoot again and then we'll get him.' And he got him, I'll tell ya. Right between the eyes. Cal Hubbard and me were standing there, watching. We weren't in the line of fire, but close enough. Too close. We got the hell out of there as fast as we could."

In all, thirty-four Detroiters—including twenty-five blacks— were killed in three days of rioting. An additional 675 people were injured, 1,893 arrested, and property damage was estimated to be more than $2 million. When the Tigers resumed play that Wednesday with a makeup doubleheader against the Indians, 350 federal troops were stationed throughout the ballpark to guard against further possible unrest.

By the following year stars like Joe DiMaggio and Ted Williams and nearly every other able-bodied big-leaguer had either been drafted or enlisted. Clubs scrambled to fill their shoes with an assortment of young, old, and infirm replacements. The war years were filled with stories of men such as Eddie Boland, who had played briefly in the Phillies' outfield in 1934. In 1944 the Senators plucked him off the New York City Sanitation Department baseball team; Boland stuck around until his summer vacation ran out and he had to return to work. The Tigers, who started the season without the services of Hank Greenberg, Dick Wakefield, Barney Mc-Cosky, Al Benton, Virgil Trucks, Birdie Tebbetts, Tommy Bridges, shortstop Johnny Lipon, and several others, signed a forty-year-old rookie outfielder named Chuck Hostetler off a Kansas semipro team and exhumed forty-year-old alumnus Elon "Chief" Hogsett, who hadn't pitched in the majors since 1938.

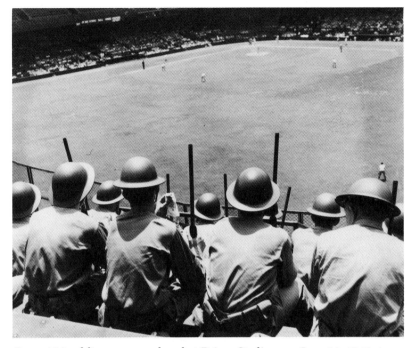

Some 350 soldiers were on hand at Briggs Stadium on June 23, 1943, to
guard against possible violence in the wake of the city's race riot. These
soldiers are watching the Detroit-Cleveland doubleheader from the
center-field bleachers. It marked the first appearance of federal troops at
a major-league game. (Copyright © 1943 by the *Detroit News*. Used with
permission.)

"It was a matter of playing anyone who was breathing," said
broadcaster Red Barber, a close observer of watered-down wartime
ball. "Nobody asked too much. It was interesting and it gave people
something to do."

Of the 14 million Americans in uniform during World War II,
about one in seven saw combat. No ball player on a major-league
roster at the time of Pearl Harbor was killed in action, though many
players saw considerable combat and several were wounded, some
grievously. The best pitcher in the game, Cleveland's Bob Feller,
was an antiaircraft gunner aboard the battleship *Alabama,* and
Washington shortstop Cecil Travis, who had hit .359 in 1941 before
enlisting in the army, suffered frozen feet during the Battle of the

Bulge. Athletics pitcher Phil Marchildron, a tail gunner on a bomber, was shot down on his twenty-sixth mission and spent nearly a year as a German prisoner of war, while pitcher-turned-infantryman Johnny Grodzicki had his promising career with the Cardinals cut short by shrapnel wounds.*

For the most part, however, major leaguers spent their days playing ball on service teams and supervising calisthenics and recreation programs. It's no exaggeration to say that the best major-league teams of the period were at training stations like Great Lakes, Illinois, and Norfolk, Virginia, where at any given time a dozen or so major leaguers could be found on their rosters. The Great Lakes team—thanks to a lineup that included the likes of Billy Herman, Walker Cooper, Johnny Mize, Denny Galehouse, and Schoolboy Rowe—was especially powerful, chalking up a 48–2 record in 1944 in exhibitions against major league and semipro teams. Fireballer Virgil Trucks racked up a 10–0 record, including a pair of two-hitters against the White Sox and Red Sox.

Mickey Cochrane was commissioned an officer to coach the Great Lakes team, and in a 1944 exhibition game against a sandlot team of Ford Motor Company employees, Black Mike proved that he hadn't lost any of his legendary fire. Cochrane, who had worked for Ford after being fired from the Tigers, made a triumphant return to Dearborn as the manager of a Great Lakes team that had won twenty-three games without a loss. Bowing to the demands of the crowd, the old Tiger favorite even got behind the plate to catch his former batterymate, Schoolboy Rowe, in what everyone understood was going to be another cakewalk, albeit a nostalgic one.

The homecoming, however, didn't go according to script. The overmatched team of Ford employees managed to eke out an astonishing 2–1 victory, the winning run coming in the bottom of the ninth when an unknown named Gene Malish crushed a blooper pitch from Rowe for a home run. The heavily embarrassed Cochrane was so mad at Schoolboy that "he could have killed him," Virgil Trucks later recalled:

[Cochrane] signed for a fast ball but Rowe throws this blooper pitch and the kid hit it about four hundred feet in an open field, an inside the park home run.

---

*Minor leaguers, lacking the celebrity of their big-league counterparts, didn't fare nearly as well. More than forty minor leaguers (and two former major leaguers) were killed during the war.

When we got back on the bus, I thought Cochrane was gonna give Rowe a dishonorable discharge, he was so mad at him. He said, "If I ever catch another ballgame and I call for a fast ball, or whatever pitch I call for, you better throw it. You'd better not throw the opposite pitch or I'll have you shipped out so far you'll never get back."

The hell with boosting civilian morale, thought Cochrane, who scheduled a rematch. This time there was no fooling around. Trucks took the mound and blew his ninety-two-mile-an-hour fastball past the Ford workers. Great Lakes won in a breeze, and Black Mike had exacted revenge.

With rosters ravaged by Uncle Sam, major-league competition actually improved. The pennant winner no longer had to be better than the rest, merely less awful. Thus occurred in 1944 an event that only a world war could bring about: the St. Louis Browns won the pennant.

The Browns, floor mats of the American League for most of their history, might have been declared destiny's darlings as early as spring training, when they established a record of sorts when eighteen men on their roster were declared 4-F, unfit for military service. Oddly reassured,the Browns then beat out the Tigers and Yankees for the flag in a barn-burner of a finish.

The Tigers were mired in seventh place as late as July, when Dick Wakefield unexpectedly received a ninety-day furlough from the navy. Wakefield made his presence immediately felt, banging out a succession of timely hits as the Tigers climbed back into the race. Wakefield wound up hitting .355 in his half-season—easily the league's highest—but he fell just short of collecting enough at-bats to qualify for the batting title.

Wakefield's bat was just part of the story, as the Tigers entered the final weekend of the season in first place on the strength of their pitching, of all things. For the first time ever, a Detroit staff led the league in earned run average (ERA), as Hal Newhouser and Dizzy Trout made up the majors' best one-two punch since the turn of the century.

At twenty-nine, Trout had his finest season. He racked up a 27–14 record, leading the league in starts (40), complete games (33), innings (352), shutouts (7), and ERA (2.12). He wasn't too bad with a bat in his hand either, pounding out five home runs and driving in nearly as many runs as Joe Hoover, the everyday shortstop, did.

The twenty-three-year-old Newhouser was equally impressive. After five straight subpar seasons, during which he had compiled an unimpressive 34–52 record, Newhouser finally learned to corral his famous temper. "From 1941 to 1943, for me those were real frustrating years," he once explained. "I probably blamed a lot of it on things I shouldn't have, felt that I wasn't getting any runs and all that. Then in the fall of 1943, after the season was over, I just shook myself up. . . . I was married then, and I just took stock of myself

The Tigers' one-two pitching punch of the 1940s: colorful but temperamental Paul "Dizzy" Trout (above) was an intimidating presence on the mound and at bat. In fourteen seasons with Detroit (1939–1952) he won 164 games and hit nineteen home runs, including a pair of grand slams. Hal Newhouser won an even 200 games in fifteen seasons as a Tiger (1939–1953), including four twenty-victory seasons. (Courtesy of the Burton Historical Collection of the Detroit Public Library.)

and said, 'Quit blaming anybody, blame yourself and don't get mad on the field like you generally do. Get ahold of yourself and start acting like a big leaguer and a professional.' So I did, and everything turned around the other way."

Also deserving credit were manager O'Neill and catcher Paul Richards, old hands with a knack for motivating moody youngsters like Newhouser and Wakefield. Newhouser, who was rejected for military service because of a heart murmur, was nearly unbeatable. He won twenty-nine and lost only nine, with many of the victories coming down the stretch. He was second to Trout in ERA (2.22) and shutouts (6) and led the league with 187 strikeouts. At season's end he edged Trout in the voting for league MVP honors. However, he would gladly have traded the award for the pennant that managed to slip through the Tigers' paws.

Going into the final weekend, Detroit held a one-game edge on the Browns. While the Tigers were finishing at home against the last-place Senators, the Browns were hosting the third-place Yankees, who still had an outside chance at the pennant. It would take a minor miracle for St. Louis to sneak in, which is exactly what happened. The Browns unexpectedly swept the Yankees four straight while the Tigers split their four games with Washington, Trout starting—and losing—twice.

The last day of the season was particularly painful, as a pair of local boys—one an inebriated prankster, the other a St. Louis outfielder—did the home team in. Detroit and St. Louis were tied going into that final Sunday, but the odds still favored the Tigers, who had Trout going against Emil "Dutch" Leonard, a knuckleballer they had beaten seven straight times. Before the game, Leonard received a phone call from a stranger offering him fifteen hundred dollars to go easy on the Tigers. Although the caller later admitted doing it as a prank, the suggestion infuriated Leonard, who pitched the game of his life. Washington won 4–1, and 45,565 disappointed fans hung around Briggs Stadium for a couple of hours to follow the St. Louis– New York game on the scoreboard. A St. Louis loss would force a one-game play-off in Detroit the following day. The Yankees jumped out to an early lead, but a pair of homers by Detroit native Chet Laabs, who had played for the Tigers in the late thirties, gave St. Louis a 5–2 win and the pennant.

Despite the bitter ending, the Tigers were preseason favorites to win the flag in 1945. That summer the manpower drain was particularly noticeable: Paul Schreiber of the Yankees, a forty-three-year-old batting practice pitcher who had last pitched in the big leagues in 1923, came on in relief against the Tigers, who also found themselves competing against a one-armed outfielder on the Browns, Pete Gray. In all, it was a fascinating flock of has-beens and never-weres that populated big-league dugouts in 1945. Of the majors' 128 starters in that last wartime season, only thirty-two were around on opening day a year later.

Washington, reinforced with a team of draft-resistant Cuban players and featuring a staff of four knuckleball pitchers, ran nip and tuck with Detroit most of the season. The Tigers swung several deals, landing Steve O'Neill's son-in-law, shortstop Jimmy "Skeeter" Webb, from the White Sox, and reaquiring their old farmhand, Roy Cullenbine, from Cleveland. The biggest acquisition, however, was thirty-four-year-old Hank Greenberg, who rejoined the team after not having swung a bat in anger in a major-league game for four years. Nearly 48,000 people turned out to cheer Greenberg's return July 1; he responded with a home run in a 9–5 Tiger win over Philadelphia. Al Benton also came home from the navy, winning thirteen games with a sparkling 2.02 ERA.

Trout wasn't nearly as spectacular in '45, winning eighteen and losing fifteen, but Newhouser won twenty-five games, including eight shutouts. "Prince Hal" completed twenty-nine of his thirty-six starts and struck out 212 batters in 313 innings. His ERA was a magnificent 1.81 and the opposition could hit only a paltry .211 against him. In each of the categories just mentioned, Newhouser led the league. It was more than enough for the sportswriters to select him MVP for a second straight year—an unprecedented honor for a pitcher—though the *Sporting News* chose the Tigers' feisty second baseman, Eddie Mayo, for their award. Mayo, who had been picked up from the Athletics before the 1944 season, didn't make Tiger fans forget Charlie Gehringer, but he did bat .285 and led the league in fielding percentage.

With Germany's surrender in May and Japan's capitulation in August, there was a palpable sense of relief in the air. Detroiters wound down from the tension of four years of war by gearing up for the excitement of a pennant race. The turnstiles hummed, as 1.3 million fans made their way into Briggs Stadium, almost breaking the Yankees' league attendance record. What they saw was another nail-biter of a finish.

The Tigers ended the season with two games in St. Louis. They needed a single win to beat out the surprising Senators, who had completed their schedule a week earlier. Rain forced a double-header on Sunday, September 30. Playing in a steady downpour, on a field that resembled porridge, the Browns pulled ahead in the bottom of the eighth of the first game, 3–2.

With darkness penciling in Sportsman's Park, the Tigers came to bat in the ninth against the Browns' top pitcher, Nelson Potter, who quickly loaded the bases with one out. This brought up Greenberg, who lashed a Potter pitch high into the misty sky. The ball landed deep in the left-field bleachers as Greenberg, water squishing in his shoes, happily made it around the bases. "That was my biggest thrill of all," he later said. "What was going through my mind is that only a few months before I was in India, wondering if the war would ever end. Now I had just hit a pennant-winning grand-slam home run. I wasn't sure whether I was awake or dreaming."

Greenberg's dramatic blast put the Tigers in the World Series against the Chicago Cubs, who got as much respect from the press as Detroit's "nine old men." To be sure, it was a sloppily played series, leading one writer to moan, "Neither team can win this Series. It is the fat men against the tall men at the annual office picnic."

Hank Borowy wasn't particularly fat or tall, merely very good. The Cubs' twenty-one-game winner shut out the Tigers in the opener at Detroit, 9–0. Newhouser, suffering from a tired wing, was shelled for seven runs before being yanked in the third inning.

Virgil Trucks, the strong-armed righthander who had won fourteen games in 1942 and another sixteen in 1943 before entering the navy, went to the mound for Detroit in game two. The Alabama native, who had been discharged just in time to start that stirring final game against the Browns, became the only man ever to win more games in the World Series than he did in the regular season, beating the Cubs, 4–1, to square the series. Trailing 1–0 in the fifth, Doc Cramer singled to tie the game, then rode home on Greenberg's three-run homer to left.

Game three also was held in Detroit, but a near-record crowd of 55,500 had to sit on their hands all afternoon as curveballer Claude Passeau twirled a one-hit masterpiece. Rudy York was the only Tiger to get a hit, lining a two-out single in the second; meanwhile, the Cubs touched starter Frank "Stubby" Overmire and reliever Al Benton for eight hits in a 3–0 win.

Because of travel restrictions, the balance of the series was scheduled for Chicago's Wrigley Field, where the Cubs had com-

September 30, 1945: Hank Greenberg is mobbed by teammates after hitting a bases-loaded home run in the rain to clinch the pennant on the last day of the season.

piled an outstanding home-field record. Ahead two games to one, the advantage was decidedly Chicago's. However, Dizzy Trout proved that he was capable of winning a big game, pitching a five-hitter in a 4–1 triumph in the fourth game. Once again, all Detroit's runs came in a single frame, as Greenberg, Cullenbine, third baseman Jimmy Outlaw, and Paul Richards each knocked in a run in the top of the fourth.

Borowy and Newhouser faced each other in the pivotal fifth game, which remained scoreless going into the Tiger half of the third. Up to this point the Tigers had scored runs in only two of thirty-eight series innings, but the drought ended as they pushed across a run in the third, four more in the sixth, another in the seventh, and two more in the ninth in an 8–4 victory. Greenberg contributed three doubles to the cause.

There had been an inordinate amount of loose play in the series, with players letting grounders through their legs, misplaying pop-ups and pratfalling on the base paths. At one point in game five a fly ball was lifted toward right-center field, where Cramer and Cullenbine converged on it.

"All right! All right!" yelled Cullenbine, as Cramer drifted over to make the catch. Cramer backed off, and the ball dropped between them.

"What the hell did you mean by that all right?" yelled Cramer.

"I meant it was all right for you to take it," explained Cullenbine.

Such slapstick should have prepared the public for game six, a three-and-a-half-hour, twelve-inning marathon in which each team used nineteen players and tried their best to throw away the game. It was the longest series game to date, with Chicago finally prevailing, 8–7.

Passeau started against Trucks, and the Chicago righthander was enjoying a 5–1 lead when Outlaw smashed a liner off his pitching hand in the sixth. The ball ripped the nail off Passeau's middle finger, and by the following inning the injury proved too much to continue. That inning, the seventh, the Tigers scored two runs and might have had more had forty-two-year-old pinch runner Chuck Hostetler not fallen flat on his face as he lumbered around third trying to score on forty-year-old Doc Cramer's single—an incident that perfectly embodied the entire phenomenon of wartime baseball.

As it was, Detroit rallied magnificently in the ninth. Losing 7–3, they scored four times, Greenberg hitting a two-out solo home run to tie the game. However, in the bottom of the twelfth Stan Hack's routine single to left became an RBI double when the ball hit a drain in the grass and bounded like a kangaroo past the startled Greenberg, allowing the winning run to score.

As the Tigers took the field on October 10, 1945, they were painfully aware that history was against them. Detroit had played in three game sevens before—in 1909, 1934, and 1940—and lost them all. However, the Cubs were forced into pitching arm-weary Hank Borowy, who had started the fifth game and finished the sixth. O'Neill, on the other hand, had a fully rested Newhouser ready to go, with Trout and Trucks available for relief.

The game was over shortly after it started. The first three batters—Webb, Mayo, and Cramer—all singled, and though Chicago manager Charlie Grimm quickly pulled Borowy, the damage had been done. Paul Derringer, the Tigers' nemesis from that seventh game in Cincinnati five years earlier, surrendered a bases-loaded double to Paul Richards and Detroit was all over the Cubs, 5–0, before most Wrigley Field fans had a chance to order their first hot dog. Backed by the big lead, Newhouser scattered ten hits and struck out ten as the Tigers captured their second world championship with an easy 9–3 triumph.

Back in Detroit the celebrating, while genuine, lacked the vigor of the all-night revelry that had accompanied the Tigers' win in '35, or V-J Day just five weeks earlier. In the light of a war that had killed 405,400 Americans, including Mickey Cochrane's son and George Kell's brother, the importance of winning what was still essentially a little boys' game paled alongside that of resolving the deadliest conflict in human history.

Despite the high cost, the war did what the New Deal had failed to do—it solved the depression. Defense plants and boarding-houses had operated 'round the clock, with men and women working and sleeping in eight-hour shifts. The gross national product had doubled, but rationing and shortages had forced Americans to sit on their paychecks. Now, with the return of peace, they were ready to cut loose.

The most obvious symbol of postwar prosperity was the automobile. In 1946, as the Motor City celebrated the Automotive Golden Jubilee by rounding up a surprising number of still-living industry pioneers for a gala banquet, retooled factories strained to meet consumers' pent-up demand for anything with four tires and a steering wheel. An early customer was the Tigers' teenage pitcher, Art Houtteman, who a year earlier had been given a $20,000 bonus to sign a contract while still a senior at Catholic Central High School. "They hadn't made any new models during the war, so I just put the money in the bank," recalled Houtteman, who had grown up on the east side, near Six Mile and Gratiot. "In 1946 I went to George Higgins' dealership in Ferndale and paid $1,614 for a brand-new Pontiac. That was a big deal, driving a new car."

Detroit was Fat City. Throughout the late forties auto sales were twice what they had been in the twenties. In 1945 there had been 25 million registered cars in the United States; within five years that number would skyrocket to 40 million. With America's emergence as the undisputed leader of the free world, and with most of the rest of the world's economies in ruins, 1946 marked the beginning of a marvelous economic bull rush that wouldn't end until the oil shocks of the seventies. The biggest beneficiaries were the thousands of unskilled workers who, thanks to steady work and increasingly generous union-negotiated contracts, were able to enjoy a standard of living that was the highest in history. Anyone who wanted a job could go to the employment office at Hudson Motors or Packard in the morning and report for work that afternoon. As the auto industry began its golden age, the city once again percolated with raw human energy. Detroiters began building families, suburbs, and freeways. That spring, the telephone directory was published in two volumes for the first time.

"It was a very special time in Detroit," Walter "Hoot" Evers, who patrolled center field for the Tigers between 1946 and 1952, reminisced years later. "The war was over and everyone was getting back on their feet and they were getting into recreation. There was a kind of general craziness about baseball in the city."

This was good news for Walter Briggs, owner of one of the richest clubs in baseball. Between 1920 and 1945 the golden-age Tigers had posted profits of at least $100,000 in all but eight seasons, a figure exceeded only by the Yankees. Twice the Tigers had turned profits of $500,000 or more, an accomplishment matched only by the Chicago Cubs. With a competitive club playing in a modern athletic facility, and drawing from one of the largest, most prosperous urban centers in the country, Briggs was poised to reap even larger profits.

In 1946 major-league attendance leaped an incredible seventy-one percent, from 10.5 million to a record 18.5 million. Along with the rest of baseball, the Tigers benefited from the return to normalcy. Four times that summer they drew more than 56,000 fans to a game. It hardly seemed to matter who the opposition was. On August 18, a record 57,235 people showed up for a doubleheader with the lowly St. Louis Browns. In all, more than 1.7 million fans made it to Briggs Stadium that first postwar summer, shattering the previous year's record. Although other forms of recreation and spectator sports were beginning to siphon off fans and dollars from the national pastime, baseball still held a virtual monopoly on Americans' affection. It was an affordable and familiar form of escapism, one that certainly was needed. For the compression of events over the last three decades was astonishing. There was the horror and disillusion of World War I; the recklessness of the Roaring Twenties; the rise of organized crime; the lawless years of Prohibition; the despair of the depression; the tumultuous labor movement; the struggles and sacrifices of World War II; a bloody race riot; the con-

The center-field bleachers are packed for a crucial late-season contest with Cleveland in 1940. Nineteen of the twenty largest crowds ever to attend a Tiger game were between 1940 and 1950. (Courtesy of Manning Brothers, Photographers.)

tinuing onslaught of new technology. Small wonder so many chose to spend an afternoon in the reassuring sunshine of Briggs Stadium, where a couple dollars bought a seat, a hot dog, and a strong sense of serenity and stability.

Although the Tigers spent only two days in April in first place, they put on a tremendous September rush, winning twenty-eight of their final thirty-eight games. They finished second, twelve games behind Boston, which had been bolstered by the acquisitions of Rudy York and Pinky Higgins. The big guns of the previous year—Greenberg and Newhouser—once again delivered. While his average dropped below .300 for the first time ever, the thirty-five-year-old Greenberg copped the home run (44) and RBI (127) crowns and trailed only Ted Williams in slugging and total bases. Newhouser, denigrated in some circles as "a wartime pitcher," showed what he could do against the big boys. He tied Bob Feller in victories with twenty-six and gave up fewer hits and earned runs per nine innings than any pitcher in the game. He also was second in winning percentage, innings pitched, complete games, strikeouts, and shutouts. All in all, it was an immensely satisfying season for Newhouser, who years later admitted, "It was a matter of pride."

That winter marked the strange, bitter departure of the final link to those storied New Deal Tigers of the middle thirties. Hank Greenberg, at seventy-five thousand dollars the highest paid player in baseball, had periodically mused about retiring. Some press reports circulated that he wanted out of Detroit, especially after not being considered for the open general manager's job. An unsubstantiated report in the *Sporting News* that Greenberg wanted to finish his career in his native New York proved his undoing. The final straw was an old photograph of the Tiger slugger innocently holding up a Yankees uniform blouse.

"This is too much," Briggs reportedly told new general manager Billy Evans. "Get rid of him!" A short while later Greenberg heard over his car radio that he had been sent to the Pittsburgh Pirates for the ten thousand dollar waiver price.

Greenberg's view of life had broadened considerably during the war, to the point that "my interest in baseball, which had been all-consuming up until then, began to wane," he admitted in his autobiography. "And after my treatment by the Tigers I was totally disillusioned and disgusted." Greenberg played one season with the last-place Pirates, then retired. For the final forty years of his life the man who had inspired Detroiters to rise and cheer him in synagogues, restaurants, and ballparks would visit his adopted hometown only four times.

With Roy Cullenbine replacing Greenberg at first base, the 1947 edition of the Tigers picked up where they had left off. They raced out to a four-game lead until a disastrous ten-game losing streak allowed the Yankees to overtake them in July. This was a gritty, talented bunch of hard losers, though. In one game Newhouser, who at 17–17 led the league in losses, stubbornly refused to leave the mound after Steve O'Neill called for a relief pitcher. And hustling George Kell, a third baseman who had been obtained from the Athletics the previous May in a straight-up swap for Barney McCosky, quickly won the fans over. Kell had hit .327 in 1946, his first of seven straight .300 seasons as a Tiger. He was easily the Tigers' best player of the immediate postwar era. "He was very aggressive and very hard-working," said his roommate, Art Houtteman. "You could tell by the type of defense he played. He was always a good third baseman. He worked hard at his hitting and got to be a very good hitter. Enthusiasm, fire, and determination. He was a real team leader."

And then there was the intensely competitive Fred Hutchinson, a hard-hitting, hard-throwing righty for whom Briggs had given Seattle $55,000 and five players back in 1939. At twenty-eight, "Hutch" was finally coming into his own. He would win eighteen games and bat .302 that season, including a game against the Browns where he tripled and then stole home. On July 18, he hurled a two-hit shutout of the Yankees, ending their nineteen-game winning streak. Two days later, 58,369 screaming fans—still the largest Detroit home crowd ever—packed Briggs Stadium for a doubleheader against DiMaggio, Berra, and Company. There were so many people club officials resorted to putting the overflow in the outfield, a practice not seen since the mid-thirties.

Once again, though, the team finished second, twelve games behind the Yankees. Kell hit .320, and Cullenbine hit twenty-four home runs and drew a team-record 137 walks. No other Tiger had any real significant statistical season of note, though rookie outfielder Vic Wertz provided a glimpse of the future when he hit for the cycle at Washington.

After three second-place finishes and a world championship in four years, the Tigers slipped into the second division in 1948, costing Steve O'Neill his job. Injuries to Kell, who had his wrist fractured by a Vic Raschi pitch in May and his jaw broken by a DiMaggio line drive in August, hurt the Tigers' chances. They stumbled home fifth, just two games over .500, despite Newhouser's league-leading twenty-one victories.

One of Newhouser's victories, however, was a historic 4–1 victory over Philadelphia on June 15. That evening the club played its first night game at Briggs Stadium—an event so overdue that the citizenry approached it like a national holiday.

At the time, every team in the majors except Detroit and the Chicago Cubs was hosting night baseball. But Briggs had put off the inevitable for years. His rationale was that used by despots in all fields: he didn't like it. However, in his old age he had become an enlightened despot. Despite a pennant race, attendance had dropped by nearly 300,000 in 1947. It was getting increasingly difficult for ordinary working men to attend ball games in the afternoon. The club had experimented with five and six o'clock starts, but by the late innings players and fans alike were straining to pick up the ball in the semidarkness.

The thought of playing ball under artificial light had always horrified purists like Briggs and influential advisers like the *News'* H. G. Salsinger. In 1935, the year Cincinnati had introduced night ball to the majors as a way of improving attendance during the depression, Salsinger wrote:

> Personally, I do not believe night baseball will remain with us. The novelty will insure patronage but when the novelty wears off, the future of night baseball will remain in doubt.
>
> Baseball was meant to be played by daylight. It just isn't as good at night; it can't be. Infielders can't get a jump on the ball at night. Ground balls go through the infield that would be fielded in the daylight. You cannot see the spin of a ball at night—only a white object sailing at you. Night baseball is a much inferior game.

If games had to be played under the lights, maintained Salsinger, separate statistics should be kept—one set for day, another for night.

As always, turnstile counts convinced disbelieving owners of the drawing power of night ball. On June 20, 1939, the Tigers played under the lights for the first time, beating the A's at Shibe Park. One week later, they helped Cleveland inaugurate its lighting system. As more and more cash-strapped clubs adopted night ball during the depression and World War II, Briggs insisted, "It's artificial without the sun."

Although it took forever for Briggs to change his mind, when he did install a lighting system he characteristically made it the best in the game. Eight steel towers rising 150 feet into the skies and containing 1,458 mammoth incandescent bulbs were erected. Head grounds keeper Neil Conway tested the illumination of the $400,000 state-of-the-art system by sitting in a chair at second base and reading a newspaper. On opening night, fans were let into the park at 6:00 P.M. This reflected the front office's ignorance about their new-fangled lights. They thought the system would not work until it was pitch black out. Meanwhile, with nothing to do, 54,480 fans huddled against the fifty-degree temperatures, munching hot dogs and sipping coffee in the gathering darkness. Finally, at 9:28 P.M. the lights, requiring 2.75 million watts of electricity, suddenly flipped on. The crowd let out a collective "oooh!" Newhouser two-hit the Athletics and night baseball was on its way in Detroit.

The Tigers played six more evening games in 1948. All of them were near-sellouts, including an August 9 contest against Cleveland that attracted 56,586, still the club record for an evening performance. The number of night games doubled to fourteen in 1949, then doubled again, to twenty-eight, in 1950. By the end of the fifties the club had reached its present level of fifty to fifty-five night games a season. The shift had an effect on newspapers heavily dependent on evening-edition sales; in 1952 the *Detroit Free Press* began its transition back to "the morning friendly," in part to take advantage of late-night scores.

Another revolutionary dimension to the game was introduced to Briggs Stadium that summer as television station WWDT (later WWJ-TV), owned by the *Detroit News*, broadcast twenty-six games. In those first primitive telecasts the station's old radio hand, Ty Tyson, handled the play-by-play as he sat alongside a camera situated behind home plate. Additional cameras were placed in center field and along the foul lines.

As with radio, WWJ was the pioneer in what was still called "video." Two years earlier, on October 23, 1946, the station had carried the first-ever telecast in Detroit—an experimental program featuring Rosie the Performing Bear and forty trained pigeons. At the time there were fewer than forty television sets in the city. That number had doubled by March 4, 1947, when WWJ became the sixth station in the country to begin daily programming. By the end of the 1948 season there were about nine thousand televisions in Detroit. Although WXYZ-TV and WJBK-TV both debuted that October and people continued to buy the expensive receiving sets at downtown department stores, most Detroiters did not yet own one. Instead, they typically flocked to their favorite neighborhood saloon to watch.

It was radio all over again, as owners such as Walter Briggs viewed the phenomenon with a mixture of fascination and trepidation. This time their fears that "free" baseball would cut into live attendance proved correct—only it was the minor leagues that suffered, not the majors. Although there were a record number of minor leagues in operation during the late 1940s, sets were still comparatively expensive and had not yet made their way into the homes of small-town America. But prices quickly dropped. By

1950 the choice between watching a major-league game in your living room or driving to a rickety park to watch the local minor-league team was really no choice at all. By 1960 there were 50 million TVs in use and the number of minor leagues had dropped by two-thirds.*

Meanwhile, major-league attendance hit an all-time high of 20.4 million fans in 1948 and approached that figure again in 1949. Studies at the time suggested that if there was any correlation between television and big-league attendance, it was that a competitive team drew well at the gate, no matter how many games were televised. As if to underscore that point, the Tigers aired thirty-five home games in 1949 and 1950, years of record attendance at Briggs Stadium. Admittedly, only day games were broadcast and cameras were barred from the better-attended night, Sunday, and holiday games. All the same, more than 1.8 million people came out to cheer a competitive fourth-place team in 1949—a figure surpassed the very next summer as the Tigers battled down to the wire for the pennant.

The '49 squad had responded well to new manager Red Rolfe, the former Yankees third baseman of the thirties. They won eighty-seven games to finish ten games behind New York. Four pitchers— Trucks, Newhouser, Hutchinson, and Houtteman—had each won fifteen or more games. Trucks and Newhouser finished 1–2 in the league in strikeouts. Trucks, with nineteen wins, also led in shutouts, finished second with a 2.81 ERA, and was the winning pitcher in that summer's All-Star Game in Brooklyn. Powerful Vic Wertz came into his own with twenty home runs and 133 RBI (third in the league), and George Kell beat out Ted Williams for the batting title by the narrowest margin in history—.3429 to .3428. Kell's two hits in three at-bats against Cleveland's twenty-two-game-winner Bob Lemon on the final day of the season prevented Williams from winning an unprecedented third Triple Crown.

---

*Radio and television had a salutary effect on sports pages. Their immediacy and availability meant fans no longer had to attend a game to follow it pitch by pitch, or wait for that evening's paper to find out who had won. Thus the traditional who-what-when-where-why approach to sports journalism became increasingly dominated by the "why?" Sports pages devoted less space to prosaic blow-by-blow game accounts and concentrated more on features, profiles, and analytical pieces. As separate sports sections became the norm after World War II, the writing became more creative and more in-depth.

This nucleus put the Tigers in first place for most of 1950. Detroit, New York, Boston, and Cleveland fought like four cats in a sack, and by the end of August only two games separated the four contenders. By September 22, when the Tigers traveled to Cleveland for a weekend series, Detroit and New York were tied for first. Ten games remained for both teams. Newspapers had Red Rolfe preferring Joe Ginsberg over Aaron Robinson as backstop. Neither one was a Mickey Cochrane behind the plate, or even a Rudy York, for that matter. But, said Rolfe, "Ginsey has been giving us some help at bat and we'll keep him in there a while."

As it was, Robinson played the third game—a fateful decision. After dropping the first two games to the Indians, the Tigers were tied in the tenth inning of the final game. The bases were loaded with one out when Cleveland's Luke Easter hit a double-play ball to Don Kolloway. The Tigers' first baseman touched the bag, then threw home. Robinson, thinking it was a force play, never tagged

George Kell hustles into third base with a triple at Briggs Stadium in 1950, the Tigers' last great season of the golden age. (Courtesy of the Burton Historical Collection of the Detroit Public Library.)

lead-footed Bob Lemon as he lumbered across the plate with the winning run. It was a demoralizing loss, one that pretty much sealed the Tigers' fate. The team lost six of its final ten games while New York won seven of ten to finish first. The Tigers, who had won ninety-five games—their most since 1934—and spent 120 days in first place, wound up bridesmaids, three games out.

"We had a real good ball club," recalled Art Houtteman, the staff's workhorse that year. With nineteen victories, twenty-one complete games, a league-high four shutouts, and 275 innings pitched (second in the league), Houtteman had his finest season, though forty years later he remained dissatisfied.

"The Yankees didn't win it as much as we lost it. We fell off a little bit at the end. I was part of that, I'm afraid. I had a pulled muscle in my side. Every time I threw a pitch it was like someone sticking a knife in me. At the end of the season I didn't win like I should've been. I wound up winning nineteen when I probably should've won twenty-three."

If there was any consolation, several Tigers enjoyed career-best seasons. Vic Wertz hit .304 with twenty-seven homers, thirty-seven doubles (runner-up to Kell), and 123 RBI, and Hoot Evers batted .323 with twenty-one home runs, 103 RBI, and a league-leading eleven triples. Evers also joined Kell in hitting for the cycle, the last two Tigers to accomplish that feat.

At twenty-eight, Kell had his finest season: a .340 average, 101 RBI (on only eight home runs), and a league-leading 218 hits. He also slammed fifty-six doubles, a figure no major-leaguer has matched since. Even more impressive were his paltry eighteen strikeouts in 641 at-bats. He played every game and led all third basemen in fielding. But in a pair of injustices that so typified that frustrating summer, Kell lost the batting crown when Boston's Billy Goodman barely qualified, and New York writers were instrumental in voting Yankees shortstop Phil Rizzuto MVP.

Nineteen-fifty would prove to be the last great season of the Tigers' golden era, though that wasn't readily apparent at the time. The following year Kell once again led the league in hits (191) and doubles (36), and he and Vic Wertz each pounded a home run in that summer's All-Star Game, held at Briggs Stadium as part of the city's 250th birthday celebration. Other than that, it was a listless summer. The Tigers fell to fifth, eight games below .500. As if to add insult to a miserable season, on August 17 the St. Louis Browns sent a midget, Eddie Gaedel, to pinch-hit against them.

After the season, apologists pointed to injuries, slumps, and the inductions of pitchers Art Houtteman and Ray Herbert into the army as the principal reasons for the Tigers' dismal performance. However, the floorboards, which had been quietly rotting in 1951, gave way completely in 1952, spilling the Tigers into the basement for the first time ever. "Everybody had gotten old," remembered Houtteman, who returned to the mound after spending a year in the army. "A lot of fellas were at their peak in '50. I won eight and lost twenty in '52, but I pitched well. That same year, Trucks won five and lost nineteen. Of the games he won, he had two no-hitters, a one-hitter, a two-hitter and a five-hitter. Now, he didn't suddenly become bad the other games. It's just that he had to damn near shut out the other team to win."

The Tigers lost a whopping 104 games in 1952. The following year they lost their first eight games and finished the summer in sixth place, by which time a series of desperate multiplayer trades had stripped the team of most of its favorites. Gone were Kell, Wertz, Trout, Trucks, Houtteman, and Evers. Newhouser was released. The front office was in disarray. Attendance plunged. Red Rolfe was fired, replaced by Fred Hutchinson, who left in a huff. Brought in to manage was Bucky Harris—the same Bucky Harris who had led the team to five straight second-division finishes in the dark days of the depression. Through 1960 the team had but two winning seasons. If there was any consolation in all of this, it was that Walter O. Briggs wasn't around to watch the deterioration of his once-proud ball club.

Briggs had died January 17, 1952. Newspapers eulogized him as "the fan who bought a ballpark." That hit the nail right on the head. To a point, it's hard to imagine how an owner could have served the fans better. Briggs had bankrolled four pennant winners, a new stadium, and whatever else was needed to put a winning team on the grass and satisfied customers in the seats. But in one key respect—the failure to even consider developing black ball players—Briggs had set the stage for the club's decade-long loss of competitiveness after his death.

Briggs's racial bias, though deplorable, was not unique among club owners. One can only sigh over what might have been if organized ball had been color blind during the Tigers' golden age. In 1924, for example, the Tigers lost the pennant when their valuable first baseman, Lu Blue, suffered a knee injury. Imagine if the Tigers had signed Edgar Wesley, the powerful first sacker of the Detroit Stars. Frank Navin certainly wouldn't have had to travel far to find the Negro league star, for the entire Detroit Stars team toiled in partner Walter Briggs's paint shop when they weren't playing ball. To stretch the fantasy, imagine having Wesley's equally talented teammate, Turkey Stearnes, playing alongside Ty Cobb and Harry Heilmann in the outfield. Or the Stars' flamethrowing Lefty Cooper challenging Babe Ruth from the Navin Field mound.

One might as well imagine Frank Navin or Walter Briggs wearing a dress. The men who ran baseball then were all products of the nineteenth century, with all the attendant prejudices. Fielding a black ball player would have required more courage and foresight than anyone in organized ball back then had. The climate for change improved dramatically with the clamor for civil rights during World War II. But, even as more progressive men such as Branch Rickey and Bill Veeck helped the majors gradually and painfully desegregate in the postwar years, the oldest Tiger refused to change his stripes.

By the 1940s Briggs was an old man, sentenced by a late attack of polio to a wheelchair. He had directed his company's war efforts with vigor, but after the Tigers' 1945 World Series there was a noticeable decline in his enthusiasm and health. A self-made man who was an unqualified success in his two favorite arenas—baseball and industry—perhaps he felt he had nothing left to prove. Despite his own blue-collar beginnings and his reputation in baseball as a populist, he apparently left his common touch at the ballpark. Chauffeured from his 148-acre estate in Bloomfield Hills to his custom box seat at Briggs Stadium, he was sheltered from the new social order taking hold. He had fiercely resisted the unionization of his manufacturing plants in the thirties, despite the company's reputation among workers as "the slaughterhouse," and ignored organization attempts by baseball players in the forties. The influx and growing militancy of Detroit's blacks threatened him, as it did all white men in Detroit's power circles. During the 1943 race riot he had used his influence to have hundreds of federal troops stationed inside his stadium. His prejudices were vocal and well known and became increasingly strident with age. But with competitive teams, record attendance, and advancing age, Briggs felt no pressure to change his ways.*

---

*During the twenties and thirties, no auto industry boss was more widely disliked by Detroit workers than Walter Briggs. Unsafe conditions in his plants produced a high turnover rate among employees and, on one infamous occasion, created a spec-

Coming at such a pivotal time in baseball, when clubs like Brooklyn, Cleveland, and the New York Giants were improving their fortunes by loading up on black talent, Briggs's attitude was more than shameful, it was almost criminal. With his deep pockets and with one of the majors' best scouting systems in place, the club could have signed several established Negro league stars—and for considerably less money than it was used to dishing out for white prospects. A change in policy after World War II not only would have improved the pennant chances of those second-place teams of 1946, 1947, and 1950, it might have kept in motion a golden era that could have conceivably stretched clear into the 1960s. Once again, imagine adding Ernie Banks, Henry Aaron, and other available black talent to a roster that by the mid-1950s included shortstop Harvey Kuenn, right fielder Al Kaline, and pitchers Frank Lary and Jim Bunning. Though the acquisitions wouldn't have necessarily guaranteed a pennant or two, they certainly would have boosted attendance, particularly among the city's ever expanding black population. By the late 1950s one in four Detroiters was black. But the club's arrogant attitude toward desegregation convinced many of them, especially the younger, more militant fans, that baseball was no longer the only game in town. By 1958, when the club finally caved into pressure by civil rights groups and fielded a token black (infielder Ozzie Virgil, who was from the Dominican Republic), it was already too late. The conspicuous lack of black patronage continues to haunt the Detroit Tigers to this day. Not that this

---

tacular accident. In April 1927, twenty-one men were burned to death and many more horribly injured during an explosion and fire in the paint shop of the Briggs Harper Avenue plant. The labor press, which charged that Briggs had been negligent in not providing an adequate ventilation system to remove flammable fumes from the shop, published a poem about the tragedy entitled "Bodies by Briggs."

In the early thirties, Briggs claimed that he had "never heard of" collective bargaining—an odd statement considering the level of union activity taking place during the depression. In January 1933, thousands of Briggs workers—many of whom were making $1.90 for a thirteen-hour day—walked out of the Highland Park plant after having their wages slashed. This kicked off the biggest strike the auto industry had yet seen and paralyzed auto production in the city. Briggs' reaction was to fill the plant with an army of deputies and strikebreakers. He refused to meet with the workers' leaders, and the strike eventually died.

By the spring of 1937, however, Briggs was forced into negotiating a contract with the United Auto Workers. Wages and working conditions improved slightly faster than the company's reputation. "If poison doesn't work," workers continued to say, "try Briggs."

would have bothered Walter O. Briggs, who continued to view himself as a sportsman and a businessman, not a social engineer, throughout the club's golden age.

That term, used here and in other books, is often a historian's device, an attempt to put bookends on a narrative. But in this case Briggs's death really did signal the end of an era. For the past half-century only two men, he and Frank Navin, had run the Tigers. They had shepherded the franchise through its wobbly formative years and into the modern age of radio, television, and night ball. Ironically, after Briggs's son, Spike, assumed the presidency of the club after his father's death, administrators of the estate ultimately decided that owning the Detroit franchise was not a prudent investment. The club was ordered sold. In 1956—two years after Briggs Manufacturing also was sold, to Chrysler—a syndicate headed by Kalamazoo broadcast executive John Fetzer bought the team for a reported $5.5 million. After almost four decades, the Briggs family involvement with the Detroit Tigers came to an end. Five years later, the name of Briggs Stadium was officially changed to Tiger Stadium.

That was in 1961, the same year seventy-four-year-old Ty Cobb died in Narrows, Georgia. After leaving baseball he had drifted, a cranky, penurious millionaire who kept an ever growing "son-of-a-bitch" list of enemies. His list of friends was considerably shorter: at his funeral, only three people from baseball bothered to show up.

One was old friend and soulmate Mickey Cochrane, who by now was as round and purple as a grape from booze. He drank to forget the death of his son in Holland during World War II and to blot out other dark episodes in his life. Although he was a parttime scout for the Tigers when he died in 1962, Cochrane "had the thought that the game had turned its back on him," Hank Greenberg said at the time. "He never got over being let out as manager by Mr. Briggs. Baseball is funny that way, especially for the great ones like Cochrane. He never got over the hurt. And this wasn't getting hit on the head by Bump Hadley. Mike's hurt was in the heart, not the head."

And what of the other golden-age Tigers? What happened to them once the cheering stopped?

A few stayed in the Detroit area, but most scattered like the pellets from a shotgun blast. Most didn't qualify for the major-league pension plan, which started in 1946. Those that did received a pittance, at most a few hundred dollars a month, but typically far less

than that. As a result, most players from the twenties, thirties, and
early forties spent the balance of their adult lives working, or at
least looking for work. In this regard, no sweeping generalizations
can be made. Some ball players, through superior drive, intelli-
gence, or connections, made a handsome living in fields other than
grass. Hank Greenberg became a part-owner of the Cleveland Indians and a stockbroker; he died of cancer in 1986 in Beverly Hills,
California, a wealthy man. Hal Newhouser became vice president
of a bank in Pontiac, Michigan, and Billy Rogell served on the Detroit City Council for nearly forty years.

Unsurprisingly, many drifted into auto-related businesses.
Charlie Gehringer owned a body trim shop; George Kell still oper-
ates a luxury car dealership in Arkansas; Barney McCosky retired
as a car salesman. Others stayed in baseball. Dizzy Trout became a
popular broadcaster, his obvious boosterism of the Tigers aggravat-
ing his partner in the booth, Van Patrick. Trout died in Chicago in
1972; six years later, his son, Steve, was pitching for the White Sox.
Marv Owen and Jo-Jo White both managed in the Pacific Coast
League, then retired as scouts. Birdie Tebbetts managed the Reds,
Braves, and Indians, and Paul Richards piloted the White Sox and
Orioles.

Some died young. Bob Fothergill, battling his weight to the end,
died one Sunday morning in 1938 of a stroke at St. Joseph's Mercy
Hospital in Detroit; he was forty years old. Schoolboy Rowe was a
Tiger scout when he suffered a fatal heart attack at his Arkansas
home in 1961, three days short of his fifty-first birthday.

Still others, like Cobb and Cochrane, grew into old men who
had simply run out of heroic opportunities. Earl Whitehill, finding
little satisfaction in his life after baseball, separated from his beautiful wife and became a traveling salesman; he was killed one autumn evening in 1954 in Omaha, Nebraska, when a driver ran a stop
sign and plowed into his car. Rudy York fought forest fires for the
Georgia Forestry Commission for $37.50 a week after being cut by
the Athletics, then came back into the majors as a coach for the Red
Sox; when he died in 1970 he was still wondering where all the
money went. A troubled Tommy Bridges turned to drink, became
estranged from his family, and died at age sixty-one in 1968 in his
native Tennessee. Dick Wakefield died melancholy and broke in
1985 in Redford, Michigan; the former bonus baby was sixty-four.
Gee Walker passed away in a Mississippi state hospital in 1981, the
day after his seventy-third birthday. "Just to show you how things

go," said Edgar Hayes, "Gee Walker was one of the most popular
players the Tigers ever had. But he was dead a week before the
newspapers in Detroit picked it up."

However they wound up, most players didn't fully realize what
they'd had until they no longer had it. "At the time, I didn't think
much about it," recalled Art Houtteman, who retired in 1954 and is
today a steel salesman in the Detroit area. "I was just playing ball
games. I was enjoying it. That was my life. It's funny, after it's all
over, you think, 'You know, some of that was outstanding and I had
quite an opportunity.' It wasn't normal."

As for the most enduring figure of the club's golden age, Harry
Heilmann remained the radio voice of the Tigers through 1950. The
familiar tug on his ever present cigarette was to cost Ol' Slug dearly,
however. By the following July he would be dead of cancer.

Such dark moments were unthinkable in the summer of 1950, a
time when the possibilities for the city and its ball club still seemed
as promising and limitless as the center-field lawn in Briggs Stadium. If one had to pick an arbitrary date when all seemed right
with the world, when Detroit and its Tigers were, for at least a day,
at their apex, one would likely choose June 23, 1950.

It's the middle of the Tigers' fiftieth season in the American
League, and appropriately enough, the Yankees are in town for
what the papers are reluctant to call "a crucial series." But inso-
much as any game with New York is a big game, ticket sales for this
evening contest are brisk—more than fifty thousand, with hundreds of walk-up sales even as the Tigers' Ted Gray throws the first
pitch to leadoff man Phil Rizzuto. A familiar voice has already introduced himself to the radio audience: "Good evening, ladies and
gentlemen. This is your Goebel reporter, Harry Heilmann, speaking
to you from beautiful Briggs Stadium."

These are good times, fat times, in Detroit. Some 8 million cars
will roll off the assembly line in 1950, more than ever before. Gas is
twenty-seven cents a gallon at the pump; it will rise a dime over the
next twenty-three years. Signs of progress are everywhere: construction of the John C. Lodge Freeway has begun, and Hudson's
has just announced plans to open a big suburban store in Southfield. The Veterans Memorial Building, the first unit of the new
Civic Center, was dedicated eleven days earlier. And the Tigers are
in first place, with a group of hustling players who like to get their
uniforms dirty. The average ball player is making a little more than
$13,000 in 1950—good money, but not so much that the average fan

can't identify with him. Autoworkers have just negotiated pension agreements with Chrysler and General Motors. Their pay, $73.25 for a forty-hour week, means they can afford the $299.50 to buy a new RCA Victor 16-inch black-and-white television—the better to watch one of the Tigers' thirty-five televised games this summer.

The Yankees chase Gray with two runs in the first and three more in the third. By the bottom of the fourth New York has built up a 6–0 lead. What happens next has the whole park rocking. Jerry Priddy, Vic Wertz, and Hoot Evers all hit home runs in the inning. The crowd has just barely calmed down when Dizzy Trout cracks one into the left-field seats—a grand slam!—giving the Tigers an 8–6 lead.

But the Yankees, who have already hit four home runs, hit two more to go on top, 9–8. The Tigers bat in the ninth. Already the ten home runs hit by the two teams have tied a major-league record. Ty Cobb would probably have a fit watching this exhilarating display of big-bang baseball, but the fans are in an uproar. Boom times deserve booming home runs. The Yankees retire the always dangerous George Kell, but Wertz follows with a double. This brings up Evers.

The crowd of 51,400 is yelling, "Hoot! Hoot!" The taciturn twenty-nine-year-old center fielder gets hold of a Joe Page fastball and sends it screaming over the head of Joe DiMaggio in center field. It lands to the right of the flagpole and, as the crowd gets on its feet, Evers steams around the bases. DiMaggio, and then Rizzuto, fumble the ball, and Evers races around third, his baggy pants billowing in the slipstream. Third-base coach Dick Bartell is a windmill, his wildly circling arms telling Evers to kick it into overdrive.

Evers never breaks stride. He scores standing up and Leo Macdonnel, the aging *Detroit Times* writer who is the official scorer, almost topples over getting out of his seat in the press box. He's waving his hand in circles and yelling "Home run! Home run!" It's an inside-the-park home run, the record-breaking eleventh of the game, and the Tigers have capped off a perfect summer evening with a golden moment that'll have a golden city buzzing for days.

In the broadcast booth, Heilmann reports the action. At fifty-five, he's been hitting or broadcasting Tiger home runs for longer than most fans have been alive, since the days of Cobb and Veach and now into the evenings of Wertz and Evers. Slug turns his microphone toward the crowd, and the bedlam rumbles through the radio like some distant traffic.

"Listen," he says, "to the voice of baseball. . . ."

PART TWO

VOICES

5

John Bogart

John Renzie Bogart
Born: September 21, 1900, Bloomsburg, Pennsylvania
Major-league career: 1920 Detroit Tigers

Had major league baseball consisted of twenty-six rather than sixteen teams in 1921, it would have created jobs for another hundred or so pitchers, and "Big John" Bogart might have enjoyed a long, productive stay in the big time. As it was, Bogart—the possessor of a lively fast ball and a "fishhook" curve—found himself the odd man out when Detroit's managerial reins passed from Hughie Jennings to Ty Cobb after the 1920 season, a season in which Bogart's pitching apparently impressed everyone but the Georgia Peach.

At the time of this interview, Bogart and his wife lived in a flat above a used-appliance store in Geneva, New York.

John Bogart died December 7, 1986, in Clarence, New York.

I got a letter about three years ago. I can't remember what it was all about, but it had a list of all these old Tigers on it. Harry Heilmann, Bob Fothergill, Ty Cobb, Johnny Bassler, the old catcher. . . .

I looked at the damned thing and I was wondering why it didn't have my name on it. Geez, I didn't read the first sentence. These were all the guys who'd played with Detroit who were deceased.

I guess I'm about the only one left who played with Jennings and Cobb. I'm a little crippled up now—got these artificial knees—but I'm still kicking around. No gripes.

Jennings was my boss my first year with Detroit in 1920 when I won two and lost one. Jennings was going to keep me with the team, but the next year Ty Cobb got the ball club. That was the first year he was manager of Detroit. I was twenty years old and he wanted older pitchers, I guess. I was there for a while in '21. Never started me a game. One day Cobb says to me, "I think I'd better farm you out. Jennings was going to keep you with the team, but as young as you are, I think it'd be better for you to get some experience." If Jennings kept the team, I might've been up there for ten years. Who the hell knows? But they farmed me out, I hurt my damned arm, and I never made it back.

I was born in Bloomsburg, Pennsylvania, in 1900, but I moved to Geneva when I was four years old. It's always been a small town. Today, look at what the kids got to play baseball with. What did I have? Had to throw the baseball off the wall and have it bounce back to me. Kids got it made now.

When I was a kid, about eleven, twelve years old, I always screamed for the Rochester baseball club. Not the majors, but Rochester. I was a paperboy those days—this was before the World War—and when the *Rochester Democrat* came out, I'd sneak a look at the sports page. When Rochester won, it'd be a red headline all the way across the page. When it was black, it meant they lost.

There wasn't any high school team then, but I started pitching for the Geneva pro team when I was sixteen. Ever hear of Heinie Groh, the guy with the bottle bat who played third base for the Giants? Well, his brother, Louie Groh, managed Rochester. I beat them one morning in twelve innings here in Geneva. Afterwards, he asked me, "Bogart, can you pitch another game this afternoon?"

So that afternoon I pitched for them down in Seneca Falls. I lost the game, 2–1. You know how I lost? There was a double steal, and the second baseman hit me in the top of the head with the ball trying to get the runner at home. The damned thing bounced over the grandstand and they won. But Groh signed me to a contract to go down to Evansville, Indiana. This was in 1920. I followed my

John Bogart in 1921. (Copyright
© 1921 by the *Detroit News*.
Used with permission.)

manager from Evansville to Ludington, Michigan, and Ludington
sold me to Detroit that year.

My first game? Geez, it was so far back. But I did good. I'll tell
you this: in 1920, I beat the best team in baseball, the world champion Cleveland Indians. I beat George Uhle. He probably doesn't
remember me, but it's in the papers. [*Allen*] Conkwright started it,
and I came on in the second inning. I beat 'em out, 6–5. I got a little
shaky near the end, I guess, but I beat 'em. I can always say I beat
the world's best team in 1920.

I had one of the best curveballs in the American League, and a
good fastball. Boy, what I could do today. I'll bet you didn't know
this: in 1935, they changed the rules to where you didn't have to
have both feet on the rubber when you pitched. Now, take a step
back or step forward and see the extra leverage you get. I always
was fast, but I'd be even faster if I could've taken that extry step. It's
like an outfielder. How could an outfielder get anything on the ball
if he stood flat-footed when he threw? I was born fifty years too
soon.

I pitched good ball [*in 1920*]. The Detroit papers even said,
"One of the bright spots was Bogart's pitching." Then I went to
spring training in San Antonio the next year and Cobb wanted more
experienced pitchers, I guess. But young guys like me—heck, we
were doing better than the older guys.

I got along fine with Cobb. I'll tell you, to me he was the greatest all-around player who ever lived. He did everything—run, hit, field. One guy's breaking his stolen base record, another's breaking his hit record, but one thing they'll never break is his [career] batting average. Imagine hitting .367 lifetime!

Cobb was a poke hitter. He'd practice that. Pitch him inside, and if the shortstop left too soon, Cobb would place it there for a base hit. If Cobb was playing today with that artificial grass, they'd never get him out.

As a manager, Cobb was all right. He was probably better than some of these dumb bastards today. See that green chair and TV over there? I watch games all the time. The other night Detroit lost a game to New York they never should have lost. Two men on base, nobody out, and they can't bunt them over. Every man on the team should know how to bunt. I don't give a damn if he's a home run hitter or what. But only a couple of guys on the whole team can

Spring training in San Antonio, 1921, Cobb's first as manager. As these unidentified Tigers are unwittingly demonstrating, a lack of communication would prove to be one of Cobb's greatest problems.

bunt. That's crazy. As a kid, you have to learn how to bunt a ball before you can hit it. So Detroit lost, 6–5. The first out was a fly ball. If they'd bunted them over, it would've scored the run. Say you lose a dozen one-run games a season. If they'd go back and see games where they should've bunted, they wouldn't have lost that many.

Like I said, I hurt my arm when Detroit farmed me out. I was warming up for a game one day and I slipped on the wet grass. I tore ligaments up in my left shoulder. I couldn't even throw a ball across the street. I saw a Dr. Knight in Rochester. I was off one year and then I started over again.

I pitched twelve years in the minors. I pitched for Topeka, Jersey City, Buffalo, Newark, and had some good years with Rochester. Once I pitched three complete games in six days with Rochester. The first two I won each, 1–0, and then I lost the third, 1–0. When you went out to pitch, you were a nine-inning man. Look at what they've got today: short relief, middle relief, long relief. Years ago you pitched the whole damn nine innings. Of course, you came in to relieve once in a while, but nothing like today. I don't even re-member a bullpen in Detroit. We'd all sit on the bench, and if Jen-nings said, "Bogart, you pitch relief," I'd run down the baseline and find some place to warm up.

Geez, the minors. . . . You'd ride all night on those trains, going through Arkansas, Oklahoma . . . all those small towns. . . . If you had to change trains, instead of going to the hotel you'd sit around three or four hours. Sleep out on the platform, for Chrissakes, and then pitch a game that afternoon. I played for Dayton in the Central League. Those small towns didn't even have a clubhouse. We had to change in the hotel. You'd play a doubleheader, take a bus back to the hotel, and come in with those old, wet, wool uniforms. You'd hang them up in your room and hope they dried for the next day's game.

The hottest place I ever played was down in Fort Smith, Arkan-sas. I got married in 1924. I took my wife and my daughter, who was a year old and in diapers, out west with me. Boy, that was a hot place. Today in Texas they don't play ball some nights. Too hot for the boys. We used to play at two in the afternoon when it might be 110 degrees. I lost as much as twelve, thirteen pounds pitching those games. We didn't have drinking fountains. We had one of those twenty-gallon milk cans filled with ice. We'd put oatmeal in it so you wouldn't drink too much and get the cramps.

I had a chance to come back to the major leagues when I was

with the Joplin, Missouri, team under Gabby Street. Ray Windsor was the owner. He had a chance to sell me to Cincinnati. He wanted ten thousand dollars for me, but Cincinnati wouldn't give it. So I went back to Joplin, and the next year my arm went dead.

I came back home and worked with the state highway department a while, and then went to Newark and played. My last year was with Binghamton in 1931 for $275 a month. What the hell, that was kind of rough going. It was the depression. I got a job peddling milk. Finally, I got arthritis in my hip and I had to quit my milk route. I loved that job. Had afternoons off, so I'd go down to the ballpark and watch the boys play. I umpired for a long time, too. I'd sit in the stands, and if they needed a substitute I'd get dressed and go behind the plate. Did that for twenty-five years.

So I had my ups and downs. In other words, I didn't get the breaks. If I was in my prime now like I was then, who knows? There's more big-league clubs and more young guys getting chances than we did years ago. I didn't make much money, but I had a lot of fun.

—July 1982

6

Eddie Wells

Edwin Lee Wells
Born: June 7, 1900, Ashland, Ohio
Major-league career: 1923–27 Detroit Tigers, 1929–32 New York Yankees, 1933–34 St. Louis Browns

Ohio farm boy Eddie Wells grew up to enjoy a unique perspective of this century's two greatest ball players. The hard-throwing left-hander pitched five seasons with Detroit and four with New York, making him one of a handful of big-leaguers to have played with both Ty Cobb and Babe Ruth during his career.

Wells's best season in Detroit was 1926, when he won twelve games and led the league in shutouts with four. Wells, who went on to post thirteen- and twelve-win seasons with the Yankees, finished his baseball career in 1937 in the Southern League. He later owned an oil distributorship in Montgomery, Alabama.

Eddie Wells died May 1, 1986, in Birmingham, Alabama.

It's a funny thing about that baseball bug, slugger. I was born out on a farm outside of Ashland, Ohio, about forty miles southwest of Cleveland. We took the *Cleveland Plain Dealer*. When I was a kid, about nine, ten years old, I'd keep up with the box scores and, why, I don't know, but I got attached to the playing of Ty Cobb. And I don't know, but he just stood for my *hero.* I was just crazy about Ty Cobb, I was just crazy about that man. I looked up to that fella. I still got his picture in my den here. In twenty-four years he had an average of .367. Yes sir.

I started pitching semipro ball when I was about fourteen. I was six-feet-one then. I was just born a pitcher. I pitched semipro ball up the Ohio River there—Steubenville, Pittsburgh, Huntington. Getting one hundred twenty-five dollars a Sunday. In other words, my name got known.

I was going to Bethany College, a little school down in West Virginia about eighteen miles west of Wheeling. Then one day in February of 1922, I was up in the chemistry lab on a Monday, and a person from the college came up to me and said, "There's a gentleman outside who wishes to see you."

So I went outside and there's a fella by the name of Billy Doyle who scouted for the Detroit ball club. He talked to me about signing a Detroit contract. I told him, "Listen, I'm in my second year of school here, and I'm on a full scholarship."

"Well," he said, "I'll tell you one thing. Mr. Navin said he'll let you finish school. We'll work it out some way." And we talked and talked. My dad never wanted me to leave the farm, but he told me, "You do what you want to do, son. I can't tell you what to do." Well, Doyle offered me one thousand dollars to sign a contract. Good mercy! At twenty-two, that was a whole lot of money to me. A lot of money. I called my dad on the phone and he said, "Do what you want." Well, I signed. And in about a week here comes a check for one thousand dollars.

After college was out, about June 7, I reported to Detroit. Didn't see Cobb or nobody on the team. I reported to Frank Navin, the owner, in his office. He said, "Ed, between now and when college starts in the fall, you go to Ludington, Michigan, and pitch." That was the Central League. I said, "Well, that's okay. I need that experience." I went up there and won thirteen games, lost ten, had an earned run average of 1.93.

Then the next year when school was out, I reported to Detroit in Boston. See, I was a country boy. . . . I hit Boston about 6:30 in the morning, at the New Brunswick Hotel where the Detroit club was. And the first thing I did, I called Cobb on the phone! He was sound asleep. Got him out of bed. Man, I didn't know ball players

Eddie Wells. (Copyright © 1927 by the *Detroit News.* Used with permission.)

didn't get out of bed 'til nine or ten in the morning. I was just a farm boy, I didn't have no sense.

Anyway, Cobb says, "Come on up." So I had breakfast with him. Spent the whole morning with ol' Ty. He asked me all about myself. Then that afternoon we go to the ballpark and—dad-gone!—come the eighth inning and I'm in the ball game! Ira Flagstead was the first batter I faced. Never will forget it. He hit a line drive right at my face and I threw my glove up and caught it. Pitched one inning. Didn't get one hit. That's my initiation into the big leagues. I was just about scared to death. Anyone who tells you they're not scared their first game is full of bull.

That night we left for New York to play the Yankees. George Dauss, the old Detroit pitcher, he liked his beer. Cobb told George, "Listen, when we get to New York, you leave the beer alone. You're gonna pitch the opening game of the series tomorrow."

So lo and behold, we get to the ballpark the next day, it's a beautiful day, and George comes in. Cobb takes one look at ol' George and he's red in the face.

He says, "You've been drinking beer!"

George says, "Yes I have."

Cobb says, "You're starting the game."

Well, he started that ball game and they got seven runs before you could shake a stick at him. There's four or five pitchers in that ball game. But anyhow, around the fifth inning Cobb says, "Ed, go down to the bullpen." By the start of the sixth inning I was in the ball game. And Babe Ruth is the first man up.

Johnny Bassler was the catcher and he come out and ask me, "Whatcha gonna throw him?"

I told him, "Nothin'." He looked at me and I said, "I ain't throwin' him nothin'." I had a whale of a slow curveball. And that's what I threw him. Struck him out. They didn't get no hits in three innings off me.

I stayed with the club until July 21. Cobb came up to me and said, "You need more experience. How'd you like to go to Birmingham, Alabama, and finish the year?" I said, "Well, that's fine." So I went to Birmingham in the Southern League and won eight, lost seven. Then the next year [1924], my senior year, I won six and lost eight with Detroit.

It's a funny thing. The opposition hated Cobb. I mean, he was a hustler and he'd spike you to get that base. A lot of the players on that Detroit club didn't like him because he was tough. Harry Heilmann didn't think much of him, and neither did Ken Holloway or George Dauss. But me and Cobb always got along great. Always did. I thought a lot of him and he thought a lot of me.

Cobb didn't hit home runs hardly at all. Doubles now and then, but mostly singles. He aimed for the pitcher's box all the time. He's the hustlingest player of all time. There's never been another since him, though Pete Rose is close to him.

I can't complain about Cobb one bit. He was real nice to me. After I graduated from Bethany College in 1924, I went straight to Detroit to report. And Ty told me, "Listen, I'm staying at Walter Briggs's house while they're away in Europe." He said, "Come out and spend the night." I said, "That's fine." Cobb treated me royally. He had his domestics [black servants] up from Georgia, and I had a good dinner that night. That evening he said, "Ed, we play Cleveland tomorrow a doubleheader. I'm going to pitch you the first game."

Anyway, the next day we get to the ballpark, and a fella by the name of Luther Roy pitched for Cleveland. I guess the Lord was with us because we won, 3–2. I even hit a double my first time up, a line drive to left field. That was my first big-league win. After the ball game Cobb comes up to me and says, "Ed, that's how easy it is

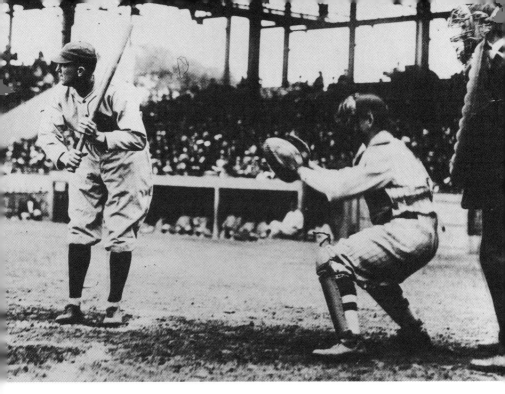

Ty Cobb at bat at American League Park in Washington in 1922. Notice the split-hands grip that Cobb used, the better to drop down a last-moment bunt or to chop the ball past a charging infielder, depending on the situation. (Courtesy of the National Baseball Library, Cooperstown, New York.)

in the big leagues to win." Well, I soon found out that he sure was wrong.

Good gosh, I happened to pitch one day against the Yankees that summer. Beat Herb Pennock, 3–2, to put us in first place. That was in August. Then we go to Philadelphia and Lu Blue breaks his ankle sliding into home plate. Man, that crumbled the ball club. Cobb wanted to buy Johnny Neun from the American Association to play first base. But old Frank Navin, I don't think he wanted to win a pennant. He'd have to pay us too much money. He wanted to stay in second, third place.

As a manager, Ty did the best he could. Cobb knew his job, which was hitting, but I remember he didn't know that much about pitching. One time Cobb and I happened to be in the clubhouse alone in New York. I was in a slump. I said, "Ty, I'm having a tough time."

Cobb said, "I know it."

I said, "What in the name of sense do you think my trouble is? I can't seem to figure out what's wrong."

Today you've got all that movie stuff. Today they can analyze a pitcher by taking these pictures all the time. Got him when he's going good and got him when he's going bad. Then they compare them, see what the problem is. They can figure out what's wrong with your stride, all that stuff.

But Cobb said, "Ed, that's something I know nothing about—pitching."

I remember one year in spring training in San Antonio. Cobb was out there standing behind the pitchers, see. Carl Hubbell was up from Oklahoma City, I think it was. Ol' Hubbell was foolin' with this darn screwball. I was standing there beside him. And Cobb told him, "Forget that screwball." He didn't want any of his pitchers foolin' around with any screwballs. And they got in an argument. Well, Carl was gone by the next week. He got with the Giants. Boy, Cobb made a mistake there.*

Back then, slugger, you had a whole lot more fastball pitchers than you have today. I mean, they were *fast*. Good mercy. Waite Hoyt—he had one of those high, hard ones. I was one of them. Lefty Gomez, Bob Feller, Wes Ferrell, Ted Lyons. Overhand high-hardball pitchers. You don't see that now. It's low, low and away. You got those sinkers, that's what they have now. We called it a two-bit curve.

Now, Walter Johnson, he only had one pitch. He was up there twenty-two years and it was twenty years before he had anything besides a fastball. His biggest worry was hitting someone. He wore a size fifteen shoe, was six-foot-two, and he could stand up straight and the tips of his fingers would touch his kneecaps. That's how long Walter Johnson's arms were.

There was some good hitters then. Now, this is funny. Remember Eddie Collins of the White Sox? Second baseman, lefthanded hitter. He was always chewing gum. Every time he come to the plate, he'd take the gum out of his mouth and put it on top of his cap. Good luck, you know. I could never get him out. He was always good for three or four hits off me. Another one was Al Simmons of

---

*Carl Hubbell went on to win 253 games for the New York Giants and was elected to the Hall of Fame in 1947.

Philadelphia. His real name was Szymanski. Doggone, I couldn't get him out either.

We had some good ball players on Detroit: Johnny Neun, Heinie Manush, Harry Heilmann, Earl Whitehill. Lu Blue was one of the finest first basemen in the big leagues. And Bob Fothergill—he was that line-drive hitter. Hit nothing but line drives. George Dauss was a very good pitcher. He had that fadeaway. He was a prince of a fellow. Most of these boys are dead.

Johnny Neun . . . I saw him make an unassisted triple play once against Cleveland. There were men on first and second and Homer Summa hit a line drive right along the line. It went right into his glove. All he had to do was touch Charlie Jamieson, who was on first. Two out. Then the man who was on second—Glen Myatt— was rounding third. Johnny Neun trots down to second and touches the base. You could hear him all over the park: "Triple play unassisted! Triple play unassisted!"*

You know, Earl Whitehill was killed in an automobile accident out near his home years ago. Whitehill was a lefthander. He had a crackerjack of a curveball. Later he went to Washington, won twenty-two games, and pitched them into a World Series. He didn't talk very much. Clean-cut fella. He was from Cedar Rapids, Iowa. I never will forget, about 1925 I was rooming with Whitey in the Fort-Shelby Hotel. It was the middle of July and he was really winning some ball games. Frank Navin called him out to the ballpark one morning, and when he came back he was all smiles. He said, "Ed, look at this." He got a check for one thousand dollars, a bonus. Man, a thousand dollars. He'd like to have passed out. That was a lot of money. That sure was.

Could you imagine how much money Ty Cobb would make today? Good God! And Babe Ruth. *Whoooo!* Dave Winfield makes a million and a half a year. Good mercy.

---

*Neun's unassisted triple play, one of only nine in major-league history, occurred at Navin Field on May 31, 1927, in the ninth inning of a game won by Detroit, 1–0. Ironically, the previous day Chicago Cubs shortstop Johnny Cooney had accomplished the same feat against Pittsburgh. Neun had read newspaper accounts of Cooney's triple play before taking the field against Cleveland and was well aware of its rarity. Neun could easily have tossed the ball to shortstop Jackie Tavener, who was standing on second base awaiting the throw, for the third out. Instead, he waved off his teammate and outraced the lumbering Glenn Myatt to the bag to complete the triple play, incredibly yelling, "I'm running into the Hall of Fame!"

First baseman Johnny Neun: "You could hear him all over the ballpark: 'Triple play unassisted! Triple play unassisted!'" (Courtesy of the Burton Historical Collection of the Detroit Public Library.)

　　I never had no trouble signing. I was just a little fella. What I got for breaking in then was four hundred dollars a month. Ten years later, when I was with St. Louis, we had one starting pitcher making four hundred dollars a month. That's right.

　　Now take the Yankees. When I was there, Babe made $80,000. Well, he was worth a lot more than that. Gehrig made $45,000. Then it dropped way down. I think the rest of us were making about $10,000 to $12,000. Most I ever made was $800 a month. Frank Navin wasn't paying much money. Heilmann was a star, man, you know he was. He made $15,000. Cobb, I think, made $50,000 to manage. All us other players, we didn't make much. Poor ol' George

Dauss, he didn't make much money. He was a star pitcher for years up there. But nobody was making any money then.

We had one left-hander by the name of Dutch Leonard. Ever hear of him? Ol' Dutch had a peculiar ball. It wasn't a slider, it wasn't a slow curve, it was something. Anyway, I was talking to Cobb one day about that. He said, "Eddie, Dutch is down there in the bullpen warming up. You go down there and ask him how he throws that ball."

Well, I did. You know what Dutch told me? He said, "What do you think I am, crazy? Let you take the bread and butter out of my mouth?" That's the reception I got from him. That's ol' Dutch. He was tough. He had a lot of bad luck after Cobb let him go. House burned down, wife died. He's the one who told Landis that Cobb bet on ball games.

See, Leonard was mad at Cobb, because Cobb let him go [in 1925]. In other words, he'd fired him. So Dutch got mad and brought that up to Judge Landis. Landis called Cobb and Tris Speaker into his office and he didn't do nothing with it. Cobb left Detroit after 1926. Cobb and Speaker went to play for Connie Mack in Philadelphia. Both those fellows broke in about 1906, something like that. That was way before my time. I can't tell you what took place on those ball clubs. They tell me these boys used to bet on themselves. I don't know. They say they did. I imagine they did. I know that when I hit the big leagues none of that was going on.

Well, I never did do much with Detroit. In 1925 I won six ball games, lost nine, and had a 6.19 ERA. In 1926 I had a thirty-three-inning scoreless streak with Detroit. Led the American League with four shutouts. I won twelve and lost ten. The next year, we were training down in San Antonio, and the first day of spring practice I hurt my arm. I threw the ball and, I don't know why, but my shoulder killed me. George Moriarty was the manager that year. He kept me until the middle of July, then they sent me to Washington. Washington sent me to Birmingham. I had tendonitis, is what I had. As soon as I hit Birmingham, that hot weather did it. I pitched the day after I reported. I lost, 4–3, but then I won thirteen straight and my arm ain't hurt since.

In 1928, the day before the season opened, Washington sold me to Birmingham outright. I won twenty-five games for Birmingham that year. Then about two weeks before the season ended, we were on a train going from Birmingham to Atlanta to play the Atlanta Crackers. I'd just had dinner on the diner and was sitting in my

Pullman seat when Billy West, our traveling secretary and business manager, told me I'd been sold to the Yankees for twenty thousand dollars. He told me I'd be reporting to them next spring training in St. Petersburg. That took a few minutes to sink in and then I became excited.

I remember during my playing days in Detroit a lot of ball players would be talking about how we'd like to be Yankees ourselves. Man, we were always in awe when we met the Yankees. There was just a certain air about them, like they were different from other ball clubs. We looked at them as being *double* big-leaguers. Yes sir.

I told you the first time I faced Babe Ruth, I struck him out. Three slow balls. In all of my career I pitched against Babe four years with Detroit and two with St. Louis. Well, he never hit a home run off me.

In 1926 we were playing the Yankees in Detroit. In those days they had to come through our dugout to get to their clubhouse. And Babe said to me, "Eddie, if it's the last thing I ever do, I'm gonna get you on the Yankees." I just laughed at that deal.

Anyway, in 1929, when I reported to Miller Huggins in St. Petersburg, Babe saw me in the clubhouse. He said, "Ed, what did I tell you that time in Detroit?" I said, "I thought you were kidding." He said, "Well, I wasn't." Well, I don't know if he got me on the Yankees or who got me on.

That ol' Babe. Man, oh man, he was something. We had a lot of fun. He'd give you the shirt off his back. I never saw a man with the constitution like the Babe had. He could put away that whiskey and beer. But listen, he could have a rough night and go out and hit those home runs like nobody's business. He swung a forty-two-ounce bat. Sure did. We called it a wagon tongue.

You know, Babe started out as a pitcher in Boston. His manager Ed Barrow's the one who saw the potential there and had him quit pitching. Barrow thought he'd do a lot better in the outfield, being the kind of hitter he was. Harold Frazee had the Red Sox. He was a theatrical man. He was going bankrupt. He was going to lose everything he had until [*Yankees owner*] Colonel Jake Ruppert bailed him out. Colonel Ruppert bought a whole bunch of ball players to get him out of debt. Then they built Yankee Stadium for the Babe. "The House That Ruth Built" is what they called it. And that's where he really went to town.

I dressed for four years between Babe and Lou Gehrig in the locker room, so I got to know those two men very well. Babe was an extrovert and Gehrig was the introvert. Babe was the idol of the fans and Gehrig was a close second. The right-field bleachers at Yankee Stadium were called "Ruthville" because that's where Babe hit ninety percent of his home runs. The fans there were just crazy about ol' Babe.

We were playing the White Sox one game in 1932. We always caught the early train from Chicago to St. Louis and here we are tied in the twelfth inning. Babe said, "Listen, boys, I'm going to end this or we'll miss our train if I don't." Well, Babe was first up and he drilled that first pitch into the right-field bleachers. Sure did. The White Sox didn't score in the bottom of the twelfth and we caught our train.

The Yankees were famous for hitting those home runs in clusters. I think that was the year Lou Gehrig hit four over the right-field wall in Shibe Park one Sunday. Lou was really a happy man in the clubhouse.

Babe was a happy guy at the right time and place. Off days and

Babe Ruth surrounded by admirers in 1922: "That ol' Babe. Man oh man, he was something."

rainy days, it was hard killing time. We just wanted to play ball, take care of the business at hand. Tony Lazzeri was one who liked to give you the hot foot when you were killing time, reading a newspaper. Or he'd light the corner of the paper and set fire to it. Another trick was spittin' tobacco juice on your baseball shoes after you'd just polished them. You can just imagine that deal, with everybody on the team chewin' tobacco.

I was very fortunate. I played for some doggone good managers. My first day at spring training in 1929 Miller Huggins told me my job was set and just go about my business. Man, that was like music to my ears. That took a lot of the pressure off, not having to worry too much about holding a job on the pitching staff.

The season opened and I just sat on the bench. Then one day Hug saddled up to me on the bench and out of the clear blue sky said, "Ed, you're gonna pitch tomorrow." Well, we were playing the White Sox at the stadium and I pitched against Ted Lyons. Anyway, I beat him 1–0 in an hour and twenty-eight minutes.

Well, we had a mediocre ball club. I won thirteen, lost nine. Then near the end of the season Hug became ill while we were playing Cleveland a doubleheader. The doctor told him to go to a hospital, and a week later little Hug died of blood poisoning. That was sad, it sure was. Ol' Hug, everybody liked him.

Bob Shawkey was my manager in 1930. He was a mighty fine fellow. We got along fine. I won twelve ball games that year and lost three. But somehow the Yankees didn't click. Philadelphia had the ball club then, and they were plenty tough. Connie Mack gave all the clubs a fit that year. Same thing in '31, when Joe McCarthy was our manager.

That Joe McCarthy, he was a real gentleman. He treated me fair. This is how fair Joe McCarthy was. In the latter part of '32, I wasn't pitching. We had a lead of twelve, fifteen games and we had a bunch of young fellas pitchin'—Lefty Gomez, Atley Donald. Lord, I didn't have a chance. One day the coach, Art Fletcher, come up to me and said, "Ed, Joe told me to tell you, you don't have to worry about not getting a share of the World Series money."

We really hit the jackpot that World Series. We played the Cubs. Beat 'em four straight. The Yankees had sold Mark Koenig, our shortstop, to the Cubs the latter part of the season. Koenig was a fine fellow, but we thought the Cubs had shorted him in the World Series shares. We rode them something terrible about that. When we hit Chicago and went to the Edgewater Beach Hotel, we really got a blast from the street fans. Babe was mainly their target.

Anyway, come the third game and Charlie Root is pitchin' for Chicago. All the Cub players were out on the bench railing, really riding Babe. Root pitched a strike and Babe stepped out of the batter's box and held up one finger. Root pitched another strike and Babe held up two fingers for two strikes. Then Babe motioned with his arm to the center-field bleachers, that he was going to hit the next pitch there for a home run, see.

Well, the Cubs really gave Babe the hah-hah. Root pitched the ball and—dad-gone!—Babe got hold of it and hit it into the center-field bleachers! That's right. I saw it. Well, the Yankee bench went wild, and when Babe rounded third base he tipped his cap to the Cubs' bench. Man, it was like a turtle had just pulled its head back into its shell, that's how quiet that Chicago bench got. In the locker room, Babe just broke down and cried. That's how happy he was.*

Well, I knew in the spring of 1933 I was going somewhere. I knew I was through with the Yankees because of all these young pitchers. I didn't know where. One day before a ball game, Joe told me to come into his room. Well, I knew I was being released. I walk in there and Joe says, "Ed, here's a letter from Wilbert Robinson, manager of the Atlanta club. He's offering twenty thousand dollars for your contract." That's a minor league team, see. He said, "I'll tell you what I'm gonna do. You've got a good friend, Bill Killefer, who's manager of the St. Louis Browns. I'm sending you over there for seventy-five hundred dollars." Joe had my release to the Browns and a ticket on the Twentieth Century Limited out of New York that night for St. Louis.

So I went over to St. Louis. Well, the first trip the Yankees make into St. Louis, I'm pitching. So I happen to pitch a good ball game. We won, 5–2. Now here's something I never heard a manager do. Joe came up to me afterwards and said, "Ed, I want to congratulate you on that game you pitched against us today. That was a good ball

---

*Ruth's "called shot" is part of baseball mythology. Observers are divided over what they really saw, but the best evidence suggests that Ruth merely gestured with his hand to indicate that he still had one swing left. Given the era and Root's ornery reputation, had Ruth really tried to show up the Chicago pitcher, the next pitch would have been directed straight at his head.

game." Now, can you imagine an opposing manager doing that? That's the kind of fella he was.

Who was greater, Cobb or Ruth? Now listen, those are two different characters all together. Now, Cobb was a dynamic ball player. He was always one thought ahead of everyone else on the field. Smart as the devil. They'd boo the devil out of Cobb, but he'd just eat it up. He liked it. If they didn't boo him he'd think something was wrong.

Me and Cobb were close. We were both Shriners. We'd go to lodge meetings a lot. That's when you had day games. We'd always go to meetings at night in different cities we were playing in. You got a big Masonic Temple in Detroit. What'd we do? Well, that's secret and stuff.

So who would I pick? Now, wait a minute. Babe won a lot of ball games for me. And Cobb managed me, and he won me a couple ball games too. They're just two different kinds of ball players. It's hard to say which one is the best. Cobb was a great man with Detroit. Good Lord! And Babe was a great man with the Yankees. I'd say it's about a tie. That's what I think.

I'll tell you one thing, slugger. Back then baseball players were dedicated. There weren't that many salary disputes. A lot of them were just tickled to death to be playing in the big leagues. Now it's money. The game's changed. I can tell by watching the ball players today. They're not as dedicated as they were. We used to love that ball game. We'd get to the ballpark at 10:30 in the morning. Now they get there in time for batting practice, if then.

I'll tell you how things have changed. One time with Detroit we was in the last half of the ninth inning, playing Cleveland, I think. We had men on and Cobb was looking up and down the bench for a pinch hitter. Cobb says, "Who here can hit?" Bob Fothergill got up and said, "I'll try."

Now, Bob's sitting there with a sprained ankle. Bad. Had it all taped up. Cobb said, "My gosh, you can hardly walk."

Bob said, "Well, I'll try." Cobb said, "Well, go on up there."

Bob was a dead-pull line-drive hitter. Everything was always to left field. The right fielder was way over to right center. This time Bob got hold of one and hit it over the first baseman's head into the right-field corner. Should've been at least a double. He got about two-thirds of the way to first and fell down. He crawled the rest of the way and got a single. Just barely.

Now, can you imagine the ball players doing that this day and age? If you were hurt, it didn't keep you from playing. They don't do that no more, slugger. But that's the way we played ball back there and then.

—*September 1982*

7

Bill Moore

William Christopher Moore
Born: September 3, 1903, Corning, New York
Major-league career: 1925 Detroit Tigers

Bill Moore's entire major-league career consisted of one disastrous outing at Navin Field. On the cold, overcast afternoon of April 15, 1925, the big right-handed pitcher entered the sixth inning of a game the Tigers were losing badly to the Chicago White Sox. Moore faced Johnny Mostil, Ike Davis, and Eddie Collins—and walked them all. After pitching a ball to the next batter, Earl Sheely, Moore was unceremoniously yanked by player-manager Ty Cobb. All told, Moore threw fourteen pitches in his sole big-league appearance. Only one was a strike.

Moore played fourteen minor-league seasons before quitting. He joined the Corning Police Department in 1936, retiring with the rank of captain. At the time of this interview, he was working as a night watchman at the Rockwell Museum.

Bill Moore died January 24, 1984, in Corning, New York.

I remember when I first joined the team down in Augusta for spring training in 1925. I was just a kid there. Ty Cobb was sitting in the hotel dining room with first baseman Lu Blue, catcher Johnny Bassler, and the third baseman—what the hell was his name?— when they all came over to shake hands with me. A young fella like myself, sitting all by myself at a table, probably lost, and they all came over and welcomed me to the club. I'll never forget that as long as I live.

The Giants were my team when I was a boy, you know. Old John McGraw, Fred Merkle, Christy Mathewson. . . . I'd check out the box scores in the paper every day, and of course I'd die if they'd lose a game.

My mother used to run a grocery store on the corner when I was going to St. Mary's School. My mother used to give me an apple or orange after school. I had a book by Christy Mathewson. Remember him? He was a great pitcher with the New York Giants. A real gentleman. The book was called *Pitching in a Pinch*. Showed you how to throw a curve, fastball, the fadeaway. I used to go out and practice gripping curveballs and other pitches using that book and holding a piece of fruit. In the winter I'd make snowballs and pitch them. That's a fact. I was nuts for baseball. That's all I wanted to be—a major-league pitcher.

I started out in 1921 when some players from Corning invited me down to pitch for Durham, North Carolina, in the Piedmont League. I was a big kid—six-foot-three, 190 pounds—and I could always throw hard. I could throw as hard as [Lefty] Grove or any of them. I don't mean that bragging, either, but I could. Durham signed me to a contract—$175 a month. Had a pretty good year there with Durham. The season was about halfway over when a Tiger scout named Billy Doyle bought me for Detroit. I was kind of disappointed with not pitching for my Giants. But I was thrilled to think of maybe one day playing with Ty Cobb, who of course was *it* in baseball.

Detroit farmed me out to Denver in the Western League, and I stayed there about a month before I was farmed out to Grand Rapids in the Central League. From there I went to Rochester. I won eighteen my first year at Rochester; seventeen the second. Got a $150 raise. What would eighteen wins be worth today? I spent four seasons in those places. In 1925 I was invited to spring training with the Tigers.

Bill Moore as a Rochester Red Wing.

I never had any use for Cobb, personally, but you had to give the devil his due. He was a great player. I remember when the Tigers played an exhibition game at Georgia Tech. On one play Cobb was going into second base, one foot aimed at the guy's face and the other at the bag. This little kid taking the throw gave Cobb the ball, whammed him with it. Cobb got up, took a handful of dirt, and threw it in the kid's face. That caused a near riot. That's the kind of guy he was. He'd cut a guy's neck to get a base.

I roomed with Harry Heilmann all through spring training. A marvelous hitter. Seems like every other year he led the league in hitting. Beat out Babe Ruth one year. Harry didn't think too much of Cobb.

Cobb didn't like me for some reason or the other. Of course, one time down in spring training I got in an argument with him. I was pitching batting practice one day to the regulars. Of course, being young, I was a little nervous. I wasn't getting the ball over just right for them, but the regulars would hit the ball anyway, you know, to help me out.

But that Cobb got up there and said, you know, "Let me at that s.o.b." Oh man, I was so mad I could've killed him.

I threw a couple over the plate and Cobb said, "What would you do now with a couple of strikes?"

I remember the first thing I learned from George Stallings at Rochester was not to let those guys get a toehold on you. Don't let them take away your bread and butter. That's the way it was in those days. No iron hat. . . .

So I showed him what I would do—I threw one right behind his head. Down he went. That's what you did in those days.

Cobb got up spluttering, "You son of a bitch!" All sorts of words. I turned around to get another ball and I could just feel the hair rising on the back of my neck. I got so mad, I took the ball and threw it over the grandstand and yelled, "Stick the ball up your ass!"

I went into the clubhouse and started packing my stuff. There was a trainer there, a little guy who used to be a pro fighter. His name was Dugan. And he looked at me and said, "Where do you think you're going?"

I said, "I'm going home. I can't take this."

He said, "Put your stuff back there! You just watch how Cobb treats me. You know, I could take that so-and-so and break him in two in two minutes. But I can't. I'm putting a kid through college and so I gotta take this stuff. So do you."

So I decided to stay.

With a month to go before opening day, Moore had his best outing yet. In an intrasquad game he retired all nine batters to face him, prompting the Detroit Times *to report:*

Moore Looks Good as "Regs" Win

Augusta, Ga. March 17.—Mgr. Ty Cobb of the Tigers may be forced to alter his pitching staff. Big Bill Moore . . . may force him to do it.

In his tentative plans regarding the building up of a pitching staff for the coming season, Big Bill didn't figure. Ty wants to carry but nine chuckers and Bill ranked tenth in his estimation. Today Ty feels that his judgement may have been faulty.

Cobb could teach you something about hitting, but he couldn't help pitchers out. Everything I knew about pitching I learned from Stallings at Rochester. He was a master. He'd always quiz you: where are you going to pitch this fellow in this situation? Okay, you've got a strike on him—*now* how are you going to pitch him? All the pitchers had to keep a book on every hitter in the league. If you pitched the way Stallings set it up, you'd never lose.

Carl Hubbell was in the Tigers' farm system the same time I was. Carl and I knew each other. We pitched against each other in the International League. Later, of course, he had all those great years with the Giants. Threw that screwball, you know. That was his bread-and-butter pitch. You know what Cobb told him to do with it? "Get rid of that damned pitch." Cobb didn't like him and Detroit released him outright. He wound up with some team in the Texas League, won ten or eleven straight, and John McGraw signed him. I was with Newark at the time. One day we had a day off, so I went up to the Polo Grounds to talk to Hubbell. He told me, "The best thing that ever happened to me was when that son of a bitch released me."

Cobb hated a colored person worse than anything. I remember once when I was with Rochester, we were barnstorming north, zigzagging across the countryside, playing games with Detroit. I can't remember exactly where it was—some small town in Georgia—but I remember the incident. We were in a restaurant after the game when Cobb asked this black waiter something. I don't know what was said, but the waiter said, "No." God almighty, you would've thought a bomb exploded in there! Cobb jumped out of his chair and grabbed that waiter by the lapels and told him, "You so-and-so nigger, it's 'No, sir' and 'Yes, sir' when you talk to a white man!" And then he went on a tirade about the blacks.

You know, I read a history—I got it around here somewhere—that when Cobb was young, growing up in Augusta, his father suspected Cobb's mother of stepping out on him. So one day he left, saying he was going away on business. But he really wanted to check on her. That night he returned, and as he was either climbing or looking through the bedroom window, Cobb's mother—wham!—killed him with a shotgun. She said later that she thought it was someone trying to break in. And many people thought that was the reason Cobb was like he was.

On April 1, 1925, just two weeks before the season opener, Moore was given the start in an exhibition game in Norfolk, Virginia. A heavy drizzle fell all through the game, and a stiff, cold

The indomitable Ty Cobb in 1917: "He'd cut a guy's neck to get a base." (Courtesy of the Burton Historical Collection of the Detroit Public Library.)

wind blew in from the Atlantic. Detroit won 13–5, but the rookie
pitcher struggled: five hits and three runs in just three innings, in-
cluding a wild pitch that scored a run.

Still, the scribes were forgiving: "Because of the conditions
under which the game was played there can be no reflection on the
work of any of the . . . pitchers." Cobb, too, must have been forgiv-
ing, or at least tolerant, for when the club moved north, Bill Moore's
name was on the roster.

The fans who packed Navin Field for the Tigers' opening day
on Tuesday afternoon, April 14, were treated to a well-pitched
game as Dutch Leonard defeated the Chicago White Sox, 4–3. Bill
Moore witnessed his first major-league game huddled on the De-
troit bench.

Earl Whitehill started Wednesday's game against Chicago, and
was shelled for seven runs before leaving the game in the fourth
inning. Cobb sent in Ken Holloway to pitch the fifth, and when Hol-
loway was removed for a pinch hitter, Cobb looked down the bench
for another pitcher. His eyes settled on Bill Moore.

Really, I really don't remember that much about it. Cobb said,
"Go in there and try to throw strikes." But I was nervous. I was wild
as hell.

"Moore was the most consistent pitcher of the lot," wrote Bert
Walker in the next day's Detroit Times. *"Only three men faced him*
and he walked them all, establishing a record for the afternoon and
season. He certainly played no favorites, although he did pitch a
strike to Collins before he sent him to first to fill the bases."

After I got a strike on Collins, he stepped out of the batter's box
and took out this big wad of chewing gum that he had in his mouth.
Then he put it on the little button on top of his baseball cap and
stepped back in.

Observed the Detroit Free Press: *"Bill Moore had a terrible time*
while making his major league debut. He walked the first three men
to face him, then was yanked after pitching another ball to the next
man." Two of the runners eventually scored, making Moore's life-
time earned run average in the Baseball Encyclopedia *∞—the sym-*
bol for infinity. Moore trudged off the field to a chorus of boos.

Cobb didn't even come out to the mound. He just hollered for me to get out of there. I remember walking off the field, and when I passed Chicago's third-base coach, Harry Hooper, he asked, "Well, kid, did you learn anything out there today?" He said, "After you walked that first batter, you were bearing down too hard. You should've thrown some slower stuff, a curve, try to get your control back." I thought that was real nice of him.

That was it. The club owner, Mr. Navin, called me up to his office and wanted to send me to Toronto. I said, "Well, Mr. Navin, I'm not going to Toronto. I want to go back to Rochester. And you can tell that so-and-so what I think about him." Boy, I was so glad to get away from him. Maybe it was foolish to feel that way, but honest to God. . . . Maybe if I'd played when Cochrane was there or anyone else, it would've been different.

I shouldn't have said the things I did, you know, but I was young and hotheaded. I think it wound up costing me. The Yankees wanted me in 1926 when I was with Rochester. Stallings said, "Come up to my room. I want you to hear this." Stallings called up Navin in Detroit, and I heard the conversation. Stallings told him that New York wanted to buy me, and Navin said, "Absolutely not."

Then in 1927 Pittsburgh needed a fastball pitcher to join them in a series at the Polo Grounds, but Mr. Navin wouldn't let me go. Cleveland and Washington were interested in me, too. Three teams wanted me. By then I'd been with the Detroit organization for six years. Why didn't they let me go? Maybe because of what I'd said a couple years earlier.

I quit about '32 or '33 and got a job with Corning Glass. Worked in shipping. Then I joined the police force. See these feet? I was a flatfoot—that's what they call all cops. I spent thirty years on the force—patrolman, then lieutenant, then captain. I passed the chief's exam, but they gave it to some other guy. So I retired.

Looking back, I probably shouldn't have said some of the things I did. From the day I told Cobb to stick that ball up his ass, I think I was cooked.

—July 1982

8

George Uhle

George Ernest Uhle
Born: September 18, 1898, Cleveland, Ohio
Major-league career: 1919–28, 1936 Cleveland Indians, 1929–33 Detroit Tigers, 1933 New York Giants, 1933–34 New York Yankees

George Uhle was nicknamed "Bull" during his seventeen-year major-league career, and for good reason. While with Cleveland he led the American League in wins with twenty-six in 1923 and twenty-seven in 1926 and twice led in innings pitched. He also was a superlative hitter. His fifty-two base hits in 1923 and .288 career batting average are major-league records for pitchers. Despite chronic arm problems, Uhle continued to perform yeoman's duty as a starter, reliever, and pinch hitter during his five-season stint in Detroit.

After leaving baseball as a scout in 1942, Uhle became a manufacturer's representative for the Arrow Aluminum Casting Company.

George Uhle died February 26, 1985, in Lakewood, Ohio.

I hurt my arm through too much work. I remember one season
in particular, 1926, when I won quite a few ball games for Cleveland. We played Philadelphia on a Saturday, the last game of the
season. The winner would finish second. My arm was tired. After
the first couple of innings, they got five runs off of me. I said to Tris
Speaker, who was managing and playing center field then, "Spoke,
I can't make it any further. I can't raise my arm above my belt."

George Burns and he were having a smoke down in the runway
alongside the dugout, and they both said, "We'll win or lose second
place with you, bad arm and all." In those days, second place was
worth about thirteen hundred dollars, I think. Pretty good money
back then.

So I pitched underhanded the rest of the ball game, and we beat
'em, 6–5. They didn't get a run off of me the rest of the way, and
that was that good Philadelphia ball club, with Jimmie Foxx and Al
Simmons and those fellows.

I used to pitch a lot of innings. When I was going good, why, if
possible, if we were going to play a four-game series in New York,
Speaker would have me miss Boston to open and close against New
York. Boston was always near last place then. Instead of an easy
outing, I had to work like the dickens all nine innings against that
good-hitting Yankee ball club. So I got my share of work and complete games that way, I'll say that.

I was with Cleveland from 1919 through 1928. During the winter of '29, Detroit traded Jackie Tavener, the shortstop, and Ken Holloway, a pitcher, for me. Cleveland liked Tavener because he hit so
well against them. But Cleveland didn't have the book on Jackie.
After I got over to Detroit, why, Harry Heilmann told me, "Just pitch
high fastballs to Jackie. That's all you have to do." And that stopped
his hitting cold.

Someone once told me that Mr. Navin had made the remark that
I was just as great a pitcher as Christy Mathewson, that I made
pitching look so easy. But that first year with Detroit I had adhesions
so bad I could hardly throw. A couple of pitchers I knew who lived
out on the West Coast tipped me off to a Dr. Spencer, who stretched
arms. I thought stretching the arm was a good idea, so Mr. Navin let
me go out a couple of weeks ahead of the team, which trained in
Phoenix that spring. Dr. Spencer stretched my arm and broke those
adhesions. And I'm telling you, the first three or four days that
you'd get a stretching from him, he'd pert near make you cry. He

could tell by your expression just where he was hurting you and where the adhesions were the worst.

The next couple springs we went out to California for training, and I got some additional stretching done while we were there. Jimmy Dugan, our trainer, watched Dr. Spencer at times, just so that he could have some idea of how to stretch an arm. He got to where he could do a fairly good job.

I pitched a lot for Bucky Harris in Detroit, and that probably didn't help my arm. We never had any relief pitching. There was only Vic Sorrell, Earl Whitehill, and myself, and no relief pitching to help us out. Back in those days, there was only one real relief pitcher in baseball, and that was Fred Marberry with Washington. They didn't start that relief business until a few years later. Now, of course, it's become a science. Today, starters are tickled to death to go six or seven innings. But then, your best pitchers started and they were expected to pitch the whole game.

I won my first nine games with Detroit in '29. Number eight was a twenty-one-inning game against Chicago. Pitched twenty innings of that game. It's my own fault that I went on for as long as I did. I got five hits off of Ted Lyons. I got a big kick out of that. Every inning after the ninth, why, Bucky'd look at me and say, "How about it?" And I'd say, "I might be up to bat next inning."

So I'd pitch and I'd get a base hit, and it'd be another couple innings or so and I'd tell Bucky, "Well, I'm going to come to bat again next inning." It kept that way all the way up to the top of the twenty-first inning, when I got a base hit leading off. Bucky put in a pinch runner for me and we were lucky enough to score. Lil Stoner came in, pitched the bottom half of the inning, and we won the ball game.

After I pitched that game, I want to tell you something, Dr. Spencer sent the most sarcastic telegram you'd ever want to read to Bucky Harris for letting me go twenty innings with my arm, as bad as it was. But the funny thing was, my arm felt fine. A couple of starts after that, I beat Washington, 7–5 or 6–4, something like that, one of those games where there was a lot of base runners on. My arm felt worse after that game than it did after the twenty-inning game.

Then something happened under my shoulder blade. I didn't know it until the same thing happened to me again later, but I had caught a cold under my shoulder.

We were playing the Red Sox one Sunday in Boston. We

couldn't play in the American League ballpark because of the church regulations in those days, so we played in the Braves' National League park. Their mound was way different from anything else in the American League. It was way high—I'd say two or three feet high, and graduated. It was built for their pitchers. Me, being an overhand pitcher, why, my fastball was high all day long. I was always in trouble, which meant that I threw an awful lot of pitches that day.

I had 'em, 4–1, going into the ninth inning. Bucky came out to the mound when he saw that I was having trouble putting anything on the ball and they were starting to hit it. He said, "How about it?"

Lil Stoner was in the bullpen. He'd relieved in my twenty-one-inning game in Chicago. I don't know, different stories that Heilmann and other players told me, but Stoner liked to get credit for games if he possibly could.* I know that when two balls were hit back to him in the twenty-first inning, he threw them in the dirt to Heilmann at first. Heilmann came up with both of them, we got out of it all right, and I got credit for the game. In this game in Boston, Stoner was the only guy we had in the bullpen.

I said, "Well, with that little guy down in the bullpen, I'd just as soon win it or lose it myself even if I can hardly get the ball up to the plate."

Bucky said to me, "I feel the same way."

Well, with each ball I threw, it hurt twice as much under my shoulder blade. Severe pain of some kind. I couldn't imagine what it was. So Boston wound up beating me. Instead of me winning ten straight and getting decent relief, I staggered through and got beat. My next ball game was in New York. Lost that game. The Yankees scored right off because I could hardly throw. So, Dugan kept on stretching my arm after that until, one day, it finally left. I wound up having a decent year.

The same thing happened to me the next season at spring training in California. One day Mark Koenig wanted to visit his home and asked me if I wouldn't like to ride with him. It was an open car and a cold day, and the next day I couldn't even throw in batting

---

* It wasn't until the 1940s that the bullpen gained universal acceptance as a strategic option in its own right instead of just a repository for failed starters. Even after saves became an official statistic in 1969, most pitchers still depended largely on their won-lost record when negotiating new contracts.

George Uhle, an early practitioner
of the "sailer." Later generations of
pitchers would call it a slider.
(Courtesy of the National Baseball
Library, Cooperstown, New York.)

practice. I immediately got on the train to see Dr. Spencer. He said,
"Well, you've caught a good cold under there." Same thing as in
Boston. Stretching took it out again, and I never had it come back
after that.

I thought Bucky was a very good manager. Bucky knew what he
was doing and I'm telling you, he was a good, smart manager. He
made it a point to look into a fellow's eyes if he was going to send
him up to pinch-hit. He wanted to check and see if they were blurry
from being out late the night before.

I had good luck pinch-hitting for Bucky. I recall one game in
particular. We beat Wes Ferrell of Cleveland the first game of a
doubleheader, I believe it was the Fourth of July. I was going to pitch
the afternoon game. I was at home, listening on the radio. The
morning game went on, no score. Finally Cleveland got one run. I
said to the Missus, "Well, I'm going to head down to the park.
Maybe I can help out in some way."

I got to Navin Field about the eighth inning, got dressed, and
went out to the bench. Ferrell was a real good pitcher and he had us
beat, 1–0. I happened to be sitting close to Bucky and in the ninth
inning he said, "How about pinch-hitting?"

I said, "Okay." I pinch-hit with two men out. With two strikes on me, I got a curveball that wasn't eight or ten inches off the ground and hit it to left field for a base hit. The next two balls Ferrell pitched went for a single and a double, two runs scored, and we beat him, 2–1. Ferrell was so mad—three base hits on three straight pitches and he loses—that he took the glove in his mouth and pulled the webbing out with his teeth.

But Ferrell was a very good pitcher and a great competitor. Don't think he wasn't. Pretty good hitter, too. He hit that long ball. I wasn't a long-ball hitter because I choked up. I didn't swing from the end of the bat. I protected home plate. They didn't strike me out very often. I used a light bat, about as light as they came—thirty-three, thirty-four ounces. A Billy Rogell model.

I loved to hit the curveball. Instead of guessing back and forth, I'd wait for it right down the line and eventually I'd get it. Speaker and I once had an argument about this business of guessing pitches, and I told him, "You're not guessing when you're waiting on one type of pitch." Until you get two strikes, of course. Then you look for anything. But you still have to favor the pitch that that pitcher throws most often. If he's a fastball pitcher, you're more apt to get the fastball, so you favor that.

Pitchers have good years and bad years because hitters catch up to the way you pitch. You have to change them. If they've been hitting your fast stuff inside, you have to switch over to let up pitches and curves.

I had a good fastball. I didn't throw *extremely* fast, by any means, but when I had to I could put an extra pound behind it. That's what Heilmann called it, "putting an extra pound" on the fastball. And if I had to, I'd put another couple pounds on the next pitch. I had a real good overhand curveball. Then towards the end, when I was with Detroit, I came up with a slider.

One day Heilmann and I were working out. Eddie Phillips was catching us. I don't know, I just happened to turn a ball loose a certain way, and it sailed. I said to Heilmann, "I've got a new one!" So I threw another one that way, and it sailed. I started using it in ball games. When I first started using it with Detroit, the batters would call time and want the umpire to look at the ball, like I had roughed it up. And Eddie would always say, "Well, that's his sailer."

Who were the toughest hitters to pitch to? Well, you have to put Ruth in that category for one. Heilmann was another. Then Lou Gehrig. But there were two hitters who used to guess me right pert near every time. One was Bob Fothergill and the other was Bibb Falk. It was uncanny the way they could guess what I was going to throw.

Fothergill was with Detroit when I went there. When I was with Cleveland, we had dinner together one night. He bet me the next night's dinner that he'd get three hits off me the next day, provided I didn't walk him. I said, "Okay"—and the son of a gun got three hits. It wasn't until I got to Detroit that I learned Bob couldn't hit those big, slow, roundhouse curves. He'd jump out of his shoes trying to him them.

Cobb? Naturally, he was real tough. His weakness was pitching inside on him. That was the one way you had the best luck with him. I hate to say it, but there weren't many umpires who'd call it a strike when it was a strike. He'd lean over home plate, and when it was on the inside corner, he would act as if the pitch was going to hit him. Billy Evans was the one umpire who would call it a strike at all times on him. Ty got to hating Billy Evans, to where Cobb challenged him and they had a fight one time, in Washington.

Ruth never could hit me. If the count was two and nothing, I would deliberately go to three and oh by pitching slow curveballs to him, try to hit him between the stomach and his knees. Let him pull it foul. If he took it, I didn't care. Then I'd throw him a change of pace, low and outside. That's the ball I made him hit all the time. I wouldn't throw him but one fastball every two games. Even then, it was only after I'd already gotten him out two or three times on change-ups. I'd throw him a high, bad fastball with two strikes on him and hope he chased it.

One of the shortest distances in any ballpark in the major leagues was left and right field in the Polo Grounds, right down the foul line. Ruth got a home run, a pop fly down the right field line, in one of my first seasons with Cleveland. He never hit another home run off of me until my next-to-last year at Detroit, in '32. I threw a good overhand curveball to him and he hit it clean across the street onto the taxicab company on Trumbull. It was the longest home run I ever gave up. I've often thought, what a fool I was. Ruth and I were such great friends. When he finally did hit one off me, why didn't I stand at home plate, give him a punch in the belly, and shake hands with him?

We all liked to have a good time now and then. Different towns, where you'd have really good company. We all had friends like Dr. Ross in Boston, who was a great friend of all the ball players. He was a marvelous fellow. He knew Ruth real well, and players like myself and Heilmann. When the clubs were in town, he'd have us out golfing. There was another dentist in Washington who had all the connections for the boys.

Ruth had good connections. Everybody liked him. He liked a lot of fun. And of course, the places that were cheating, the speakeasies, they were tickled to death to have Babe Ruth come there. They'd put us in a side room so the public wouldn't know he was drinking there. There was a place in New Jersey, for instance, that had an upstairs room where they served good beer and had really good food. Babe would invite a player or two from the other ball clubs and take them over.

He loved to eat. One time at the end of the season I had Speaker and his wife and Ruth and his wife over my house for dinner. Babe was crazy over pig knuckles and sauerkraut. Every time I'd go over to his apartment for dinner, it'd be pig knuckles and sauerkraut. So I had it for him. He ate so many, it looked like he was throwing them over his shoulder. This was during Prohibition, so the local brewmeister brought a keg of beer over the house. Babe really enjoyed all that. My daughter Marilyn, who was only about seven or eight at that time, got together all the kids in the neighborhood and charged them each a dime to look through the window and see Babe Ruth. She didn't let her two brothers in on it, though.

Back in Prohibition days, the baggage handlers would test your luggage with stethescopes. If they heard any gurgling, why, they'd open up your trunk. I'll never forget once in Hot Springs, Arkansas, where we used to go for the mineral baths. You couldn't buy any beer down there. It was a case of having some moonshine fixed up with either some grenadine syrup or Coke to disguise the taste. Right after we got there, Ruth said, "I'll give you guys a good drink. Come on up to my room."

So we went up to Ruth's room. Babe got the hotel boy to give him a claw hammer to open this crate that he'd had shipped over. But when Babe opened it up, instead of the twelve bottles of booze that were supposed to be inside, there was one broken bottle sitting there. The rest had been stolen. Somebody else had opened it up.

I know over in Pennsylvania, where Stan Coveleski came from, they made real good moonshine. They'd bury the kegs and everything to age it. Covey always used to have a couple half-gallon bottles in his trunk for road trips. He'd pack chewing tobacco all around them so they couldn't move and gurgle around.

Of course, you could go across to Canada and go to a roadhouse, have your beer, a highball, whatever you wanted. And you could bring a bottle back across the Ambassador Bridge in your car, if the guys didn't want to take it away from you. But you'd get to know those fellows pretty good, so you could bring a bottle back.

I grew up on the west side of Cleveland. My father was an engineer on the New York Central at that time. I was crazy about baseball as a little youngster. When I was only seven or eight years old, my parents bought me a glove and ball. No one could get hold of them—I put them under my pillow at night.

I followed the Cleveland ball club in the papers. They were called the Cleveland Naps then, after Nap Lajoie, the great second baseman. I didn't get to see them very often at League Park, just once in a while when someone would take me. Joe Birmingham was the manager and played center field. Addie Joss and Joe Jackson were there, too, but Vean Gregg was my favorite because of the curveball he had. He was a lefthanded pitcher, though. That was the funny part. I was a righthander.

I got started by playing semipro ball after graduating from high school. I went up the ranks, through D, C, and then B leagues, and then with a class Double-A team. This was at a time when companies hired ex-ball players and paid them to play ball for them. These were the days when they were getting crowds of seventy thousand at Brookside Park, this big, circular park in Cleveland. You may heard of when White Motor played Omaha in a game at Brookside Park around 1915 or so that drew more than a hundred thousand people.

I played for Standard Parts, which later was bought by Eaton. This was 1918, the year before I joined Cleveland. We had two Delahantys on the team.* Del Young played right field and he was our manager. He was formerly with Cincinnati. We had a fellow by the name of Young on second base who had played a little bit with St. Louis. Our catcher had been sold to Chicago, reported, and, well, that's about all. But at least he'd had that advantage. Our third baseman had been in the American Association. Then we had a center fielder who had been sold to the big leagues twice out of the Central League, and each time in the fall of the year he was unlucky enough

---

* Five Delahanty brothers played in the major leagues at the turn of the century.

to slide and break a leg. So we had a pretty fair—*pretty fair*—amateur team.

Glenn Liebhardt and Heinie Berger, both ex-major-league pitchers, were our pitching staff at Standard Parts. Liebhardt recommended me to the Cleveland club, and they called me over for a conference. I made them sign an agreement that if I didn't make good with them right off of the rail, that they would have to give me my release, not send me to the minor leagues. Dough back in those days was real tough. I was working during the week at Standard Parts and also getting paid for two games a week, a Saturday and a Sunday. Then we cut in on the gate receipts when we went out of town to play. We made fairly good dough, more than what the Cleveland ball club offered me to play for them. What did they offer me? Nothing, or next to nothing, let's put it that way.

Tris Speaker was my manager when I joined Cleveland. He also played center field. A marvelous player. He'd play a shallow center field and make these shoestring catches, sliding on his knees; many times you didn't know whether he had trapped or caught the ball.

"You didn't catch that ball, did you, Spoke?" I'd ask him.

"They called it out, didn't they?" he'd say.

Joe Jackson was on the Cleveland team before I got there. Shoeless Joe. Somehow or other he got over to Chicago. He was a terrific hitter. My first year in the league, 1919, was when the Black Sox threw the World Series. But Joe was too dumb to get involved in that. He didn't get into it, he really didn't. He wasn't that smart. I mean, they may have talked to him about it and all, but it didn't sink in. He didn't try to do anything to lose. He had a hell of a series. In fact, he didn't have anything to do with the planning of it. I know that from conversations with other players at the time, some of who knew some of the stuff.

Jackson and Eddie Cicotte and the rest of the Black Sox weren't suspended until the 1920 season was just about over. But they had a good ball club, I'll say that. It's too bad. It was one of those things where they weren't making any money, I guess, and they were going to try to make a few bucks extra. Hard way to do it. But you know, back in my day, if a fella was making five thousand dollars a year, he was getting a big salary from most of those owners.

I played with Smoky Joe Wood on Cleveland. His arm went bad to where he couldn't pitch anymore. But he could really throw hard at one time. Had one year [1912] where he won thirty-four games with the Red Sox. He hit pretty good and he was a good outfielder, so he alternated with Elmer Smith in right field for a few years. I got a letter from Joe last September when I was in the hospital. He's up in Connecticut somewhere. Going to be ninety-three. He said to hang with him.

Stan Coveleski's still around, too. He's close to ninety, I guess. Up to last year, he fished every day, winter and summer. Never kept any fish, either. Gave 'em to the neighbors every time. But now he's laid up.

Covey was a great spitball pitcher. He knew what to do with a spitball. He could throw it better than most spitball pitchers because he could throw it different speeds—slow, slower, and then really break it off when he had two strikes on you. We beat Chicago out for the pennant in 1920 and Covey beat Brooklyn three times in the series.

I was home in bed when Ray Chapman was killed that summer by Carl Mays. I didn't make that trip to New York. I came up with water on the knee. Right before that I was pitching in Detroit. They had this clay in front of the mound. With a man on first, I had a ball bunted to me. I tried to throw to second base, but when I turned, my spikes got caught in the clay and my knee twisted. When I got back home the doctor had me put packs on my knee and told me to stay in bed.

Chappie was a great bunter, one of the best in the business of pushing the ball between the pitcher and first base and making the second baseman field it. He could really fly. Ran like a deer, so he beat a lot of bunts out for base hits. He never moved his head, they tell me, to get out of the way of the ball. I have a hunch that he froze because he had in his mind the idea of starting to bunt. Maybe just starting to lean a little and then he didn't know what to do to get out of the way of the ball. He didn't move his head or do anything.

Mays could've been throwing under his chin to stop him from bunting. But I would never accuse Carl of deliberately trying to hurt him. I don't think any pitcher wants to hurt a batter. You might throw under his chin to keep him from leaning over the plate and taking advantage of you. Mays had that reputation, along with a few other pitchers back then, of telling batters from the mound to get ready, that he was going to throw at them. He'd yell, "Get ready to duck!"

Chappie was a marvelous person. He had a real good voice. There were three or four fellows on the ball club who could sing a

little bit. They'd always have a quartet together. On the day he was
hit they rode the elevated out to the Polo Grounds. They told me
afterwards that they knew Mays was going to pitch. Chappie made
the remark, "Well, I'll do the fielding. I can't hit him, so it's up to
you fellas to do the hitting today." Kidding, you know, about it, and
then he turns around and gets hit and gets killed.

We brought up Joe Sewell from New Orleans shortly after that
to play shortstop. A good hitter right off the rail. He helped the ball
club a lot. We got into the World Series that year against Brooklyn,
and we beat them five games to two. That was a best-of-nine format
that year because of the size of the two ball parks. Neither ball park
could seat even thirty thousand. In fact, Cleveland put up temporary stands in right center, and roped off the outfield in left center,
and even then it wouldn't hold more than twenty-seven thousand
fans.

I relieved in the two losing ball games. I know they didn't hit a
ball out of the infield off of me. I came pert near starting the last
game, but Speaker told me, "If I do, George, and something goes
wrong, they'll all accuse the club of trying to make the series go an
extra game or two."

I was in the bullpen when Bill Wambsganss made that unassisted triple play in the fifth game. Jim Bagby pitched that game. We
won, 8–1, but he gave up a lot of hits. Brooklyn hit into a triple play
and three double plays and they were all line drives. Brooklyn finally got one run in the ninth inning and Bagby popped off afterwards that they wouldn't have gotten that if Speaker had fielded a
ball cleanly in center field. That didn't set too well with Speaker. In
fact, he pitched Bagby very little the next year.

Revenge? Well, I remember one game a couple years later, just
before New York sent Carl Mays to Cincinnati, where Miller Huggins made Mays pitch the whole ball game against us with a tired
arm. We beat him badly, 13–0. I pitched for Cleveland and drove in
six runs that game. Huggins and Mays were having some sort of
feud, I guess, so Huggins let him take a beating. Mays was just tossing the ball up to the plate, his arm was so tired.

I played for Detroit 1929 through the beginning of '33. Detroit
was a marvelous city then. Downtown was wonderful. You had
no worries about walking around. The Missus used to go over to
Hudson's and parade around. The Tigers were always a very good

Detroit owner Frank Navin and manager Bucky Harris. (Courtesy of the Burton Historical Collection of the Detroit Public Library.)

drawing ball club. In Cleveland, if you had six thousand people at a ball game, it was marvelous. Heck, in Detroit it was always a case of seven thousand to ten thousand people, and I mean during the week. There was a lot of difference.

I know Bucky said to me one rainy Sunday in Detroit, "Do you want to play?"

I said, "We've got a pretty damn good crowd here. Why not start? I'll tackle it in the rain."

So we played. I think we got beat. But we played.

Jumpin' Joe Dugan was a coach with Detroit then. I can't remember now exactly why they called him Jumpin' Joe, whether it was because he jumped ball clubs so often or was always hoppin' mad. But he was a real clever fellow. And real nice.

I'll never forget one incident. We stopped to get a beer once in Chicago—Charlie Gehringer, Johnny Grabowski, Dugan, and myself. Al Capone's name came up in the conversation and one of us made the remark that "we'd love to meet him."

The fella who owned this saloon kind of worked for Capone— a collector or something. Anyway, he says, "Would you really like to meet him?"

We all said, "Yes."

"All right," he says. "I'll arrange it for tomorrow night then."

So the next evening we stopped by his place and he drove us to the Lexington Hotel, which was Capone's headquarters. He had it all arranged. When we walked into the lobby of the Lexington, the guy running the elevator stepped away and let us stand there for about five minutes. We stood in the hallway until he must've gotten the okay to come on up.

When we got on the elevator we were searched. Then when we got off on the floor where Capone had his suites, we were searched again. We went down this hallway to a door that led to a corner suite. We went in and there was a guy by that door. And then there was a guy by the door that led into the next room. I'd say we were searched four times by the time we got into Capone's office.

We sat down alongside the wall right inside the door. Capone was a little busy with a fella at the time—Ed Strong, a promoter. Before we were introduced, we had a chance to look around. Capone was sitting at this big desk. On the wall behind him were hanging these great big paintings of Lincoln and Washington. Dugan took one look and said, "Look at this: Washington, Lincoln— and the king sitting in the middle."

Capone didn't hear that. But he was glad that we came up. He was a big baseball fan. He wanted us to go out to dinner with him. He was going to some show that he owned, taking the troupe out, all the girls, and he wanted us to join him. We didn't want to do that, so we said thanks, but we can't.

We were leaving for Cleveland after playing Chicago, about the time a big fight was on, Stribling versus Max Schmeling. Capone turned to Strong, who owned a racetrack at that time and was backing the fight, and said, "These boys are going to be in Cleveland shortly. See that they get in to see the fight. Take care of them."

Never met him again. But he was fine with us. You know, they rave about all the money Capone made, but I don't about just how tough he was. He gave money away hand over fist to poor people. I heard he took care of a lot of people that way. He was sent away to prison a little while after that. Income tax evasion. Off the record, you know, he died of softening of the brain. Syphilis.

Detroit sold me over to the New York Giants in 1933. Bill Terry wanted a pinch hitter. I went over there with that purpose, but my back was so bad I could hardly move. I didn't last very long with the Giants. When they released me, I went to an osteopath by the name of Dr. Fields in Lakewood. Dr. Fields found out what was wrong right off the rail. My sacroiliac was out. He worked on me for about ten days. I worked out with a fellow down in one of the city parks, to find out if it was all right to pitch. It was coming along fine and I got a call from the Yankees. So I reported three or four days later, and I think I won six straight ball games for them.

Then the next year they wanted me to be the long relief man, and I was never able to do that. You know: get up, warm up, sit down. I was always able to throw a dozen balls, get into a game, and I'd be fine. Just like I used to for Bucky Harris. I remember saving two ball games in a row for him one season in Detroit, and in bad situations—bases filled, a two and zero count on the batter. Then the very next day, New York is in town, and the same trouble in the ninth inning. This time it was a tie ball game. So instead of getting out of it in the ninth, I pitched until the sixteenth. All of these relief appearances were after taking my regular turn. Finally Bucky said to me, "Go on and go fishing for a couple of days. Every time I look up, I have to use you." That's the only vacation I ever got in baseball.

But I had a lot of fun. In fact, I've got to tell you kind of a cute story. At the end of one summer in Detroit, the club had these contests on the last Sunday of the season to draw people to the ball park. Fungo-hitting, circling the bases, fastest hundred-yard dash, four or five contests like that.

Bucky Harris came up to me and said, "Let's win at least one of these contests. Take a dozen balls home and bake them overnight. We'll win the fungo-hitting contest." Baking the baseballs made them lighter, so they'd go further when they were hit. As it turned out, that was the only contest we *didn't* win. No kidding. Joe Vosmik won it for Cleveland.

Anyway, the following year, the Missus was out at Navin Field with our daughter, who was about six or seven years old at the time. We were playing Boston. I went up to pinch-hit. I hit a line drive to right field, and at the last moment it curved away from the outfielder. It broke so fast, it went off his glove and they gave me a three-base hit.

My daughter turned to Helen and said, "Will they give Daddy a hit on that?"

"Sure," said Helen. "It was too hot to handle."

"Oh," said my daughter. "Did they bake that ball, too?"

—July 1982

9

Charlie Gehringer

Charles Leonard Gehringer
Born: May 11, 1903, Fowlerville, Michigan
Major-league career: 1924–42 Detroit Tigers

Nicknamed the *"Mechanical Man"* because of his consistency and effortless grace, Charlie Gehringer is arguably the finest all-around second baseman in American League history. In nineteen years with the Tigers he compiled a lifetime batting average of .320; hit 184 home runs; stole 182 bases; and banged out 2,839 base hits in 2,323 games. He batted .321 in three World Series, started the first six All-Star Games, and was voted the league's Most Valuable Player in 1937, the season he won the batting championship. He also was amazingly durable, twice compiling consecutive-game playing streaks of more than five hundred games.

Charlie Gehringer was inducted into the Baseball Hall of Fame on June 18, 1949—a ceremony he missed because he was being married in California. Today the Gehringers live in a large, secluded house in Birmingham, Michigan.

I think it was Lefty Gomez of the Yankees who gave me the "Mechanical Man" name. He made the statement to the papers once that "you wind Gehringer up in the spring and turn him off in the fall and in between he hits .340." Unfortunately, it's not quite that easy. Like anything, it's a lot of hard work and practice.

Looking back, I'd have to say that starting in pro ball was plain luck. I grew up on a farm outside Fowlerville. It was a big farm, fifteen cattle and about 230 acres, and it took two or three people to keep it going. My parents had a feeling that I wasn't going to like it on the farm. My older brother was doing most of the heavy work, driving the tractor, and running the heavy equipment. My dad was still alive and we had a hired man, too, so it gave me a chance to go away to college for a year.

I had an idea that I'd like to be in sports, maybe coaching. I took phys ed classes at the University of Michigan. I went with more or less a baseball background, but I went out for football. I remember Ray Fisher, who was coaching baseball then, caught me on the sidelines one day at practice.

"Don't get too excited about this game," he said.

"Don't worry," I said. "I won't."

Funny thing is, I won a letter in basketball but I didn't get one in baseball.

I'd pitched all through high school. Just lost one game. That was 2–1 to Detroit Northern, who always played us in a doubleheader whenever they came out to play Howell, the next little town. I pitched a little bit in pro ball, but after they started knocking me around pretty good I said, "Well, there must be a difference." So I decided to try second base. I always could hit pretty good.

We used to have a super fan back home who hunted with Bobby Veach, the old Tiger outfielder. He asked Veach if it was all right for me to go down to Detroit for a workout. Today, of course, you couldn't hide a prospect if you wanted to. But this was 1923, and it was possible to get a tryout with a major-league club fairly easy, providing you had some potential. They didn't want you cluttering up the field. So I went down for about a week in the fall of the year.

Ty Cobb was the manager then, and apparently he was so impressed he went up in his uniform to Mr. Navin, the club owner, and got him out of his office to take a look at me. I signed a contract with the Tigers, and I can't remember if I got a bonus. Maybe five hundred dollars. But I would've signed for nothing.

When I was a kid, you see, I used to keep a kind of scrapbook. I used to paste newspaper pictures of Cobb and Veach and Harry Heilmann, and here I was going to play with them.

Cobb was a hateful guy. I think he wanted it that way; felt it made him a better player. I never heard him say anything good about anybody. He died a pretty bitter man. I think he had so many regrets it made him pretty miserable. Nobody liked him as a manager. He was such a great player himself, he figured that if he told you something, there was no reason why you couldn't do it as well as he did. But a lot of guys don't have that ability. He couldn't understand that.

Cobb was jealous of everybody and a strict disciplinarian. He had very few friends. All players shrunk away from him, especially the pitchers. Golly, he wore a path from center field to the pitcher's mound. When he'd relieve a pitcher, he'd just *grab* that ball away from him.

But he was super for the first couple years I was up. Golly, he was like a father to me. He took care of me, coached me, rode with me on the train and all that. He even made me use his own bat, which was kind of a thin little thing. I said, "Gee, I'd like a little more batting space," but I didn't dare use another one. He would've shipped me to Siberia. Then all of a sudden he got upset with me about something. To this day I don't know what it was. He would hardly speak to me. He wouldn't even tell me what signs I was going to get from the coaches. Weird. But he kept playing me, so it didn't really matter whether he talked to me or not.

The only thing I can think of that might have ticked him off is a game we played coming north from spring training. Nobody cared too much, really. It was hot and we were tired of exhibition games by that time. All of us stood out on the field and more or less didn't holler or cheer it up. Cobb yelled, "C'mon, let's have a little life out there!"

When I came back to the bench he yelled again: "C'mon, get some life out there!" I said, "I'm making as much noise as anyone else." Of course, none of us were making much. So maybe that set him off. He was a hard fellow to figure, to say the least.

I played parts of three seasons with Cobb as manager. Cobb played a few games and did fairly well. He'd have been all right if they'd had the designated hitter back then, because at that time Cobb couldn't field or run. It was pretty hard to use him in a crucial spot. He was still intimidating, though. I remember in the fall, when the rosters got bigger and rookies came into town, Cobb would sit on the bench with a file, sharpening his spikes. In the old days, you had to go through our dugout to get to the visitors' dugout. All these kids would get the message. Their eyes would bulge out a little. Of course, at that time Cobb was over the hill and he didn't play much. But he'd still cut you to pieces if you got in his way, and they all realized that.

Yeah, he had a super career. He made a lot of money. I guess he got to know some people here who gave him some good tips. I remember when I first came along as a kid, making four thousand dollars a year, and he was telling me to buy General Motors and Coca-Cola stock. Which was good advice. But you had to live, too, besides buying stock.

I think my first contract was for thirty-five hundred dollars. That was my first year, 1924, when I played for London in the Michigan–Ontario League. They only paid two hundred dollars of it monthly, and Navin had to pick up the rest. I remember my father died that year and I went home three days for the funeral. When I came back I discovered the London club had docked me three days' pay—which I thought was pretty chintzy.

I lived in Detroit with a family from Fowlerville my first couple of years. Lived in a great neighborhood at that time, but it's deteriorated a little since: Twelfth and Pingree Street. Gee, there were some nice little bungalows. Think I paid ten dollars a week and got good food and lodging.

Mr. Navin was like all the owners then. He was in it to make a living. He was hard to deal with. In those days an owner didn't need millions, but it took some money to move ball players around and what-not. I remember one year during the depression he had to borrow money from the bank to take us to spring training. The situation had to hurt you salarywise, but then, you were happy to play for most anything. Today, everybody's got an agent and he's only too happy to say how successful he is. In those days, you didn't know what anybody made and didn't really seem to care.

Second jobs? I think you had to have one. Very few players stayed here during the winter. Most of them were from the south in those days and they were all pretty much small-town kids. I think they all went back home after the season. Of course, you always had guys who liked to hunt and fish. I didn't care too much for hunting.

I never had a gun, and I could never have shot anything if I'd had one. I always said I'd never shoot anything unless it chased me, and so far that hasn't happened.

In the off-season I'd work at J. L. Hudson's, during the holidays. I enjoyed that, gave me something to do, and I met a lot of nice people. I used to take the Trumbull streetcar down. Didn't have a car in those days, so I always jumped on the streetcar and went downtown. Seems like that was the way everybody was going. Good service. At least we didn't know any better. I used to even take the Trumbull streetcar and go back out after a ball game. If you had a bad day, though, you had to put some plugs in your ears. The fans were getting on the same car and you'd hear about it. They'd say, "Who was that turkey playing out there today?"

I used to go on barnstorming tours every year. At that time you didn't have television, so people were curious to see major leaguers play ball. Out west, up north, through the Dakotas. . . . We went through Canada one year. We used to draw a lot of people and have a lot of fun. We'd have a good club—Bill Dickey, Heinie Manush, George Uhle—and play the local teams or another club that traveled with us.

Most of those little-town teams didn't give you much trouble, but those colored teams would. I traveled one year with Satchell Paige and his group of colored boys from Chicago. We went up through the Dakotas and Minnesota and Kansas. Got to bat against Satchell every other day, which wasn't much fun. He could throw that fastball. He also had this hesitation pitch where he'd step forward, hang onto the ball for a second, then let it float up there. Kind of a change of pace. Satchell pitched almost every game. He'd generally start and pitch about three innings. Everybody wanted to see him pitch, so he had to. He was a clown.

They had some great players—Oscar Charleston, Buck Leonard. . . . It's a shame they couldn't have played in the major leagues. There was a little infielder named Judy Johnson. A super base runner. Leonard was a big husky guy. Pretty potent with a bat. I don't know how well he did, since I never did read his statistics. I don't know how well they were kept. I'm surprised they kept any at all. I remember that Chicago team had a big first baseman by the name of Mule Suttles. Gol, he could hit a ball nine miles. I remember [Earl] Whitehill was our pitcher, and he couldn't get Suttles out. And Whitehill was a good pitcher. Suttles wore poor ol' Whitehill out.

My first full season was 1926, Cobb's last season in Detroit. For

Charlie Gehringer, circa 1926.
(Courtesy of the National Baseball
Library, Cooperstown, New York.)

Bob "Fats" Fothergill in 1929.
(Courtesy of the National Baseball
Library, Cooperstown, New York.)

the next several years we generally had a heavy-hitting ball club,
but we couldn't win anything because of our pitching. When I first
came up we had Heilmann, Cobb, and Veach in the outfield, and
guys like Heinie Manush and Bob Fothergill sitting on the bench,
even though they were hitting .350. Now, when you see kids hitting
.240 playing regularly, it's laughable.

Fothergill? I don't know if you ever saw a picture of him, but he
was about as round as he was tall. Had a terrible weight problem,
but he could really run. He came from Massillon, Ohio, where he'd
been a great football player. I remember seeing him punt a football
once—golly, he punted it as far as anyone I ever saw.

But he was a great hitter, especially against left-handers. A lefty
couldn't get him out without him hitting a line drive. They might
catch the ball, but he'd really smash it.

He had a time keeping his weight in shape, but he still ran
pretty good. In fact, I remember we were in Philadelphia once and
we were getting beat about 13–0 going into the last inning when he
hit a home run. He's rounding the bases nice and easy—and then

when he gets to third base he comes running like a freight train and does a complete flip in the air and lands on home plate! Never saw him do that before. Man, he brought the house down!

Fothergill was a funny guy. I remember when the Boston ball park had a little knoll that went up to this short fence in left field. They've taken it out since, but back then, an outfielder had to run up the knoll because you couldn't back up it. One day Fothergill misjudged a fly ball. He ran up the knoll, then he ran down it, and as he started coming down the ball hit him in the head and bounced away. We were going to Philadelphia next. They must have read about it in the papers because before the next game, some guy presented Fothergill with a football helmet at home plate.

Heilmann was another super guy. He played a little first base, but mostly right field. He was a good fielder with a good throwing arm, but he was slow and couldn't cover a lot of ground. But he sure could hit. Seemed like every other year he'd win the batting championship. He'd hit .390, .395, and over .400 one year. A tremendous hitter. Cobb couldn't hit any better than that, so he didn't fool with him. Besides, Heilmann was so big and strong I don't think Cobb would get very nasty with him.

I don't know why the averages were so much higher then. Golly, the pitchers back then used to cheat, used to keep the ball in play forever. It'd get so black you could hardly see it. They threw a lot of spitballs, knuckleballs. . . . You talk to a modern ball player, and he thinks the pitching must've been horrible with the averages we compiled. But it really wasn't. You saw Lefty Grove and Bob Feller and Red Ruffing—they were no picnic.

I hit Feller halfway decent, but golly, it was tough. He'd curve you 3–0 and 3–1, and that's not in the Bible. He was just wild enough so you had to be kind of loose and easy up there.

Grove of the Athletics was probably the toughest. He could throw so hard. Rarely would you get a curve from him. He'd just fire the ball and defy you to hit it. I always said that by the time you made up your mind whether it was going to be a strike or not, it was too late to swing. He just poured them in. They used him as a relief pitcher, too. He'd come in when it was a little dark—in those days they didn't have lights—and, gee whiz, that was a disaster! Lucky to foul one off.

Grove hit me in the elbow once. By the time I got to first I couldn't get my shirt over it and I had to quit. Oh, dear. By the time I got to first base I had tears this big in my eyes. That was about the first time I ever hit against him. The guys had told me, "Well, one thing about Grove: You don't have to worry about him hitting you. He's never wild inside." After I came back to the bench, I said, "Well, boys, he's wild inside."

Cobb left after 1926 and played his last couple of years with Philadelphia. George Moriarty took over as manager and he hated Cobb's guts. He'd sit in the dugout and call Cobb every name in the book as he ran to first. Cobb would hear, of course, but Moriarty was one guy he'd never challenge because Moriarty was a tough cookie. Ordinarily, if the guy was smaller or less able to defend himself, Cobb would've come over and cleaned the bench out, I guess.

Bucky Harris came over from Washington to manage in 1929. Bucky was a little too nice. He was a super guy to play with. Wouldn't scream at anyone. Not like Cochrane. He'd get you and let you know what the score was. I suppose you've got to be tough in a way, because you've got all kinds of guys to handle. But I never heard Bucky Harris second-guess anyone. The fact that he was so easy to play for probably didn't help his managing, but you'd never want to work for a nicer guy.

Mickey Cochrane turned it all around in 1934. We were that close and we needed a catcher badly. We got Cochrane from Philadelphia and then we got Goose Goslin from Washington; in both cases it worked out well. Mickey was a super guy and we needed him so badly, what with these young pitchers we had coming along, like Schoolboy Rowe and Tommy Bridges. It was like getting a good quarterback in football. You're dead without one, and it's the same way with a catcher.

He helped straighten Schoolboy Rowe out. He would've had some great records if he hadn't hurt his arm. He was off to a super start and then he ran into some problems. We'll never know just how great he could've been.

Schoolie was a great all-around athlete. He'd played football, basketball, everything in high school. I remember he once hit a golf ball 315 yards on the fly at Lakeland. He could hit a baseball as far as Ruth. He hit one in the center-field bleachers in batting practice in the Polo Grounds later when he was with Philadelphia, and I think only two or three other guys have done that. A great athlete. Died young. Only fifty-one when he had a heart attack. You'd think a guy like that would last forever.

Schoolie almost broke [Lefty] Grove's record for most consecutive wins. Grove had won sixteen in a row, and Rowe had sixteen going on seventeen [*in 1934*] when he pitched against the Philadelphia A's. He'd won his last outing in Washington in the ninth inning on a home run by Greenberg, tying the record, and he looked like he was going to be the guy to break it.

But the newspapers were driving him crazy. He wasn't getting any sleep. They were in his room and calling him at all hours of the day and night. The A's wound up clobbering him. As I remember it, we were never in the game. It started off badly, but Cochrane left him in. In those years we had such good hitting we figured we were never beat until the final out. We'd come from behind so many times. I don't know how long Rowe stayed in, but it was pretty obvious that he didn't have it that day.

I always thought Schoolie had a fastball as good as Grove's. He was so tall, that when he'd stand on that mound and start his delivery from way up here, from second base you'd swear that the ball was going to hit the ground before it reached the plate. Just sizzle. Never saw anyone throw harder than he did when he first broke in with the Tigers. He hurt his arm in spring training trying to field a bunt. He pitched quite a while after that with the Phillies, but never with the arm he once had. It's sad when you go that route.

Tommy Bridges? I was always glad that he was on our side. A super little pitcher. In fact, I'd have to say he was as good as Hal Newhouser. Maybe his record wasn't as good, but he had some great years. He had probably the best curveball I ever stood behind. I've seen him throw that curveball at a guy's head, and the batter would fall flat on his rear end thinking it was going to hit him, and then the ball would go over the plate for a strike. You think he didn't make the batter look silly?

Billy Rogell came over from the Red Sox in 1930 and he left in '39. Those ten years were fine. Got along great. Before that I'd played with something like twenty-two different shortstops. It was fantastic the way they were coming and going. It was Bill Rigney and Jackie Tavener when I first got here, but then it was a constant stream. I don't think anyone stayed a year until Rogell came.

Billy was pretty good to play with. We would get along great until the scorer made a bad call and gave him an error on a ball that got by him. That would upset him badly. With a runner on first, I used to give the signs on who was to cover second [*on a steal attempt*]. But Billy wouldn't even look at me, he'd be so mad and cussin'. He wouldn't look my way, so I'd have to holler at him. Even then I was never sure that he'd heard me. So maybe a time or two

Curveballer Tommy Bridges: "I was always glad that he was on our side."
(Courtesy of the Burton Historical Collection of the Detroit Public
Library.)

Cochrane would throw the ball down and nobody'd be covering. So
that'd set Mickey off. You can imagine the turmoil.

Rogell and Cochrane were two of a kind—they were both a little
short-fused. I'll say one thing about Billy: I don't think I ever got to
the ballpark but where he wasn't already there. I don't care how
early I got there, he was always ahead of me. That's how eager he
was to operate. He was a real nut for baseball.

I had a reputation for always taking the first pitch, but that was
only partly true. I hit a lot with men on base. In those days we had
a lot of knuckleball and spitball pitchers. You're in trouble with two
strikes against those kind of guys, so I didn't take too many pitches
from them. They would try to get ahead of you with a fastball and
so I was pretty much inclined to hit that one.

But against the average pitcher, I thought I was a better hitter
with two strikes. Many times you go up there and think, well, I've

got two or three more pitches, and you get careless. You swing at bad balls and make an out. With two strikes you concentrate more, you cut down on your swing and put the ball in play.

Look at Joe Sewell. He struck out only four times one year with the Indians. Best I ever did was thirteen. But Sewell, I think he struck out thirty times *total* in one five-year span.

Joe was a punch hitter. He choked up on that bat. A lot of guys did. You have control of it. If you're any kind of a hitter, and the pitcher's overpowering you, you can still at least foul off the pitch. That's what makes me so mad today. The guys who can't hit home runs are still swinging for them. With a runner on third and less than two outs and they don't get him in, I just . . . cringe. How do managers put up with that? And you see it so much today.

When you choke up on the bat you don't have to start it so quick. These big guys now, once they start their swing they can't stop it. There's so many strikes called on that half-swing, it's ridiculous. The first-base and third-base umpires are now doing most of the umpiring. In the old days you could get away with that pretty good. Back then, all the umpiring was done behind the plate.

We had very few run-ins with umpires in my day. I never got thrown out of a game. I could never understand what an umpire's ancestry had to do with a call, anyway. I felt you had to be friendly with them or you're not going to get the best of it. I would never turn around and tell them that they did this or that wrong. If I wanted to say something to them, I'd say it out of the corner of my mouth or look the other direction. Try showing them up, and you'll be in the showers.

We played the Cardinals in the '34 World Series. To this day I think Brick Owens, the umpire, beat us out of the championship. We had St. Louis down, three games to two, and we should've won the sixth game. Late in the game, Owens called Cochrane out on a play at third even though all of the photographs show that he was safe by a mile. We wound up losing to Paul Dean by a run. Had Cochrane been called safe on that play, we would've had the bases loaded with nobody out and we could've had a big inning. Then in game seven, Dizzy Dean shut us out, 11–0, and that was that.

That was the game where we had all of the tossing of the fruit. Ducky Medwick of the Cardinals slid hard into Marv Owen in a play at third, and that started it. At that point, the game was all but over, and the fans were venting their frustration. I never saw so much fruit in my life. There must've been a fruit truck out in left field making deliveries because the fans kept throwing stuff and finally they had to take Medwick out of the game just to restore peace.

It was very frustrating to come so far and then lose. We were just as good as St. Louis, though that Gas House Gang had some great pitchers—the two Deans, Bill Hallahan, and Bill Walker. The Deans, of course, each won two games in the series, though we beat Dizzy one game in St. Louis, 3–1. Paul could throw harder than Dizzy, but he didn't have the curve or know-how. He was just a Dizzy Trout-type pitcher—just go out there and throw as hard as he could for as long as he could. I still say we should've beaten Paul Dean in that sixth game.

We won again in 1935, even though we were in sixth place as late as May. We played the Cubs, and Greenberg got hurt in that series.

Hank, of course, was our big gun. A strong guy. He had long arms and a big arc to his swing, so even if he was fooled on a pitch he could still hit the ball a long ways. His famous saying to me was, "Just get the runner over to third." Hank loved those RBIs. He had 183 one season. Just get 'em over to third, so Hank could drive 'em in. I told him once, "You'd trip a runner coming around third base just so you could knock him in yourself."

We had to use Flea Clifton in the series to replace Greenberg. Clifton wasn't much of a hitter, but he fielded well and we won in six games. Goslin drove in the winning run, though I thought I was going to. We were tied 3–3 in the ninth, and Cochrane led off with a single. I hit after Mickey, and I lined a pitch down the first-base line that nine times out of ten is at least a double. But Phil Cavaretta, the first baseman, hadn't moved off the bag. He knocked it down in the coach's box and got me, but Cochrane went to second. Then Goslin brought him home. Every time I see Cavaretta I say, "You killed me. You kept me from being a hero."

But winning that first World Series was a big thrill. The entire town was ga-ga. I tried to take a friend downtown, but golly, everything was blocked up. You couldn't cross the streets, the city was such a mess. First world championship for Detroit. Seemed like everybody was downtown, whoopin' and hollerin'.

Rudy York came up a year or two later. He came up as a catcher, but he wasn't very good. They tried him at third, and he was even worse there. They finally moved Greenberg to left field and put Rudy at first base. They had to find some place for Rudy because he was such a good hitter.

I roomed with Rudy for about a year. He used to like to drink his beer, and he'd smoke cigarettes when he went to bed. If the cigarette burned his fingers, then he'd wake up and put it out. But quite often he'd fall asleep and then he'd drop that burning cigarette. I don't know how many mattresses he burned up. We always said he led the league in burned mattresses. I finally moved in with someone else. I wanted a little better chance of getting out in case he burned the hotel down.

But I liked the baseball life. We traveled by train: two private coaches along with a diner on the back. The food was super and we'd play bridge, pinochle, and hearts en route. We all had our own berths; no upper deckers. I'd prefer to travel that way than fly.

Of course, you couldn't cover the ground you have to cover today. The league was pretty compact then. You could make the four eastern clubs within three hours. Boston to Washington would be the longest trip you'd have. From Washington to Philadelphia and then Philadelphia to New York would be maybe an hour.

In every city we stayed in a nice hotel. You'd eat dinner in style and a good orchestra would play dance music. Gee, it was super. Chicago was a good town. New York was good for a day or two. I didn't care for St. Louis and Washington. They were pretty hot and sticky all the time. They finally got night ball about 1937 or so, which made it better.

Detroit was the last club to install lights, so I never played night ball at home. But there were four clubs that had it in the American League—Philadelphia, St. Louis, Washington, and Chicago. They could only play fourteen night games a season, though, because that was the limit. I didn't like it too well. I thought it screwed up your eating habits. You never knew when you could eat a full meal. You didn't want to eat before a game and you didn't want to eat too much after a game. You'd just be nibbling off and on, here and there. I thought it was upsetting. Then you got to bed at one or two o'clock in the morning. Of course, you slept in late, but then you had all day to loaf around, looking for something to do. I preferred it the old way—day games.

I was the on-deck hitter when Cochrane got hit by Bump Hadley in Yankee Stadium. My goodness, he went down like someone had hit him with an ax. He got hit right above the ear. The ball bounced right back to the pitcher. Some doctor said that if it'd been an inch lower he probably would never have awakened. He later tried managing from the bench, but I think he had too much time to think on the bench. He'd outguess himself. On the field he was able to make instantaneous decisions. Whether the beaning had any effect on it, I don't know.

Mr. Navin died the winter after we won the World Series and Mr. Briggs, who had been a silent partner, took over. He fired Mickey halfway through the '38 season. You would have thought that somebody with Mickey's record would find a place in the Tigers' organization. Of course, Mickey was pretty quick on the draw with his temper, as was Briggs, and I guess Briggs and Cochrane had a word fest that didn't help matters.

Del Baker replaced Cochrane. He was the last manager I played for. I liked to play for him. He was all baseball, morning, noon, and night. He was pretty experienced. He'd never played much major-league ball, but he was connected with it all his life.

We surprised a lot of people, including ourselves, when we won the pennant in 1940. The Yankees had won four straight World Series, and most of our team was over the hill. Cleveland had such a great team. We nosed them out in the last series of the year. They thought they had it all wrapped up until the last couple weeks of the season, when everything fell apart over there.

We got Bobo Newsom, who had a big year. He also was probably the biggest character on the Tigers. He was a funny guy. A great jokester. He could do Amos and Andy so well that if you didn't look at him, you'd think you were hearing the radio. He was always pulling some trick, especially on Schoolie. Schoolie wasn't too quick with a repartee, so Bobo was always getting the best of him. Nailed his spikes down to his locker once, and things like that. Just drove Schoolie crazy.

Good pitcher, though. He probably was on more ball clubs than anybody that ever pitched, but he certainly had a great arm and a great heart for the game. Pretty good beer drinker, but other than that, he really put it all out.

I remember him pitching against Greenberg once before he came over to our club. It's a hot day, he's got two strikes on Hank, and all of a sudden he just walks off the mound. He didn't even give the umpire a sign or anything. Just took off for the dugout. Everybody said, "Well, where's he going?" Bobo goes into the dugout, and we see him going over to a big pail of water, and he's washing his face and he's toweling it off. All this time Greenberg's just waiting, probably thinking Bobo had hurt himself. Finally, after he's all washed up and dried off, Bobo trots out and throws one strike and Greenberg's out. I'd never seen anyone leave quite like that before. Or since. I forget whether he was with the Browns or Washington then, but Bobo was in a class by himself.

We played Cincinnati in the World Series. Bobo's father died during the series, but he said he still wanted to pitch. He beat the Reds the first two games he pitched against them, but then he lost the last game, 2–1. We could've won it, if Dick Bartell hadn't been asleep.

We were leading 1–0 late in the game, when Frank McCormick

The 1940 Detroit lineup and batting order. From left: center fielder Barney McCosky, right fielder Bruce Campbell, second baseman Charlie Gehringer, left fielder Hank Greenberg, first baseman Rudy York, third baseman Pinky Higgins, shortstop Dick Bartell, catcher Birdie Tebbetts, and pitcher Bobo Newsom. (Courtesy of the Burton Historical Collection of the Detroit Public Library.)

led off with a double. The next guy up hit a ball over Bruce Campbell's head in right field. Campbell picked it up right away and threw it into Bartell. Bartell thought, "Gee, with that double McCormick must've scored," but McCormick had waited to see whether it was going to be caught. So McCormick, who was no speed demon, was just rounding third when Bartell got the ball. I kept yelling, "Home, home, home!" Gee whiz, with Bartell's arm, he's a dead pigeon. But he never did throw the ball. Even after he looked and still had a chance, he didn't throw. And to this day, I don't know why. I'll have to ask him some day. Must have bet on the other team.

I had a fair year in '41, but in '42 I didn't hit for much of an average. Jimmy Bloodworth came up from Florida and played a little bit. Guess it was better than me at my age. You get thirty-seven or thirty-eight, it doesn't seem to be too old, but it is in sports, I guess. I'd played eighteen years and it takes a lot out of you. You lose your zip in hitting and you lose a certain amount of speed fielding. I didn't notice any fielding change, except I assume I covered less ground. I'm sure balls got through there that wouldn't have ten years earlier. I suppose the fans and the manager notice.

Infielders are rarely spectacular. I've always said infielders don't win games, they save them. It's all mechanical. If you had to stop and think, "Now how am I going to field this ball?" it'd be past you. Your reflexes take over. You have to think before the ball is hit. That's where a lot of mistakes are made. You've got to see what the potential is beforehand and then say, "Well, I'm going to throw to this base if I get the ball." You can't be thinking, "Gee, what am I going to do tonight after the game?"

I'd say Al Simmons hit the hardest ball to second. He swung late at the ball a lot of times. With that long bat he stayed away until the last second, put his foot in the bucket a little. But he was so strong that you couldn't really throw it by him. He'd hit what we call in golf a "fade." The ball would come at you, and you'd think you were in front of it, and it'd keep going, going towards first base. And he'd hit it hard. No wonder he had the years he did.

We kept up on our stats then, but not like they do today. I don't think anybody thought about getting three thousand hits in those days. In fact, the Hall of Fame wasn't even around till I was finishing up, so you didn't give that much consideration. As it turned out, I needed just a few more hits to reach three thousand. I might've gotten them if I didn't have to go in the service in World War II.

After Pearl Harbor, I signed up for the draft. But instead of waiting to get drafted, I enlisted in the navy. I was thirty-eight at the time, and I wasn't about to go in as a foot soldier at that age. I thought I'd get into something better.

We had enough training to do as it was. But I enjoyed it. In fact, I came out of the service in such good shape that I felt I could've played a few years. But we had a good business going by that time, so I said what the heck. We were selling fabrics to automobile manufacturers. I started that in '38, so when I came back in '45 it was really going good. Rather than get involved in baseball again and more or less start over with new management, I decided to stick with what I got. So I retired.

The most I ever made? About forty thousand. I probably got more than anyone on the club with the exception of Greenberg. I think Hank got a little more. Of course, you have to think that in those days you could buy a brand new Cadillac for two thousand dollars. In fact, I bought my first house in Detroit, a brand new place on Grand River out near Rosedale Park, for $10,500 in 1934. It was a nice house, never even lived in. It was built by a builder whose **wife** died the week he finished it. After my father died my mother

Charlie Gehringer and his mother.

was up on the farm pretty much by herself, so I moved her in. She was a diabetic and needed someone to look after her. I might've married sooner than I did but I couldn't see bringing a wife into that kind of situation. But she was a great fan. She'd come out to the ballpark or listen to the games out on the porch.

Then in 1950 Mr. Briggs asked me to be the general manager, which was the last thing in the world that I wanted to do. I tried that for two years and got out as soon as I could.

It was a nightmare. We had a lousy ball club, and I'd been away from baseball at that time for ten years. I didn't know who was and who wasn't. But he invited me down and we chatted a while and finally he stuck his hand out. I left it hanging there for fifteen minutes. I thought, "Geez, I don't want this." But it got so embarrassing that I said, "Okay," and shook hands.

Brother, what a headache! We couldn't beat anybody, and I made several trades, but it still didn't get us anywhere. I didn't wish Mr. Briggs any ill will, but he died my second year and, boy, that let me off the hook. Mr. Briggs's son, Spike, took over the club. I figured I could get away from him. At that time I had Muddy Ruel as my farm director, and he was a great baseball man. Muddy wanted the job, and they wanted Muddy, so. . . . I guess a lot of people like that job, but I don't see how you can sleep nights. I would've had ulcers if I'd stayed another year. So much going on, so much turmoil. After '52 I went back to my business. I stayed there until 1974 when I sold out.

My greatest thrill? You know, people ask me that all the time, and I've got to say that every day in the major leagues is a thrill, and the next game is even bigger. Still, one that I'll always remember is back in 1929, when the folks from my home town of Fowlerville had a day for me at Navin Field.

They presented me with a set of golf clubs. They were beautiful: matched Spalding irons and woods with a beautiful leather bag. They also were right-handed, and of course I'm left-handed. But I learned how to play the game right-handed, those clubs were so nice. Anyway, we played the Yankees that day and we won big. I started off with a home run. I had four hits and almost hit for the cycle, and to top it off I stole home. I probably had some better afternoons, but that was kind of a special day.

—January 1982

10

Art Herring

Arthur L. Herring
Born: March 10, 1907, Altus, Oklahoma
Major-league career: 1929–33 Detroit Tigers, 1934, 1944–46 Brooklyn Dodgers, 1939 Chicago White Sox, 1947 Pittsburgh Pirates

Art Herring may have been short in physical stature, but he was long on perseverance. After a five-season stint with the Tigers in the early thirties, the peppery right-handed pitcher spent all of the next ten years in the minor leagues, save for seven token appearances for the White Sox in 1939. Herring, who was alternately known as Art, Bill, or Sandy, finally made it back to the big time for good with the Brooklyn Dodgers in 1944. He stayed in the majors until 1947.

Herring later played two more years of semipro ball in Indianapolis before retiring and starting a second career as a carpenter. Today he and his wife live in a mobile home park near Gas City, Indiana.

Let me tell you a story about Ty Cobb. In 1919, he come to Oklahoma to visit his sister. Back in that day and time they had just amateur teams, you know. Every town had one. And they had good ball clubs. That's all they did was play ball.

They got up a couple of teams to play a ball game. One team only had eight players. I was a kid, about thirteen years old. They lacked one player, so the guys around there said, "Let that kid there play. He can run like a jackrabbit and catch that ball."

I went out there and I slid on my elbows and caught two line drives. I went in and sat right on Ty Cobb's knee. Right today I can feel Ty Cobb run his fingers through my hair. He said, "Those are two of the best catches I ever seen, boy, big league and all!" He said, "You're gonna be a big leaguer."

And you know, I'd get my dad's old socks and tear 'em up and sew 'em with a darning needle and go out and throw them against a wall and catch 'em all the time. Never thought I'd be a big leaguer, but that's all I did was play ball.

In 1946—I was with Brooklyn then—Ty Cobb was in our club-house, visiting with Leo Durocher. After a few other guys got done talking with him, he started out of the clubhouse. I said, "Can I talk to you a minute?"

I introduced myself. Cobb said, "Hey, you're the best relief pitcher in baseball, you know it?"

I said, "Well, I'm doing all right."

Cobb said, "There's one other Bill Herring that I know of, and he used to be a pitcher with Milwaukee."

I said, "You don't remember me, do you?"

He said, "No."

"Remember one time you come to visit your sister in Oklahoma and they had a ball game out there?"

Cobb said, "Whoo, let me tell you something. I seen a little kid out there make two of the most doggone catches. I'd give anything in the world to know where he is."

"Well," I said, "you're looking at him."

Boy, the papers played it all up. The next day there was a pic-ture of Ty Cobb and Bill Herring, meetin' again after all those years.

I went by Bill in Oklahoma. Bob Fothergill gave me the name "Sandy." I was just up with Detroit. He'd say, "How's it going, Sand-blower?"

I was just a kid, you know. One day I said to him, "How come you call me Sandblower?"

He said, "You're so short, every time you let a tootie, you blow sand in your shoes."

I'm five-foot-seven. I wore a size 4, 4½ shoe, so I sent it to the Hall of Fame. They got it along with those shoes that midget wore for Bill Veeck once. Being short, I'd have my picture taken all the time with tall guys like Buck Morrow or Schoolboy Rowe. But heck, there's plenty of ball players who were small and did good.

We lived on a farm about three and a half miles south of Altus, Oklahoma, where I was born. Nobody had any money in that damn time. We'd get to go to town about once or twice during summertime. That was in the covered wagon days. My daddy'd give us kids a nickel. We'd buy a box of Cracker Jack and shoot marbles all afternoon long until four o'clock. And we was happy.

I had three brothers and two sisters. We all went to a consolidated school in Friendship. We had about fifteen consolidated schools in a twenty-mile radius. All those people at that time was sports-minded. They wanted their team to win.

My daddy was a catcher, and he caught left-handed. He was one of the best, and not because he was my dad. Hit, throw, he could do it all. Like Willie Mays—he could do it all, and do it better than anybody I ever seen. That inspired me.

We had a good baseball team then. In high school, I'd strike out anywhere from fourteen to twenty players every time I pitched a game. We should've won the state tournament in Oklahoma City. I struck out the last batter with a curveball that our catcher dropped. Instead of tagging the batter or throwing to first base, he rolled the ball out to the mound. Of course, we all thought we'd won the ball game. We were all on the sideline celebrating. You'd think we'd won the World Series. Anyways, the coach made the guy who struck out go to first base. Then he went to second. I saw him doing this, so I went back out there and got the ball. They resumed play and they beat us.

Cecil Foster, who managed a team in Snyder, come to watch some of the games I pitched in the Friendship league. He said, "I'll give you $7.50 to pitch and your brother, Elmo, five dollars for catching."

My daddy didn't want us to play Sunday ball. All of us kids went to church. Sunday school. He wouldn't let us kids play ball or even play catch in the yard. So I'd tell my daddy and mother that I was going over to a friend's house or somewhere and Cecil Foster and me, we'd go down the road to Snyder about twenty miles away and I'd pitch a Sunday afternoon ball game.

Later, when I got to Detroit, Cecil Foster used to come visit me in the clubhouse. I'd leave passes for him at the gate. One day Bucky Harris come up to me and said, "Art, I can't let Cecil Foster come in the clubhouse anymore."

I said, "Why? He's the first manager ever I had."

So Bucky showed me a picture out of the paper where Cecil was a-smugglin' booze across the Detroit River. In a speedboat. I didn't know he was that kind of guy. So they wouldn't let him in anymore.

Anyway, at the breakfast table one morning I heard my daddy say to my mother and all of us kids, "Well, I gotta go to town and borrow some money." That was because of the grasshoppers. They ate about a hundred yards out of our fields all around. They was on

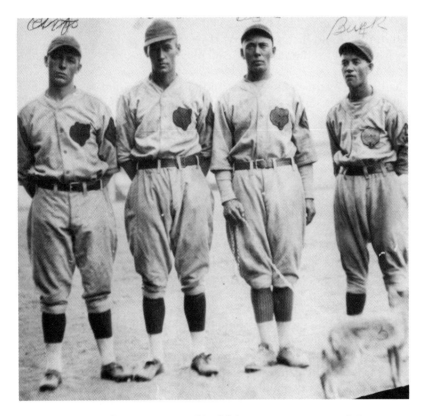

The Herring brothers in Lone Wolf, Oklahoma, in 1925. From left: Art, Elmo, Dick, and Buck.

the fence posts, locus trees, everything, just thick as the hair on a dog's back. Just eatin' all the crops in the field. He said, "I got to get some arsenic to poison them."

My mother said, "How much is that gonna take?"

My daddy said, "It's gonna have to be a hundred dollars."

Well, I had over a hundred dollars buried out there in an old can. I didn't want my daddy to know anything about it. I wouldn't spend it or nothin'. Boy, he'd tear me to pieces, taking money for pitchin' ball on Sundays. I was scared to death.

Finally, after my dad left, I told my mother, "I can't let my dad go borrow any money when I got that money out there." She said, "Where'd you get that money?" And I had to tell her.

Daddy got us four boys together. He said, "I'll tell you what, boys. I don't want you to play Sunday baseball. It's against my wishes. But you're big enough to know right from wrong. If you're determined to do that, you do what you want."

My oldest brother, Dick, started playing semipro ball with Lone Wolf, Oklahoma. One Sunday, I went with him up there. He started a ball game against the Gotebo Indians. Those were *real* Indians playin' at that damn time. Lived on a reservation. Never been beaten. Anyway, Dick pitched three innings and they knocked him out. Earl Forbas was their manager. He had a big left-hander down there, Slim Love, warming up. My brother said, "Why don't you let this kid brother of mine pitch? He's striking out all these high school kids."

I went out there and you know I struck out thirteen of the fourteen men I faced. Lone Wolf signed me. Three hundred bucks a month—and I was still going to high school. I was fifteen.

My three brothers played with me. Dick, Elmo, and Buck. Elmo could do anything. He weighed 200 pounds. He pitched for ten dollars every day, got his arm like that. He threw his arm out; otherwise he would've been one of the best. Buck was a little bitty guy. He didn't weigh but 130 pounds, but boy, he was one of the finest little catchers you ever seen. We went to the Amarillo tournament and won that. Went to the Denver Post tournament—won that. Austin, Texas—won that. Oklahoma City—won that. I'd pitch, play the outfield. I was a pretty good hitter.

At the end of '28, I got a tryout with Beaumont as an outfielder. My first time up was against Jimmy Walkup with Fort Worth. They'd won three flags in a row. Well, I hit a home run my first time up. The next year I went to spring training with Beaumont.

Black or white, mascots were a
staple of baseball teams from
the sandlots to the major
leagues. Here Beaumont pitcher
Eldon Auker poses with his
"good luck charm" in 1932.
Perhaps there was something to
it: the Tigers' farm club won
the Texas League pennant that
year and Auker went on to
spend the next ten years in the
major leagues.

We'd go out at ten o'clock and we wouldn't sit down until four.
I mean, it was 110 degrees in the shade. Our shoes would be sop-
ping in water. Hot, man, it was *hot!* I had a handkerchief under my
baseball cap. My eyes were peeling, my nose was peeling, I was
peeling all over. We had a fifty-gallon barrel of water, filled with
lemons and oatmeal so you wouldn't drink a lot of it. You'd drink a
little of that, that's all you had. We couldn't sit down.

They had cliques on that ball club: George Watkins, Three-
Finger Simon, Chick Galloway. They went right from the ballpark
to the saloon. One game I hit a home run. They say it's the longest
ball ever hit at Beaumont Park, better than five hundred feet. I was
going to make the ball club, see, so they got to pinching me and
tripping me, got to threatening me. The river's right outside the ball
park. They said, "We're gonna drown you. You hit another ball like
that, we'll drown you." I got to where I struck out. I was afraid to
hit. And they released me. And George Watkins was one of them
responsible.

Well, I got to the big leagues. I was with Brooklyn and Watkins
was with New York then. Boy, he come to bat that first time and I
unloaded four right at the back of his head.

After Beaumont released me I signed with Oklahoma City. Jack
Holland was the owner. It was independently owned. Lefty Leifield

was our manager. He was an old pitcher for the St. Louis Browns. Oh, he was a mean guy. He was a beer-drinking guy and I tell you, every other word was a cuss word. He had me scared to death.

I was having a pretty good year in 1929. I'd won nine straight games for Oklahoma City. Johnny Holland had me sold to the Yankees for thirty-five thousand dollars and three ball players. That was a lot of money in that damn time. Anyway, I lost a ball game—this was the Western League—to Denver. I walked a guy and then the next guy—a real good hitter—hit a fastball out of the park to beat me. Ol' Lefty Leifield said to me, "You come out to the ball park the next day. I want to talk to you."

I lived right next to the ball park, about a half-block away. I boarded in a private home, me and another guy. How Lefty Leifield found out where I lived, I don't know, but he was at my door the next morning at nine o'clock. Woke us up.

He got me out to the bleachers, next to the clubhouse, and just hollered, "Base on balls! Base on balls!" I pitched 389 innings one year and walked forty men. I had pretty good control. But it just so happens I walk a man and here he's hollerin' "Base on balls! Base on balls!" at me.

Well, I lived just about 150 miles west of Oklahoma City. I had me a 1927 Ford touring car. I got in my car and went home. Meanwhile, Eddie Goosetree, a scout for the Yankees, came down. They'd already had me sold to the Yankees, see. Eddie Goosetree wanted to know what was the trouble. They told him, "Well, he jumped the ball club."

Eddie said, "Well, we don't want no maniac like that, jumping the ball club." But he didn't know the story about it.

I went back to Oklahoma City. Lefty Leifield didn't cuss at me the rest of the way. I won nineteen, lost thirteen, and set a [single-game] Western League strikeout record; I think it was thirteen at the time.

I went to Detroit at the end of the year and won two and lost one. By the way, the first big-league ball club I beat was Boston. I beat Big Ed Morris that day. First ball game I pitched in the big leagues.

Here's a picture of Earl Whitehill. Wasn't he a good-lookin' guy? He married a beauty queen, Violet. She was that girl on the California raisin box. He was a real good left-hander. He'd turn around and face second base when he pitched, like [Fernando] Valenzuela does for the Dodgers. He was kind of uppish. He didn't run with rookies. He got killed in a car crash in St. Louis a few years later.

Heinie Schuble was on the team. He played shortstop, third base. He was a small guy, smaller than me, but he had pretty good power. Funniest little guy you ever saw, but he didn't like to listen.

I remember one time we were playing New York and we were three runs behind. Herb Pennock, that real good left-hander, was pitching. Heinie got up there with the bases loaded and a three and oh count. Jewel Ens, the third-base coach, gave Heinie the take sign. Instead of taking, Heinie swung and hit the next pitch into the seats—a grand slam.

Man, him and Jewel Ens got to fightin' right there in the dugout. "That's the lousiest play in baseball," he's yelling at Heinie. "You could've popped up." He's going on and on.

Heinie just looked up with those possum eyes of his and said, "Yea, by gravy, but you're not three runs behind now, are you?"

When I first come up with Detroit, I didn't know the batters. I had this little black book I'd put in the pocket of my baseball uniform. They only had two umpires then—one behind the plate and one out by second base.

So come a batter I didn't know, I'd turn my back and take a look into that book. I'm looking down there, you know, when I hear, "Pitch inside to him." There'd be George Moriarty or George Hildebrand out behind second base, whispering under their breath, telling me exactly how to pitch to him. They'd help me out. Wasn't that something?

I had a good fastball. Henry Ford had me come out one day to the proving grounds for a demonstration. They had just come out with shatterproof windshields and they wanted me to try and throw a baseball through it. They clocked me at ninety-four miles an hour. That's pretty fast for a little guy. Well, I could make the windshield crack, but I couldn't throw a ball through it. Henry Ford gave me a dime. Boy, I treasured that. Had it in a steamer trunk in my barn until it burned down a few years ago.

Frank J. Navin was the owner then. Oh, he was a wonderful guy. The finest man in baseball ever I know. Let me tell you an incident.

In 1931 I made forty-five hundred dollars. Whitehill, Vic Sorrell, Waite Hoyt, and those guys were working on a bonus then. See, in that time a player might not get a raise, but he might get a bonus for winning a certain number of ball games or hittin' so many home

Spring training in Palo Alto, California, in 1930. Bottom row, from left: Art Herring, Ray Fritz, Hughie Wise, George Susce, and Gene Desautels. Top row, from left: Vic Sorrell, Nolen Richardson, Charlie Gehringer, Earl Whitehill, and Ray Hayworth.

runs. You know, if a fella was trying to lead the league in something, and the Yankees or Philadelphia came to town, he'd come in and tell the trainer, "Oh, I didn't sleep any last night" or come up sick, and Bucky'd have to find another pitcher or starter.

This one day in the clubhouse I'd heard the coaches and Bucky Harris talking. They had a little compartment office at the end of the clubhouse, right by my locker. We were getting ready to play the Yankees. Bucky said, "Never again will I let Mr. Navin sign these guys to a bonus contract. When the Yankees come into town, nobody wants to pitch. But when Boston comes into town, everybody wants to pitch."

I wasn't pitching. This was June, and I knew it was cuttin'-down time. I thought they were gonna send me out someplace. So when Bucky and his two coaches stepped out of their office, I said, "Bucky, could I talk to you a minute?"

He said, "Sure."

I said, "Let me pitch today."

Anyway, the Yankees beat me, 2–1. Ruth hit a home run to beat me a ball game. I'd pitched a three-hitter up to that time. I had 'em beat, 1–0, two men out and Gehrig at bat. Ninth inning.

Bucky stopped the ball game, came out to the mound and said, "Art, make Gehrig hit a bad ball or walk him." Gehrig had two triples off me, so I walked him. I'd struck out Ruth three times that day. But the first ball I pitch him is this far outside and he hits it over on Trumbull Avenue. We went in the clubhouse after the game and down come a message from Mr. Navin: "Tell Art Herring I'd like to see him after he's dressed."

So I went up to Mr. Navin's office. On the walls were all these pennants and pictures of Ty Cobb and mooseheads. I'd never seen all that stuff before. It being near the fifteenth of June, I said to myself, "Well, if I'm going to Toronto, I might as well look around and make myself at home."

But Mr. Navin came out and said, "Boy, what a ball game you pitched!" He said, "I just love to watch you work, the pepper games and all. You just run all the time and keep yourself in good condition." Then he asked me what Bucky Harris had told me out on the mound. I didn't want to tell him, but he wiggled it out of me.

He hit the ceiling. He said, "If Gehrig hits a home run, it only ties the ball game. You got Ruth out three straight times. But you know that big guy. He'll hit 'em off anybody—high, low, any way." He talked around a little bit more. Finally he said to Charles Navin, who wrote the checks, "How much is Art making?"

Charles said, "Forty-five hundred."

Mr. Navin said, "Give him an extra twenty-five hundred."

I shouted, "Besides my salary?" Boy, that was a lot of money then.

He said, "You keep pitching this way, and I'll give you another bonus at the end of the season."

I beat Chicago and I beat Cleveland. I beat several clubs. The best pitchers, too. Whitehill and those other guys wouldn't pitch against them. That summer Lefty Grove won sixteen in a row for Philadelphia. I had Grove beat one game in that streak until Dale Alexander threw a ball away at first base. I won seven, lost thirteen, and we finished seventh. I was tenth in the league in ERA. At the end of the season, the twenty-seventh of September, me and my wife got in the car and drove to his office and he gave me twenty-five hundred dollars more. I went home that year and bought me forty acres of land outside Friendship. Built me a new house. The next year I bought a 160-acre farm. I had 200 acres. Grew cotton.

People didn't have no money in the depression. Things were bad in Detroit with the car factories closing, and they were bad in Oklahoma. I know my dad had eight hundred acres of ground there. Had crop failures, so he didn't have no money to farm with. I loaned him twelve hundred dollars. Man, that was a lot of money. But he was a big farmer then. Think what you could buy then.

You know, my daddy, he lost all of his money. He inherited thirty-three thousand dollars and he lost that in fifteen days' time. The Citizens State Bank went busted in Altus, Oklahoma. We bought a little grocery store for him in Friendship. There was a couple cotton gins there and a church, a couple grocery stores, a couple filling stations, a blacksmith shop, and just a few houses.

Me and my wife, Ruth, could pull a bale of cotton a day. Two thousand pounds. I'd pull twelve hundred pounds, she'd pull eight hundred. We went to high school together. We went together seven years before she asked me to marry her. And you know something? We've just been married fifty-six years, and we went together seven years, and we went to grade school together before we started to date. And listen, let me tell you something about her. She made the All-State basketball team two years in a row. She's the only woman living who made one hundred points in one game. Ruth was playing for Friendship and they beat Roosevelt. The score was 116 to 50-something. That team won two state championships. Us boys wouldn't play them. We were ashamed. Those girls would've beat the dog out of us.

We was just country kids. Heck, Ruth hadn't been to Oklahoma City but once before we drove up to Detroit. Tommy Bridges and his wife were from the country, so we were friends. Me and Tommy'd go fishing on Belle Isle and all those lakes around Detroit. I liked to hunt quail and rabbit when the season was over. I stayed in shape year-round. I'd throw and my wife would catch me. When I went to spring training, man, I was ready.

I'd had a good year in '32 if they'd pitched me. I wouldn't get in a ball game for ten or twelve days. I started very few ball games. All I did was relieve, relieve. Pitch mop-up. Maybe I'd pitch two innings if the score was 10–1 and we were behind. Didn't make any difference to me whether we were ten runs behind or it was 1–0, I just shut my mouth and worked. I was just glad to be a big leaguer.

Detroit sent me to Beaumont in '32. I lost the first three games I pitched down there. Some little colored guy saw me outside the park one day. He said, "Art, come here. Rub my head." I rubbed his head—won seven in a row. We won the pennant that year. So when we were having our pictures taken, I said, "Come out here, Tom Mix." I had a picture made and give it to him.

In the fall of '33, Brooklyn bought me from Detroit. I played for Casey Stengel. Everybody was a dummy to him. But we had some players on that ball club—Van Lingo Mungo, Al Lopez, Hack Wilson.

I roomed with Hack Wilson. I mean, I roomed with his suitcase. He was small, but built like a wrestler. He hit fifty-six home runs one year [1930] with Chicago. Interesting? Sure. He liked that whisky.

We got into Chicago our first road trip. The road secretary had told me, "Art, you're a clean-living guy. I want you to room with Hack. I want you to talk to him, maybe stop him from drinking."

I thought, "Shoot, man. That bulldog?"

Anyway, we checked into our room. Hack came in and put his suitcase down. I told him, "Now, I go to bed about nine o'clock, Hack. Here's the password." I give him a little note. I wrote on it, "Aunt Fanny from Hillsboro, Texas." I told him, "If you're too drunk to say 'Aunt Fanny from Hillsboro, Texas,' you won't get in."

I didn't see him again until five o'clock the next morning. He knocked at the door and I said, "What's the password?" Well, he didn't get in.

We had to report for a game at eleven o'clock that morning, and you know what? He hit two home runs that day. I roomed with him for three days in Chicago and then I asked waivers on him. But he was some guy.

I went to Sacramento in '35, then I was in the American Association nine years with the St. Paul Saints. We won the pennant in '38 and I won three games in the playoffs against Milwaukee. George Blaeholder taught me to throw a slider later on. I went back to the big leagues on my slider. Branch Rickey came down and signed me to a Brooklyn contract. I pitched from '44 to '46 with the Dodgers.

No, I didn't play with Jackie Robinson. But I pitched against him my last year with Pittsburgh. He got some hits off me. He's one of the greatest second basemen I ever saw play. He took a lot when he first came up. They'd knock him down, throw at him, yell "nigger" from the bench. He didn't say anything. He'd just go out there and play.

But that's the way it was in that day and time. Man, them bench jockeys. Of course, with Pittsburgh, it couldn't be worse. We had Jews, Polacks. . . . You'd have two teams going at each other all afternoon. I know when I'd be pitching, they'd be yellin' at me, "Hey, sardine! Hey, kipper!" But I didn't care. I thought I was lucky. I just thanked the good Lord I was up there.

—December 1986

11

Marv Owen

Marvin James Owen
Born: March 22, 1906, Agnew, California
Major-league career: 1931, 1933–37 Detroit Tigers, 1938–39 Chicago White Sox, 1940 Boston Red Sox

The starting third baseman on the Tigers' 1934–35 pennant-winners, Marv Owen will forever be known as the man whose tussle with Joe Medwick of the "Gas House" Cardinals in the seventh game of the 1934 World Series precipitated a riot at Navin Field. The incident overshadowed the taciturn infielder's steady glove work and reliable run production, which included a .317 average and 96 RBI in 1934 and a .295 average and 105 RBI in 1936.

Marv Owen retired as a Detroit scout in 1973. He died June 22, 1991 in Mountain View, California.

Letters? Geez, I've seen more in the last five years than I saw in all the years before that put together. That's because guys like me, we're antiques now. That's true.

I'd say I get maybe ten a month. And this bothers me, see? A guy might send me three postcards to sign and I'll send him back two. Or one guy the other day sent me a large envelope with a couple pictures of me and Billy Rogell sitting together in the dugout, and I signed them both. I put 'em in the envelope, seal it, and all of a sudden I see this plastic cover for these pictures. And there's another envelope some other guy sent me. I can't remember which guy sent me what. I don't want one guy grumbling, "Geez, look at that damned cheapskate, he's taking my damned cover." I don't know what's going on. And it bothers me.

The only newspaper guys I used to know around here are all gone, they're all retired like I am. Some ex-newspaper guy burned me up. He told these young guys at this little grocery store I like to go to that I used to play. I used to walk in there and I was a nobody before that. And I liked it that way. Now some guy will walk up to me and say, "I hear you used to play for Detroit." I tell them, "No, I used to play for the Gilroy Haymakers" or something like that. He's gonna tell me about his career, see? I'm not interested in his goddamn career.

One guy was saying, "I want to tell you my theory on how I teach my Pony League hitters how to hit." I said, "I'm not interested at all." He said, "I'm gonna tell you anyway. . . ."

I've seen about eleven thousand professional baseball games, including as a scout. I don't want to see any more of them. I used to go to Candlestick to watch the Giants, but that was years ago. Too goddamn cold. I've finally decided that I'm allergic to cold. I do. Anytime I get someplace and I feel cold, I get the hell out of there. I had the flu twice in three months and I don't want that goddamn thing again. I'm cold now. I've got two sweaters on, a pair of long johns, and two pairs of socks.

I've had enough of that stuff. Even when the Tigers won the World Series [in 1984]. I was interested, sure. I'm a good newspaper man. But TV drives me crazy. I want comedians. I don't get any comedians anymore. What's his name, Buddy Hackett? Or Milton Berle. Red Skelton. But those guys are all retired now. Even Joey Bishop. My kid bought me a new TV. Every time he comes over, he says, "Well, have you turned the TV set on yet?" I say, "No." Unless some comedian gets on there.

Did you talk to Charlie Gehringer? I called him "Champ" when we played, because he was the best. Still call him that. Did he give you any of his wit? Charlie was my best man when I got married at Saint Aloysius in Detroit. My wife was only five-foot-three, so I had this tiny little ring. The priest asked, "Have you got the ring?" Charlie takes it out of his pocket and looks at it for a second. I thought, "Oh, he's gonna give me a good one now." Charlie says, "That's the smallest horse collar I've ever seen in my life."

My first wife was a schoolteacher. Her name was Violet. Somebody told a friend of mine that she wanted to meet me. He was the manager of a hotel where all the single players stayed at. We called it the Wolf House, because that's what it was. He gave me the number. So one evening about three weeks later, there's nothing to do, so I said what the hell and called her on the phone.

When I told her my name, she said, "Oh, no, Marv Owen wouldn't do that." I said, "How can you say that? You haven't met him yet." She said, "Well, give me your number. I'll call you back in fifteen minutes." So I did. She called and she started asking me all sorts of questions about my career, like what you're doing. Finally I said, "What's the chances of seeing you tonight?" She could've looked like old Mother Hubbard for all I knew.

We agreed to meet by the Fisher Theatre on Grand Boulevard. I stood there and watched this green Pontiac go 'round the street, this woman in a big straw hat looking like she's looking for someone. So I stopped the car and said, "You Violet?" and then I got in.

About a year and a half later we got married. But she couldn't get the east out of her system. We moved out here after I left the big leagues. She always went back east. We had a kid and she deserted me, then six months later she deserted him. He was seventeen. So that's when I said the hell with it, I'm getting a divorce. To do that to me was bad enough—and I wasn't the kind of guy who was going out with every girl in the city or something like that. It hurt my kid. I said, "Goddamn, she can't do that to my kid." Kid's got no mother.

I got married again in 1973. She was eight years younger than me. Funny thing is, my older sister says, "Well, I'm glad you got married. Now she can take care of you when you get old." Two years later, she died. Cancer of the breast. I've been a widower for seven and a half years. Someone said, "Why don't you get married again?" I said, "Well, every time I get stuck with a babe, the first thing she says is, 'Let's take a big trip.'" I don't want to do that. I'm tired of traveling.

I've got a fathead book. That's what ball players call their scrapbooks. See what it says on mine: "This contains only good days." One day my son says to me, "Didn't you ever have bad days?" I said, "Hell, I could fill fifteen books with those."

I was born in Agnew, a town about nine miles outside San Jose.

I had four sisters. My dad was a chef and a realtor. He used to play semipro ball, but I was too young to remember. I'll give him credit for one thing. Usually a father tries to teach his kid how to play ball and the father doesn't know a goddamn thing. My dad never tried to help me with anything. I remember when I was only nine years old and he'd pitch to me and my sisters. You'd think he'd make it easy for me at the bat? He'd sidearm me all the time!

I got my height from my mom, but I got my quickness from my dad. He was quick as a jackrabbit. He could run. A little guy, about five-foot-eight. He was a clever guy. My dad could walk on his hands for a block. I was thinking about that the other day. Here I am, seventy-nine years old, and if I was fifty years younger I'd have him teach me how to do that. That way the next time I hit a home run, after I got halfway around the bases I'd finish by walking on my hands.

Did you know I could grab seven balls from a box and hold them? Once when I was in high school I was reading the evening newspaper and here's Dazzy Vance—a good pitcher with Brooklyn, a Hall of Famer—holding six balls in his hand. I studied Vance's hand. I had big hands and I had a bureau drawer full of baseballs, so I put seven in my hand. I knew a sportswriter quite well, so I called him and told him. He said, "Bring seven balls to my office. We'll take a picture." It was in newspapers all across the country. I got all kinds of publicity.

I was eighteen in that picture. They called me "Freck" because I had freckles all over my face. The kid who gave me the name had one less freckle than I did. They asked me when I joined Detroit, "What's your nickname?" I told the writers, "Freck." They said, "Oh, we don't like that. We'll call you Marv."

I played college ball at Santa Clara College. I got half a scholarship—fifty dollars a semester for my tuition. I would've gone to San Jose State otherwise, since that was about fifty yards from my house. This was 1926. I got my phys ed degree. Only reason I took it was because it was the easiest class. I just went there to play ball.

I signed with Seattle in the Pacific Coast League. I think I joined them on a Tuesday and the first day I'm playing third base. I'd never played third base in my life. I'd been a first baseman in high school and college. But the manager said, "Can you play third?" I said, "Yeah, I know where it is. I can field a ground ball." I was scared to death, see?

But then that Sunday we had a doubleheader and our shortstop

Marv Owen at eighteen.

hit a ground ball leading off the first game. The pitcher covered the bag and they collided. So the manager says to me, "Can you play shortstop?" I gave him the same answer: "Yea, I can field a ground ball." I played the rest of the season there. The other guy never came back. Broken clavicle, I guess it was. His bad break was my good break.

I guess I lived up to my name—Owen—because Seattle owed Detroit $100,000. The Tigers had the option to pick anybody off the club, so they picked me. This was in '31.

I'll say it was the depression then. I signed up with Seattle for four thousand dollars. The first check they gave me for a thousand dollars bounced. That's the best thing in my fathead book, that rubber check. The best money I ever made with Detroit was nine thousand dollars. But hell, I could buy a brand-new Pontiac for $850. Later, I got ten thousand with the White Sox.

I'll be truthful—I was scared. When I joined the Coast League, I thought, "Oh, I can play as well as some of those bums out there." But in the big leagues, you think you're in another world. In the Coast League you might face two good pitchers in four games. In the big leagues, you face a good pitcher every day. So it took a little while to convince myself that I was capable of playing in the big leagues. After that, it was duck soup.

I played all four infield positions with Detroit that first year. Bucky Harris was the manager. We were in seventh place then, I think. We had good crowds when we were winning. Of course, the wolves are the same in every town. I remember before I became a regular, I'd make a boot and the fans would yell, "We want Schuble! We want Schuble!" So they'd bench me the next day and put Heinie in. Schuble boots one and suddenly it's "We want Owen! We want Owen!" So they're never satisfied. But you can't answer them because ten other guys will get on you.

I was playing first base when I collided with the concrete wall by the first-base dugout in Detroit. I had dinner with Wally Schang, the Yankees' catcher, in the hotel after the game and he said, "You'd better go soak your foot." So I said okay and went up in my room and soaked it. I couldn't get my shoe on the next day. I'd broken my goddamn foot.

So I talked to Bucky Harris. I said, "Bucky, I can't get my baseball shoe on."

He says, "You have to play."

I said, "Play? I can't run."

Bucky says, "Well, you can catch a ball, can't you?"

I said, "Yeah."

"Well," he says, "you'll play. I'll take care of you."

This was mid-July. At that time I was hitting over my head, about .319. I'm playing, but I can't run, I can't stride, and so I drop right down to .223. Then one day I'm standing there reading a newspaper and Bucky puts his arm around me and says, "I think you'd better go to Charleston, get some more experience."

If I wasn't a rookie, I would've said, "Listen, you said you were going to take care of me. Hell, you're not taking care of me by shipping me to the minor leagues. If you'd put me on the bench for four weeks, I'd been okay and I could've played." But I went.

They shipped me out to Toronto in '32 as a third baseman. Funny thing is, the Tigers were playing me a little bit at third base

in '31 and I didn't like it. It was a hard throw, a difficult throw. You
have to angle it to the first baseman. But Detroit gave me the job the
next year in spring training. That was 1933, Bucky's last year in Detroit. I think he was told to quit. Then they got Cochrane that winter.

Cochrane was a good ball player. And he bought something over
to Detroit that we didn't have. He told all of us one day in New York
that first season, "You fellas are accustomed to losing. There's not
much difference between winning and losing. I don't want you fellas to talk about losing. We're playing the Yankees today. When you
see that 'New York' on their uniforms I want you to see 'St L.' " He
meant the St. Louis Browns, see? I don't know what the hell happened, but since that time on we all believed in ourselves. We
started clicking.

I remember Crowder was pitching this game in Yankee Stadium
and—bing, bing, bing—they got five runs off him in the first inning.
So Cochrane goes to the mound. All four infielders came to the
mound, too. And we're talking there and everything, and Cochrane
says, "You haven't got it today, General. I'm gonna have to make a
move."

I don't know how come, because I was never a pop-off guy, but
I said, "Why don't you give him a chance? We'll score more than
five runs anyway."

So Cochrane says, "Okay, finish the game." And we beat 'em
out, ten to eight.

Our starting staff was Schoolboy Rowe, Tommy Bridges, General Crowder, and Eldon Auker. Cochrane was a fastball catcher because he caught fellas like Lefty Grove and George Earnshaw in
Philadelphia. Bridges came to him once and said, "You don't call
enough curveballs." Tommy had a hell of a curveball. So Ray Hayworth would catch Tommy quite often, because he called for more
curveballs. I think Tommy won over twenty games three straight
years for us.

Schoolboy could've been a third baseman, a first baseman, or
an outfielder. Good hitter. Good power. I remember in '34 when we
were fighting for the pennant and he got into a game against Chicago as a relief pitcher. I'm guessing now, but I think he'd won thirteen consecutive games at that point. So Rowe pitches a couple innings, and they score a run off him. Now it's 3–2, we're in the ninth
inning, and I'm the first batter.

Rowe was getting ready to hit and he says, "Hey Merv, come

over here." He called me Merv half the time. Now, Rowe wasn't a bragger. But he said, "You get on and I'll hit a home run." I singled and Rowe hit one that went forty miles in Comiskey Park to win it.

Greenberg always gets a lot of credit for his bat and power, but he was a good runner, good fielder. He didn't run like a big man. He was six-three, about 210 pounds, but he had a short man's coordination as a runner. He was a good guy going from first to third. A good man to throw to, too. Good man on a ground ball.

Rogell was a much better player than he gets credit for. He's the only ball player I ever knew who could catch a bad hop. I asked him about it one day and he said, "I don't know. Whatever the ball does, I do." If I'd get a bad hop, I wouldn't catch the damned thing. I don't know how he did it.

Billy was a switch-hitter. I was surprised when I saw his career batting average. He was much better than .265. He must've had a couple bad years to pull his average down. He was temperamental. He must've broken twenty-five bats a year across home plate. He'd strike out or pop out and come back to the dugout. We knew what was coming next. We'd say, "Oh-oh, here comes the old theme song: 'Bullshit, I'm going fishing!' "

You know about Charlie. The two best ball players I ever saw were Gehringer and Ruth. It's too bad Charlie didn't play in New York with the years he had. He could do anything. Ruth, too. He could steal a base when he wanted to. I never bragged about a hitter beating out a bunt on me 'cause I always thought I wasn't doing my job. About five times in the three years I played against Ruth, he'd drop a bunt down the third baseline and beat it out. If the ball game was won or he needed a base hit, he'd dump it down there. I'm playing shortstop, Rogell's halfway in center field, Gehringer's halfway in left field, and Greenberg has to hang and pray by first in case he might hit a ground ball to one of us. Ruth would drop a bunt, get to first base and stand there: "Ha-ha-ha."

I knew I was a pretty good ball player. I had good hands. There was no one better than me in picking up a bunt on the run. Funny thing is, even when I was a kid I used to practice that, even when I was a first baseman. I could do any damn thing any third sacker could do. Dykes had a super arm, he could outthrow me, but I had a good arm, too.

I don't know if I was tricky or not. I don't think I was a dumb player. One time Joe DiMaggio's on first in Yankee Stadium and someone hits a single to right field. He's coming into third and the ball hits him. I don't know where the ball is, see? I said, "Well, I'll take a chance." So I put a decoy on Joe and he knocked me down. I rolled right over on his goddamn body and I got up. So the next day, the same play happens with Red Rolfe. This time the umpire says to Rolfe, "You score." I did it in the World Series with the Cardinals, too. Ernie Orsatti was coming into third base and I didn't know where the ball was. I put on an act and rolled over him. No one told him to score.

All four infielders played every game [in 1934] except Hank, who asked for Yom Kippur off. It's too bad he did because all of us infielders would've played all 154 games. Towards the end of the season, after we had the pennant clinched, I went to Cochrane and said, "Mickey, I'm worn out, I'm pooped. I gotta get a rest, but I wanna play all 154." He said, "Just start and get out." So I got in the lineup for an inning or so and got out. I'm the low man on the totem pole as far as runs batted in go. I had ninety-six. If I'd known I had ninety-six RBI at the time I would've stayed in. I could've picked up four in a week.

Gee Walker? I roomed with him with the Tigers and later when we went to the White Sox. We had nothing in common at all. He was great friends with Jo-Jo White. They were both from down south. They called each other "nig-gah." They'd gamble on any goddamn thing—horses, cards, dice.

I remember one time in Boston. Cochrane had very few meetings. But he called one. He said, "I'm not going to talk long, but if there's anyone on this ball club who has a set of dice in their pockets they'd better get rid of them right away." Jo-Jo White went to his coat and got something. Then he went into the bathroom and you could hear the toilet flush. See, they used to roll dice at five o'clock in the morning.

Walker had as much ability as anybody in the big leagues. He could run, he could throw, he could hit, he could hit with power. He was a good outfielder. But he never got out of it what he should. One time he got picked off second base in Yankee Stadium, but Frankie Crosetti dropped the ball and Walker was safe. The ball was about three feet from Walker. Crosetti tried to get the ball, but Walker would keep running in front of him and try to block him like a football player. He did that about five times until the umpire called him out for interference.

But Walker couldn't do anything wrong in Detroit. He gave the fans excitement. If he had one chance in ten of catching a difficult

"The people's choice" in Detroit during the depression was the talented but erratic Gerald "Gee" Walker. Gee (second from left) is pictured here with his brother, Hub, and Pittsburgh's own brother act, Lloyd and Paul Waner, before an exhibition game at Navin Field in April 1931. (Courtesy of the Detroit Tigers.)

ball in a tight ball game, he'd take the gamble. You can't do that. He was like a nervous racehorse. He'd get on first and he couldn't wait to get on second. He'd end a rally all the time.

I remember once in St. Louis in '34, when we were fighting for the pennant. It's the eighth inning, tie game. There were men on first and second and I was gonna bunt. Walker's on first. The pitcher threw me a high curve, so I stopped. The catcher threw to first and

Joyner "Jo-Jo" White. (Courtesy
of the Burton Historical
Collection of the Detroit Public
Library.)

picked Walker off. Naturally, the guy on second base gets in a rundown to save Walker and he gets tagged out.

So now Walker's on second and the bunt's off. I ground out to
the shortstop. Now there's two out and Walker's still on second. But
before the pitcher throws a ball to the next batter, he picks Walker
off with a throw to the shortstop.

Walker caused two outs. He was playing right field and Goslin
was playing left. So when the inning was over and they were going
out on the field, when they got about fifteen feet from the dugout,
Goose says, "What the hell are you doing on the bases? You're running like a goddamn drunk or something."

Walker says, "You big-nosed son of a bitch, get off of me."

Cochrane gets in it. He says, "That's gonna cost you 250 bucks."

"I don't care if it costs me 350," says Walker.

Cochrane says, "Well, we'll make it 450 and you're suspended."

They sent him back to Detroit. Then Cochrane called a meeting
without Walker. He said, "We're trying to win a pennant and we got
someone on the ball club who doesn't care if we win or not. I don't
want the man on the ball club, but I'm gonna be fair with the guy.

We're gonna vote. If you want him on the club, vote yes. If you don't, vote no."

Well, there's twenty-four ball players, two coaches, and Cochrane. That's twenty-seven people. They counted the votes and there were three no's—the coaches and Cochrane. Afterwards Cochrane said, "All I can say is that you guys certainly disappointed me." But we all figured, hey, one of these days we might be in the same position. So Walker rejoined the ball club when we got back to Detroit.

Cochrane wouldn't play him much in the World Series that year. But in the second game against St. Louis he pinch-hit in the ninth inning against Bill Hallahan. He singled to tie the game. They brought in Bill Walker, a left-hander, to pitch. We're all in the dugout, seeing what the hell's going to happen. We were saying, "Well, it won't be long now." And *bing!*—he was picked off, first pitch.

They were a good ball club, St. Louis. They had Dizzy and Daffy Dean and Bill Hallahan, a left-hander. Frankie Frisch was at second, Leo Durocher at shortstop, and Pepper Martin was the third baseman. The Gas House Gang had more color. Dizzy was half nuts. Medwick was too, in a different way. Medwick was different from most ball players. He was hard, tough. And he slid like a football player. I found that out in that seventh game in Detroit.

They always put on some big dinner in Detroit. What is that, the outstanding Polack or something? Do they still do that? Anyway, I was scouting and living in Hollywood when I got a phone call from Ed Katalinis, my boss. This is sometime in the late fifties, it's gotta be. He says, "You be right here at this phone two weeks from now." I said, "What's going on?" He said, "They're gonna honor Joe Medwick as being the outstanding Polack athlete of the year."

So I talked to Bill Norman, the manager, and then Spike Briggs. Then George Kell came on the line and talked to me. Kell said, "Well, I gotta go now, but the phone's going to be alive. Don't hang up." I sat there like a dummy for a half hour with a dead phone. So finally Kell gets on the phone and says, "It's your turn to speak."

So I praised the guy for playing hard, for winning the extra dough. I said, "I don't hold nothing against the guy." More bullshit like that.

A few years later, I think the Giants are in the World Series, and so that afternoon I went to the game and some scout from Santa Clara saw me there. He said, "Did you hear Joe Medwick on the pregame show?" I said, "No." He said, "Boy, did he make hamburger out of you."

How do you like that? I praise him at that Polack banquet in Detroit and here he cuts my goddamn throat. His side is that I more or less stepped on him on purpose. He said I gave him a decoy and that's why he slid. I didn't give him a decoy because I caught the goddamn ball. As I caught the ball he was all over third base. As I bent down to catch the ball, my toe spike landed on his right foot. I felt myself on his right foot. So I threw myself on my haunches to get off his foot.

That's when he kicked me three times, called me a son of a bitch. He just grazed me, though. And that made me mad. When a guy slides hard, but clean, that's okay, you don't give a damn. But when a guy slides hard and gives you a few little extra digs, well, you get a little mad.

He thought I did it on purpose. I was frustrated, yea. But I had

Medwick's hard slide into third baseman Marv Owen caused the fans to riot in the final game of the 1934 World Series.

to catch the goddamn ball. I didn't know where his foot is. After he stood up and I went to my position, he stuck his hand out. He wanted to shake hands with me. He wanted to forget about it. But I was mad about it then, see. Well, I made a mistake—maybe, I don't know—and I said, "Ah, bullshit with that."

Then all the fans booed him, too, when he went out to left field. They started throwing fruit, vegetables, all kinds of garbage. They wouldn't let us play the game. Took the ground keepers three different times to clean up the garbage. Took seventeen minutes to clean the field.

I'm sitting in the dugout while they're cleaning up the stuff in left field. I'm sitting there with the other players and someone says, "Hey, Judge Landis wants to see ya."

The foul line along the third baseline went right to the judge's box. That was the longest walk I ever made in my life, walking to Judge Landis's box. I get over there, and here's Frisch, Cochrane, Medwick, and the three umpires. Bill Klem was one of them. So I get over there. I smile at the judge. He's like this, a piece of concrete. He says, "What happened at third base?"

I didn't know what the hell to say. I just said, "You saw what happened."

Then he said, "Medwick, what happened at third?"

Medwick says, "I slid into third."

The judge says, "What else happened?"

"Nothing."

"You're out of the game."

Frisch turned around fast and said, "What's he out of the game for?" And Klem grabbed Frisch by the shoulders, yanked him back and said, "He's out of the ball game. Let's play ball."

It didn't matter. We got shellacked. I saw Medwick years later in Modesto when I was scouting. He was a Cardinals instructor. I saw him after a game. I shook hands with him. I thought everything was okay. He was still mad. If he'd gotten one more hit in the series—he would've been up one more time, anyways—he would've tied the record for most hits in a World Series.

Was St. Louis the better club? The best way for me to answer that is to say we won it all the next year. We played the Cubs in the '35 series. Greenberg hurt his wrist in the second game sliding into home plate. Hartnett, the catcher, was as big as Hank.

The next day during practice, Mickey says to me, "How'd you like to play first?"

I said, "Ah, Mickey, they said I can't play first. I don't want to play it."

He says, "Well, you have to play it."

So we get through with batting practice and we start going into the clubhouse and who's sitting in the corner of the dugout but Mr. Navin, the owner of the ball club. I start walking nonchalantly down the steps and he says, "Hey, Marv, I want to talk to you." He says, "We got you from Seattle as a first baseman. Now prove that we were right."

Well, that's that. Greenberg had a great big glove with a net that big. I'd watch him spend two hours on the train fixing that web the way he wanted. That was too goddamn big for me. So I went to Mickey. "I can't use Hank's glove at first," I said. "I'm going to use my finger glove."

Commissioner Landis confers with St. Louis manager Frankie Frisch (left) and Medwick. Unwilling to forfeit a series game, and with the Cardinals comfortably ahead, Landis finally ordered Medwick's removal to restore peace. (Courtesy of the Burton Historical Collection of the Detroit Public Library.)

Cochrane said, "You mean to say you want to use your finger glove at first base in the World Series?"

I said, "Yeah."

He said, "How bush do you wanna get?"

I said, "Well, at least I can catch the ball that way."

So the next day I'm at first base in the World Series, using Hank's glove. They put Clifton at third base, and Flea threw me a ball. It was a pickup, and I had to go into foul territory to catch it. The umpire says, "Yer-rr out!" I looked in the goddamn web. I didn't even know I had the goddamn ball.

They all hit ground balls to me. I had eleven assists. Eleven! But I was a first baseman in high school and college, so it all came back.

Marv Owen (far right) and four future Hall of Famers in 1935. From left: Mickey Cochrane, Charlie Gehringer, Goose Goslin, and Hank Greenberg.

I had a hell of a time hitting, but we beat the Cubs and won the series in six games.

The next year Greenberg broke his wrist when Jake Powell was running crooked. We were playing Washington early in the season. Powell hit one to me and I threw the ball on the runner's side of the bag. The umpire's already called him out when he runs into Greenberg and breaks his wrist. Hank got as white as a sheet, it hurt so much. I played against the same guy years later in the Pacific Coast League. He got in a rundown with me and tried to run me over. I said, "Hey, Jake, cut out that goddamn baserunning. You're not in the goddamn big leagues anymore. We're just trying to survive now."

We had an average first baseman, Jack Burns from the Browns, replace Hank. But he never hit with Hank's power. I think the Yankees beat us by fifteen games that year. We finished second in '36 and '37. We missed Hank and we missed Mickey.

I remember when Mickey was hit in Yankee Stadium. I remember that distinctly. He hit a home run his previous at-bat, so some said that Bump Hadley was throwing at him. But the count's three and one on him. Three and one is no beanball, you know that. Cochrane moved his elbow half a second late and by then the ball was past his elbow. The ball hit his head and it sounded like it hit a sack of sand. You could put Cochrane, the bat, and the ball inside a six-foot circle at home plate. In the clubhouse the doctor kept saying, "How many fingers?" He wanted to see if Cochrane's brain was okay. Cochrane gave him the right answers.

I think Cochrane was in the hospital in New York for six weeks before they moved him to Ford Hospital in Detroit. Then I got a broken hand. So the doctor treating me said, "You want to see Cochrane's X ray?" He showed it to me. The fracture was spread like a triangle. The doctor said that's what saved his life. Took the pressure off his brain.

I don't know if we would've won even if they'd played. DiMaggio was the difference. Joe came up in 1936. Now, I'm going to tell you something and you're going to say the guy must be nuts. The best curveball I ever saw in my life I had my glove on. Joe DiMaggio hit a ball—hit the hell out of it, a real grass-cutter. Before I could even move my hands, the ball was out in left field. The goddamn ball broke like a curveball. Only ball I ever saw hit like that.

Boots Poffenberger came up about that time. He was a little rocko. But he was a good guy. A little stubby guy. He'd short-arm

the ball. Had a sneaky fastball. He came up in '37, I think it was.
The first game he pitched, he was nervous and got into trouble.
Cochrane's catching. I thought, "The kid's in trouble and no one's
going to the mound." So I went out there and talked to the kid. He
told me later that he never forgot that.

He couldn't hang onto any money. He was married to a nice
little gal. They stayed at the same hotel we did. She wouldn't let
Boots have any money for booze. So Boots would go up to the front
desk and say, "Give me fifty bucks and put it on my bill." He was
something. I guess he once called room service and told them to
bring up "the breakfast of champions."

"What's that?" they asked him.

"A couple eggs and a bottle of beer," he says.

One day we were all in the hotel in New York. He was pitching
that day. We all had to be at the ballpark at a certain time. Well, no
Poffenberger shows up. So Mickey says, "Anybody want to substitute?" Auker would always substitute, so he pitched.

I was the first guy back to the hotel, and here in the lobby is
Boots. I said, "Where the hell were you? You're supposed to be out
pitching today."

"Oh," he said, "last night I tipped a few."

I said, "Well, you better tell Cochrane."

He said, "Ahh, that big-eared son of a bitch, I'll tell him anything I want to." Boots got sold to Brooklyn.

Charlie and Chief Hogsett tried to convince me to take a bottle
of beer to relax. They could drink a bottle or two and within thirty
minutes the tenseness would be all gone. It'd take me half the night
to get rid of the stuff. My dad hit the booze kind of hard, so I'm kind
of negative towards booze. He'd get mean, see? Wine all the time.
One drink and he'd go bananas.

That stuff could ruin your career. We had a pitcher named
Clyde Hatter in Detroit once. I was friendly with the guy. He didn't
show up at the ballpark for a couple days, so I go up to his hotel
room in Detroit and say, "What's the matter, Clyde?"

"Oh, I'm sick," he said. "I'm pooped." So bighearted me, I call
the team doctor. He goes up to see Clyde, he looks in his eyes, and
he knows right off the bat that the guy was drunk. He pulls open the
bureau drawer and there's two glasses of whiskey. He told me, "The
guy's drunk."

I said, "Holy Almighty, I probably ruined his goddamn career."
So the doc told Mickey he was drunk. I guess Clyde got shipped

down to Louisville. He went home that winter and they found him
dead in back of his father's car. From booze.

Me, Walker, and Mike Tresh got traded to the White Sox in '38.
I always had a feeling I was going to be traded, but I thought it'd be
Cleveland. I played regular in '38 and '39. My first year with Dykes
I hit .281 with about sixty RBI. That's a lot of RBI for a leadoff man.
The next year we're playing the Yankees and somebody hits a
swinging bunt to me with a runner on third. I thought the runner
was gonna slide, but he probably figured I wasn't even going to
throw it home, I guess. Anyway, I throw a strike to home plate and I
got the guy right in the middle of his back. The ball goes to the
grandstand and a run scores. I never started another ball game.

I was mad. So one day in St. Louis, we're getting ready to play a
doubleheader, and I caught Dykes by himself in the clubhouse. I
said, "Hey Jimmy, I make a goddamn boot and you put me on the
bench. When you used to play with the A's, I saw you make errors
and Connie Mack didn't throw you on the goddamn bench." So he
says, "Okay, you're playing the second game today."

Dykes was going to take Eric McNair—who took my job—and
put him at second and put Ollie Bejima on the bench. But you know
what Bejima did that first game? Hit two triples and a home run. I
never saw another game after that.

I was with Boston in '40. I got hurt one day with a foul tip off
my foot. Joe Cronin made me a coach. I said, "I don't want to be a
goddamn coach. You're tipping off the National League that I can't
play major-league ball. Maybe I've still got a chance to play." I was
trying to catch on, maybe with the other league, see?

I left in '40. Then I went to Portland in the Coast League. I became manager in '44 and finished second and first. Then the war
was over and all the players came back in '46. I had just one mediocre player come back, so I finished in a tie for last with Jo-Jo White.
He was managing Sacramento. The player pension came in the winter of '47. When I was playing and managing at Portland, the general manager said there was a possibility I might make it back to the
big leagues in '45 because I had a good year. Didn't happen. I wound
up scouting. I've been retired since '73.

I was in baseball forty-five years and I get $132.88 a month. It
stays the same. It doesn't go up. I'm glad to get it. I get social security—$660. I'm all right that way. I got a three percent raise, twenty
bucks. I have three rentals and a house in Santa Clara. I'm okay. But
I could always use more.

A couple years ago the All-Star Game was at Candlestick. Hank was the honorary captain. So I got the idea, what the hell, all four infielders are still alive, I'm going to get this ball autographed. I sent it to the Giants and they got Greenberg to sign it. I had to call them and they said, "Yea, yea. We're sending it." I got it a couple weeks later. Then I sent it to Charlie in Birmingham. Then I mailed it to Billy in Florida. I had to call a couple times: "Where the hell is it?" He says, "Oh, don't worry about the ball. I sent it yesterday." So I got it. Now I don't know where the hell the ball is the last six months. It must be somewhere in here.

I take credit for this bat. It's got the original signatures of all four infielders. I sent one to Rogell. He's like me, he doesn't have all the cups and bats that Hank and Charlie have. It cost me ten bucks for the bat, including the lettering, and $2.50 for the postage.

I ordered it from Louisville Slugger. It took 'em a while to get it right. The first time they didn't have the stats on it. Then they spelled Greenberg with a u. That got me so goddamn mad. I called them in Louisville again. Guy said, "What's the matter now?" I said, "Greenberg doesn't have a u in his name." He said, "Are you sure?" I said, "Goddamn, I can still see."

I've got a 1934 Detroit road uniform. I got it in the hope chest with the mothballs. Santa Clara College always opens the season with an alumni game, so I pull it out and wear it. I don't feel at home in it anymore. I feel like a stranger in it. I don't play because I can't judge the speed of the ball anymore. I coach first base the first couple of innings. And I'm so goddamn old, when a left-handed hitter gets up there, I just pray he doesn't hit a line drive because I can't get out of the way of it. I'm going to do this a couple more years, I'm thinking, and then I'm going to give the uniform to the college. Then I'll really be retired, I guess.

As far as the baseball books go, most people will just remember me for Medwick's slide. It doesn't bother me. Otherwise, they wouldn't know who the hell I was.

—*January 1986*

12

Flea Clifton

Herman Earl Clifton
Born: December 12, 1909, Cincinnati, Ohio
Major-league career: 1934–37 Detroit Tigers

Although he hit only .200 in an unremarkable four-year career with Detroit, and went hitless in sixteen at-bats after an injury to Hank Greenberg pressed him into duty in the 1935 World Series, Herman "Flea" Clifton enjoys a distinction denied countless ball players with longer service and more impressive credentials: for one week that long-ago October, the seldom used utility infielder was the starting third baseman on a World Championship team.

Flea Clifton entered the insurance business after leaving baseball. Today he and his wife live in their hometown of Cincinnati, Ohio, where he continues to coach sandlot teams.

Ty Cobb was my patron saint, and he got me into more damn trouble than I could shake a stick at. What I was doing, I'd get a base hit or walk and I'd give the pitcher hell on my way to first base. I'd steal second and then I'd give the catcher hell for having a goddamn pretzel arm. And I couldn't understand why these old pitchers who had real good control kept hitting me in the ribs. I was hit by a pitch nineteen times in the first half of my first year at Raleigh.

We had an outfielder on the team named Bill Lewis. He was from Ohio. Nice fellow. So I'm sitting there one day and I get to reminiscing with Bill and I said, "I don't understand this. No one else gets hit but me."

He looked at me funny and he said, "You don't know why?"

I said, "No, I don't."

He said, "Then repeat after me: 'I give the pitcher hell, I give the catcher hell, I give the infielders hell, I give the outfielders hell.' You're giving everybody hell, so their control's not so good when you come to the plate." So then I started to keep my damn mouth shut.

I got mixed up in two or three fracases every year in the minors. Seems like I always wound up with some guy who was six-foot-one and 190 pounds. I watched a supposed fight—a shoving match, really—the other night on television. I said to my wife, "These people didn't play in the Texas League." She said, "What do you mean?"

I said, "Well, if two of us got to jukin' like that, it would've been a real fight." If you went out after the pitcher in the Texas League in 1932, the players would form a ring and if you wanted to fight, you fought. You either won or got the hell kicked out of you. The big policeman who was there on the field would surround the group and see that it was a fair fight. Now, if *you* saw a partner that you'd like to tangle with, then they made another ring and you two squared off. So, none of this bullshit about pushing and shoving and stomping on people like today. Makes you sick.

Texas is my favorite state, for a number of reasons. The beer tastes better and the women are prettier. And I love the heat. Always did. The thermometer down there looked like it had blood poisoning. It was always one hundred degrees. But I put on ten pounds, grew an inch and a half. I was a late grower. I was about five-ten, 160 pounds when I left Beaumont for Detroit.

Texas would've adopted me, I'm telling you right now. I would've been a good ol' Texan. Fact of the matter is, the owner of the Beaumont team wanted to adopt me. He liked me. He had a string of oil wells as long as your arm. He said, "Hell, none of my kids are home anymore. Come live with me. Hell, I'll adopt you and we'll have a ball." I would've, too. But I got married that winter and he didn't know that.

My wife's name is Marcella. When we got married, I said, "Honey, you go with me, you're liable to get killed. But when I go to the big leagues, I'll take you."

After she got there she cried a bathtub full of tears. I guess maybe that ol' Ty came back in me. I used to play every pitch and after the game I'd come home and make a photostat of it in my mind. Even today I do it. I told my three daughters when they got married, "When your husband first comes home, give him a kiss, give him a can of beer, and let him alone for a half-hour."

But Marcella, two or three minutes after I was home, it was "let's do this, let's do that" and so on. So after a while I had to raise up and say, "Why don't you shut your goddamn mouth?" I said, "Honey, I don't want to hurt your feelings. But goddamn it, when I come home, just give me a kiss and a can of beer and let me alone."

But she never learned it. I told her the same thing the other night after the kids' game. I wouldn't be talking like this except she isn't home. We've been married over fifty years. Like I told her, "I never got rid of you 'cause I'm liable to get one worse and I don't think I can get one better. If you can put up with me, I can put up with you."

We grew up in the same neighborhood in Cincinnati. The west end. Nice people then, but it's developed into the bottom of the barrel now. I was an orphan, but I didn't grow up in an orphanage. I lived with an aunt one time, lived with my grandma, and so on. But I got by.

My father was killed in the First World War. Somewhere in the Argonne Forest. That was my understanding. He was six-foot-two and 175 pounds and that's all I ever knew. My mother died in 1925. She was killed by a friend of the family—*supposedly* a friend of the family. He was a friend of my stepdad. When he wasn't drinking, he was as nice as pie. But this one time he got to drinking and what-have-you and strangled my mother. With my school tie. They gave him life and sent him up to the pen. He got friendly with one of the guards up there and they made him a trustee. The guard was taking him home with him and finally one day he got to drinking and he killed the guard's wife. So they put the juice to him.

Right after my mom died my stepdad kicked my ass out into the snow. He never liked me, anyway. Rightfully so. He wasn't worth a nickel. That was 1925. I'll never forget that year. For a year it was tough, but I toughened up pretty quick. I was living behind a garage in the back end of town, across the Ohio River in Ludlow, Kentucky.

The guy was pretty nice about it. Had a big potbellied stove, so it wasn't too bad. I was stealing milk bottles off stoops and there was a restaurant owner who'd give me something to eat so I could go to school. That's the thing I really wanted to do—go to school. I wouldn't go home to my grandma. I was trying to stick it out and she finally came looking for me, found me, grabbed me by my ear, and dragged me to her house.

Then I got a break. I read a book on Ty Cobb. He became my patron saint. I tried to do every damn thing he did. My philosophy was to hitch my wagon to a star. I played like Cobb, with larceny in my heart. I was fast, so I raised myself to outmaneuver the bigger guys. I figured a small bullet can kill you just like a big bullet. I didn't have nobody to tell me to come home at night, but I didn't stay out all hours, didn't drink, chew or smoke or chase the broads. I made up my mind I was going to play for Detroit. When the time came, I could've gotten more money from that nickel-pinching, old s.o.b. from St. Louis, Branch Rickey, but I took less money to sign with Detroit. I figured, "I'm going to Ty Cobb's home. He took me there. I'm gonna make it come true."

I was playing semipro baseball here in Cincinnati. We had very good baseball at that time. It wasn't uncommon to have five or six thousand people out at a baseball game. We'd won the city championship, so we went to the National Baseball Federation tournament. I was voted the outstanding shortstop of the tournament and Billy Doyle, a scout for Detroit, started talking to me. He was from Detroit, that's where I always wanted to go, so Billy and I hooked up and away we go.

They sent me to Raleigh, North Carolina, in the Piedmont League. This was 1929. Raleigh at that time mostly had fellas who had been up to the majors or who had played higher minor-league ball. Now they were playing, I guess you might say, for a ham sandwich and a case of beer.

That infield at Raleigh was one of the most interesting infields I ever played in my life. The park was built over an old brickyard. Once in a while you'd get to digging around with your toe out there and you'd run into a brick. They worked their way up. So you'd have to pull that brick up, throw it on the side, fill the hole up, and continue the game. Now there was a fast infield. But you know what they'd say: "If you catch them here, you'll catch them in the big leagues."

Raleigh's where I met Hank. I'll say one thing for Hank Green-berg, he worked his ass off. I played with him two years in Raleigh, two years in Beaumont, and four years in Detroit. Didn't give a damn where he was, he worked at it. He was a made ball player. When he started he couldn't hit you if you ran up to the plate with the ball in your hand. By the end of the season, those fences started to run in. He started to hit that ball.

We'd get some bats and balls and go out there before anyone else. One time we happened to get out there at the same time and there was some question over who was going to hit. So one word led to another and the next thing you know, Hank grabbed me. Now, Hank was six-four, so he just reached over and pulled my head into him. It's a good thing he did 'cause I was going to hit him with the damn bat. As it was, I beat the shit out of his shins.

Right after that, Hank's parents came down from New York and they wanted to meet me. When they took one look at me, they jumped all over Hank for picking on me. His mother said, "You ought to be ashamed of yourself, picking on that little guy." They were giving Hank hell and he's trying to show them his black-and-blue shins. I can still hear Momma Greenberg calling Hank a brute.*

Second year at Raleigh, I hit over .300. I was an upright batter, nothing fancy. Used a thirty-four-ounce bat for a fastball pitcher and a thirty-five-ounce for curveballers. I was a right-hander, but I could've been a left-hander, and this is the mistake they made with me. It happened that second year. Of course, I was a left-hander as a kid, and schools at that time broke you as a right-hander.

Anyway, I was hitting left-handed around town here, and doing a good job with it. Detroit wanted me as a right-hander. Finally, one day I told the manager at Raleigh, "I can hit left-handed. Did you know that?" He said, "No. Why don't you go and try it this game?"

Well, big Bill Lee happened to be pitching that day. Bill Lee at that time could drop that curveball of his over the plate like no-

---

*In Greenberg's autobiography, Clifton is remembered as a product of hard times and a true child of the depression: "He was a tough little guy, even though he weighed only about 150 pounds. On the road, he used to eat nothing but doughnuts and bananas. He said they were cheap and filling and stretched his meal money. Flea was the only ballplayer who could show a profit on $1-a-day meal money."

body's business. But when he wound up with that fastball, if he hit the backstop, he had good accuracy.

So he threw a couple right behind my ears—accidentally so, 'cause whenever Bill Lee threw a fastball at that time he didn't know where the hell it was going. I was the only rookie on the ball club that year. This manager was responsible for me, so he cut me off right there. He said, "Hell, if I get you hurt, the club up there is gonna kill me." So he stopped me from hitting left-handed, which was unfortunate. I could run. You give me that other six feet on the other side of the plate and I could have given some people some misery going to first base.

I went to Beaumont in 1932. Del Baker was our manager. We had a championship ball club. Me, Hank, Schoolboy Rowe, Eldon Auker, Pete Fox, Frank Reiber—I think eventually the majors got about ten ball players from that team.

I roomed with Schoolboy Rowe. He was a good ol' country boy. He had one of those tough backs, like those guys who lift all those weights to build up their shoulders. Every once in a while School-boy would stretch one of those knotty muscles out and then he'd have some problems. At night I'd knead those shoulder and back muscles on him, try to keep them from seizing on him so he could get some rest.

A lot of those towns in the Texas League were oil towns. If you made a good play they'd throw silver dollars on the field, even if you were on the other team. Hell, you could eat for a month. We had some battles in that Texas League. See, at that time the Gas House Gang was coming up through Houston, which was a Cardinal farm team. So when our two teams met, there was a ball game. But Dallas was our big rival. We played each other at the end of the season, fighting for first place, and that's when Hank got into it with Zeke Bonura.

See, Dallas and Beaumont were mortal enemies. When we came to town they always put us in hotel rooms where the most noise was. There'd be those bucket brigades outside your window, banging on pots and pans and buckets all night, trying to help their team out.

It was one of those muddy games. Maybe it shouldn't have been played. Hank hit the ball and was marching down that first base-line, and Hank was no gazelle. Of course, Zeke Bonura always led the league in fielding percentage for a very simple reason: Ol' Zeke,

Texas Leaguer Herman "Flea" Clifton outside the Beaumont ballpark in 1932.

he just couldn't get off a dime to get anything. He was in Hank's way and there was no way he could turn one way or the other. Zeke happened to be in the middle and Hank had no choice but to run into him.

So the crowd got into it, naturally. You get two dogs and say, "Sic 'em, boy," and eventually you get a fight. Well, they played it up in the Dallas papers. Next game we played, John King was the umpire. He was an old Texas Leaguer who hated all left-handers because he couldn't hit them, and that's why he never made it to the major leagues. He owned a string of oil wells and was a million-aire, so once in a while they let him umpire. He wore a six-shooter when he did, but I think he wore that just to have some fun.

Down in Texas, anything might happen. They almost shot Hank in the head down in Galveston after a ball game. What the hell, we were leaving the ballpark after a fight on the field and some of the fans got enthused. Somebody shot a rocket or something through the window of the bus. Fortunately, it didn't hit anybody. Hank was the tallest one in the bunch. That's why I always said Hank was slightly stooped.

We played Chattanooga that year in the Dixie World Series. They beat us. We had a pretty good ball club. That was the year I sprained my knee sliding, so I wasn't able to play. I was All-Texas League shortstop. Maybe I would've made a difference, maybe not. That's when I got my nickname, "Flea." I'd hurt my right knee and I was trying to run and run and run. I wanted to get in there. Finally Baker said something like, "You're worse than a goddamn sand flea," and it stuck. Someone else said, "Give him a chew of tobacco and shut his damn mouth. I'm tired of being cussed out." So I started to chew and I've been chewing ever since.

I came up to Detroit in 1934, a year after Hank. I was always taking up for Hank. He was a person to me, he wasn't Jewish. As long as he didn't flaunt it, it was none of my damn business. I remember that year there was a Jewish holiday coming up and we were playing the Yankees. Hank had a problem. There was quite a to-do about it. Hank wanted to play in the worst way. The papers stressed that religious angle, and I don't agree with that. I was as close to Hank as anybody could get and I didn't see that much of it.

Of course, some wanted Hank to play. There were some things said behind his back. Hank didn't know it, but that's when Jo-Jo, Walker, and me got into it. Those good ol' southern boys. Oh, they had to get along with Hank. Hank'd beat the shit out of them. But in my opinion, they didn't give a damn about Hank. I just told them, "Where in the hell would you guys be if it wasn't for Hank up to this time? Hank has really been putting the bucks in our pockets. Hell, don't kick the horse you're going to ride." That was my opinion anyway.

Of course, other teams rode the hell out of Hank for being Jewish. I remember that Gas House Gang—Leo Durocher, Pepper Martin, Dizzy Dean—really put it on him. He was a no-good kike and so on. Hell, that was part of the game. Like when I walked out there in the World Series in '35. What was that little tune that the Cubs sang to me?

Pappy's in the poorhouse,
Sister's in jail,
Momma's on the front porch,
Pussy for sale.

Now, there's some prose for you. And I never forgot that. But if you think I was going to pay any mind to that, you're nuts. That agitating went on all the time. You didn't pay no mind to that. If you did, you were dead. It's just like that little ditty someone came up with on the Cubs. Anything they thought could get you riled up, they'd try. They'd talk about your mother, your father, your sister.

But they rode everybody. Oh, sure. Shit, these bench jockeys, they'd call their friends from down south "nigger lovers." Tried to get them stirred up. They'd holler some of the same things we used to holler at some of our friends in the west end. We didn't call the Italians "Italians," we called them "wops" or "dagos." The Catholic boys were "kneebenders" and "crossbacks." We had one Jew in our group, so he was "the kike." I was "Mohammed." Why? Well, I had to be something. Nobody ever thought anything about it.

Cochrane would let you know what was what. I liked Cochrane very much. Was he like Cobb? I would say yes. He was smart and he could handle people. I don't know much about Cobb handling people, but if you could handle people like Jo-Jo and Walker and some of these other guys, then you've got something going there.

I'll never forget when I scored from second on a groundout, just like Ty Cobb. This was in late September in '35 and we just about clinched the pennant. We were tied 1–1 with Washington in the eighth inning and I was on second. Jo-Jo White hit a three-two pitch that hopped three or four times. I was off with the pitch, so by the time Buddy Myer threw to first, I was sliding across the plate.

Cochrane came up to me in the dugout and patted me on the head. "You know, son," he said, "if you wouldn't have scored I would've shipped your ass so far away it'd cost you seventy-five dollars to mail a postcard from there."

Hank hurt his wrist early in the series against the Cubs. He tried to play with it, but that's when they had to make a change. Marv Owen went to first base and I took Owen's place at third. I remember the guy who owned the Red Sox, Tom Yawkey, came up to my room one night. He was out there for the series, browsing around, and I'm asleep. He said, "Did I wake you up?"

I said, "You sure as hell did."

"At ten o'clock at night?"

I said, "Yes sir, I got a job to do tomorrow, so no fun time here." Tom told me about that years later. He said, "I was the most surprised guy in the world, finding you in bed two hours before midnight." Well, that's what ol' Ty would've done, so. . . .

I never hit the ball harder than I did in the '35 series, but I couldn't buy a base hit. We beat the Cubs, and that's the important part. Nervous? I never really thought about it—until I got the check in February. Then I got to thinking about it, how I had the chance to throw a few million dollars away with a boot.

My last year at Detroit was 1937. Then I played at Toledo, Syracuse, Minneapolis. I got out of baseball for good in '44. I could've gone back to Minneapolis, because I had a really good year. They were going to make me manager, but then they gave it to Zeke Bonura, who was coming out of the service. I said the hell with it. I had three kids and I didn't like to travel. I started in the insurance business, another career.

I've been running kids' teams for forty years or better. Now you have to be a Ph.D. to deal with these mothers and fathers when you're teaching their kids manners. That's my program. The first thing they learn is to say, "Yes sir," "No sir," "Thank you," and "Please." Then I teach them to take care of their bodies. Then I teach them baseball. In that order. I had a group this year I called "the league of nations." Every color and nationality under the sun. It was knothole baseball, fourteen- and fifteen-year-old boys. No eyes, no ears, and a big mouth. They had never played together, for one thing, and they hadn't any training in the fundamentals, which is a direct road to stupidity. They get into a bad groove and you know how that is. They want to be big-league ball players. But they were a good group of kids.

As far as the big leagues, today they give them pool tables to play on, they give them golf balls to hit, and the powers-that-be believe that this is what the people want. Trying to dress the game up. But my opinion is, if you want to go to sleep, go to a ball game. They took all the color out of the game.

I've made this prognostication several times: it's not too far in the future when you're not going to have these stadiums. All you're going to have is a ball field and TV cameras and you can sit home and pay to see your baseball game. It'll be two teams with four fences around them, and you can have your peanuts and beer in your home. I think that's what it's heading to.

—*February 1983*

13

Chief Hogsett

Elon Chester Hogsett
Born: November 2, 1903, Brownell, Kansas
Major-league career: 1929–36, 1944 Detroit Tigers, 1936–37 St.
Louis Browns, 1938 Washington Senators

Although he was only slightly more native American than a Cleveland Indian, Elon "Chief" Hogsett invariably was greeted with war whoops from Navin Field fans whenever he took the mound during his eight-year career with the Tigers. Hogsett, a submarining left-hander, was the club's premier relief pitcher during much of that time, twice leading the league in relief wins and finishing runner-up in saves in 1933 and 1935.

Hogsett became a liquor salesman after he left baseball and today lives alone in a small frame house in the college town of Hays, Kansas.

I got a call the other day. Some guy from Denver. Goddamn, I don't know how they get my name, always trying to sell me something. Anyway, this guy wanted to sell me some books on the Old

West. Pretty soon I just told him, "Goddamn it, I am part of the Old West!"

I was born on a farm just outside Brownell, Kansas. Had ten brothers and sisters, and I'm the only one left. In fact, I'm the only Hogsett here in Hays. I'm known all over town: "Chief."

If anybody can't remember my name or they're in doubt, I ask them right away, "You ever been on a farm?" Well, lots of people from these parts been on farms. Then I say, "You ever see a hog settin' down? Well, that's my name: 'Hogsett.' "

I know when Eldon Auker was visiting this way about two or three years ago, he stopped by the fire station on the corner.

"You know where Chief Hogsett lives?" says Eldon.

"Chief?" they told him. "Why, he lives right down there in that green house."

Hell, and I don't even know any of those firemen up there.

I hated the farm. Part of the problem was my step-dad. My mother remarried when I was three. He liked the cathouses and drinking so there was always some sort of arguing going on. He used to keep five or six gallon jugs of whiskey hidden around the farm. I used to swipe a taste myself, only I'd swipe just a little bit from each jug so he wouldn't notice.

I left home when I was fourteen. We had a herd of cows in the corral. One day I opened the gate, took them out to pasture, and never came back. I rode horseback into Brownell, stayed with my sister in a hotel where she was working. My old man didn't give a damn. Probably glad I left.

I pitched for the Brownell high school team and for town teams in the area. I was wild as hell, too. I'd walk eight, strike out ten, hit three, and throw a few wild pitches. That was because of my pitching motion. I was known as a "submarine" pitcher, sort of how Kent Tekulve pitches today. It's a strange way to pitch, I guess, but it seemed real natural to me. It was from growing up on the farm. I was so bored I'd always be skipping stones or trying to hit something. Wasn't a stone that I didn't pick up and throw when I was a kid.

I turned pro for a team in Independence, Kansas. After they cut me, I signed on with a team in Cushing, Oklahoma. That's where they first started calling me "Chief." I roomed with a full-blooded Kiowa Indian and the nickname just kind of stuck. Am I really Indian? Well, I'm one-thirty-second Cherokee on my mother's side.

Elon "Chief" Hogsett.

Maybe more, but whoever figured that out quit checking. Probably afraid of what they might find.

Detroit picked up my contract in 1925. I won twenty-two games at Montreal in '29, so the Tigers called me up in September. Those Indians around Montreal were big baseball fans. Before I left, the Iroquois tribe had a ceremony at home plate where they made me an honorary chief. They gave me the name "Ranantasse." It means "strong arm."

After my first season with Detroit I pretty much stayed in the bullpen. I'd come in and pitch to those left-handers. Goddamn, the Yankees had five of them in a row those days—Ruth, Gehrig, Lazzeri, Dickey, and Combs. How'd I pitch Gehrig? Not very good. He hit me a hell of a lot better than the Babe. Babe liked that live fastball, high. And I was a sinker ball pitcher, so it's understandable, I guess. I didn't give up a hell of a lot of home run balls. Didn't give up a whole lot of fly balls to the outfield, either. It's funny how these things work. I had pretty good luck against the Babe, but someone like Ossie Bluege with Washington could hit me in the dark with a strand of barbed wire.

Gehrig could cut your legs off, he hit the ball so hard. But what I remember about Gehrig is how he used to murder cigarettes. He'd come into the visitors' clubhouse and duck down in the tunnel. His image was everything they said about him, but God, he smoked cigarettes. He'd always come in between innings for a smoke if he wasn't due up.

Lou wasn't too popular with his own teammates. He was a loner. Good guy—kept care of himself. Didn't cause anybody else no trouble, but he wasn't a socialite. But he was the "Iron Man." We used to try to step on his feet at first base and everything, but he'd play with a broken thumb, broken fingers. Stayed in there for 2,130 straight games. Kind of had the same image Steve Garvey had with the Dodgers.

The Babe would get his base hits. Oh, goddamn, he hit one back at me one time, right back by my ass after I'd delivered the ball. A

Chief Hogsett is made an honorary member of the Iroquois tribe at the Montreal ballpark in 1929. Once, when the good-natured pitcher failed to hold a lead against Cleveland, a reporter wrote: " 'The cheerful Cherokee' was not equal to the task of checking the uprising of the palefaced Indians from across the lake."

terrific line drive—if it would've hit me, Jesus Christ, they would've had to amputate my cheek. It was a sinker ball he hit that time, and the line drive was still sinking when it hit second base. It hit the bag, bounced straight up into Charlie [Gehringer]'s hands, and Charlie threw him out before Babe was halfway down to first base.

Babe stopped in his tracks and said, "You big son of a bitch, I've got enough trouble hitting you without that!"

Oh hell, everybody liked the Babe. Wasn't any pitcher knocked Babe down. All the players kind of gave him credit for raising the salaries. I never heard any ball player say anything bad about the Babe.

Babe was a mixer and a rounder. In those days, I think Babe's top salary was eighty-five thousand a year. You've heard the story where somebody told Babe, "Goddamn, you're making more money than the president of the United States."

Babe supposedly said, "Well, I had a better year."

I guess Miller Huggins tried to quiet the Babe down when he managed him, but without much success. Once he fined him five thousand dollars. About a full year's salary for a lot of players then.

My top salary was seventy-five hundred dollars a year. Shit, I didn't have any money. Just my baseball salary. Even then, I was buying a new Buick every year and going to Florida every winter on that salary. Every day, weather permitting, I'd be fishing. Every day the weather didn't permit, I'd be in some saloon, drinking double martinis. Of course, I was a little bent come spring training time. But a dollar was a dollar then. A dollar's about twenty-nine cents now.

We got about thirty-five hundred dollars for a World Series share in 1934 and about sixty-five hundred the next year, when we beat the Cubs. That's when I bought a couple of lots down in Florida. Shit, if it wasn't for a gold mine, oil well, and an okra farm—tore my playhouse down a little bit.

We used to get a lot of guys pitchin' things in the clubhouse. I've been taken a few times in my life. Ball players are pretty gullible, and I've been gullible a few times, I guess. I was going to get rich in the oil field, going to get rich on my okra farm. . . . I bought five acres worth with my series share. I knew where Appaloocha Bay, Florida, is, but I never saw the farm. The feds had their nose in that one for a while.

I had a seventy-five hundred dollar gold mine in Texas. *Did* have. I was with the St. Louis Browns then, training in San Antonio, when this guy started talking. Hell, I went out there and started panning gold myself. The guy was a pretty good mining engineer, I guess, but ain't nothing ever happened. My wife was still in Florida and I called her. We had some bonds, and I said, "Send me thirty-five hundred dollars' worth of bonds." Cashed those s.o.b.'s in. Then I wintered there part of one winter and sunk the rest of my dough in there.

Did I throw at hitters? Not at their heads. I'd throw at their feet or their knees. That was part of the game back then. The good hitters expected it. Of course, some took exception to it.

But I've thrown at guys. Oh yeah. I lowered the boom on Heinie Manush one day. That's when I was first up with Detroit. Heinie was with the Browns at the time. I hit him his first time up; it was very unintentional. Oh geez, he exploded! He got about halfway down to first base before he turned and yelled to me, "You son of a bitch! You better go back to the minor leagues and learn how to pitch!"

I didn't say a thing to him. But I said something to myself: "You s.o.b.—if I'm in the game the next time you're up, I'll let you know."

And I did. Floored him the second time he was up. Went down like a shot hog. He didn't say anything after that.

It was a good life. I wouldn't have had any of that, if it hadn't been for my wife, Mabel. I knew my gal for over sixty years. I was married to her for over fifty-two years. In those days we paid pretty good rent. My wife and I had a little apartment on Chicago Avenue in Detroit during the season. Paid $125 for a one-bedroom apartment. This was during the Dirty Thirties. The ballpark was called Navin Field then. We were finishing around fifth or sixth those years, but come a Monday, we'd have fifteen thousand out there during the depression. Detroit's always been a good baseball town.

It was fun while it lasted. I remember around 1930 we had an outfielder by the name of Elias Funk join the team. Liz Funk. He was involved in about the funniest thing I ever saw on a baseball field.

We were up in Boston playing the Red Sox, and you know how Fenway Park used to have all those pigeons around center field? Well, Liz was playing center one afternoon, and it was bright and sunny out. Earl Whitehill was pitching for us, and Earl Webb was the batter.

Webb smacked one out to center field. Ol' Liz was out there picking his nose or eating peanuts or something—not paying attention, in any case—when the ball was hit. Liz looked up into the sun and couldn't find the ball. Just at that time some pigeons went flying in front of him. So Liz took off in one direction after the pigeons, while the ball went sailing past him the other way.

I guess those Boston fans must've been wondering, "Look at that crazy son of a bitch chasing pigeons." John Stone, who was playing left field, finally ran down the ball, but by that time Webb had already circled the bases for an inside-the-park home run. The fans really let Liz have it. I think if there'd been a hole in the outfield, he'd have buried himself in it.

Things turned around when we got Cochrane. Playing manager—you don't see that too often. When was the last one? Right off the top of my skull, I can't remember. I know Bucky Harris was still a playing manager when he came over from Washington. But hell, he wasn't going to move the Mechanical Man out of there at second base.

Ol' Mick never let you fall out of sleep out there. I remember sometimes I'd come into a game and feel like trying out a new pitch. Mickey would call for a fastball and I'd cross him up. God! He'd come stormin' out halfway to the mound and fire that ball back to me.

"Wake up, you big Indian son of a bitch!" he'd yell. I knew what he meant: quit experimenting out there.

I was more or less a loner. Always have been. Outside of Charlie [Gehringer] and me. We roomed together for five years. We both had the reputation of being real quiet. I've read that one story about a thousand times, I suppose, the one where we're having breakfast together and I supposedly say, "Pass the salt, Charlie."

"You could have pointed," Charlie says.

Charlie and me would go out at night and have our fling, of course. Hell, we wouldn't know each other the next day. We didn't pass our stuff on to the other ball players. Charlie and I always clicked together. I used to kid Charlie. He'd say, "Fix me a drink, Chief." I'd say, "What the hell do you think you are—a star?"

We'd go out and hang on a pretty good one some nights. Charlie would be out there at second base the next day hung over. He'd be all right as a rule. But there was one time in Boston when we were out all night with Father E. J. Reed, a good friend of Charlie's. He liked to sing. Liked to drink, too. The next day we didn't get back to Fenway until infield practice was over.

It was cloudy, but the elements looked very favorable for a

game. Charlie started the game, but he just couldn't do it—he had
to upchuck. But the elements saved him. Went ahead and washed
us out that game. Call it divine intervention.

Well, as I've said before, it's a different school than when I was
playing. But it's still in my blood. My daughter will call me up
maybe two, three times a week. "What are you doing, Dad?" she'll
say. I tell her, "I'll give you two guesses. Take away one of them, and
what've you got? Watching baseball."

I'm on cable here. I can get ESPN, but I can't get the Atlanta
Braves station, even though they're in the *TV Guide*. I can't get
WGN—that's Chicago—but I can get an independent out of Kansas
City. I don't know what the hell's going on.

I've been bugging to go visit, maybe see my daughter in Illinois.
I just don't feel like going anywhere, damn it, since my wife got sick
on Mother's Day, 1979. The thirteenth of May she started feeling
bad. Took her to the hospital where she had her first stroke. She was
in the hospital forty days. Got her home. Nurses were coming out to
the home three times a week. Took care of her. I finally saw . . . hell,
I could do or had been doing everything they'd been doing, so I
finally told them I can take care of my wife. Got along pretty good.

Lou Gehrig: "His image was everything they said about him, but God, he
smoked cigarettes."

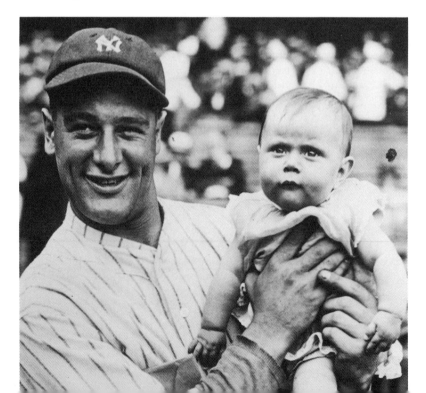

Got her out in the backyard. Her right side was kind of affected, paralyzed a little. I'd get her down those steps there, walk her around a little bit.

Then she was feeling a little tough again. Got her back in the hospital. She wasn't there any length of time at all when she had the final, the second stroke. Shit, *flattened* her. Just flattened her.

You just don't know. That's where I say *justice*, goddamn it, it should've been me. I've done everything to deserve it. But she never did.

That old ball takes a bad bounce once in a while. . . .

I sleep downstairs now. Got a phone down there. Got my TV set down there. I'm not independently rich by a damn sight, but gettin' along. When I get to feeling a little dumpy, I don't need a doctor to diagnose my case. Sleep when I want to. I like to stay in the sack. Hardly ever go to bed before midnight. Hardly ever get up before nine o'clock. I putsy around, do my own cooking, own laundry, mending, everything. I'm housebroken.

I've had a gal or two say, "Chief, you need somebody around the house?" I told them, "Well, I don't need a woman around the house to touch, but maybe once in a while it wouldn't hurt to have a woman's touch around the house." That reminds me, I've got to wash my living-room curtains, if the weather ever opens up.

Well, I've been through the mill. I've slept on the ground, in straw stacks, depots, and boxcars. I've slept in the richest homes, and I've slept in the poorest shacks. I don't think I'd change anything I've been through. I've got no regrets. *Que sera, sera.*

—June 1982

14

Billy Rogell

William George Rogell
Born: November 24, 1904, Springfield, Illinois
Major-league career: 1925, 1927–28 Boston Red Sox, 1930–39 Detroit Tigers, 1940 Chicago Cubs

The one constant of Billy Rogell's half-century in Detroit was his irascibility, a trait that served him well on the diamond and inside city-council chambers. A sure-handed shortstop, Rogell at various times led the league in assists, putouts, double plays, and fielding percentage. He also was a reliable clutch hitter, knocking in one hundred runs in 1934 despite hitting but three home runs. Remarkably, he played the last month of the season and the World Series on a fractured ankle that remains painful and terribly disfigured.

One of the most popular players ever to wear a Detroit uniform, Rogell parlayed his fan appeal into a long political career, serving on the Detroit City Council from 1942 to 1980.

Today Billy Rogell and his second wife live in an apartment in Port Richey, Florida.

Compare the '84 club with the '34 Tigers? They don't even come close. I'm sorry to say that. For one thing, we had a hell of a lot more hitting. If you remember, on that ball club we had four players who are in the Hall of Fame—Mickey Cochrane, Charlie Gehringer, Hank Greenberg, and Goose Goslin.

It's awfully hard to compare fifty years ago with now. But my big argument is this: expansion. Today there's what, twenty-six teams? That means there's about 250 more ball players. There's a lot of good ball players today, no doubt about it. But there's not as many on every ball club like in our day. There's not that much good talent.

You know, it was a little different in my day. We didn't look at that money so much. Money wasn't the big thing. It was the ball club that you played for. You wanted to win. All these guys talk about today is money. Run to the bank. They've got agents who negotiate for them and all that bullshit. Hell, I didn't give a damn about the money as long as I played. I wanted to play baseball.

Of course, ball players in my day were a lot closer than they are today. We traveled by train. We sat there and talked baseball. Always talked baseball: "How you gonna pitch this guy? What can we do to beat this team?" And so on. Today, they get on an airplane, they sure the hell ain't walking around the airplane talking baseball. Hell, we'd get on the train at 125th Street in New York after a day game and wouldn't get home to Detroit until eleven o'clock the next morning. So what the hell are you going to do except sit there and talk baseball?

I was born in Springfield, Illinois, but I grew up on the south side of Chicago—102nd and Wentworth. My parents died when I was eleven, so I lived there with my older sister. I wasn't an incorrigible. I was a loner. Even today I'm a loner. I'm not in the habit of having people make a fuss over me. I don't like it.

I dropped out of high school after a couple years. Hell, I was on my own ever since I was eleven. I started working when I was thirteen. I had to support a couple kid brothers. I did anything I could do—peel onions, clean doorknobs, any damn thing to make a few bucks. I used to pick up bottles, bones, and papers, sell them to the ragman and get myself some money to watch the White Sox play. Of course, in those days they had Chick Gandil, Eddie Collins at second, Swede Risberg, Buck Weaver at third, Shano Collins, Ray Schalk. They had a good ball club.

So, say I worked my ass off for forty or fifty cents. The ballpark was a long way, so I'd ride the streetcar to Thirty-fifth Street for five cents, get a hot dog for ten cents. And for two bits I could sit in the right-field bleachers, right behind Shoeless Joe Jackson. The greatest hitter I ever saw. That bastard could really hit that ball. And the first player I ever saw who used a black bat.

The Black Sox? Hell, I was still a kid then. Well, sure, it bothered me, 'cause those guys were my idols. They kicked 'em out of baseball, yet these bastards today take dope and they're still playing.

I knew a guy who was one of the Black Sox. Eddie Cicotte. Knew him very well. He was from Detroit. In fact, he and Cobb played together in Detroit [*as rookies in 1905*] before he went to Chicago. I used to visit him all the time. He ran a strawberry farm off Six Mile Road. One of the nicest guys God put on this earth.

A lot of old-timers from the early years would come around the clubhouse when I played in Detroit. We loved those guys. We'd sit around and b.s. with them. There used to be a catcher, lived over in Canada. I can't remember his name. Little guy. Nice guy. He played in the big leagues. Guess he needed a handout because every once in a while someone handed him a twenty-dollar bill. Guess he needed a little help.

I always wanted to take Cicotte to the ballpark, maybe see Cochrane. I'd invite him, but he'd never go. I guess he wasn't allowed to go. He and the rest of those Black Sox were thrown out of baseball for life, but the lousy son of a bitch was Chick Gandil. He got all the money. Joe Jackson, that poor guy couldn't even read or write, they tell me. He hit .375 that series, but they said he was a part of it. Look at Cicotte. He was winning twenty, thirty games for the White Sox and having to take a pay cut. But that's the way it was in those days. A guy would work all week for a lousy twenty dollars a week. Today, for chrissakes, a kid wants twenty dollars for cutting your goddamn lawn.

Was he sorry about what he did? Well, what the hell, I never asked him. Listen, he was my friend. I liked the guy. We never talked about it. I didn't look at him as an old Black Sock. I liked the guy, that's all. Anyway, look at these guys today taking that dope. They should kick all these bastards out. They don't deserve to be making that kind of money and be in that profession. What the hell are these young kids coming up going to think? I'll tell ya, when I was a kid I used to sit there in those bleachers and my eyes used to pop out of my head. I'd say, "Jesus, one of these days I'm gonna play here." And sure as hell, I did.

I played high school ball and then some semipro ball around Chicago. I was only about fourteen or fifteen years old, playing with all these older guys. About four or five had played some professional ball. They said, "Jesus Christ, you've got a good chance of playing major-league ball." Next thing I know, I went to a club in Coffeyville, Kansas, where the Dalton boys rode.

I was a second baseman then, but the manager was a second baseman, so he put me in the outfield. In Coffeyville we used the state fairgrounds. There was no fence, because they ran racehorses out there. One day we went to Muskogee, Oklahoma, to play, and Muskogee had a short right-field fence. Some guy hit a high fly ball and I ran after it. I forgot where I was. I hit that fence and busted three ribs. Of course, I couldn't play much after that. I couldn't swing the bat and then the league blew up.

The next year I went to Salinas, Kansas, in the old Southwestern League. I hit .317 and the next thing I know, I was sold to the Boston Red Sox. How much? A couple horses, I guess. I was eighteen years old.

I came up with the Red Sox in 1925. Christ, we had about twelve guys on the ball club who were just about twenty, twenty-one years old. We had too many kids: Jack Rothrock, Charlie Ruffing, Jack Russell, myself. The team was too damn young to be a major-league club. I think we finished last every year I was there.

I played against guys like Cobb and Walter Johnson and George Sisler. First game I played, Lefty Grove was pitching. I wasn't nervous at all. Maybe I should've been; I struck out four times. After that I hit him pretty good.

I remember playing against Cobb once when he was with Philadelphia. He was in a terrible, terrible slump—one for about twenty-nine. He hit a blooper into left field and he had to slide into second base. He hit the bag and that bag *flew*. He tore that bastard right off. He got up, sparks in his eyes. "Jesus Christ," I thought to myself, "I don't want to tangle with that old bastard." He was a big man, about six-foot-one, two hundred pounds.

My first year up, I hit .195. I batted both ways. Boston tried to make me a right-handed hitter because of that big wall they have in left. I don't know why I had to go to the goddamn minors to do that. So I was with Jersey City for a while, then I went back to the Red Sox. I was traded to St. Paul in the fall of '28. Ben Chapman was

Billy Rogell. (Courtesy of the Burton Historical Collection of the Detroit Public Library.)

there. He played third and I played shortstop. I hit about .336 and that's when I came to Detroit, from Toronto. That was 1930.

We trained in Tampa that spring. Hank Greenberg came up that year, too. He was only nineteen years old. He was from New York, and this was the first time he'd been away from home. In fact, I'm the guy who saved him for the Detroit Tigers.

Hank was at batting practice one day, and he hit a line drive that hit one of our pitchers on the knee. The pitcher grabbed a ball and threw it at Hank, yelling "Goddamn Jew" and all that shit, you know, that goes along with it.

Hell, Hank can't help it if he's Jewish. We stayed at the Tampa Bay Hotel then. So I'm walking down the canal there that night and there's Hank standing there, crying. I said, "What's the matter with you?"

"I'm leaving the Tigers," he says. "I'm gonna quit and go home."

I said, "You're gonna let that guy run you out of baseball? Don't be silly. Go out and outplay the bastards." And he did. I'll tell you, I used to hit ground balls to him after everybody'd left. My hands got sore, for chrissakes. But it helped make a good first baseman out of him. He was not a natural. He worked at it.

Of course, Detroit's as different as night and day from when I first came to town. There weren't any freeways then; I helped put them in later when I was a councilman. All the blacks lived east of Woodward Avenue. Today the city's about seventy percent black. The far northeast, where the Belgians are, is the only predominantly white area in town. The streetcars are all gone. Hell, I used to take them all the time. Why pay a buck for a cab when I can take a streetcar for ten cents? I wasn't in any hurry. Crime? No, the Purple Gang took care of all that.

I lived on Rochester and Linwood in the early thirties. There used to be a bar there that had good food. I used to go and have dinner there once in a while. One day I went in there and this guy came over and introduced himself to me. I can't remember who the hell he said he was. I'd had a good day, so he said, "Congratulations. I saw the ball game today. You had a hell of a game."

After he left, I asked the owner, "Who was that guy?"

He says, "Oh, that's one of the Purple Gang."

Turned out this bar was a hangout for the Purple Gang. I never went in there after that.

Gehringer lived on Winthrop and Grand River. I almost bought his home one time. You know where Saint Mary's of Redford is? I used to go to church there. Ushered there. That's where Charlie and his mother used to go to mass every morning. Then my wife spotted this one home on Glastonbury, by Six Mile, right behind Saint Scholastica. I bought that for $13,300 in 1934. Beautiful home. Today it would cost you over $100,000 to build that home.

Most ball players lived in the city then. I was never concerned with people calling me. Even when I was a councilman I had my name in the phone book. If anybody called me I'd tell them, "Listen, my office hours are so-and-so. Come down and see me. We can argue all you want on the damn phone, it ain't gonna do you any damn good. I'd rather do it face to face." They never bothered me, not that much. In fact, I get more phone calls here since I retired than when I was in Detroit. Really.

I get along with everybody. I just mind my own damned business. But I don't let anybody run over me. Like Ben Chapman. He was one of those guys who'd go out of his way to hurt you, but if you ran into him on the bases, he'd scream and holler like hell. I remember when he came up with the Yankees. Huh! He was going to try and knock every infielder into left field.

He hit Gehringer one time in New York. Cut him all the way up to his shinbone. What the hell, Gehringer never said a word. But I told Chapman, "You ever try sliding like that on me, you know what I'll do? I'll hit you right between the eyes."

Oh, I got him. Oh yeah. He gets on first and he hollers to me, "Rogell, tie your jockstrap on 'cause I'm gonna put you in left field!"

I said, "Okay, you nigger ball player!" He was from down south. He hated blacks. That's what got him kicked out of baseball. So I called him a nigger. You can't do that today.

So, the next ball was hit right at Gehringer. *Bing!* A perfect double-play ball. Charlie throws to me. Just as Chapman started to slide I jumped up and threw and I kicked him right here in the face with my spikes. Boy, the blood started coming out of his mouth. He's spitting blood and he says, "Rogell, you son of a bitch. . . ." I turned around and laughed at him. I said, "That's for you. Next time, it won't be that easy." He didn't knock anybody down on our ball club after that.

I replaced Bill Akers at shortstop. From 1933 on it was Greenberg playing first, Gehringer at second, me at shortstop, and Marv Owen at third. We had a hell of an infield, and not because I was on it. For two years there, boy, there wasn't any better. In fact, in 1934 and '35 our infield drove in more than four hundred runs each year. You never hear a damn word about it. But Jesus, if we'd been the Yankees, there'd be headlines all over the place: "The Greatest Infield in Baseball."

If a newspaperman liked an athlete, he could make a hell of a star out of him. Who the hell is Iffy the Dopester today? I see he's back in the paper. Malcolm Bingay was the original Iffy. He was with the *Free Press*. He drank like a fish.

I'll never forget when we played the Cubs in the '35 series. My first wife and I were staying at this nice hotel on the northeast side of Chicago. Bingay came into the lobby. He was walking towards us. God, he looked like he'd vomited all over himself and slept out on the street. My wife said, "My God, don't tell me they let these drunks in here." Bingay and I got along good before that, but he heard her, I guess. He must have. From that day on I was on his shit list. That's what I mean about having the newspapers building you up and tearing you down.

We got Cochrane and Goslin in '34. No one was like Mickey. I can truthfully say that for all the men I played for, he was the best. And he didn't hold any malice, that's one thing I can say for Mike. If you could play, you played. Not like Del Baker and the great Hartnett.

Only one time did we get into it. Gehringer and I screwed up on who was covering the bag on a hit-and-run. Goddamn, the guy hit the ball right through where I was standing. Mickey comes charging out to the infield, those eyes flashing. And they did, too—those eyes used to spark.

"What the hell's going on out here?" he yells. "Can't you guys get together out there?"

I got pissed off. I looked at Gehringer and he didn't say nothing. Charlie wouldn't say boo if someone kicked him in the rear end. So I looked at Cochrane.

"Goddamn you, don't come charging out here," I said. "You go back and do the catching and I'll play this position. If I'm not good enough, you can find someone else."

Mickey just said, "Okay, red ass." And that's all that was said.

Goslin played left field and batted cleanup. He was a good hitter, a left-hander, but he was slowing up in the field. Goslin would never come in on pop flies. I used to have to run my ass off into left field. One day him and Owen almost got into a fight over it. Owen caught the ball, but he jumped all over Goslin. You know, a guy running in can come in twice as fast on a fly ball as a guy going out. First time I ever saw Marv Owen get into it. He was one of those nice guys. Never said boo.

Most of my career with the Tigers I was the leadoff man. One day in 1934 we were going to Washington and Cochrane came up to me on the train and said, "Come on. I'm gonna buy you dinner." While we were sitting there he says, "Tomorrow, you're hitting fifth."

That was Greenberg's spot in the order. I said, "Geez, Mike, you must be crazy. I'm 155 pounds. I'm not a home run hitter." But he said, "Greenberg strikes out and gets doubled up a lot. Billy, if you make up your mind, you can drive in those runs."

The next day at the batting cage, Jo-Jo White is batting first, so he gets up and hits. Then Cochrane, then Gehringer, then Goslin batting cleanup. After Goslin bats, Greenberg is getting ready to step in and Mike says, "Uh-uh, Hank. You're hitting sixth. Bill's hitting fifth." Greenberg's face dropped about that far. Later, me and Gehringer's standing out there by second, and Charlie asks me, "What's going on?"

I said, "Ask Cochrane. He told me I'm hitting fifth, so I'm hitting fifth. I don't belong there. I'm not a home run hitter."

Charlie says, "Well, you won't hurt the ball club."

I drove in a hundred runs in 1934 with my lousy three home

runs. That was one hell of a year. So much excitement. Goddamn, the World Series was over before I even realized I'd played in a World Series.

I can remember one day that summer when we played the Yankees. This was late in July, and Navin Field was packed. They had the goddamn outfield roped off, mounted cops, everything. Gomez was pitching, and I think he'd only lost once or twice all season. At one point they were beating us 9–1 and we came back to win, 12–11. We scored four runs in the bottom of the ninth. Goslin doubled in a couple runs to tie it. I drove in the winning run. I hit a single between short and third, a line drive, and Goslin slid home safely.

I only got to first base. I was jumping up and down, yelling "Run, Goose! Run, Goose!" We beat 'em and that put us in first place. Jesus, after the game the fans stayed on the field and were yelling, cheering like you wouldn't believe. After we came into the clubhouse, Mickey says to me, "Where the hell were you?"

I said, "What do you mean, 'Where was I?' "

He said, "You should've been on second base. Suppose they'd thrown Goose out?"

I said, "Excuse me." He was right. That's where I should've been going on the throw home. But I was so excited, I was egging Goose on. I was saying, "Put the wings on, boy, go like hell."

There used to be a beer joint on Grand River, between Warwick and Outer Drive. Elsie's Bar. God, I've known them since the early thirties. They had a picture of all the .300 hitters on that team, all eleven of us. At one time in '34, that's how many of us were hitting .300. I wound up at .296. At the time I fractured this ankle I was hitting about .313.

I broke this ankle the first week of September. I hit a double to right center and I was rounding second. Del Baker, who was coaching third, was waving me to third. All of a sudden he threw his arms up. I stopped, and as I wheeled my ankle popped. Sounded like a damn .22 going off. Christ, I had a hell of a time with it. Swelled up like this. If they'd put a cast on it, I wouldn't have been able to play. Hell, in those days you didn't want to get out of the lineup. Someone might take your job.

Denny Carroll wrapped that thing with eight layers of tape. I walked around like a damn horse. I played the rest of the season, the World Series, and didn't take that tape off until February of 1935. Yeah, it looks like hell, all right. I knew a bone doctor down in Texas that I did a lot of fishing with. He wanted to grind that bone down, but it was 60–40 that it'd be stiff. Once in a while it bothers me, if I do a lot of walking. I like to walk. I figured if I was a woman, okay. But who the hell wants to look at *my* damned ankle?

I think we won the pennant by seven games over the Yankees. We were coasting the last couple weeks, so we didn't play good ball in that series. The Cardinals won the pennant on the last day of the season. I think they won twenty-one of twenty-eight to close the season, so they were hot. They were up and we were down.

They had a lot of bugs on that St. Louis team. Jack Rothrock, Dizzy and Daffy Dean, Medwick, and that third baseman, Pepper Martin, they were all half nuts. To show you what I mean, I hit Dizzy in the head in that series. He had no business being out there as a pinch runner.

This was in the fourth game. We beat them quite bad—ten to four, I think it was—and they needed a runner. Frankie Frisch was looking around the bench, and before he could say "I need a runner," Dizzy was running out to first base. To me, that was the silliest thing I ever heard of. It was Dizzy's idea. I know Frisch wouldn't send his best pitcher out there.

So, the next ball's hit to Gehringer like a bullet. A double-play ball. I could see Diz coming. He was running on the inside of the base path, instead of out near the edge of the grass. Then he veered my way. He got in his fool mind that he was going to break up the double play. When I caught the ball, I didn't look. I threw right at Greenberg, 'cause I knew where the hell he was. And I wound up hitting Diz.

So, he staggered around a little and fell down. I looked around and said, "What happened to him?" They said, "You hit him in the head." I said, "If I hit him in the head, then I didn't hurt him."

They carried him off the field. He was all right. The next day, they took a picture of me giving Dizzy an old steel army helmet. The funny part about all that was he pitched that day, and about my third time up I hit a line drive to center that just missed his bottom. He sat down right on his ass. There's thirty-eight thousand people in the park and they all go, "Oooh." Then one guy out in the bleachers yells out, clear as a bell, "Hey Diz! Jump in a barrel! That Rogell's after you again!"

Well, we beat Diz that day, but we let the series slip away after that. We had them down, three games to two, with the last two games in Detroit. We got robbed in the sixth game on a bad call on Cochrane, then the seventh game they beat us bad.

Rowe pitched against Paul Dean in the sixth game. We were losing 3–2 in the sixth inning. We had Cochrane on second and Gehringer on first, no one out, and Goslin bunted the ball. The catcher, Delancey, threw the ball to third base. I've got pictures that shows Cochrane's feet on the bag, with the ball still coming. But Brick Owens, an American League umpire, called him out. Instead of having the bases loaded with no one out, it was still second and first with one out.

I was the next hitter. I hit a long drive to right center. Gehringer went from second to third. That was two out. Greenberg followed

Dizzy Dean, one of the storied Gas House Gang, at the 1934 World Series: "They were all half-nuts."

me with a single to score Gehringer, and then the next guy, Owen, hit a long fly ball which would've scored a third run. Instead, it was the third out of the inning. We lost that game four to three to Paul Dean. He wasn't half the pitcher his brother was.

Auker pitched the seventh game against Diz. We were in it until the third inning. Dizzy Dean hit a pop fly to left field. Nobody covered second base. I back-pedaled for the ball. Goslin nonchalantly went after the ball. Dean never stopped. Gehringer was standing between first and second. Why, I don't know, but that's the way it happened. Seemed like everything just fell apart. Dean gets on second, the next guy hits a ball down to Greenberg, and no one covered first. Rothrock walked to load the bases, then Frankie Frisch hit one on his fists just over Greenberg's head, one of those bloopers, and all hell broke loose. Before the inning was over they'd scored seven runs. That just shows you it's the little things that hurt you.

We were getting beat about nine to nothing when Medwick hit one out to right-center field. Medwick was fancy-danning it. You know when you're out in front like that, I guess your hat gets that big. I never cared too much for him. He was one of those types of guys who liked to run over you, like Ben Chapman. I was out there waiting for the relay. But hell, there wasn't going to be any play on Medwick. Owen was standing there when he slid into third base. He must've bumped or kicked Owen with his spikes. Owen, to keep from falling on him, tried to step around him. They called each other a son of a bitch probably, but no one threw any punches. Medwick caught hell when he went to left field after their side was out. I don't know where the hell all the garbage came from. Grapefruit, apples, oranges, everything. If somebody had an old Ford they would've thrown that out at him. Never saw anything like that before. They didn't quiet down until the commissioner of baseball kicked Medwick's rear end out of there. Threw the showboat out.

I'll tell you one thing: that '35 Cub team was better than the '34 Cardinals. Tommy Bridges was the hero that series. I'd like to see some of these free swingers today swing against his curve. Tommy was a high-class boy. He came from a hell of a family. His father was a doctor in Tennessee. Tommy was one of those silent guys. He was a silent drinker. He liked that scotch. I tried to get Bridges straightened out once. I got him a job with Pfeiffer's, but he never showed up. Oh, God, he got bad. I felt sorry for him. He gave me my greatest thrill in baseball.

That was the sixth game of the '35 World Series against the

Cubs. We were tied 3–3 when Stan Hack tripled to lead off the top of the ninth. Tommy struck out Billy Jurges, Larry French bounced back to him, and then Chuck Klein flied out to Goslin in left field. Then we won the ball game in the bottom of the ninth when Goslin hit that blooper over the head of Billy Herman into right field. A broken-bat single. But it counted.

The city went crazy. Christ, they were driving down the streets, on the curbs, over the curbs, everything else. But it was just good, clean fun, everybody happy and nothing vicious. You know, I was in Detroit in 1984 for the last game, when they won the series. We left after the eighth inning. We grabbed a cab on Trumbull and went to where our car was. By then kids were acting like a bunch of wild animals. Fifteen-year-old girls running around with six-packs. Never saw anything like that. Terrible. It's a goddamn good thing it rained like hell that night or there would've been a lot of damage done. It's good to have fun, but where the hell do they get a kick out of tipping someone's car over?

Pitching? Oh, they had so many good pitchers in those days. Seemed like every ball club had three or four outstanding pitchers. You went to New York and they had Ruffing, Gomez, Pipgras. You went to Philadelphia and they had Grove, Earnshaw, Walberg, and Mahaffey. Detroit had Rowe, Bridges, Auker, and Crowder. Cleveland had Ferrell and later, Harder, Johnny Allen, and Bob Feller.

There was a guy in Cleveland, a humpty-dumpty pitcher named Joe Heving, that I never could hit. You know, he was just one of those kinds of guys. Sneak up on him, sneak back, that son of a bitch could read my mind. Others guys would wear him out.

First time I faced Feller, I hit a home run. Second time, I doubled. The next three times he hit me in the back. I was leading off that game, and Rollie Hemsley was the catcher. The sixth time I came to bat I turned around and said to Hemsley, "If that son of a bitch hits me this time, I'm gonna hit you right over the head with this bat." Then I looked at Feller and told him, "I'm gonna come out there and kick the shit out of you." He didn't throw one near the plate. And that son of a bitch could *throw* it.

I punched Boots Poffenberger in the eye once. I was a veteran, so they had me room with him one year in spring training. He was all right the first week. I talked to him like a Dutch uncle. He raised coon dogs, so I kept preaching, "Jesus Christ, if you're smart, you'll take that money, buy some land, and when you're done with baseball you'll have a nice farm for yourself." He'd say, "Oh yeah, yeah."

Then one night about a week later, I get up about eleven o'clock and he's shaving, slapping all that good-smelling shit on him. We had a twelve o'clock curfew. So I said, "Where the hell are you going?"

"Oh, I'm gonna take a walk," he says.

"What the hell you getting all dolled up for?" I asked. He was running around with some gal. She was a telephone operator and she got off at twelve o'clock. They'd go out and drink beer. Christ, he plows in, three or four o'clock in the morning. He stunk like rotten beer. You know how that is, it smells like hell.

I didn't say nothing the first or second day. Finally, the third day, I said, "Now listen, Poffie, you dumb shit. Someone ought to punch you in the eye and knock some brains into your goddamn head. Here you've got a chance to make some money, buy that farm, and you're pissing it away."

So this one night he came in. He staggered over to me and grabbed me by the toe. "Rogell, you awake?" he says. "Punch me in the eye." I said, "Oh, go to bed, you drunken bastard."

He grabbed me by the foot again and shook me. "Punch me in the eye," he says. I said, "Oh, go to sleep."

He grabbed me a third time. He grabbed me that third time and I got up and punched him in the eye. He fell flat on his ass. I don't know where I got the strength—he was no small guy, you know; he was built like a damned ape—but I grabbed him by the ass and the neck and threw him on the bed. Ripped his goddamn pants and everything. He kept moaning all night. When I left in the morning, I got a pitcher of water and threw it all over him and got the hell out of the room.

Poffenberger's on the first squad, so he's got to be out there at practice at nine o'clock. I'm on the second squad because I'm a regular, so I didn't have to be there until ten o'clock.

Jesus, I hurt my hand. It swelled up. I thought I broke a bone in it. Christ, and here I am leading off. I'm batting, but I'm not swinging, 'cause I couldn't get hold of the bat. I bunted about six times. Del Baker was the manager. He said, "What the hell's the matter? Why aren't you swinging the bat?" Then he saw my hand. He said, "What's the matter with your hand?"

"Oh," I said. "I must've hurt it somewhere." Pretty soon Poffenberger shows up. Hell, his eye was out to here. Right away Baker says, "What happened?" I said, "I don't know." That same day, that evening, the deal was made and Poffenberger was sent to Brooklyn. Even then he didn't show up in Brooklyn until ten days later.

When it came to drinking, you should've seen Pete Fox and that

Indian catcher we had, York, one day in Cleveland. After the game was over, I'd always find Denny Carroll. He was the trainer and my roommate. There was a bar right across from the hotel. We'd stop and have a beer, then we'd go have our dinner. After that we'd go to a movie or take a long walk.

This one day, we went into the bar and just those two were sitting there, Fox and York. They'd had ten, twelve bottles of beer already. So Denny and I, we had our beer, left, had our dinner, went to a movie, came back a few hours later—and they were still sitting there. They had two cases of empties sitting in front of them. I said to them, "Jesus Christ, did you guys eat?" They said, "No." I don't know how they could drink so much. But most of them in those days were beer drinkers. Rowe was a good drinker. Gerry Walker drank pretty good, too. They could go out the next day in that sun and boil it out of their systems.

I'll never forget one day when Bobo Newsom was with the Browns. There was this place out on Grand River, had rides and everything. Oh, what's the name? It's not there anymore. Anyway, we're all guests out there one night. Tiger Night. The Browns are in town, so Bobo, he had to come out. He got stiff. And he's pitching the next day.

Christ, we beat them about 18–0. The manager was so goddamn mad at Bobo, he made him stay in there. Every time he made a pitch he'd fall flat on his face. We felt sorry for him. It got to where every time we hit the ball, we'd run until someone tagged us out. He was a rounder if there ever was one. But he was a pretty good pitcher, too.

I wasn't a drinker and I wasn't a rounder. I always figured, I'm married to one woman, that's all I care about. One's enough. Take care of her, you're doing a hell of a job.

But listen, a lot of these southern boys—goddamn, they got up there, they'd go crazy. Never saw the big city. I roomed with this goddamn Rudy York. He was the silliest bastard I ever met in my life. He was a third-string catcher at the time and I was a regular, and all night long that goddamn phone was ringing. He knew every whore in New York. That was in '34, our second trip east. We went to Cleveland from New York and I told the club, "When we get to Cleveland, I don't want to room with him. If I have to pay for a room myself, I'll pay for it. But I'm not rooming with him anymore." That's when I started rooming with Denny Carroll. He wasn't one of these cunthounds.

Rudy York in 1938: "He was the silliest bastard I ever met in my life." (Courtesy of the National Baseball Library, Cooperstown, New York.)

Jesus, we had a good ball club then, even if you never hear about us. We won two pennants and might've won another if Greenberg didn't hurt his wrist. And don't forget, we lost Mickey and Rowe and we still finished second in '36 and '37. Mickey could still have been a hell of a catcher if he hadn't been hit by Bump Hadley. Sounded like someone hit a steer in the head with a sledgehammer. He just stood there, rocked a little bit, then down he went.

That deflated the ball club. Oh yeah. You know, you can't lose a guy like Mickey. You can't lose your manager and the best catcher in baseball. He came back to manage, but he was not the same Cochrane. He couldn't play, so he was not the same man. He was canned for his own good. Otherwise, the poor guy might've died, he was so high-strung. I think he then got involved in something with the Ford Motor Company, a manufacturer's agent or something.

He lost his son in the war. Gordon, Jr. He was on a tank destroyer when it was hit by an eighty-eight-millimeter shell. Blew it all to hell. They never found nothing of him. The only thing they found was his dog tag. That's what I've been told. That affected him, no doubt about it. Nice kid, too, damn it. It's just one of those things that happen.

Hell, I lost my oldest boy. He was thirty-four. A jet fighter pilot.

It's May 25, 1937, and a Bump Hadley fastball has just crashed into Mickey Cochrane's right temple, severely fracturing his skull and ending his career. Rushing to his aid is catcher Bill Dickey. Despite tragedies like this, it wasn't until 1952 that batting helmets were worn for the first time in the major leagues. (Courtesy of the National Baseball Library, Cooperstown, New York.)

He had leukemia. He was a squadron commander, a major. He was a professor at Central Michigan University. . . . Ahh, that's neither here or there. But those things have an effect.

You know, every once in a while I give a lot of thought to my oldest boy. He was a good kid. Never hurt anybody, helped everybody he could. They were on maneuvers up in Alpena. He was flying when he blacked out. Everybody's screaming at him and he finally got out of it. They took him to that hospital in Bethesda, Maryland, for ten weeks. Doctors there told him he had leukemia. . . . I sure miss that boy.

Baker took over as manager after Cochrane. He'd been a coach for the Tigers for a long time. I can tell you a story about Del Baker, when Cochrane was still managing and Baker was coaching third base. That's where I got in the crapper with Mr. Baker.

We were playing Washington and Jimmy DeShong was pitching. We were tied 3–3 in the last inning. The first batter up singled. Now I'm up. Baker was on third, giving signs. He touched blue on his uniform. That was the bunt sign. If he touched blue again, that meant "hit away."

Well, the first pitch was a ball. He didn't touch blue, he didn't change it, so the bunt was still on. On the third pitch, he touched blue. That changed the bunt to a hit. I got out of the goddamn box. Who was following me, but Gehringer and Cochrane. There's only one damn thing to do and that's bunt. Well, he'd changed the bunt to a hit. I'm looking down at Baker and he's giving me that goddamn blue, he's touching blue like crazy. I got out of the box twice and finally the umpire said, "For chrissakes, get up and hit, will ya?"

DeShong throws the next one in, I hit it in the second deck, and we win the ball game, five to three. So when I round third base Baker hits me in the ass and says, "That's the way to bunt the ball." Well, I stopped. I said, "What do you mean, bunt? You gave me the goddamn hit sign." I went in, touched home plate, and went into the clubhouse.

Cochrane's office was here and Baker's locker was here, the first one as you got in the clubhouse. Baker's standing there. I went over to Cochrane. I said, "Mike, tell me, what the hell was I doing? I don't think Baker knew what the hell he was doing." Of course, that's the worst thing I could've said with Baker standing there.

Mike said, "You did exactly what Baker told you to do. You hit the ball. You won the goddamn ball game, that's all." Right away I thought, "Oh, I'm in the doghouse with Mr. Baker."

He had that grudge against me from that day on. And the day Mr. Baker became the manager of the Detroit ball club, he and I had words. He said, "Your days are numbered on this ball club."

That last year I played with the Cubs, you might as well throw that damn year out. Can I tell you a story about that? It's amazing how managers—Del Baker was one of them—if they liked you, they played you. If they didn't—boom.

In 1939, I had a chance to manage a minor-league team in the Cleveland organization. So I went to Detroit at the end of the '39 season and asked for my outright release. If I'd gotten it, I would've gotten the managing job. But no, they wanted to hold onto my rights. A little while later, I was up in Bay City, duck hunting, when I got a call from the Associated Press saying that I was traded to the Chicago Cubs for Dick Bartell.

Well, they didn't trade Dick Bartell for a broken bat. I went to spring training. That first day I'm sitting there, eating a sandwich and drinking a pint of milk after the morning workout, and Gabby Hartnett's talking about the '35 World Series. Hartnett was the manager, and he's saying how lucky we were to beat them.

I said, "What the hell are you guys talking about? We lost Greenberg with a broken wrist and we still beat you in six games."

Hartnett looked at me and said, "You don't belong here."

I said, "What do you mean?"

He said, "You're still an American Leaguer."

I said, "Well, if that's the way you feel, Mr. Hartnett, give me my outright release. Because I'll get a job—in the American League."

From that day on I was in the crap house. And I could've helped that ball club. He didn't play me and I got to where I didn't give a goddamn. I went back home to Detroit a couple times. Finally, the day the Green Bay Packers played the College All-Stars was the day I quit. This was late in the summer of 1940. They gave me my outright release and they paid me in full. I said the hell with it.

You know, I love hockey. I prefer hockey any day to baseball. I really do. I used to coach some high school hockey in the winter. Those guys are magicians. They have to be, on those skates. So one day I'm at a game and our family doctor said, "You're gonna run for city council."

I said, "What the hell's that?" He said, "You're gonna run and you're gonna win." So I said, "Okay." I ran for council in 1942 and I finished third behind Johnny Smith and John C. Lodge. And I stayed there for the next thirty-eight years.

I don't know what to attribute that to. Of course, naturally it had something to do with baseball. There's no doubt about it. But Dizzy Trout and Harry Heilmann both ran for sheriff once and they didn't make it. Detroit's Democratic and Trout ran on the Republican ticket. You know how much chance he had. If you're not Democratic, you can't get to first base in that town. But I'd win. I was the only guy on the whole goddamn council who was Republican. I went out and made speeches and talked with a lot of people. I didn't spend five thousand bucks my first election.

Everybody talks to me about baseball. They don't say nothing about my council work. I worked my ass off as a councilman. I know a lot of people have said, "How can a dumb goddamn ball player stay on the city council so long?" I tell them I must've been awful dumb—or smart as a fox. Must've done some good in thirty-eight years. I was chairman of the Roads and Bridges Committee for Wayne County and also the Airport Committee. I was the one who built Metro.

At this particular time the county airport was only a mile square. I had to fight all those millionaires out past Eight Mile and Schaefer. I guess some of them had bought a lot of land out there. That's where they wanted to build it. Wanted to make a quick deal for themselves. Of course, I was a no-good son of a bitch to them, and all three newspapers said I was just a goddamn dumb ball player, but I got the airport where I wanted it. And a good one. One of the finest airports in America.

The one thing I was terribly disappointed about not getting my own way was the expressways. I wanted five lanes instead of three, with fifty feet on both sides for public transportation. They kept on saying, "Well, the money. . . ." But at that time, the forties and fifties, there was plenty of money. I'm chairman, but in a committee, the majority rules. That's what you have to go by. You just try your best to convince the others. And of course, the Southfield Freeway, they call that "Rogell's roller coaster." That expressway cost $15 million a mile to build. You know what? I saved $7.5 million a mile. Didn't have to excavate it.

I liked the job. You know why? Because you could help a lot of people. You'd be surprised.

When I'd drive down to council meetings, I'd go down First Street. That was a one-way street. There was a sporting goods shop. One day, as I was crossing Michigan Avenue, I noticed this guy lying by this store. I drove about two stores down and I thought, "Goddamn, that looked like Bridges." So I backed the car up and got out and sure enough, it's Tommy Bridges. Jesus Christ, he looked terrible.

So I took him over to City Hall, the old one, and got him cleaned up. Got him some coffee to drink, took him out to breakfast, talked to him. I said, "Tom, where the hell do you live? I didn't know you were in Detroit." He says, "I live in Toledo." See, he'd gotten divorced from his wife and married this waitress he'd met in Seattle or some damned place. The husband was after him to kill him and all that crap. He came to Detroit looking for a job.

Well, at that time some of these breweries had guys going

around selling. I got hold of the guy who owned Pfeiffer's. I said, "Listen, you're hiring this guy and that guy. Why don't you hire Tommy Bridges? What the hell, here's a star pitcher for Detroit for what, twenty years?" He said, "That's a hell of an idea. Where can I get hold of him?"

So I got Tommy all set up. Gave him some money and sent him back to Toledo and then I called him. "Listen," I said, "I got a job for you. Two hundred a week, all expenses paid. You'll be traveling around Detroit, and every other week you'll go upstate."

"Okay. Good, " he says. I said, "Now be sure you make that appointment." I talked to his wife, too: "Make sure Tommy is here."

Well, a few days later I get a call: "Where the hell's Tommy?" It's Pfeiffer's. Well, how the hell do I know where Bridges is? He never showed up. He went way down. It was terrible to see that. But nice guys go, too, you know.

I remember getting in a hell of an argument with Joe Cronin over Gerry Walker. Walker was out of baseball by that time. He'd dove into a pool and broke his neck and was paralyzed from the neck down. I got a letter from his family, asking for help. So what the hell, I went to bat for the guy. Or tried to.

One day something was going on in Detroit and Cronin was in town, so I talked to him about Gerry Walker. I said, "Jesus, this All-Star Game was set up for the ball players' pensions. Walker's got a broken neck and he's paralyzed. Can't something be done for him?"

Cronin said, "The All-Star Game was not meant for pensions." I said, "You're a goddamn liar. It was." Him and I almost had a fight at Briggs Stadium. Cronin was president of the American League at the time and he never did anything to help Walker.*

I never liked Cronin anyhow. I ran into his catcher once, Rick Ferrell, when they were with Boston. I was scoring from first on a long double off our left-field scoreboard. I'm running with my back to the ball and no one's at home telling me what to do. Slide, stand up—what the hell, the next hitter should've been there telling me

---

*Most of the proceeds from baseball's annual All-Star Games were earmarked for the Association of Professional Baseball Players of America, a welfare organization formed in 1924 to aid indigent ex-players and umpires. At the time of the first All-Star Game in 1933, forty-five men were receiving monthly stipends from the organization. Since then, radio and television money, as well as a share of postseason revenue, has been added to All-Star Game receipts, building a financial base from which modern pension and retirement funds have evolved.

what the hell to do. And Ferrell's standing there at home plate, doing nothing. So I ran into him.

The next thing I know, Ferrell throws the ball at me and comes charging at me. I punch him in the mouth, knock him on his ass, and Cronin grabs me right away. So he's got me pinned and the other guy pops me. Hell, I didn't know what happened. But what I should've done was stomp on Cronin's goddamn feet. He would've let go of me in a hurry. Hell, I didn't know what happened, these guys picking on a little guy like me. I was an innocent man.

Same thing happened once when I was a councilman. Hell, I'd been out of baseball fifteen years. One night I'm in bed with my wife and I get a call. It's Cochrane, saying he's up at the Blue Danube on Seven Mile Road. So I put on my clothes and go meet him. He's with this other guy, some big guy who was the traveling secretary of the ball club. This guy thought he could run over everybody.

Muddy Ruel was the general manager then. So this guy said, "Why don't you get together a petition saying we'll get rid of Muddy Ruel and give Mickey Cochrane the job?"

I loved Cochrane. I thought he was a hell of a guy. But I looked at this guy and said, "Man, you must be crazy. That ball team is eight games over .500. For what reason would you want to get rid of Muddy Ruel?"

So he says to me, "Oh, you little shit, you ain't got a gut in your body."

I looked at him and said, "Listen, there must be something wrong with that brain of yours." And with that he takes a swing at me. I'm sitting down. Well, I just moved my head, his fist went by, and I hit him. Knocked out some teeth. I really cold-cocked him.

The next day I'm in my office and my hand is all swollen up. People are asking me, "What happened?" And I'm telling them, "Oh, I caught it on a nail." But pretty soon I figure I'd better go see a doctor. He wants to know what happened.

"I caught it on a nail," I said.

"Okay," he says. "What really happened?"

I told him, "I caught it on a goddamn nail."

He says, "How many teeth did you knock out?"

"Three or four," I said.

"I thought so," he says.

I played in the big leagues for fourteen years. I don't get a pension. They picked that pension deal up in 1946. You had to have been playing then to collect anything. Today's players don't care about us. "I got mine," they say. "Who cares about them?" They've got so much money in that goddamn pension fund. . . . Listen, some of these guys today making $900,000 a year are going to get a pension of $96,000 a year. It's a joke.

I remember when Ty Cobb would come by the clubhouse when he was in Detroit. We were always glad to see the guy. The old-timers were something special to us. Not these bastards today. They don't know who the hell we are. We made this damn game for them. If it wasn't for us they'd be picking sugarcane instead of making a million dollars a year.

Don't get me wrong. I don't want someone saying, "Oh, here's a Blue Ned." I'm not a Blue Ned. That was the times. You didn't have pensions and endorsements and all that other crap to fall back on. One winter I worked for Drewery's, going out and meeting people. I sold cars with George Higgins Pontiac for a while, then I got to be a manufacturer's agent, those "five percenters" or whatever you want to call us. And I saved my money. I wasn't one of those guys pissing his money away.

I used to barnstorm every fall—Birdie Tebbetts, Taft Wright, myself. We were allowed up to three players from each club. A lot of people would come watch us play, visit with us. They'd say, "These guys are human just like us. They're no different." Hell, we brought baseball up north. We'd play Alpena, Bay City. We didn't make any money, but we had a hell of a lot of fun.

The men are different today. They're supposed to be bigger, faster, but I don't think they can take it like we did. Gehrig gave me eleven stitches once. I was standing on third, trying to get the ball on a triple, and the next thing I knew I was on the ground. This was in New York. Little guy like me . . . boy, did I want to fight that guy. I grabbed him by the hair, stuck his nose in the dirt. Forty thousand people booed the hell out of me. I got eleven stitches, three inches of tape, kept on playing.

The competition was so much keener when I played. And we played smarter. You watch these games today? These guys today, they want to steal bases when they're losing fifty to nothing. Now, what good's a stolen base when you're winning or losing by ten runs?

Or they'll hit when the count's three and oh. I remember Ted Williams did that when he was a rookie. We had 'em beat about ten to one, ninth inning. He was the first guy up. Got three balls on him. Three and nothing he hits, knocks it over the third deck in right field. The first time anyone drove a ball out of the ballpark. So he went to first and as he got near second base, I'm standing there. "Well," I said, "now the score's 10–2. Jesus Christ, no wonder you can hit .350, hitting three and nothing."

The big idea is to get men on the bases. You weren't allowed to hit three and oh. If you did, you got knocked on your ass your next time up. These .230 hitters today are swinging three and oh. We got guys playing major-league ball today that we wouldn't have even let in the ballpark in my day. It's a lousy way to say it, but it's true. I played in the best era in baseball.

I've been down here seven or eight years now, ever since I retired from the council. I got a letter from the commissioner's office. Asked if I wanted to take part in these old-timers' games. I put down on the sheet: "too old." I don't want to get involved in any of that crap.

You know, I want to tell you something. I saw a couple of old ball players play one of these games. These guys were good ball players, but now they're seventy-five years old. And to see some of them falling, stumbling, crawling . . . I'll never do that. I want them to remember me as I was. Maybe I wasn't the greatest, but I wasn't the worst. I didn't have to take a back seat to any of them, believe me.

—July 1986

15

Barney McCosky

William Barney McCosky
Born: April 11, 1918, Coal Run, Pennsylvania
Major-league career: 1939–42, 1946 Detroit Tigers, 1946–48, 1950–51 Philadelphia Athletics, 1951 Cincinnati Reds, 1951–53 Cleveland Indians

Barney McCosky was a fleet center fielder and leadoff batter who immediately made his presence felt in the Tiger lineup. In 1939, his rookie season, he hit .311. The following season he hit .340 and had a league-leading two hundred hits and nineteen triples to help propel the team into an unexpected World Series appearance against Cincinnati. Although McCosky lost some of his speed because of military service during World War II, he still compiled a .312 lifetime batting average over eleven major-league seasons.

McCosky became a car salesman in the Detroit area after leaving baseball. He and his wife currently live in an apartment in Vero Beach, Florida.

After I got out of baseball I had a party store on Joy Road, between Greenfield and Southfield. One day in the late fifties one of the lawyers in the neighborhood asked me if it'd be all right to use my name for a youth baseball league. I said okay, so they brought in the paperwork and everything else and I signed them. And after more than thirty years, the Barney McCosky Baseball League is still going strong.

The teams had their own managers and coaches. I'd just go out and talk to the kids, hit them some ground balls and fungoes. One day I went around the field and came in and sat down on the bench. This little fella was sitting next to me and he had some nice, brand-new batting gloves on. I said, "Well, I see you've got your new batting gloves on."

He said, "Oh yea, I've got a couple pair. These are for opening day."

And I said, "Where do you play?" He said, "I play first base."

We talked a little more. Finally I said, "Do you know who I am?" He looked at me and said, "No, sir."

I said, "Well, I'm Barney McCosky."

He straightened up and looked at me. "Barney McCosky?" he said. "I thought you was *dead!*"

I almost fell off the bench laughing. Here I am out of baseball only a few years and already I'm supposed to be dead.

I was born in Coal Run, Pennsylvania. There were nine kids in our family and I was the baby. I was just a year old when my mother died. I think she was just wore out from having all those kids. Mother was only about thirty-six or thirty-seven, I think, when she died. My dad never remarried. My older brothers and sisters raised me. Then my older brother, Tony, came to Detroit and got a job. He bought the family in. I was probably four years old when we came to Detroit.

We moved to the·southwest part of town, out by Schaefer near Fort Street. I went to grade school at Oakwood School, and from Oakwood I went to Southwestern High School.

Tony worked on the line at Dodge Main. Dad worked at what they called the carbon works in Delray, by the river. The depression affected our family just like everyone else. Nobody had any money. We took mustard sandwiches and ketchup sandwiches to school. We made sandwiches out of bananas. When supper time came we always had soup. Whoever worked—that was my brother Tony and my dad—got the meat off the soup bone. Five brothers and four sisters. But we survived.

I always liked baseball. Basketball, too. I was All-City and captain of the team in both sports at Southwestern. I was a guard. At that time there was no running up and down the court like racehorses like it is now. Back then it was basket, tip-off, basket, tip-off. If you had a tall guy you had a good team.

My first year of baseball I played second base, and then I played the outfield. I still have the city high school record, I think, for highest average. I hit .727 my senior year. Funny thing is, we played five or six exhibitions prior to the season and never got a base hit. I was hitting the ball good, but it was always at someone. Once the regular season started, they couldn't get me out.

Charlie Gehringer was my big hero. I copied his batting style all the way through. I forget which newspaper it was, but when I first came up with Detroit they had pictures of us two without the numbers on our backs. It said, "Who is who?" Then on the next page they had the photos with our numbers on. I was number twenty-one and Charlie was number two. But you could tell because Charlie was a little more bowlegged than I was and I was a little taller. But the bats were right in the same position and everything else.

Wish Egan signed me up. I went to spring training at Beaumont, which was the Tigers' Double-A team. I'd just turned eighteen. I hit about .450 and they kept me on the team. I played about the first ten games and then I made a mistake. I dove for a foul ball with a man on third. I caught it and when I looked up, the man was scoring. Well, that's experience, and I didn't have it. So I sat on the bench about a week. Finally, I got hold of Wish Egan. I told him, "Wish, I came down here to play ball, not sit on the bench." So he said, "Okay, I'll see what I can do."

He got me a ticket and I went to Charleston, West Virginia, in Class C ball. Lots of good ball players in that league: Phil Rizzuto, Jeff Heath, Jim Hegan. I wound up hitting .400 on the nose. Led the Mid-Atlantic League my first year in baseball.

Then the next two years I went back to Beaumont. Hit .311, .321, something like that. In 1939 the Tigers invited me to spring training in Lakeland. I was hitting the ball good there, so they said, "You're going north with the team." They had Earl Averill and Al Simmons in camp, but they were getting up in age. And Jo-Jo White was just traded. I was young, so I could outrun them, I could do everything. So on opening day in Detroit, I was in center field.

Barney McCosky in 1940: "I never could get enough baseball." (Courtesy of the National Baseball Library, Cooperstown, New York.)

When I heard that I was going to start in center field in front of my hometown, I had stomach quivers. Until that first pitch went by. Then it seemed like just another ball game.

Johnny Rigney was pitching for Chicago. I lined out my first at-bat, then I got a single and a double. I remember they had Jackie Hayes playing second base, and I hit a ball down to him. He nonchalantly picked the ball up and when he looked, I was already across the bag. He didn't know how fast I was, see? The next time I was up, I looked and he was ten steps in. So that first year I hit .311, the next year .340, and I kept going.

I was the baby on the team. Guys like Rudy York, Hank Greenberg, Pete Fox, Billy Rogell, Pinky Higgins were there at the time. These guys had been up eight or nine years. Here I am just a rookie, so when we'd go on the road they went their way and I went mine. I didn't go out with the guys and go around town. Most of the time I went to a movie, came back to my room and went to bed. They didn't want me because I was just a baby. But I didn't mind. I was still playing ball, I had a place to sleep—hey, I'm glad I'm here.

I roomed with Dizzy Trout. We got along real good. He'd give you the shirt off his back. And if you were going out somewhere, he'd give you his tie, too. A real nice guy.

Diz's real name was Paul. How'd he get his name? Well, he'd do crazy things. He'd be out there pitching and if the mound wasn't right, he'd run off and grab a rake and fix the mound the way he wanted. Things like that. He had a big red bandana that he always carried in his back pocket. He'd pull it out and wipe his sweat off. Sometimes he'd flip it around or drop it, just to draw attention.

But he could throw. He could hit, too. Big guy, about six-foot-two, weighed about 220 pounds. Diz used to throw a fork ball. Now they call it a split-fingered fastball, but it's the same pitch. He could control it. He had big hands, so he could spread those fingers across the ball.

Diz could be mean out there. There was one game where Luke Appling of the White Sox was fouling off pitch after pitch. He was good at that. He could stand at the plate and do that all day long, until he got the pitch he wanted. Diz was getting madder and madder. Finally he yelled from the mound, "You son of a bitch, let's see you foul this off!" And he wound up and threw his glove at Appling. Damned if Appling didn't swing and foul *that* off, too. Diz got tossed out of the game for throwing his glove.

I remember when Diz met his wife, Pearl. It was on his birthday. The game was over and Diz and I were leaving the clubhouse. Pearl was standing right by the clubhouse door. She stopped him. "Diz, I baked you a birthday cake," she said. "Here it is." He said, "Oh, fine. I'll see you later, Barney." I kept going and he was talking to her. They went out and after the season he married her. Pretty girl. They wound up having ten kids. One of them later pitched for Chicago. They called him Rainbow Trout.

I've been married forty-four years now myself. Jane's maiden name is Malicki. I knew the family. Her mom and dad owned Joey's Stables down in Delray. I met her, went off to the war, and we wrote back and forth. I gave her an engagement ring when I got back in '45 and we got married in '46.

We lived in Dearborn, a couple blocks west of Telegraph between Cherry Hill and Michigan Avenue. Right around Divine Child. That's the church we went to. My sister lived just east of Telegraph. She told me, "Buy yourself a lot over there. It's a real good

spot." Lots back then were cheap, so I did. I bought the lot when I
was down in Beaumont. I was getting paid $350, $400 a month,
something like that. The first couple years I sold Fords in the off-
season at Southwestern Motor Sales, right by Southwestern High
School. Then I worked as a security guard at the Ford Rotunda on
Schaefer. I saved my money. Finally, my World Series check in 1940
was about $3,500, which was enough to have a house built. Then I
married Jane and moved her right in. I think I paid $17,000 for the
house, and when I sold it I got about $110,000.

I'd take Michigan Avenue straight on in to the ballpark. On the
way down I'd pick up Johnny Lipon. He was a shortstop for Detroit
at the time. He lived right around Junction and Michigan. He'd be
waiting at the corner. I'd stop and pick him up. Detroit was safe
then. You could go downtown at midnight and not be afraid to walk
the streets. You can't do that now.

My family would go to the ballpark and see me play. All except
my dad. I don't think he knew baseball all that much. He was a
foreigner, you know. He was from the old country, Lithuania. He
didn't want me to play baseball. He'd say, "You go work. Everybody
else in the family working, you go work, too. Baseball is just fun
game." He didn't realize you got paid for playing ball.

I took care of my dad. I was the youngest, so he was my responsibility. He lived with me and Jane until he died. After I'd been
playing for a while he saw a couple ball games and kind of knew
what I was doing, but I don't think he understood what was going
on. But he was proud of his son. Oh yeah. Get a couple drinks in
him and he'd talk about me.

Ted Williams came up with the Red Sox my rookie year. He was
one heck of a hitter. In fact, if I had to pick my choice of all the
hitters I played against, I'd have to pick Williams first. He could do
whatever he wanted to. Probably could've hit .400 every year if he
wanted to, because teams shifted over to right field on him. They
wanted him to hit it to left field. There was no one on the left side
of the field. The shortstop was behind second base, the third baseman was playing out in left field, the left fielder was in left center,
the center fielder in right center, and the right fielder stood on the
foul line. He'd still rip them through there or over their heads. It
was about 440 feet to right field in Fenway Park, and he was still
pulling home runs. We used to talk about it on the bench: what
would he hit if he played in Detroit, with that short right field? How
many home runs would he hit? My God.

I remember when I first saw Ted. I think Roxie Lawson was pitching. I'm in center field, watching this skinny kid hitting, and—*boom!*—he swung and I watched the ball go over the right-field roof in Briggs Stadium. It was foul. I said, "Nobody can hit a ball that far." Two innings later, he hit another one right out of the stadium. This one was fair. I just shook my head: *no way*. That's a good drive in a Model T Ford.

There's something else I remember about my rookie season. In May New York came into Detroit to play its first series with us. We got through with our batting practice and I was sitting alone. The Yankees had to come through our dugout to get to their dugout. One

Boston's "Splendid Splinter," Ted Williams: "We used to talk about it on the bench: what would he hit if he played in Detroit?" In his rookie season, 1939, Williams became the first player to hit a fair ball completely out of Briggs Stadium. Two year later, his dramatic home run with two outs in the bottom of the ninth beat the National League in the first All-Star Game played in Detroit. (Courtesy of the National Baseball Library, Cooperstown, New York.)

of the sportswriters said, "Mr. Gehrig, would you mind posing for a picture with Barney McCosky? He's just starting out." I looked and there was Lou Gehrig. He said, "Oh, I'd love to."

Many a time I seen him and Ruth play at Navin Field when I was a kid. In his prime he was about 220 pounds with muscles all over him. He'd hit line drives. *Zoom.* They were gone. Good fielder, good runner, could do everything well. But now his legs were just giving out. He couldn't control his muscles. He could barely make it up the clubhouse steps. He put his arm around me and they took the picture. Then he went across the field and sat down and that's when he broke his consecutive-game playing record. Babe Dahlgren took his place and I think he hit a triple, home run, and two doubles that day. That's the first time I met Lou. Only time I met him. After that he lasted what, a year?

Nineteen-forty? Well, everything just happened that year. We had Tommy Bridges and Bobo Newsom pitching, and Schoolboy came back from Beaumont—he'd had arm problems—and won a lot of ball games for us. We had Al Benton in the bullpen, and Al was a good stopper. When we got ahead, we'd put him in for an inning or two and it was our ball game.

Del Baker was managing the Tigers then. He was a coach under Mickey Cochrane, and when Cochrane got hit by Bump Hadley in New York in '37, he took over in midseason. And then the following year, when they fired Mickey, Del Baker took over the manager's job. We finished fifth, I think, my first year, so Del made some moves in 1940.

Rogell was slowing down at short, so they traded him to the Cubs for Dick Bartell. Gehringer and Bartell worked together well, and we had Pinky Higgins at third. That year we took Greenberg off first base and put him in left field because we wanted more power in the lineup. Rudy York, who had been catching, couldn't play the outfield. He'd get hit in the head out there. So they put York on first and Greenberg in left. Birdie Tebbetts moved behind the plate. Everybody just seemed to click.

Hank asked me for help in playing the outfield because he'd never played there before. So I'd come down to the ballpark about 10:00 or 10:30 in the morning and throw balls against the left-field fence and tell him what base to throw to. I'd yell "second base!" and he'd wheel and throw. Stuff like that, you know. That lasted about five or six days.

Hank was pretty good, but he wasn't that fast in the outfield. On

anything that was hit to left center, he'd yell, "Come on, Barney!"
All I could hear was, "Come on, Barney!" I'd come over and get it
and he'd look at me and give me the high sign: *all right.*

Then one day we had an off day. Hank called and said, "Whatdya doing?" I said, "Nothing. Just sitting around the house." I
thought maybe he wanted me at the ballpark again. He said, "Can
you meet down at the Michigan Theatre?" I said, "Sure I can."

So about noon I met him there and he took me up to the fourth
floor to his tailor. He told the tailor, "Make a suit for Barney." So he
measured me up. That was my first tailor-made suit, for helping
him out in the outfield. That's the kind of guy he was.

Rudy was a problem. He liked to drink. They did everything to
keep him sober. They'd give him bonuses and everything else. He'd
be all right for about a week or ten days, then he'd go right back on
the sauce again. He'd never give anyone any trouble, but he was just
that kind of guy, you know. He could play with it.

He was a good hitter. Rudy probably swung the heaviest bat on
the Tigers—thirty-eight ounces and thirty-five or thirty-six inches
long. Strong son of a bitch, I'll tell ya. I remember when we were on
the train going down to play Cincinnati in the World Series. There
was a little, narrow passageway. I was coming one way and he was
coming the other way. He had a few drinks in him and he grabbed
me by the arm. He said, "McCosky, we're going down to play the
World Series. I've been in them before and you haven't. It's just like
another ball game." And all the time he's talking, he's squeezing my
arm. I'm halfway down to my knees. I said, "Rudy, for God's sake,
let go of my arm. You're killing me." My whole arm was numb.

I was six-foot-one, about 184 pounds. I could always run. I
never stopped at second base. I'd hit second and say, "Now throw
me out." I just kept going. My first year up, I hit fourteen triples, just
behind Buddy Lewis of Washington. And then the next year I led
the league. I hit nineteen. Greenberg liked that. I was standing on
third base. That was an RBI for him.

I batted first or second. I'd switch with Pete Fox or Bruce Campbell. Gehringer would hit third, Greenberg fourth, York fifth, Higgins sixth, right down the line. At one time, in the middle of our
pennant year, we had nine .300 hitters in the lineup. That was when
Bartell and Tebbetts were hitting .300 and we had Schoolie, a good
hitter himself, pitching. We wouldn't think anything of being six,
seven runs behind going into the seventh inning. The feeling was

that everyone would start hitting and we'd come out on top. Big innings all the time.

Birdie Tebbetts was our mainstay as a catcher. He'd go in against left-handed pitching. We had Billy Sullivan, he was our left-handed-hitting catcher. But Birdie, he really knew how to handle the pitchers. He was a great guy. How'd he get his name? Well, he chirped back there. He had a high-pitched voice. Always talking,

Catcher George "Birdie" Tebbetts, so named because of his squeaky voice and incessant chirping behind the plate, played eight seasons with Detroit in the thirties and forties. He was once ejected for suggesting to the home plate umpire that he look through the open spaces of his mask when calling balls and strikes. (Courtesy of the National Baseball Library, Cooperstown, New York.)

always chirping back there, so someone named him "Birdie" and that stuck.

I remember when Birdie just about got knocked out with a grocery sack of vegetables. That was in Cleveland in 1940, when we were playing the Indians the last series of the year for the pennant. That was the game where Floyd Giebell beat Feller.

When we went in there we were, what, a couple games ahead? Cleveland had to win all three games to win the pennant. They were opening with Bob Feller, who of course was their ace. We didn't want to throw one of our best pitchers against Bob in the first game. So we had a meeting. We had Newhouser, Hutchinson, and a young guy called Floyd Giebell. We took a vote and we picked Giebell.

No one knew Giebell. He'd joined the ball club for the last month of the season. He'd pitched a couple of good games against the White Sox. So we put him in there, thinking we could take a chance on losing that game and come back with our best—at the time, Schoolboy Rowe, Tommy Bridges, and Bobo Newsom. But the kid won the ball game.

I think it was a 2–0 game. Rudy York hit a home run. But the guy who really helped us out was that Giebell. Ben Chapman came up with men on second and third with one out, and then with a man on second with nobody out, and Giebell got him each time. That was the big turning point of that game. If Chapman would've gotten a hit or two, then we would've been out of there—fast. After that Giebell went to spring training the next year and then you never saw him again. We stopped down in Virginia once to see if he was still there. We looked in the phone book, but no luck.

That was some game. Cleveland had just played us a series in Detroit, and I guess there was a little argument about someone dropping fruit in our ballpark, throwing stuff at the outfielders and infielders. So that first game in Cleveland someone in the upper deck dropped a bag of fruit and bottles on Birdie while he was sitting in the bullpen. It hit him in the head and the shoulders and it pretty much knocked him out. So that wasn't so good. But we were going down to the wire. Everything counted, you know.

I was going for my two hundredth hit. I think I got two that day and the next day I got my two hundredth hit. I didn't have too much trouble hitting Bob. In fact, that one year that he struck out all those hitters in the American League [*a record 348 in 1946*], in his book he said the only one he couldn't strike out was Barney McCosky.

I'm one he didn't get. I was no home run hitter. I just choked up, but I made sure I always had good contact with the ball. Not that I owned him. He got me out, too. Plenty of times.

Bobo opened the series for us against Cincinnati. Bobo was a real character. He'd been around the league twice. And he had a real rubber arm. He didn't have to warm up with the catcher. He'd take a ball from the bullpen and on the way to the mound he'd just throw it back and forth into his glove. "I'm ready," he'd say. He'd throw a lot of slow stuff, then bust a fastball in on you. He had an exceptional year in 1940. Everything that was hit was right at somebody, so he piled up the wins.

You know that Bobo's dad died during the series. We thought it might affect him, but he said, "No, I'll pitch." There weren't any travel days that series, so he pitched the final game with only a day's rest. And he pitched a hell of a ball game, too.

We were ahead 1–0 in the seventh. Frank McCormick led off with a double. Then Jimmy Ripple hit one between me and Bruce Campbell in right. McCormick held up a little, I guess because he thought it might be caught. Campbell picked the ball up and relayed it to Bartell at short, and he hesitated. The runner, McCormick, kept coming around third, but there was no throw at the plate. If Bartell had thrown it just when he got it, it probably would've been close, because McCormick was a big, slow runner. He should've thrown it, he didn't, and that was the tying run coming in. Ripple got sacrificed to third, and then Billy Meyers hit a long fly ball that I caught at the fence to score what turned out to be the winning run.

It's just one of those things. A couple of months ago we had a golf outing around St. Petersburg. Johnny Vander Meer, who played with the Reds, was sitting by a table. I said, "Johnny, can I see that World Series ring?" He put his hand over and I said, "That son of a bitch should be mine, you know it?" He laughed and said, "I know. I'm glad I have it."

Sure, I would've liked to have won. But thank God I played in one. I'm tickled to death. It was a thrill to be a hometown boy and get in a World Series.

I went into the navy in 1943. There were ball teams for the soldiers and the navy. We had Vinnie Smith, a catcher for Pittsburgh, Tom Ferrick, a pitcher for the A's, and other big-leaguers. The army had Joe Gordon, Joe DiMaggio, Bill Dickey's brother, Skeeter. I played in Hawaii and then we had kind of a tour of the Pacific

October 6, 1940: Hank Greenberg has just gotten hold of a Junior
Thompson pitch in the fifth game of the Detroit-Cincinnati World Series
and sent it screaming toward the left-field seats at Briggs Stadium. Along
with 55,189 fans, teammate Barney McCosky (edging off third base)
watches the ball land in the deep reaches of the upper deck. The
tremendous third-inning blast broke open a scoreless tie and gave Detroit
all the runs it would need in an 8–0 shutout. (Copyright © 1940 by the
Detroit News. Used with permission.)

islands—Guam, Tinian, then Saipan for fourteen months. You'd see
some Japanese up in the trees, watching the games. The islands
were pretty much secured by then, but they didn't want to give up.
A lot of them were wearing navy dungarees. They liked baseball,
you know. The MPs would be up in the hills, what we called the
bleacher seats, and they'd be grabbing four or five Japs while the
game was going on.* But we didn't play much over there. Mostly
softball, because they didn't have the diamonds there. You'd hit a

---

*The Japanese were ambivalent about their enemy's national pastime. There were
several accounts of Japanese soldiers screaming "Babe Ruth eats shit!" as they
charged American lines. (When told of this, Ruth replied, "I hope that every Jap that
mentions my name gets shot and to hell with all Japs anyway.") And yet many ser-
vicemen stationed on Pacific islands recalled seeing bored Japanese discreetly
watching games during lulls in the fighting.

ball and it'd land in the ocean. But we had our jobs to do. We were part of Gene Tunney's physical fitness program. We'd have the boys run, give them exercises, umpire games.

When I enlisted I wanted to be a pilot, but I could tell I was in over my head. So I called Mickey Cochrane at Great Lakes—he was a commander in the navy—and I got transferred there. I'll say that officers took their baseball seriously. I remember when I was playing on a navy team on Treasure Island, by San Francisco. Admiral Nimitz was in Hawaii and he wanted us ball players out there. But our captain wouldn't let us go. Then one night we were all told to report. The next day we were on board the USS *Birmingham*, on our way to Hawaii. That's the kind of pull Nimitz had, putting the best ball players in Hawaii.

I managed Aiea Barracks in Hawaii. Remember Bobby Riggs, the tennis player? I had him in my barracks. Jesus. He was in my platoon. He just couldn't march in a straight line. Honest to God, he duck walked. That was because of all that tennis training, where you're always moving sideways. Finally I had to put him in the back of the line.

We had a league and we'd play other service teams, like Kaneohe airbase and the sub base at Pearl Harbor. Johnny Mize of the Cardinals and Hugh Casey of the Dodgers played for Kaneohe. I got into it with Casey one game. He was sore because I always hit him good, I guess. One game I hit a home run off him. So the next time up, while I was bending over, rubbing some dirt on my hands, he wound up and threw the damn ball and hit me right in the middle of my back. So I went out to the mound and punched him in the jaw. We had a fight right there on the mound.

I figured I was a goner, you know, that I'd be shipped out for fighting. I was told to report to our captain. So I did. I saluted him, said, "Chief Specialist McCosky reporting as ordered, sir."

He told me to relax. Then he says, "You know why I called you in here, don't you, McCosky?"

I said, "The fight on the field, right?"

He says, "That's right. If you hadn't gone out after him I would've shipped your ass out of here." After that he shook my hand and that was that.

I went to spring training with Detroit in 1946. We had about nine good outfielders come back from the war—Dick Wakefield, Vic Wertz, Pat Mullin, Roy Cullenbine, myself. First thing I knew, I was traded. In May the Tigers sent me to Philadelphia for George Kell.

I couldn't believe it when they first told me. The A's were in town to play the Tigers. I was just putting on my shoes when one of the coaches came up to me and said, "Barney, you won't have to put those shoes on. You won't be playing today. You've just been traded. They want to see you at the Book Cadillac." That's where Connie Mack was. So I went down there to talk to him.

Mr. Mack had wanted me when I was in Beaumont, but the Tigers wouldn't give me up. He looked at me and said, "I finally got you, McCloskey." He never did get my name right. I said, "Thanks a lot, Mr. Mack. I didn't want to go." He said, "I know you didn't want to go. But I've got you now."

Later I told Jane, "Well, I've got to play somewhere, and they're still in the big leagues, even if they are the A's and don't have that much." I just made up my mind that I was going to play as hard there as anywhere else.

Mr. Mack, of course, was managing Philadelphia. When I got there he was well up in age, in his eighties. He was still wearing those stiff collars and hat instead of a uniform. It was his habit to

Barney McCosky slides in under the catcher's tag in this game against the St. Louis Browns, circa 1941. Notice the photographer with his large-format camera right on top of the action. Through the 1950s photographers were allowed to ply their trade within several feet of the batter's box.

wave his outfielders into position with his scorecard: go to left center or right center or whatever. But by then he didn't know the ball players. We knew who was pitching and where the ball would probably go. As soon as he'd look the other way, we'd move back. Half the time we'd catch the ball and he'd be happy because he'd moved us over. But everybody respected him, though.

Embarrassing moments? Oh, there's a couple that come to mind. I remember once in Philadelphia, when we were getting ready to play the Yanks. We had a meeting before the game about the guy who was pitching for the Yanks, Bill Wight. He'd just come up and we were talking about what a good move he had to first.

So I singled off him and I'm on first base. Earle Mack, Mr. Mack's son, was coaching first base. He comes up to me—I'm maybe eight inches away from the bag—and says, "Barney, watch this guy. He's got a good move to first base." And I looked at him and said, "I know. And it's too late. He's tagging me out right now."

Another time when Detroit was playing the Yankees, I was on first when Gehringer ripped the ball down the first baseline. I took off for second base. I'm standing on the bag and Phil Rizzuto and Joe Gordon are yelling "foul ball! foul ball!" I was running, so I couldn't see where the ball was. I stepped off the bag to go back to first when Rizzuto tags me and says, "You're out!" Ohhh, I looked for a hole to crawl in.

Based on what they're paying .210 hitters today, I'd be making two or three million a year. My top salary was $17,500. I made that with Detroit. I didn't even get that when I hit .328 in 1947. I finished second to Ted Williams that year for the batting title. I went up to see Mr. Mack about a raise. I told Mr. Mack what I wanted and he started crying. He said, "I'd give it to you, McCloskey, but I don't have it." Finally, he gave us $500 for me and Jane to find a house in Philadelphia to stay in.

But I never got a raise from Mr. Mack. The A's weren't drawing that good. The A's were sharing Shibe Park with the Phillies. The A's would go on the road and the Phillies would move in for a home stand. That's when they had a winning club, the Whiz Kids. They won a pennant in 1950. The same fans are going to the games, so they're gonna pick the team that's winning. That's what hurt them. Mr. Mack just didn't have the money. Every time he had any kind of ball player, he'd sell him. Jimmie Foxx, Jimmy Dykes, those guys. That's how Detroit got Mickey Cochrane back in the thirties.

Philadelphia sold me to Cincinnati in 1951. I was there about six weeks, hitting .320 or so, when Hank Greenberg bought me back into the American League. Hank was the general manager of Cleveland then, and the Indians needed a utility outfielder and pinch hitter. I stayed with Cleveland until 1953. Greenberg wanted me to go to Indianapolis, Cleveland's Triple-A team in the American Association. He said, "You can go down there and play and coach. If we need you we can call you up." I threw up my hand. I said, "No thanks, Hank. I've had enough." I didn't want to go to the minor leagues, not after playing all those years in the big leagues. And I was getting up there in age.

I went into business with Jane's father. After I sold the store I sold cars for about seventeen years. I liked it. I met a lot of people. We talked baseball a lot, and that helped. I sold cars at Fort-Park Chevrolet on Fort Street, then Walt Lazar in Taylor, then Les Stanford in Dearborn. From there we came down to Florida in '82.

I still follow the game. Oh yeah. I think there's a lot of good ball players playing today. I don't think they have their heart in it like we did. They don't care if they hit .300 or win twenty games. It doesn't matter what they do, they still get paid. When we played, you had to earn your money. You got paid for what you did, so you hustled all the time. You tried to get better. If you had a good year, you got paid accordingly. If you had a bad year, they'd take ten or twenty percent off it. Today, there's no way. You look in the paper and one guy's jealous of another guy. They sign a contract, but once they see that someone's getting more, they say, "Trade me or give me another contract." That's not right. Heck, you signed a contract.

I know that playing in Detroit, I couldn't get enough baseball. We played nothing but day ball then, so after the game I'd leave the ballpark, drive home, and go out behind the school where the kids were playing. I'd bring plenty of balls. The kids loved it. Instead of taped balls, they had balls with covers on them. I'd bring some broken bats and we'd fix them up with tape. I'd get extra batting practice hitting fungoes to the kids. I wouldn't get home till six-thirty or quarter to seven. I'd stay out there two hours and never think anything about it. But I just loved it. I couldn't get enough baseball.

—*April 1990*

16

Doc Cramer

Roger Maxwell Cramer
Born: July 22, 1905, Beach Haven, New Jersey
Major-league career: 1929–35 Philadelphia Athletics, 1936–40
Boston Red Sox, 1941 Washington Senators, 1942–48 Detroit Tigers

Durability and consistency characterized the twenty-year major-league career of Roger "Doc" Cramer, who stroked 2,705 hits in 2,239 games, batted .290 or better a dozen times, and led the league in at-bats a record eight seasons. A five-time All-Star for the Philadelphia Athletics and Boston Red Sox during the 1930s, he was traded to Detroit in 1942; three years later, the forty-year-old was still patrolling center field and batting third for the Tigers, helping the team to a World Series win over the Chicago Cubs in the last wartime season.

Cramer was a carpenter during the off-season and after his baseball career ended. At the time of this interview he was living alone in a house in Beach Haven, New Jersey, that he built himself.

Doc Cramer died September 9, 1990, in Manahawkin, New Jersey.

I came up with Philadelphia in 1929, so I played in Detroit when it was Navin Field. Then it became Briggs Stadium. That's one of the best ballparks in the country. It'd be a shame to tear it down. The outfield was just like a carpet. You could dive for a ball out there and you'd scoot across that grass. You wouldn't stick in the ground. A lot of these ballparks, the ground gets a little wet and you wind up sticking your shoulder into it. That's how I broke my collarbone.

Did that in Shibe Park in 1932. Dove after a ball that Lou Gehrig hit. Caught the ball, and that bone came right through my shirt. Funny the way it was then and how it is now. I walked off the field, came into the clubhouse, and they cut my shirt off and tied my arm back. My wife took me to the hospital. Those players now, all they have to do is get a hangnail and they're in the hospital.

I watch quite a lot of baseball. I don't know, they play it so much different than we did. Take running out a ground ball. When I played, the runner always turned to the right. You never went across the diamond back to the bench. Now, that holds up the game. I've hit ground balls, got thrown out, and by the time I'd turned around and got behind home plate the pitcher was pitching to the next batter. I'd have to stop.

All this showboatin' and walking around. . . . They'll swing at a ball, then they'll walk around. . . . We never did that. The umpire wouldn't let you. No wonder these games today last forever.

This dope, too, I don't understand it. When you trade a million-dollar career for some coke, there's something wrong with you. I can't see that at all. If you get a kid to reach eighteen years old without touching that stuff, I think you're lucky. Damn lucky. The high school up here—they sell it. I can understand a bottle of whiskey or a couple of beers. But that dope—that kills them.

We'd have a beer after the ball game or with supper, but that was about it. You had some guys who drank to excess, like Rudy York and Rollie Hemsley. Rudy was a Cherokee Indian and they like to drink. But Rudy would give you everything he had.

When I was with Philadelphia, we'd go out together—Jimmie Foxx, Mickey Cochrane, myself. It's a life you have to learn to control yourself. You go out in those barrooms, you've got to be careful. That's what the boss, Connie Mack, told us: "I don't care what you boys do after a ball game. You'd just better be able to play tomorrow, that's all." We generally were.

I played twenty years in the big leagues. Hit .296 lifetime. I was hitting .300 when I quit playing regular. Then I started pinch-hitting my last couple years with Detroit, and that knocked me below .300. Otherwise. . . . Where was I? You get eighty years old, you can't think of nothing.

The Hall of Fame? It don't even enter my mind. I don't care if I'm in or out, to tell you the truth. I know a lot of guys in there who don't belong. To tell you the truth, I don't know if I'd even go if I was elected. Doesn't make a bit of difference to me. You know something, when you look things over, that Hall of Fame, that's a tough job. A lot of those guys doing the picking never saw a lot of us play. Never seen me play.

I coached a couple years with Detroit, then I retired in '49. I worked some as a carpenter. See, my daughter got sick and my wife got sick, so I had to quit that. She had bone cancer. It was the worst thing I ever saw. She'd be in bed and roll over and break a bone. She was forty-two when she died. My wife died in '79. I had to just quit to take care of them, that's what it amounted to.

There's a Doc Cramer Drive here in town. A political job. They wanted to name this street after me. I said, "I don't care, just don't mix me up in the politics." Well, they had a big send-off. There's five baseball fields up the street, so that's why they named it. This was about three years ago.

I built this house all by myself. I was a carpenter. Fifty years in the union. There was nothing here then. Well, the road there, but it was gravel. Now they're coming in just like that. We went from fifteen hundred to thirty thousand people around Manahawkin. They come here to get close to the beach.

Philadelphia's sixty miles away, so I always followed the A's. We didn't have radio at first, so when I was a kid I'd have to look in the next day's paper to see how they made out. They had Eddie Collins, Stuffy McInnis, Home Run Baker. Rube Waddell was one of the pitchers. He was something. Later, when I was with Philly, Connie Mack would tell us stories about him. One time they were training down in Fort Myers and they were all supposed to be showing up for some parade. Everybody's there except Waddell. They're all wondering, "Where is Waddell?," when the parade starts coming down the street. And there's Waddell, tossing a baton, leading the parade. But he was some pitcher.

I grew up right here in Beach Haven. My father was a butcher.

Roger "Doc" Cramer. (Courtesy
of the Burton Historical
Collection of the Detroit Public
Library.)

How'd I get my name? Well, the guy across the street used to be a
country doctor. I used to hang around him all the time, so they
started calling me "Doc." I was only about ten or so.

I played shortstop on the high school team in Barnegat when I
was still in eighth grade. I don't know how they managed that. They
approached me. I did all right. I was hitting third. See, they didn't
have too much to draw from. We only had about twelve kids. We
had to play these bigger towns around us, like Tom's River and
Lakewood.

I didn't finish high school. They threw me out after a couple
years. I had to go to work, so I got a job in carpentry. I started playing
semipro ball in Beach Haven. I pitched on Wednesday and Sunday
and on Saturday I played shortstop. I was making big money then,
or what I thought was big. I got fifty dollars for pitching and twenty-
five for playing shortstop. That's in 1926. That's more money than I
was making working. I'd work half a day and then play ball the
other half. I'd change into my uniform in whatever house we were
building.

In those days you couldn't play Sunday ball in Philadelphia, so one time Cy Perkins and Jimmy Dykes came out to a ball game I was pitching. They asked me if I'd come up to Philly. I didn't want to take a day off, but I went up there for a workout. The old man, Connie Mack, was out there, looking everything over. He told me to get a room, stay in Philly. They signed me up the next day. Big sum of thirty-five hundred dollars. That was in 1928.

I spent the rest of the year working out with the A's. Never got into any games. The next year they sent me to Martinsburg, West Virginia. The Blue Ridge League. I thought I was in a foreign country, to tell you the truth. But I stuck her out. That's the best year I ever had, my first year out. Hell, I hit .404, won twelve and lost one.

The A's brought me up the next year. They were winning the pennant that year, but in July they sent me to Portland. The reason was, we were playing in Washington one day and they sent me up to pinch-hit. Fred Marberry was the pitcher. I had Marberry, three balls and a strike. Eddie Collins, the third-base coach, gave me the sign. I thought they gave me the "hit" sign. I swung and popped up.

Well, it was the "take" sign. That night, going back to Philly on the train, the old man called me over to his seat. That's when he told me I was going to Portland. I said, "How come? I thought I was doing all right."

He said, "You were. You're going out there to learn the signs—and also how to field."

I told the old man, "I'm not going to Portland." He said, "Yes, you are." And I said, "Oh no, I'm not." And we went back and forth. Finally I said, "Portland, *Oregon?*"

He said, "That's right."

I said, "By God, you kept me in the United States, didn't you?" But I was on the train the next morning. Took four days to get there.

He called me into his office the next year. Then they had Al Simmons, Mule Haas, and Bing Miller in the outfield. He named those fellows and he said, "Now, you beat those fellows out and you've got a job." I said, "Well, that's not too much trouble"—to myself.

I'll tell you, in those days a rookie didn't have a chance. A rookie never hit batting practice with the regulars. He hit in the morning. Yes sir. You went out there at 10:30 in the morning. But you couldn't let them push you around. If you did, in those days they'd push you all the way back to the Blue Ridge League. You had to let them know who you were, too.

Simmons was a little rough. I remember when I first started

playing regular. It was in Boston, on a Sunday. The Red Sox played
at Braves Field then because it was a bigger field, held more people.
The boss called me in and said, "You're playing center field and
hitting second until you show me you can't play." He said, "Hit
with the regulars."

So I go out to hit that day. Max Bishop's the first batter and I'm
second. Simmons is standing there and he says when I step in,
"What the hell are you doing in here?"

I said, "The boss told me to hit second."

"Oh," he says, "who am I around here?"

Remember, this is Al Simmons. What'd he hit every year—
about .390? Anyhow, I said, "I don't know who you are. Just another
ball player as far as I'm concerned." That Cochrane, I thought he
was going to die laughing. But that was that. Simmons was the best
friend I had after that.

Lefty Grove? He's another one. He was a dandy. I remember
when we were playing a game in Fort Myers in spring training. That
was my first year. The Yannigans—the scrubs, we called them the
Yannigans—we were playing the regulars. I hit a line drive off
Grove that got between the outfielders for a home run.

Boy, that didn't go. I come up to hit the next time and Cochrane
says, "Boy, you better be ready. He's gonna throw at you." I said,
"Oh, he wouldn't do that in a game like this, would he?" Cochrane
said, "Yeah, he would. You don't know him."

My God, Grove hit me right here, in the back. Knocked me
down. Didn't break nothing. Anyhow, they took me out of the game,
put me on the rubbing table with a bag of ice. That's about all they
did then. Grove pitched his three innings and came into the clubhouse. He comes by me and says, "You didn't hit that one, did you,
busher?"

He was the hardest thrower I ever saw. I remember once in Yankee Stadium when he came in to pitch with the bases full and nobody out. We had a one-run lead. He struck out Ruth, Gehrig, and
Lazzeri on ten pitches. Lazzeri fouled a ball.

Another time we were in Detroit to play a series. This is when
they first came out with this shatterproof glass in cars. Grove said to
me, "The Buick people want me to throw a ball at this shatterproof
glass. Will you come out and warm me up?" I said, "Yeah, all right."

So we went out there and the first couple times Grove just kind
of lobbed the ball. The head guy for Buick says, "No, Mr. Grove, we
want you to *throw* it."

Robert "Lefty" Grove: "He was a dandy." (Courtesy of the National Baseball Library, Cooperstown, New York.)

"Okay," he says. "I'll throw it." So he got out there and picked up the ball and let her go. He threw it through the front windshield and out the back window. Left a little hole about that big.

That was some team in Philadelphia. Grove, Earnshaw, Cochrane, Simmons, Jimmie Foxx—they were out to beat you. We all were. That Cochrane was a hell of a catcher. He was the best I saw in my time. Better than Dickey. Good arm. He could run, too. I played against Bill Dickey, Luke Sewell, Rick Ferrell, all those good catchers. But he was ahead of all of them, no question.

You didn't have to make a perfect throw to Cochrane. He'd get the ball and dive into the runner. He didn't care if the runner hit him in the mouth or whatever. Dickey'd give us the plate, Cochrane wouldn't. He wouldn't let you have it, no way. You had to take it away from him.

I know when he went to Detroit and I was still with Philly, we played a close ball game. I was on third and someone hit a fly ball. I tagged and came home. The ball went this way, the glove that way, and his mask was over there. "You son of a bitch!" he said to me. By God, it was like hitting a wall.

He was a leader. He'd come back to the bench yelling, "What the hell's the matter with you guys?" He was from New England, you know, so he'd talk in that New England brogue: "*Gawd*-damned *cawk*suckers!" He'd stir you up.

We lived together in Philadelphia—my wife and my kids and his wife and his kids. Had this big double house in Bala-Cynwyd. He lived in one side and I was in the other. Cochrane's wife's name was Mary. They had a daughter named Joan. In fact, that's who my daughter was named after.

Cochrane had a son, Gordon, Jr. I knew that boy well. He wasn't a hard-driving guy like his father. He was more easygoing. He got killed in the war. He was in France in the army. That killed Mike. That hurt him something terrible; the mother, too.

Foxx? He was a big right-handed hitter. Just all muscle. Lefty Gomez once said even Foxx's hair had muscles. I saw Foxx hit a ball off Gomez once in New York. You ever been to Yankee Stadium? You know that wing that sticks out in left field? It's in the third deck. That's what he hit. Paint fell off it for ten minutes.

Jimmie was a good guy. He was another fella who hurt himself with whiskey. He choked to death, you know. Some restaurant in Miami. He had a piece of steak in his mouth and it got stuck in his throat. He wasn't very old.

Foxx hit fifty-eight home runs one season [1932]. We thought he'd break Ruth's record, but he didn't hit any the last few games of the season. I know, because other pitchers have told me this, that they laid the ball right down the middle for him. But he'd pop it up. Just overtrying, I think. He just couldn't get those two to tie.

I played with Foxx and Greenberg, but Ruth hit 'em further than both. He was the best ball player there ever was. No question about it. He was a hellraiser. He was all that and a little worse. I've been barnstorming with him through Canada. He used to come down hunting with me. Cochrane, too. Both were good shots. But Ruth was crazy. He was wild. I've got a shotgun in that other room he gave me. Ruth was walking along, using it like a walking stick. Packed the barrel with mud. He fired it and it exploded, just like that. Lucky he didn't lose an eye.

But he was the best. Hit, run, throw, a great pitcher. Twenty-nine scoreless innings in the World Series. That ain't bad. He could field, too. If you were on first and a guy hit the ball to right field, you didn't want to try to go to third. You'd never get there. Ruth would throw you out—on the fly. It'd be a strike, too.

Gehrig? Nobody liked Gehrig, not even his own players. I know that to be a fact. Tony Lazzeri, he couldn't stand to be near him. He was too cheap, that's what it was. And he was self-centered. I always got along with him. He'd have a beer and drink with you, if you bought it. Otherwise, he wasn't buying you one. The only guy that got along with him was Bill Dickey. They roomed together. Well, I'd just as well not talk about Gehrig anyhow. No sense burying somebody after they're dead.

That Philadelphia team won three pennants in a row—'29, '30, '31. I played in the '31 World Series against the Cardinals. We got beat that series. That was a good St. Louis team. They had Bill Hallahan, Jesse Haines, Paul Derringer, and Grimes on the staff. Pepper Martin had a big series. They blamed Cochrane, but he ran on the pitchers—Earnshaw, Walberg, and Quinn. The only one he couldn't run on was Grove.

I pinch-hit against Burleigh Grimes both times. He was a tough son of a gun. First time up I hit a line drive that Frankie Frisch made a good play on. Next time I come up, it's bases full, two outs in the ninth inning of the seventh game. We were losing, 4–0.

I'll never forget the boss crooking his finger at me. Kid Gleason was sitting next to me. He said, "He wants you. Get up there." So I went over and Mr. Mack said, "You're going to pinch-hit for Walberg." Liked to scare me to death. But I got a base hit. Scored two runs. That's the only runs we got that game. I'll bet Grimes threw me ten spitballs. I saw him years later and I said, "I kept waiting for you to throw me a fastball." He said, "You'd still be waiting. I wasn't going to throw it."

In Philadelphia, Cy Perkins, Cochrane, and Mr. Mack were in the stock market. My locker was right by Perkins's and Cochrane's. I heard them talking about it, that when this stock hit $100,000 they were going to cash it in. And that day, the market went to hell and they lost everything. That's why Connie Mack started selling off all his players, to get back even. Attendance was falling off, too, and he couldn't afford to pay those big contracts with the depression on. He sent Simmons and Jimmy Dykes to Chicago and sold Cochrane to Detroit. I wound up on Boston with Grove and Foxx. They got there a year before me. After the '35 season, Mr. Mack sent me and Eric McNair to the Red Sox for pitcher Hank Johnson, Al Niemiec, and some cash.

Cochrane tried to get me into Detroit many, many times. Del Baker was the manager when I finally got there, and later, Steve

O'Neill. All three of those fellows were catchers, so that might've had something to do with their record. They knew how to handle a pitching staff.

Detroit's always had good pitchers, going way back. That Earl Whitehill, he was a hell of a pitcher. Tommy Bridges was 150 pounds of guts. He almost had a perfect game against Washington once. Dave Harris got a pinch hit with one out to go. Schoolboy Rowe . . . Bobo Newsom . . . and Dizzy Trout and Hal Newhouser.

That Newhouser. . . . When I was with Boston I got a hit off of him. I'm standing on first base and I'm watching him swear and stomp around that mound, glaring at me. I said, "Who do you think you are? Isn't anyone ever supposed to get a hit off you?" He walked over. He was a cocky guy at that time. But he got to be a good boy and a good pitcher.

Newhouser used to tell me that story after I got with Detroit. That was in '42. I'd gone to Washington for Gerry Walker in '41. Then they traded second baseman Jimmy Bloodworth and myself

Mickey Cochrane and his wife, Mary, attend a World Series game between the Giants and Yankees in 1936.

to Detroit for shortstop Frank Croucher, and Bruce Campbell, an outfielder.

A lot of the players were gone from that Detroit team—Greenberg, Tebbetts, Pat Mullin. The army was taking them all. I remember one pitcher we had, Joe Orrell. He went down and took his examination one day before the game started. We figured he was gone, too. About the fifth inning, he was back in the clubhouse, putting his uniform on. Someone said, "Joe, what happened?"

"Oh," he said. "Short war."

Wakefield was another one in the service. Did I read in the paper that Wakefield died? He was one of the first bonus boys. He hit pretty good when he first came up, but I don't know what happened after that. Was he worth that kind of money? No. What he was, he was O'Neill's boy. He was a good boy. He didn't deserve what he got, but it's his own fault.

I had good years in Detroit. But it wasn't like it was before the war. Or after. See, I played when it was good, with Ruth and DiMaggio and Simmons. Goddamn, we were lucky to get nine men to put on the field some times. We had guys on the field, to tell you the truth, I couldn't tell you who they were right now. I think we had some boy from New Jersey, Bob Maier, on third base. Skeeter Webb was at short, Eddie Mayo at second, and the Indian, York, was on first. Cullenbine, myself, and anyone else who wanted to play were in the outfield.

That staff we had then was pretty good. Newhouser, Trout, Virgil Trucks, three or four other guys. But the guy we depended on if we wanted to win a ball game was Trout. Doggone, he wasn't afraid out there.

He had that one year [1944] where he won a lot of ball games and we just missed the pennant. The Browns beat us by a game. They were a wartime team. Nelson Potter and Jack Kramer were the pitchers. That's the only pennant that club ever won. When I was with Philly, they'd always be in last place or close to it. But hell, that's what a war will do for you.

I think we were a game up going into the last weekend. The Browns beat the Yankees three or four straight and we were closing against Washington. Washington had all those knuckleball pitchers—Nigeling, Leonard. They had four, I think. I had trouble with 'em. The key to hitting a knuckleball? I don't think anyone has found out yet. They wound up beating us out of a pennant.

The next year Greenberg came out of the service; sometime in

July, I think it was. He had a big effect. As nice a fella as you'd ever meet. He comes fishing down here in the summer, the next town down. I haven't seen him in a long while.

Anyway, it came down to the final game again. We played the Browns a doubleheader that last day. It rained like hell that week and it was still raining when we played. Nelson Potter pitched and they had us going into the last inning. Then we got runners on second and third and I was up.

I like to kid Hank about what happened. I was batting third, so they walked me to set up the double play. Greenberg was batting fourth and before you know it, he's hit one into the bleachers for a grand slam and we win the pennant.

After that, whenever I was somewhere and Hank was there, I'd remind him: "Remember the time they walked me to pitch to you?" That'd get him going: "Hey, tell them what really happened." I don't, of course.

The Cubs? They were about as bad as we were. We played three in Detroit and four in Chicago. That was because of travel restrictions.

We beat 'em in seven games. Hank Borowy won two games and came back to pitch the last game with a day's rest. Yeah, Hostetler was on the team. He cost us a game. All I know is that I hit the ball and he tried to score on it and he fell down. Naw, he shouldn't have been there. He couldn't play.

We beat Borowy the last game in Chicago. His arm was tired, I guess, because we didn't have any off days. We scored five or six runs in the first inning and we wound up clobbering them.

The war was over then. We came home. That was the end of it.

—April 1986

17

Eddie Mayo

Edward Joseph Mayoski
Born: April 15, 1910, Holyoke, Massachusetts
Major-league career: 1936 New York Giants, 1937–38 Boston
Braves, 1943 Philadelphia Athletics, 1944–48 Detroit Tigers

*A journeyman infielder when he came over to Detroit in 1944,
Eddie Mayo's glove helped solidify the Tigers' infield in the middle
forties. Although his statistics were ordinary, the scrappy second
baseman's true value to the Tigers is best measured by results. During his first four seasons with the club, the Tigers won a World Series and placed second three times. In 1945, the Sporting News recognized Mayo's contributions by selecting him as the American
League's Most Valuable Player.*

*A successful sales career has enabled Eddie Mayo to enjoy a
very comfortable life-style. Today he and his wife divide their time
between homes in Berlin, Maryland, and Palm Springs, California.*

I don't even watch the game anymore. There's so many . . . absurdities in the game today. The lack of discipline. These guys don't
even know the fundamentals. Some of my golfing partners talk

313

about that outfielder on Philadelphia. What's his name, Lenny Dykstra? "Oh, what a ball player!" they say. "He dives into bases. . . ."

Well, Christ, four hundred guys played like that back when there was sixteen teams. *Everybody* dove into bases, *everybody* came in spikes high, *everybody* ran out a ground ball. If you didn't play ball like that, you didn't stick around. But, compared to some of the clowns out there today, you find some guy like Dykstra is such a standout.

In my den here I've got a letter from Will Harridge, who was the president of the American League, when he fined me twenty-five dollars for knocking Skeeter Newsome on his ass. He was a shortstop for Boston. What happened? Well, we were playing in Detroit and he hit one to left center. A three-base hit. One of the tricks of the trade when you're a second baseman is to stand on the inside of the bag as the runner comes around. That way he has to make that wide turn. He can't cut it short.

So I'm just standing there, watching the outfield, and Newsome's got to make that wide turn, which made his three-base hit a two-and-a-half-base hit. He sees he can't make it to third. So, as he turned around and came back to second, he tossed out a couple expletives and popped me in the chest. I don't know why the hell he didn't throw a haymaker, 'cause he had me there, I wasn't even looking for it. I threw off my glove and—I remember it like it was yesterday—three jabs and a hook and he was on his ass. He was one guy I really wanted to demolish. But big Cal Hubbard, the umpire, jumped between us.

The *Sporting News* named me MVP and gave me a watch in 1945. We beat Chicago in the World Series that year. I was aggressive and I played every day and I think I contributed to the team winning the championship. I *contributed,* I wasn't responsible. We had a lot of great ball players on that team—Hal Newhouser, Hank Greenberg, Rudy York, Dizzy Trout, Roy Cullenbine, Doc Cramer, Paul Richards. But I fought every pitch. I was a fighter. I had to work hard for everything I got.

I guess I sound like an old-timer, don't I? My father came over from Poland in 1890 when he was about eighteen. The family name was Mayoski, but he recognized he was coming over to a new country, so he shortened it to Mayo. He settled in Massachusetts and learned the language. My dad did a little bit of everything. He was like a mechanic and a carpenter. My family moved to Clifton, New Jersey, when I was about six months old. I guess I was yelling so much that the mayor said, "Get him out of here."

I was born in 1910. Who knew baseball then? When I was four, five years old, the houses were few and far between, so most every kid had a ballpark right alongside his house. The ballpark consisted of an open lot and four stones. That was baseball then. I had a brother and two sisters. We were an athletic family. My brother played ball, and my one sister, who's still living, she was kind of a tomboy. My dad may have been an immigrant, but he knew enough baseball to hit a lot of fly balls to me when I was a kid.

We lived a block or two away from a beautiful park in Clifton. It was a double-decker from first base to third base, and the bleachers went all the way around to deep center field. Are you familiar with the blue laws? In the 1920s, in Brooklyn and Philadelphia, they were forbidden to play baseball on Sunday. As a result, the teams that were not playing in Philadelphia or Brooklyn always came into Clifton on Sunday and played strong semipro teams. That's where I got my exposure to major-league baseball.

I would say that park held twenty-five thousand people. You'd have fifteen or twenty trolley cars lined up on the streets on Sunday. These open trolley cars would come in from Paterson or Passaic and every town about five miles in every direction. Baseball was a big thing in Clifton, New Jersey, at that time.

You know, in those days before television, semipro baseball was a way of life. Every community had a team representing them, and they weren't shy about importing players from wherever. In fact, I played for eight different teams in eight different cities. A different team each day and twice on Sunday. We'd play in Paterson, then hightail it up into New York state. It was quite common in north Jersey. You'd see the same fellas but on different teams.

Semipro was the birth of a lot of ball players at that time. There were scouts all over and my exposure playing for eight different teams all over north Jersey helped me get noticed. One day a Detroit Tigers scout, a fellow by the name of Ike McAuley, came to the house. I was going away that fall on a basketball scholarship to Providence College in Providence, Rhode Island. I was to leave right after Labor Day, and a week or two before that he said, "How'd you like to play for the Detroit Tigers?"

Well, you know what that means. I gave up my scholarship and went to play in the minor leagues. They farmed me to Huntington, West Virginia. That was a Class C team in the Mid-Atlantic League.

That was 1932. That was the year the depression really set in. As I recall, the number of minor leagues had dropped to fourteen or fifteen. A lot of teams were folding. I'd signed with Detroit for $175 a month. Midway through the season—we played a split season—the owners called us in.

"You know what's going on all around," they said. "We don't know whether we're going to make it, but we're going to try. The only hope we have is if you agree to take a cut in salary of fifty percent."

Thank God they didn't know math. They offered me one hundred dollars a month. That's twenty-five dollars a week, and you had to pay for your own room and board. Of course, when you went on the road you stayed at the best hotels and the club paid for your room and board. I always got a dollar and a half a day meal money. You couldn't tip very well on that.

You ever been to Beckley, West Virginia? The Beckley Hotel is about two blocks long with twenty rooms on the second floor. It had a men's room and a tub at one end of the hall and a ladies room and a tub at the other end. They filled the tub up one time, that was it. At the end of the game, fifteen muddy, clay-clogged kids jumped in and out of the tub and then went across the street to Greasy John's, where you spent the balance of your dollar and a half a day on a hot dog and a Coke.

We had three Model A Fords at the time, with running boards on the side. They had an expansion luggage rack on the running board on the left side. You put your suit roll in there. After you'd played a night game you'd travel from Huntington, West Virginia, to Johnstown, Pennsylvania. That was about 350 or 400 miles. You'd drive all night long and get in Johnstown just in time to play another game. But that was baseball then. And you loved it. That was great.

I was a third baseman at that time. I also played some shortstop. In 1936 I was purchased by the Baltimore Orioles of the International League for the great sum of twenty-five thousand dollars and a player. Joe DiMaggio was purchased from San Francisco by the Yankees that same year for the same amount of money, but I commanded a higher purchase price by one player. But from that point on, all similarities cease.

I came up with the Giants. Bill Terry was the manager. I was a left-handed hitter, and at that time they needed someone with a little power. I used to hit twenty-five, twenty-six home runs a year. I was to fill in for Travis Jackson, who had been an All-Star shortstop for New York before he switched over to third base. He was having knee problems, so whenever he tired I guess I was supposed to fill in.

I went three for five my first game in the Polo Grounds. I would've been four for five, except I backed the right fielder up against the fence. He made one of those stretch catches. But it was a memorable day as far as I was concerned. We won the pennant that year and the Yankees beat us in the World Series in six games. I played a little. One time at bat and a couple innings in the field.

I never really got nervous. You get excited. Talk about nervousness, though. . . . I remember Doc Cramer, who was a great ball player. We started off this one season when we were both with Detroit. He was the first hitter and I was second. I was in the on-deck circle and I could actually see where Doc, his whole body was shaking on that first pitch. Now, Doc had been a veteran for fifteen years then. After that first pitch, though, it's all over. I guess it's like going to see a dentist the first time.

New York was overloaded with left-handed hitters—Terry, Mel Ott, Jo-Jo Moore—so they traded me to the Boston Braves after '36. I played a couple seasons there. Bill McKechnie was the manager that first year, then Casey Stengel the following year. I don't think I was given an honest chance to prove myself. Not really. Joe DiMaggio had a great rookie year with the Yankees. Then the following year his brother Vince came up with Boston. He was an outfielder and they tried to make a third baseman out of him. They were trying to capitalize on the name. I don't want to sound like sour grapes. I'm happy the way things worked out.

I was sold to Los Angeles, the Cubs' farm team in the Pacific Coast League. They kept me down there for five years. I was playing third base, shortstop, second base, and on occasion, first. If you check the minor-league records, you'll see I had some great years. Lots of home runs and hitting and everything. But there was no future with the Cubs because of Stan Hack at third and Billy Herman on second. They were fairly young, so I could've been with Los Angeles until I died of old age.

Back then, the Pacific Coast League didn't even know the majors existed. That was the major leagues out there. A very strong league. If you were a club owner and you had some players out there and you're making some money, you're not about to get rid of them. Los Angeles wasn't about to sell me because it was a profitable operation.

But in 1943 I was drafted by the Philadelphia A's. I was thirty-three years old then. And talk about bad breaks. The Sunday before the start of the season, we were playing an exhibition game in Bloomington, Delaware. I played third base then. I had a fellow in a rundown and the ball hit the runner's head and caromed off and hit me in my left eye. Caused a retinal hemorrhage. I opened up the season with a patch over my eye. I continued the entire season with a blind spot in my eye. I still have it. If I focus with my left eye, there's kind of a gray area there.

Philadelphia tried to send me to Louisville, but Detroit claimed me. That was in 1944. I played for Steve O'Neill. In my opinion, he was the greatest humanist and manager of ball players that I've ever known. A great strategist and a very understanding man. He was the kind of manager who said, "You're a major-leaguer, you know how to play ball," and left you alone.

I played second base and Skeeter Webb was the shortstop. He was married to one of Steve O'Neill's daughters. A great shortstop. He wasn't a good hitter, but a good base runner and a fine fielder. I enjoyed playing with the guy. But the fact that he was Steve O'Neill's son-in-law was just blown out of proportion. He came over from the White Sox and replaced Joe Hoover at shortstop, but that had nothing to do with it. I don't know how the press, how they distort things. If he's doing the job, who cares? With the bases loaded and the last ground ball of the World Series coming down to shortstop, I'd want him out there. He's going to handle it for me.

Rudy York played first base. I don't know what his IQ was or if he ever graduated from grammar school, but he was the smartest base runner I ever saw. You know how intricate the signs can be, the take-offs and everything. They change according to the inning or the situation. Rudy would get on second base and it was fabulous how he could steal their signs. You could count on it. He'd be on base and rub his shirt: *I've got 'em.* He'd tip off the signs and you could go to the bank with it.

Those first two years I was with Detroit, we had great pennant races. I remember 1944 vividly. We had a one-game lead over St. Louis with four games to go. Washington came into town, and we had beaten them sixteen of eighteen games that summer. We're thinking, we win two out of four, we're home.

Meanwhile, the Yankees went into St. Louis, through Cleveland. They'd had a very successful series in Cleveland. Yankee pitchers had a two-hitter, a three-hitter, and two four-hitters in St. Louis—and lost all four games. We won two out of four and the Browns won four straight. That was a crusher, a real crusher. Spoiled the whole winter for me.

We won the pennant the following year, however, by a game and a half over Washington. That was a rather unique situation there.

Eddie Mayo in 1945. (Courtesy of the Burton Historical Collection of the Detroit Public Library.)

Washington had finished the season a week earlier because the Redskins were starting their football season. We were ahead of them by a couple games in the loss column, I believe, so there were several scenarios possible. We could win the pennant, we could lose it, or we could tie, depending on what we did that last weekend in St. Louis.

We had two games with the Browns. The Saturday game got rained out, so we had a doubleheader for Sunday. It rained like hell all night. In fact, the field was inundated. They had to delay the game because they had to bring straw and tons of newspapers out on the field to soak up the water. It was still drizzling when the game started. I think it was Cal Hubbard behind the plate, and he said, "Once we start, we're going to go through without stopping."

As the game started, it really started to pour. It just poured all day long. Of course, Greenberg hit that tremendous home run and won the game for us. That clinched it for us. St. Louis was battling the Yankees for third-place money—a couple hundred dollars difference—and they would've dropped into fourth place if we beat them the second game. I remember Luke Sewell, the St. Louis manager, decided, "Well, it's raining now," so they called the second game off.

The Cubs had Stan Hack, Phil Cavaretta, Swish Nicholson.

Great guys. What I remember about that series is that it was cold, very cold. I remember Claude Passeau pitched one game in Detroit. He was a great pitcher, but I think he pulled a snow job on the umpires and us. He had rheumatic hands and he had to kind of twist the ball in his glove to get a grip on it. We were all so naive. He's saying it's cold, he's got arthritic fingers, but he must've had sandpaper in there because he shut us out on one hit.

Our two workhorses back then were Hal Newhouser and Dizzy Trout. Trout was overpowering. He'd break the bat off in your hands. Entirely different pitcher than Newhouser. Hal would finesse you, whereas Trout would challenge you. Trout was a good hitter, too, and a lot of fun to have on the team.

Hal was a great pitcher. He wasn't a thrower like some of these guys in baseball today, he was a pitcher. He had all the ammunition that goes with a great arm. I watch an inning or two today and these guys have no idea what they're doing out there. They're just throwing the ball.

But not Hal. As an infielder you'd get into a situation where the game is on the bases. You'd go out to the mound and say to Hal, "How are you gonna pitch to this fella?" He'd say, "How do you want me to?" I'd say, "Look, I'm gonna play in such and such a place. Make him hit the ball to me and we'll get a double play for you." It was a pleasure to play behind him.

Paul Richards was probably the smartest catcher that I ever played in front of. I remember vividly the seventh game of the World Series in Chicago. We'd each won three games, and we jumped out to a five-run lead the very first inning. Hal was pitching.

Hal went out to the mound to pitch the bottom of the first. Having played behind Hal, you could almost sense how long he was going to last. When he was on, his fastball wouldn't just sail in there, it had a hop. And his curveball wouldn't roll, it would snap. I took my position at second base in the first inning. I was watching him throw to Richards and I said to myself, "Oh-oh, I hope Steve's got somebody warming up because Hal's ball isn't hopping." Apparently, Richards sensed the same thing about Hal's pitches not moving. I looked at the bullpen and there were five pitchers warming up already: Trout, Trucks, Benton, Bridges, and I forget who else. Not one guy, but five.

The Cubs were laying back, waiting for that fastball. Well, Richards called change-ups on about four of five pitches, a completely different pattern from Hal's usual kind of pitching. Then the third or fourth inning, Hal got his second wind and his ball started to come alive. Richards sensed this and after that it was fastball, fastball. The Cubs were standing in there, waiting for those change-ups, and they just kept fouling those fastballs off. That's why I say Richards was a great catcher. He could sense every mood of the pitcher.

Our check for winning the series was about $6,500. That was about half of what I was making then, which was about $14,000. I remember when I was with the Giants in '36 the loser's share was $4,600. Of course, at that time you could buy a Cadillac for $1,100. Taxes were two percent. In 1945, that same Cadillac cost $1,500. You could buy a three-bedroom home for $5,500. It's all relative.

There were no endorsements in those times. I think it wasn't until 1947 or '48 that the bubble gum cards came out. Topps gave us two or three hundred dollars, something like that. There was no TV then. Television didn't come in until '48. I got a raise after we won the World Series, but I really don't know what it was. We're talking about forty-five years ago, aren't we? I can't even remember what I had for breakfast.

I played regular through 1948. I was in spring training with the

On behalf of the defending world champions, manager Steve O'Neill accepts the traditional floral horseshoe from the Detroit Fire Department on opening day, 1946. Directly behind O'Neill is Hal Newhouser, who won two games in the series. Eddie Mayo stands at the extreme right of the group. (Courtesy of the Detroit Tigers.)

Tigers in '49. The Tigers had acquired the Toledo franchise from the Browns in the fall of '48. Billy Evans, who was the general manager, said, "Ed, we're looking for a manager. Would you be interested?" I said, "Sure." Starting at Triple-A? I jumped at the chance.

They were training at Bartow, about twelve miles from Lakeland. I packed my bags and got over to the ballpark that morning. Slick Coffman was the pitching coach. I said, "Slick, the only way I can get a line on these ball players is to have an intrasquad game." Slick said, "Ed, if you and I play, we'll have enough for one team." We had seven players. That was it. The Tigers had bought the franchise, not the players.

One of the players was Ray Herbert, and another was his brother, who was a catcher. He had limited talent, but the only way the Tigers could get Ray was if they signed his brother, too.

Ray was a kid right out of high school in Detroit. Good kid, good stuff. Never lost a ball game until he turned pro. That was up in Minneapolis. A powerful hitting team. I had to take him out and, oh, that hurt me. He went in the clubhouse and I went in after him. This was during the ball game. He was sitting in there, crying. Boy, I had to tell that kid everything I knew, that this wasn't going to be the last time he was going to get his brains beat out. Ray was a kid who listened. He was hungry for advice, and it paid off. He was up in the major leagues in a year and a half and he had a successful career.

I managed Toledo in the American Association for two years. Then I coached with the Red Sox in '51 and with the Phillies from '52 to '54. But then I realized that in baseball, you're vulnerable as hell. As a coach, your future lies in the success of the manager, and the manager's future lies in the success of his players. I had an opportunity to get into private industry and make a hell of a lot more money. A lot of responsibilities, a challenge—that's what I wanted. I don't think my baseball background helped me, not in the business I went into, which was selling ceramic tile.

I was preparing myself. I realized I wasn't going to last forever in baseball. The company to whom I went, I knew some people who were in that business. So in the fall and winters I used to go and visit with them. I learned all the intricacies of installing tile. It's entirely different now, but back in the fifties, the ceramic tile business were essentially masons, Italian people. Mostly it was masons who came in, put mortar on the wall, threw tile on the wall and on the floor. It was interesting. It was fascinating to hear those guys talk. In fact, my ambition at that time was to open up a distributorship in the ceramic tile business. Then this other sales opportunity opened up, so I grabbed that instead of investing my own money. People didn't know who the hell Eddie Mayo was when I talked to them. It was just a business proposition. It was a good company with quality service, and that's what we did. I made a good living.

It's ironic—*criminal*—that a lot of the ball players who contributed to baseball, so many of my older friends who were in baseball and got out of it before the pension plan started in 1946, got no credit for their service. Yet so many of these fellows were out giving speeches night after night during the winter, putting on clinics, and never got paid for it. And they've never realized a dime from the pension fund. It's a damn shame.

You know, two years ago I was out in California during the winter. An old friend of mine, Johnny Vander Meer—double no-hit Johnny—called me up. Johnny grew up in north Jersey and pitched for Cincinnati. He was out at a card show. We went out to dinner and we were cutting up old times when he said, "Why don't you get into this card thing? You know, I made more money last year signing cards than I ever made when I was playing."

I said, "John, I get anywhere from six to eight requests a week for autographs and I'm tickled to death. I don't charge. Those that want to charge, fine. It's against my philosophy."

I guess there's a big address book of players past and present that shows who their agents are and what they charge. I guess they have my name and it says "no charge." That's why they want my autograph. So, anyway, these promoters get these ball players and. . . well, let them do their own thing. It's not for me.

The thing I want to point out is, Johnny's also on this baseball old-timers committee that gives relief to some of these old-time ball players. It would spin your head to know some of the ball players that are on welfare. I'm not free to tell you who they are. It's a damn shame these same fellows who contributed so much of their time in the promotion of the game should be on baseball welfare.

As I said, I had an opportunity to get into private industry with a ceramic tile manufacturing company. I was vice president of sales. We had corporate offices in Boston and plants and warehouses coast to coast. I was with them from 1955 to 1970, and then I became president of Pedersen Golf Corporation, a manufacturer of custom-built golf clubs. It's a regional golf company in Wilton, Connecticut. After that I owned a couple steak houses in New Jersey. I retired on my sixty-third birthday and I've been retired ever since.

We have a couple of homes. Both are on the golf course. We have a house here on the eighth tee. The house in California is on the third tee. Both are planned communities, not senior communities. I get out maybe three, four, five, six times a week. Get out there and just hack away. I haven't worn a watch in years. But don't tell the *Sporting News* that.

—June 1990

18

Ed Mierkowicz

Edward Frank Mierkowicz
Born: March 6, 1924, Wyandotte, Michigan
Major-league career: 1945, 1947–48 Detroit Tigers, 1950 St. Louis
Cardinals

Ed Mierkowicz played parts of three seasons as an outfielder for Detroit during the 1940s, hitting .177 in a total of thirty-four games. "I was a typical wartime ball player," he said. "Really, if it wasn't for the war, I probably never would've been called up." Mierkowicz spent fourteen years in the minors, emerging for one final major league at-bat with the Cardinals in 1950. He struck out.

In 1984 Mierkowicz retired after working twenty years at the waste treatment plant in Wyandotte, Michigan. Today he and his wife live in an apartment on nearby Grosse Ile.

You know, it's a funny thing. Maybe the younger ball players will feel, "Well, here's an old-timer talking." But you know, I never really thought that much about money, because I loved to play base-ball. Hey, that was better than carrying that lunch bucket. Where the hell could you get paid to play a sport? That was really something. To me it was.

I played against fellas from Pennsylvania in the minor leagues. Their fathers worked in the coal mines, they were being groomed for the coal mines, and they'd say, "I've got to make it. I don't want to have to work in those mines." It was their goal. The odds were very heavy against them making the big leagues. Even playing minor-league ball was something.

Do you know a fella named King Boring? I played sandlot ball around Detroit for him. He started me about 1939, 1940. Super guy. A lot of b.s. Made you feel like a superstar, even if you weren't. He was that kind of guy. I was just a kid in high school, you know. Whenever you did something, he'd say, "You're the greatest." Which was good. Built your confidence.

I can remember in 1940 when I was playing for King and he used to run me over to Toledo. He had a working agreement with the St. Louis Browns as a scout. One time we worked out when Toledo was playing Columbus. This was when Columbus had all these good future Cardinal players, guys like Harry Breechen and Harry Walker. Fred Haney was the Toledo manager, and before the game he took me up to the batting cage during batting practice.

Here I am, just a kid, and Fred Haney said, "Let the kid hit a couple."

Those guys took one look and said, "Get that little bastard out of here!"

It was a little different then, see? They didn't want me taking up their time. As the years went along, players accepted these things a little better, but at that time they always felt that insecurity, always felt that somebody was going to take their jobs.

I attended Roosevelt High School in Wyandotte. I was a three-sport man. I had eight or ten scholarships, but I wasn't a great student. I was all sports. My dad always wanted me to go to college. He would've been so proud. He always wanted one of us to go in our family. He worked in the gasket factory all his life, so when I got the scholarships he said, "Now it's easier for you to go." But it wasn't in me to go to school. In those days, a lot of us didn't go to school.

I got a big break my last year in high school. We played Dearborn Fordson, and there were some Tiger scouts there to watch the Fordson pitcher. I hit two long home runs and a double, drove in five runs, and we beat the guy, 5–2. First game that pitcher lost in four years of high school. I heard later that he got killed on Iwo Jima. Anyway, I caught the eye of Wish Egan, the Tigers' chief scout.

First there was the army. I got called up in 1943. I wanted to go in anyway because all my friends were in. It was different in those days. It was a world war. You couldn't run to Canada because Canada was fighting too. You went because you had to. Hell, Greenberg was in and he was thirty-four. He didn't have any business being in there. He had flat feet.

I went to Little Rock, Arkansas, for training, and that's as far as I got. I was in for eight months and my outfit went to Africa. I had rheumatic fever and got discharged. Pretty soon after I got home, Wish Egan signed me up. He had stopped by the house and talked to my parents. He said, "How about playing ball for us?" I said, "Sure." This was 1944, and most of the good players were in the service.

They assigned me to Hagerstown, Maryland, in the Interstate League. Then I went to Buffalo the next year. I came up to the Tigers in August 1945. Me and Billy Pierce, Art Houtteman, and Johnny McHale all got called up from Buffalo together. All of us were Detroit kids. We all had a chance to sit there.

It was a real tight race that summer. We beat out Washington by a game. Greenberg came out of the service the last half of the season and helped us win it. On the last day of the season we had a one-game lead, and we had to beat the Browns to clinch the pennant. Greenberg hit one off of Nelson Potter, a grand slam in the bottom of the ninth when we were behind, and that put us in the World Series against the Cubs.

We won in seven games. Newhouser beat 'em 9–3 in the final game at Wrigley Field. I took Greenberg's place in left field in the last inning of that last game. Nervous, you know, but a big thrill. In fact, it was so much that I couldn't handle it. My folks in the stands . . . hell, you go from high school to the majors in a couple years and you're in all this excitement. But it was a nice break for me. I got a World Series ring. Some guys play ball for thirty years and never get one. We came back that night on the train and, Christ, there were ten thousand people waiting for us at Union Station on Fort Street.

The next year I went back to Buffalo, Triple-A ball. They had super ball clubs. Guys who were in the service for three or four years had to play some place before they came back to the big leagues. Guys like Hank Sauer, Eddie Majeski, Ewell Blackwell. Every club had at least three or four guys who were big-league ball players. Triple-A ball in '46 was better than major-league ball had been in 1945.

Vic Wertz and I played the outfield in Buffalo, and we both

came up at the end of '46. I stayed until 1948, and Vic stayed what—nineteen or twenty years?

I played against left-handers for the Tigers. I'd get a couple hits, and I figured I was going to play. Then I'd sit on the bench for a month.

Vic and I used to room together, and I remember there were nights when we'd go out—Neil Berry, Vic, and I—and have a couple of beers. We'd talk, you know how guys are: "I think I'm going to play a little bit more." And Vic would say, "Yeah, you're going to play, Merk."

After I hit a home run off the Yankees' Eddie Lopat here in Tiger Stadium, we went out that night and I said, "Yeah, I think I'm going to play more now." But I didn't play for a whole month then. The next time I played, I got a double and single off Mel Parnell up in Boston, and back on the bench again.

I always felt that I came up too fast. Of course, sitting there wasn't helping me. I sat a lot. I wanted to play. I think that if I

Ed Mierkowicz with fellow Wyandotte native Bob Kuzava at Briggs Stadium in 1946.

could've played, at least I could've satisfied myself that I couldn't make it. But this way, I never proved it.

In 1949 I got sent to the Cardinals organization, and I had a good year at Rochester playing under Johnny Keane. I hit .300, hit about forty doubles, eighteen home runs, and they brought me up. But who did St. Louis have in the outfield? Stan Musial, Enos Slaughter, and Terry Moore. I'm there, you know, but what the hell am I doing here? I want to play. It's nice, but you're not going to play very much with those guys in front of you. And in the old days you stayed with one ball club until you died.

I can remember going down to the offices in Briggs Stadium once to see [Tiger general manager] Billy Evans about a raise. I was a kid, I walked in, and that son-of-a-bitchin' room was as big as this house. It scared you. Billy would sit back in his chair with that long cigar and give you a hard time for what—a hundred dollars?

In Buffalo that year I hit about twenty-five home runs, drove in one hundred runs, hit .325. And he don't even know my average!

He said, "What are you asking for?"

I told him, "I'm asking for about two hundred extra a month." A twelve-hundred dollar raise.

Well, for chrissakes, he jumped that high!

You know what he told me? He said, "Can you do anything else besides play baseball? You want to go work at Wyandotte Chemicals over there?" You know, made you feel like a real asshole. In other words, if you don't want what we're offering, get going. Get your lunch bucket.

I feel great for ball players now because they don't have to take that huff. Now a ball player will say, "My time is limited as far as playing and making money, so I've got to make it fast." I can understand that point. It's just like you working for somebody. Of course, I don't think I have the right to say, "Hey, I want half of your business." After all, the person that I play for, he started that business. But he's going to pay me a fair wage, and if I think I should make more I can quit and go someplace else. Well, that falls under today's free agency clause. Which is good. It's like everything else in life— things have gotten better. Kids go to school, they've got something going, they can say, "Hey, I don't have to play baseball." Of course, they can say that because they know the owners need the good ball players.

I finally quit playing in 1957. I'd already played in Mexico and Cuba and for a half-dozen minor-league clubs. I finished up that year with San Antonio, Baltimore's Double-A club. A good team, too. Had Brooks Robinson at third and Boog Powell playing first. We won the pennant that year, but lost the play-off. I had a pretty good power year, but I was slowing down. Hell, I was thirty-four, and getting tired. Anyways, the big leagues is where you want to play. The minor leagues and all that, it's nothing. It's shit really. I'd known for a long time that I'd never make it back to the majors. I was playing simply because I loved playing.

I'm working for the county now. I'm a mechanic here at the waste treatment plant. My job is to rebuild these big pumps. Got some heavy ones. I didn't know anything about mechanics, but after seventeen years, I do now. I make good money—twelve bucks an hour, plus overtime.

They had a reunion for us last summer back at Wrigley Field. The 1945 World Series teams. Geez, I couldn't believe it. Out of our group, eleven Tigers were dead. Doc Cramer was seventy-four, could hardly walk. Jimmy Outlaw, Paul Richards—old men. I looked at those guys and I closed my eyes and envisioned when I used to play by them. Turn the clock back thirty-five or forty years. Those guys were young guys.

I knew Doc Cramer's family. His wife just passed away. We were talking and I said, "Doc, remember when we were in Detroit and your daughter was graduating and you bought her that convertible in Pontiac as a present?"

And he said, "You know, Ed, my daughter died about three years ago." And that was sad.

We played a three-inning game. I hit against Dutch Leonard and he walked me twice. Billy Pierce pitched for us, and Paul Richards caught him. Man, I told him, "Paul, that's really something for someone your age to go out and catch." He was seventy-nine.

These days I always think of baseball. You're a ball player and that time goes by so fast. Just like a shot at the World Series. It's only one moment, really, and it's over. You know what I'm trying to describe? It happens, and then it's over. There's six or seven days of it, and you think it's going to last forever, but it doesn't.

—June 1981

19

George Kell

George Clyde Kell
Born: August 23, 1922, Swifton, Arkansas
Major-league career: 1943–46 Philadelphia Athletics, 1946–52 Detroit Tigers, 1952–54 Boston Red Sox, 1954–56 Chicago White Sox, 1956–57 Baltimore Orioles

George Kell came to Detroit from the Philadelphia Athletics on May 18, 1946, in a trade for Barney McCosky. He quickly fashioned a reputation as the game's finest all-around third baseman. The perennial All-Star was a slick glove man that at one point led the league in fielding seven straight seasons, as well as a line-drive spray hitter that batted over .300 nine times, including all seven seasons with Detroit. He hit .343 in 1949, becoming the first American League third baseman to win a batting championship. Kell twice led the league in hits and doubles; no major leaguer since has matched his fifty-six two-base hits in 1950.

Kell finished his career in Baltimore. "After I saw Brooks Robinson play third base, I decided it was time to retire," said Kell, who along with Robinson was inducted into the Baseball Hall of Fame in 1983.

George Kell has been a broadcaster for the Tigers since 1959. Today he and his wife live in a sprawling brick ranch in their hometown of Swifton, Arkansas.

I've always thought that the best years of baseball were the 1940s and '50s. There were just so many great, outstanding ball players playing then. Williams . . . DiMaggio . . . Berra . . . Rizzuto . . . Feller. I could just go on and on. I felt even as I was playing that this was major-league baseball at its absolute finest.

And I think about those days. Oh yeah. I remember the dirt and the sweat, how the grass smelled all freshly mowed. I think about the Yankees coming to town for a big series and those big crowds . . . the sun shining and the players hollering . . . the umpires wearing those suits and ties on a hot afternoon. When I'm broadcasting a game in Tiger Stadium—or what used to be Briggs Stadium when I played—I find myself thinking about some play or game that happened thirty years ago on that same ball field. The time I dove and grabbed a line drive off Lou Boudreau in the ninth inning with the bases loaded. Or the home run I hit here in the '51 All-Star Game. I don't know if that kind of feeling is possible at most other ballparks. I *know* it's not.

I can truly say that I'm happy I played when I did. I honestly am. I can watch a game at the park or back in my hotel room and I've got to wonder if the ball players today are having any fun. They're better athletes and they're making so much money, but I don't know, the atmosphere that I loved is just lacking for some reason.

I grew up in Swifton, which was just a little farm community then. Still is. My dad would take me and my brothers out on those rocky old fields and play ball with us. We had a radio then and I remember how I could hardly go to bed at night not knowing all the scores from the big leagues. St. Louis is about two hundred miles north of here, so I was always a Cardinals fan. When I was about fifteen or so my aunts gave me "knothole passes" and I'd take the trolley down to watch that old Gas House Gang play: Pepper Martin, Dizzy Dean, those guys. I think I knew right from the start, right from when I was small, that I wanted to be a major-league ballplayer.

See, my father was a pitcher and a shortstop and just an outstanding amateur athlete. That's the way he got to Swifton. He was

George Kell in 1950. (Courtesy of the Burton Historical Collection of the Detroit Public Library.)

a barber at a town up in the hills in Arkansas. The local team used to hire him to come down and pitch on Wednesdays and Sundays when they had their big games against the other towns. Back in those days, every small town had a baseball team, and they were very competitive. They finally told him, "Hey, we'll buy the barbershop here in town and give it to you and pay you to pitch if you'll just come down and be part of us." He moved down here and stayed . . . well, I've been here every day of my life.

My father raised three sons fully convinced that they were all going to be major-league baseball players, if not Hall of Famers. The three of us played ball together all the time. My middle brother, Frank, and I were only eighteen months apart. My other brother, Skeeter, was much younger. Two of us did play in the major leagues. I played, of course, and Skeeter played one season with Philadelphia. Frank was killed in World War II or else my father may have been right.

I started off playing American Legion ball right here in Newport in 1937, '38, and '39. I graduated from high school in '39 and went to Arkansas State at Jonesboro for one year. The Brooklyn Dodgers had a minor-league club in Newport. I came back here and signed with the Dodger chain. They released me, so in 1942 I went to Lancaster, Pennsylvania. In '43 Connie Mack bought me.

I'd just finished up a big year at Lancaster. I'd batted .396 and we'd won the pennant and the play-offs. Towards the end of the season Mr. Mack came down to see me play a doubleheader. They tried to keep it secret, but my mother and father were there and they told me, "Mr. Mack is in the stands to take a look at you."

Well, that day I got five base hits, including three home runs, and I wasn't even a home run hitter. Mr. Mack came through the dressing room after the game. He was shaking hands with everyone, and when he came up to my locker he said, "Young man, I've just purchased your contract. You're coming to Philadelphia with me."

Lancaster was only sixty miles from Philadelphia, so I drove up and reported to Shibe Park and played one game against St. Louis. It was the end of the season—a weekday—and the Philadelphia A's were probably in last place, or close to it. No big crowd, best as I can remember. Maybe seven thousand people. I really don't remember a lot about it. I don't remember being nervous or scared or anything. I don't know, maybe I was a little cocky. I felt that I could play with anyone, that I belonged up there. Even though I was coming from a Class B league into the majors.

So I stepped right in. A big left-hander by the name of Al Milnar was pitching for the Browns that day. I had a three-base hit my first time up and that was the only hit I had. I had this schoolteacher's contract so I drove home to Arkansas after the game and started teaching school.

I'd gone to college just that one year, but during the war they issued emergency certificates. They were just huntin' all the teachers they could get. My wife Charlene was teaching school—second, third grade. I was doing nothing during the wintertime, so I just got my certificate and started teaching. I taught high school phys ed and various classes.

The miracle is, looking back on it now, is how we played baseball at all with a war on. How we traveled, how we could justify burning the lights, how people got to the ballpark with rationing of gasoline. I don't see how we justified it all. We traveled by train then. We didn't have berths all the time. Didn't always have compartments. I know we made some trips where we stood all night or slept in our seats. But that was travel. Travel wasn't always that easy in those days.

I remember when we were in the play-offs in 1943 against York. I was playing for Lancaster. It was the final ball game of the year. In the middle of the game we had a blackout. All the lights went out, so we sat in the dark for thirty or forty-five minutes. When the lights went back on, second base was missing. Somebody took it as a prank, I guess. It took another thirty minutes to find a bag to put out there so we could finish the ball game.

When I went to spring training the next year with Philadelphia, we had to train in the east, at Frederick, Maryland, because of the travel restrictions. And it was cold. We worked out in extremely cold weather. You can imagine what the weather is like in Detroit or anywhere else in the east in March. We played a lot of games in the snow.

Our exhibition games were mostly against service clubs. We played the Coast Guard Academy and we went to the navy base at Annapolis and played the teams over there. I remember playing a game in Frederick one Sunday afternoon and it snowed the whole ball game. We didn't even stop playing. We had old wood heaters in the dressing rooms beneath the stands. Those old concrete floors and everything . . . I remember how cold it was to shower and dress before and after the games. It seemed like it was always cold. But, Christ, I couldn't gripe about that. With a war going on, certainly we weren't going to be griping.

My brother Frank went through the war. He was a pilot and died in the Army of Occupation [in Germany] six months after the war was over. He was just fixin' to come home when it happened. He and three other pilots were living in this house. I don't know exactly what they did in the Army of Occupation, but they did fly. One crew flew at night and the other two flew during the day.

It gets awfully cold in the wintertime there. They had these old gas stoves heating the house. These other two pilots came in one morning and found Frank and another boy dead from fumes. They think it was sabotage, that somebody had turned the gas off from outside and then turned it back on. Of course, it was devastating, as you can well imagine. My father arranged to bring Frank back home for a proper burial.

Like everyone else, I'd registered for the draft. In 1944, my first full year with Philadelphia, I was called up. I'd had a bad knee all through high school and college, so they rejected me. I don't know why, it wasn't that bad. I know my draft board kept reviewing my status and I'd report to them. I'd get notices from them and I'd be shifted from 2-A to 1-A to this, that, and the other, but I was never put on any kind of permanent status. I was so young and gung-ho then about everything . . . I was gung-ho about playing major-league baseball, if they'd called me into the service I would've been gung-ho about that, too. There were guys being called up every day during the season and we talked about it: "You going next?" "Yeah, I guess. Whenever I get my call."

The caliber of play was down, absolutely, looking at it now. Mayo Smith was on the team with me in '45. He was an outfielder called up from the minor leagues. A typical wartime ball player. He never would've played without the war. As soon as the fighting was over, he was back in the minors. But I didn't know any different because I'd come from a Class B league. To me it was still the major leagues and much better than what I'd been playing against.

The Browns used a one-armed outfielder for a season. Pete Gray was an oddity, to say the least. A one-armed man just can't play major-league baseball. A one-armed man can't play good minor-league baseball. But this was during the war, and I imagine Pete Gray was first signed as a sort of drawing card.

The strange thing about it was that the fella could hit with that one arm. And he could run like a deer. So this helped him a lot. But in the outfield he had his problems catching the ball and throwing

The Browns' one-armed outfielder swings a bat in 1945: "Pete Gray was an oddity, to say the least."

it, especially if somebody was tagging up to advance a base. He'd throw his glove under that stub real quick and bring the ball out real quick. He had it down to a science. He'd come up with the ball throwing, but there was a delay there and it bothered him. He didn't have real good power, but he swung the bat pretty good. I don't know what he hit. I can't imagine he hit a whole lot, about .220 or so. He went back to the minor leagues after the guys came back from the war.

Hell, I was in over my head, coming from a Class B league to the majors. My first year up I hit .268 and the next year .272, which by today's standards is good, but in those days wasn't all that good. Those two seasons, 1944 and 1945, I spent growing up and learning the pitchers, so by my third season I was hitting .320.

The first time I really realized the difference was in 1946 when everyone began to come back from the service. We opened the season in Philadelphia against the Yankees. There was a tremendous crowd on hand, of course. DiMaggio was there, and Rizzuto, Dickey, and guys I'd always heard of and never thought I'd have the chance to actually play against. That was when I realized I was in the big leagues.

Mr. Mack had about six or seven infielders coming back after the war—Pete Suder, Jack Wallaesa, there was a bunch of 'em. Everybody kept telling me, "When all these guys get back, there won't be a place for you because they played regular before you got here." That's what they kept telling me.

Well, when they came back, they didn't beat me out. I was the regular third baseman. But Mr. Mack had a shortage of outfielders and had a surplus of infielders. We went into Detroit one weekend in 1946 to play a series. The Tigers, who needed a third baseman badly, told Mr. Mack he could have their pick of any of their outfielders, except Dick Wakefield, for me. He had two or three third basemen, so he said, "Fine."

Detroit swapped Barney McCosky for me. I was just a kid when they traded me, and I remember Mr. Mack telling me, "I hate to get rid of you, son, but this is the best thing that's ever happened to you. You're a good ball player. You'll go to Detroit where they'll draw a lot of people and they'll pay you a lot of money."

I thought, "Well, that's just a lot of talk from an old man who feels sorry for me right now." But it turned out to be exactly like he said. I had a lot of good years in Detroit, they drew a lot of people, and they paid me a lot of money.

I made $3,000 the first year I played in the major leagues. I got $5,000 the second year and then the third year I asked for $8,500. Mr. Mack offered $6,500 and we wrangled around. I finally went to spring training and he said, "I'll give you the other $2,000 if you have as good a year as you had the first two." We left it at that. Then he traded me to Detroit in May and the first thing they asked me is, "How much money are you making?" I said, "Sixty-five hundred. But Mr. Mack said he'd give me $8,500 if I had a good year." The Tigers told me, "When we trade for you, you've already had a good year."

I believed it. When I walked into the Detroit clubhouse I felt for the first time that I was playing for a big-league team. It was just a completely different atmosphere from Philadelphia. Here's a team that had won the World Series the year before. I remember Dizzy Trout coming up to me, putting his arm around me and saying, "You're just what we need. We can win this thing with you at third base." So the Tigers gave me eighty-five hundred right there, retroactive to the start of the season. Then at the end of the year, after I'd hit .320, they gave me twenty-five hundred more and raised my salary to fifteen thousand for 1947. I was on my way then.

Detroit was more of a working-class town then. Everything revolved around the automobile. We didn't play night games because we didn't have lights. The ball games didn't start until 3:05. We started at that time because the shifts at the factories changed at three o'clock, so this gave people a chance to get off work and stop by and see the game. It was really an automobile city in those days. This was right after the war, and Detroit was a going, growing city.

Mr. Briggs finally put in lights in 1948. Everybody was in kind of awe over it. The year before we had started playing what we called twilight games that started at five o'clock. They were a big success. We drew a lot of people. We had a couple that had to be called because of darkness when they ran a little bit long. But you have to remember, we played games faster in those days, and it didn't get dark until 8:30.

Three hours is a common game today. In those days we had a lot of ball games that were played in two hours. Two and a half hours was a long game. Of course, you have more strategy today, more players being used, certainly more relief pitching. In those days, boy, if you started Hal Newhouser on the mound, you didn't go and get him unless he was really getting bombed because you didn't have anybody in the bullpen better than him. Or better than Trout or Houtteman or Hutchinson.

But today it's a specialized game. You've got your middle reliev-
ers who are poised to go at the first sign of trouble. In the eighth
inning, if you've got a one- or two-run lead, here comes your stopper. They figure it's better than leaving a tired starter in there. And
it is, it is good strategy. You didn't do that back then. You pitched
your starter until he just couldn't pitch anymore, really.

But I remember it very well, that first night game. It was June
15, 1948, and we played the Philadelphia A's. Newhouser pitched.
The first thing that struck me was the brightness of the lights.
I thought, "Man, it's almost like daylight out here." They'd
done a great job arranging the lights. It was the best-lit field I'd ever
played on.

There was a lot of excitement before the game. Almost like a
carnival. The funny thing is, I didn't realize the size of the crowd at
first. In fact, I got a call from the front gate that some friends of mine
from Arkansas were in town and wanted to watch the game. I told
them they shouldn't have a problem getting seats, but they were
told that the game was sold out. I went out on the field and looked
around, and when I saw the size of the crowd, I got a chill. Just
packed in there. We won that game, 4–1, and we continued to draw
big crowds at night.

We had good ball clubs in Detroit. Guys like Vic Wertz, Hoot
Evers, and Johnny Groth were in the outfield, and we had Hal Newhouser, Freddie Hutchinson, Dizzy Trout, Art Houtteman, and Virgil Trucks pitching. We finished second practically every year I was
there. We finished second in '46 and '47, and we almost won the
pennant in 1950.

Freddie Hutchinson was one of the greatest competitors you'd
ever see. At one time he could throw real hard. Then he hurt his
arm and he became one of the best at mixing up his pitches. Absolutely fearless out on the mound. A little bit too much sometimes—
he'd get himself in trouble with the umpires. But he'd win you fourteen, fifteen games every year. Later he managed the Tigers, then the
Cardinals and Cincinnati. He died young. Cancer of the lungs. He
smoked a lot. In fact, his brother's a doctor and he set up a founda-
tion in Seattle, the Fred Hutchinson Cancer Research Center out
there. It's a whole wing of a hospital.

Hutchinson was pitching the day DiMaggio broke my jaw in
Yankee Stadium. This was in 1948. It was the second game of a
doubleheader, and he had 'em beat, 2–1. Freddie had a great change
of pace, so three or four times they'd hit the ball off the end of the
bat and topped it down to third. And now all of a sudden they've

Freddie Hutchinson:
"Absolutely fearless out on the
mound." (Courtesy of the
Burton Historical Collection of
the Detroit Public Library.)

got the bases loaded in the eighth inning with one out and Di-
Maggio's up.

Normally, you'd play DiMaggio just as deep as you can, but I
was playing in. My thinking was if he tops it, I've got to throw home
and cut off the tying run. Anyway, he hit a line shot that hit right in
front of me. It wasn't a pickup or a long hop, but an in-between. I
had to go down to block it. I remember thinking, "Just get in front of
it, knock it down."

It took a wicked hop and came up right at my face. Of course,
your head is the easiest thing in the world to get out of the way;
that's why more batters don't get hit in the head. I whirled, and it
caught me just on the side of the jaw. I fell down, stepped on third,
and I would've had a double play, but I guess I passed out. I don't
remember, but they said they had to pry the ball out of my hand.

But that was pure instinct. I had my mind made up what I was
going to do. I always played double-play situations that way. If they
hit it hard to my left, I'm going to second. If it's hit down the line to
my right, I'm going to step on third. If it's hit slowly in front of me,
I'm going home with it. You've got it planned what you're going to
do before the ball is even hit, then you expect the ball to be hit to
you and you react accordingly. That's why not too many guys catch
them today. They're not expecting the ball to be hit to them.

Vic Wertz? As good a clutch hitter as I've ever seen. Vic Wertz
was an outstanding ball player. You know, I talk a lot on broadcasts
about not getting that runner in from third with less than two outs.

Well, with Vic Wertz, it was a *challenge*. He'd get him in if he had to get hit in the head with the ball. Great clutch hitter. I batted third, Vic generally batted fourth, and Hoot Evers batted fifth.

I remember when Hoot Evers hit that home run to beat the Yankees in 1950. I think there were eleven home runs hit that night, which was a record at the time. The Yankees hit six of those, I believe. It was unbelievable the way they were flying out. Even Dizzy Trout got into the act and hit a grand-slam. We'd fought back from about a seven-run deficit, but then New York scored a couple runs and had a one-run lead going into the bottom of the ninth. We got a man on against Joe Page, who was always tough. He had that good fastball. Evers got hold of one and drove it over DiMaggio's head in center field. It just bounced around out there, and by the time Rizzuto got the relay he'd circled the bases for an inside-the-park home run. There were probably fifty thousand people in Briggs Stadium that night, and the place was just going crazy.

That 1950 season was a heartbreaker. We were tied with the Yankees that year with one week left in the season. We were in Cleveland on a Sunday; the season ended the next Sunday. We felt that if we won that day we had a good shot at the pennant. We went into the bottom of the tenth inning tied, when Cleveland loaded the bases with one out. Luke Easter, a big left-handed hitter, hit a sharp ground ball to Don Kolloway at first base. Instead of throwing home first, Kolloway touched the bag—which is all right, except that Aaron Robinson, our catcher, didn't see him.

So Kolloway brushed the bag—out—and threw home. He had the guy out by ten steps at home. Robinson stepped on the plate and fired it back to first for the double play. But the force play was off when Kolloway touched the bag. The runner from third scored and that was the winning run. Everybody really maligned Aaron, but he just didn't see it. The ball was hit right down the line and Easter, a big left-hander, was probably running inside the line. That put us a game behind and we lost another the last week and finished three games out.

That was the biggest disappointment I ever had. I had primed myself for playing in a World Series, but it wasn't to be. I probably had my best season. I hit .340, had fifty-six doubles, played in every game. I always thought I should've been Most Valuable Player that year, but they gave it to Phil Rizzuto instead. That's one of the advantages of playing in New York, or of playing in a World Series. You've got a showcase. If I would've played in New York and had

the years that I had in Detroit, I would've gone into the Hall of Fame
the first two or three times I had the opportunity. The guys in Detroit who covered the club, like Watson Spoelstra of the *Detroit
News*, they touted me because they saw me play. They knew what I
did for the ball club. I could field, I could hit, I could *win*.

I was a line-drive hitter, a spray hitter. Didn't hit many home
runs. I hit out of a low crouch, crowded the plate all the time. I
never did strike out much. I went several years there where I struck
out less than twenty times each year. In fact, I could never figure out
why I *ever* struck out.

I always played hard. One year Vic Raschi broke my wrist with
a pitch. I came back and Joe DiMaggio broke my jaw with that line
drive. I hated being out of the lineup. Hell, I wanted to *play*. I don't
care if I was playing today and making a million dollars, I'd still
play the same way, because I had a lot of pride. I never wanted
someone watching me on that ball field to go home and say, "I saw
George Kell doggin' it out there today." To me, nothing could hurt
me worse than some kid going home and saying that.

We started going downhill after '50. Attendance was off. The
Tigers had to do something to shake up the ball club, so they set up
a blockbuster of a deal with Boston. Detroit got Johnny Pesky, Walt
Dropo, Fred Hatfield, Bill Wight, and Don Lenhardt, and Boston got
me, Hoot Evers, Johnny Lipon, and Dizzy Trout.

This happened in the middle of '52. Ted Williams was there
when I got to Boston. I played the rest of the season with him, then
in '53 he was called back to the service for the Korean War. Then he
came back at the end of the '53 season. I played with Ted until 1954,
when I was traded to the White Sox.

Ted was a real nice guy, one on one. You'd like him. He's a very
private individual. He's very leery of the press. A lot of things have
been written about him that aren't true. The press just maligned
him. He didn't win the MVP when he won the Triple Crown or the
year he hit .406. Even the first year he was eligible for the Hall of
Fame, he wasn't selected. What the hell, what *are* the qualifica-
tions?

I beat out Ted for the batting title in 1949. Williams and I were
nip and tuck all season, and it all came down to the last day of the
season. I was a couple of points behind and I really thought he'd
win the thing. Boston was in New York, playing for the pennant,
and I knew Ted would be sky-high for it. I figured he'd have a big
day. Meanwhile, we were closing out the season in Detroit against

Cleveland. Bob Lemon was pitching for Cleveland, and he was the toughest pitcher I ever faced.

But I got a double and a single my first couple times up. Then the Indians, who were trying to clinch third place, brought in Bob Feller, and he fanned me the next time up. In the press box, they were keeping up with the averages, and they sent word down to the dugout in the ninth inning that Williams had gone hitless in New York and that I was ahead of him by two-thousandths of a point.

Cleveland was ahead of us, so we had to bat in the bottom of the ninth. There was some question as to whether I was going to hit or not. I was the fourth batter due up. If we went out in order and I didn't bat, I'd win the batting title. Johnny Lipon grounded out, but then Dick Wakefield pinch-hit for the pitcher and got a base hit. There was only one out, so I was gonna have to bat. Red Rolfe was the manager, and he asked me what I wanted to do.

"Do you want to bat?" he asked. I really didn't, but I couldn't see putting in a pinch hitter for me in that situation. So I told him, "I've got to hit."

Then Eddie Lake hit a ground ball to Ray Boone, the shortstop, right near the bag. He stepped on second and threw to first for the double play. I couldn't believe it! Man, I threw my bat about fifty feet in the air, I was so happy. I don't think I'd ever been happier in my life.

I guess they still give a silver bat to anyone who leads all the minor leagues in hitting. I got one in '43 when I hit .396 for Lancaster, and of course I got one in '49 for leading the American League. I was the first player to lead both the minors and major leagues in batting. Isn't that something? Guys like Andy Pafko, Dick Stuart, Lou Novikoff, and Lew Flick, guys who were fantastic in the minor leagues, never did anything in the major leagues. You'd think it would've happened more often, but so far Tony Oliva's the only other one to do it since.

I got into broadcasting almost by luck. I had gone up to the booth my last season in Baltimore when I was hurt with a bad ankle. I did some color work with Ernie Harwell, who was covering the Orioles then. At the end of the 1957 season I told [manager] Paul Richards I was going to quit. My family wanted me to quit, and I had this farmland in Swifton to make a living.

Paul said, "Okay, I'm not going to fight you, but I know where you can pick up $15,000 to $20,000 on weekends, if you're interested. CBS is looking for someone to work with Dizzy Dean and Buddy Blattner on 'The Game of the Week.'"

So I went to New York and auditioned. Hell, I thought they were just going to give me a job, not go to New York and audition. Anyway, they set up a dummy interview and told me to do a little play-by-play. I didn't know anything about it. I just sat there, thinking "wow."

When I came home my wife asked me, "Did you get the job?"

I said, "I don't see how I could get that job, telling me to sit down and start interviewing some guy I never heard of before. I couldn't get that job."

A week later, CBS called and said I had the job.

So I worked for CBS in 1958, just weekends. Then that winter, Mel Ott, who had been broadcasting for Detroit, was killed in an auto accident. The Tigers called and said they'd like me to work for them. I asked if that would be full-time. They said yes. I told them I couldn't do that, but [club owner] Mr. Fetzer kept on wanting me to come up and work, so I finally signed a contract and went to work full-time.

The first year I was there with Van Patrick. At the end of that season Stroh's bought the rights—Goebel's had had it for twenty years—and Stroh's didn't want Van because he'd been with Goebel's. So they released Van and kept me. They asked me who I'd like to bring in with me, and I said Ernie Harwell. So they brought Ernie in from Baltimore and he and I worked together for five years. We did the radio and the TV.

No, it wasn't simulcast. We'd shift booths—we had radio in one and TV in the other—at the end of four and a half innings and trade broadcasts. Then it got to the point where I was just gone too much. My family didn't like it, so in 1964 I quit. Man, they were paying me $50,000 a year then. That's a lot of money to walk away from. But my son was graduating from high school, my daughter was a sophomore, and they just didn't want me gone all the time. So I quit, but Mr. Fetzer said, "Sit tight. We'll work out something."

Then about December that year, ABC called me and said, "We've bought the rights to 'The Game of the Week' and we'd like you to do the play-by-play for us." I said, "That's great. That's weekend work and that's what I like to do." I called Mr. Fetzer and he asked, "Have you agreed to it?" I told him, "Well, I told them I would do it." Mr. Fetzer said, "You'll hear from us by morning."

That night, Hal Middlesworth, the public relations man, called me. "Here's what you do," he said. "Mr. Fetzer's got it set up where we're going to divide our broadcasts. You're going to take over the television and Ernie's got the radio. And it's going to be all weekend broadcasts. Would you rather work here or at ABC?" I said that I'd rather stay with Detroit. So he said, "Here's a night letter you send ABC, telling them that you can't sign a contract because you're going back to Detroit where you belong." So I did, and I've been here ever since.

I enjoy broadcasting so much, it's just a lark to me. I really leave here for a telecast looking forward to it. Can't wait, like looking forward to a golf game. I'm relaxed, I'm in my element. I don't think I've ever been nervous broadcasting. I don't think there's anything in that TV booth that can throw me, because I know what I'm talking about. I go in the booth, they say "You're on," and then it's just, "Good afternoon, everybody. . . ."

If there's anything about it that's tough, it's filling during a rain delay. We dread a one-hour rain delay. At one time we had to fill continuously. I've filled as long as two hours, just talk and talk. Today, we're a bit more sophisticated. We've got films and we can use interviews that aren't dated, so we don't have to fill that much.

I know a lot of people prefer to listen to me and [broadcast partner] Al Kaline talk. I get more mail on that than probably anything else. People write: "I wish it wouldn't have quit raining. We enjoy listening to you and Al talk." And it's not that tough when me and Al are sitting there, talking. You know, we've got so much we can talk about, just like we're in our living rooms. But it can get to be tough when you have to start groping for things to say, hunting up statistics and so on.

Al is more relaxed in the booth now. He has really made great strides. At first he was nervous, unsure of himself, unsure of what he should and shouldn't be saying. He made the statement once, "If I ever get to be as relaxed as Kell up there, I'll be okay. It's not the end of the world with him." I heard that and told Al, "Boy, it shouldn't be the end of the world with you either."

Heck, he was worried about losing his job, even up to last year. I finally told him, "Al, the Detroit Baseball Club is looking, first, for someone who can do the job. You can do the job. Second, they're looking for name recognition, and you've got it. And third, they want a ball player to do the color, and you're a Hall of Famer. You fit every criteria they've got, and as long as you do the job they're not going to be looking for anybody else."

Al said, "Well, I hadn't thought about it that way." And now, I believe, he's a lot more relaxed.

I try not to be a "homer," but I'm sure for the Tigers. I work for them, and I feel that ninety-nine percent of the people I'm talking to are Tiger fans. But when I go on the road and listen to Harry Carey and Jack Brickhouse in Chicago, and Jack Buck in St. Louis, and Phil Rizzuto in New York. . . . These guys scream and yell and rant, "Let's get a rally going!" And I say to myself, Kell, they're not talking about you when they call you a homer, because the last thing I'm going to do is embarrass myself. I guess I'm a little too conservative, but I'm not going to be a cheerleader. I think as far as I go for rooting for the home team is saying, "We're behind," "We need a rally," or "We need to get going." But I'm not going to cry and moan and lead the cheers, and Kaline's not either. He's as conscious of it as I am.

Al is more apt to criticize a player. He tries to get away from it, but I tell him that it's all right, if that's what you want to do. I just try to report the game, I really do. I'm not going to knock 'em, as long as they're *trying.*

Now, I've knocked some ball players that I just absolutely felt were dogging it. But I'm more inclined to ignore those that dog it. I get to the point where I hardly recognize them. Here's this guy, he's at bat, and if he gets a base hit or strikes out I'm not going to brag on him and I'm not going to knock him. Guys that don't hit to right field with the tying run on second and nobody out, who don't even *try.* . . . I'll mention that he should be hitting to right, but if he doesn't, doesn't even try, well, I've already said it once and then I just ignore him. If he's a dog to me I just don't have any use for him. I didn't play baseball that way and I know it's just not the way to play the game.

—December 1980

20

Bob Cain

Robert Max Cain
Born: October 16, 1924, Longford, Kansas
Major-league career: 1949–51 Chicago White Sox, 1951 Detroit Tigers, 1952–53 St. Louis Browns

Though Bob "Sugar" Cain hooked up in several memorable pitching duels during his five seasons in the majors, it was his role in an otherwise forgettable midseason contest between the Tigers and St. Louis Browns in 1951 that earned him a footnote in baseball history. On August 19 that summer, at Sportsman's Park in St. Louis, Cain pitched to three-foot-seven, sixty-five-pound Eddie Gaedel—the only midget ever to bat in a major-league game. Ironically, Cain was traded the following season to the Browns, bringing him in daily contact with the man who dreamed up the stunt, maverick owner Bill Veeck.

After leaving baseball, Bob Cain became a salesman for Kraft Foods. Today he and his wife live in the Cleveland suburb of Euclid, Ohio.

A lot of people that I run across, when they hear my name, they say, "Oh, are you the one who pitched to the midget?"

I say, "Yes, you're right." That's the only way they can remember me.

I think that stunt brought me more notoriety. It's helped in that respect. But I think my accomplishments have been kind of overshadowed by this. I've pitched some awfully good games in my career. I remember my first year with St. Louis, in '52. Bob Feller and I tied up in a pitching duel and we each gave up one hit. I beat him that game, 1–0. I pitched a lot of low-hit games. I pitched a lot of high-hit games, too, I guess. But I was proud to be one of the few able to make the major leagues when I did. There were only eight clubs and two hundred players in each league then. So it was rough getting up there and *staying* there.

I was born in Longford, Kansas, but I was brought up and raised in Salinas, which is just a few miles away. Went to high school in Salinas. I was playing midget-league ball there and then I went into American Legion ball. From there I jumped into professional ball with the Giants organization. I never pitched for New York, but I was in their organization in Jersey City up until '49.

I was traded to Memphis, which was a White Sox farm club, that year. I did pretty good with Memphis, so I came up with the White Sox in '49. The very first game I ever pitched in was at Boston and the first batter I faced was Ted Williams. I'll never forget it. At that particular time we were getting drubbed pretty bad. Fenway Park isn't the greatest park in the world to pitch in, especially for a left-hander. I was lucky enough to strike Williams out the first time I faced him, but I think that was the last time I ever got him out.

The next year in spring training we had about eight left-handed pitchers, and I had to try and break into that group. We had Billy Pierce, Gene Bearden, Mickey Heffner, and a bonus boy, Jack Bruner. Seems like we had nothing but left-handers. But I was fortunate enough in spring training in 1950 to stay with the team.

I played all of '50 with the White Sox. I had a pretty good year, considering the type of ball club we had. I had good luck with the Yankees, who won the World Series that year. I beat them four times that season. As a matter of fact, my first major-league start was in Yankee Stadium, and I think it's still in the record books as one of the worst beatings they've ever had. We beat them, 15–0. From then on I pretty much started for the White Sox.

Then during the first part of the '51 season I was traded to De-

Bob Cain warms up before a
1951 start. (Courtesy of the
Burton Historical Collection of
the Detroit Public Library.)

troit for Saul Rogovin, a pitcher. We had just a mediocre ball club
that season. I think we finished about fifth place. I remember having
a lot of trouble with Cleveland that summer. Bob Feller pitched his
third [career] no-hitter against me down at Cleveland Stadium. I
lost that ball game, 2–1. A short while later, Bob Lemon pitched a
near-perfect game against me in Detroit. Lost again, 2–1. The only
man to get on base was Vic Wertz, who hit a home run around the
eighth or ninth inning. I wound up winning twelve games that year,
all but one with Detroit.

Cain's tenth win of the season came on August 19, 1951, when
the Tigers and St. Louis Browns squared off in a Sunday doubleheader. With the Browns headed for yet another last-place finish,
owner Bill Veeck attracted the largest crowd to Sportsman's Park in
four years—18,369 people—by promising fans "a festival of surprises," including a between-games show of jugglers, jitterbug
dancers, and a ragtime band.

We were playing a doubleheader that Sunday. I was warming
up to pitch the second game when they wheeled a big cake out to
the field. And out of the cake came Eddie Gaedel.

Eddie Gaedel was a twenty-six-year-old Chicago native whose growth was stunted at age three by a thyroid condition. He was working as an errand boy at a Chicago newspaper when Veeck signed him to a one-hundred-dollar contract. "You see, we weren't drawing anybody in those days," Veeck explained years later. "I promised our sponsor, Falstaff Brewery, that if their salesmen would go out and push tickets for this doubleheader, I would do something that would get us national attention. Of course, I didn't know what that would be. But I would think of something."

The whole thing was a promotion for the fiftieth anniversary of the Falstaff Brewery. I had met Bill Veeck before. Had a wooden leg. Lost it in the war. That didn't stop him. He'd go swimming and everything else. He was a great guy. He'd been doing a lot of, well, what some people thought *strange* things in baseball to attract attention.

He'd made a fortune in Cleveland, setting all kinds of attendance records and winning the World Series in 1948. He'd put on all kinds of promotions, like fireworks and "Black Cat Night" and everything else. He was always thinking up some kind of promotion to get the crowds in. In St. Louis, they were desperate for crowds. They weren't drawing anybody. I think if it wasn't for the vendors and players' wives coming to the park, they wouldn't have had anyone in the stands. He irritated a lot of the owners, I think, with the stunts he was pulling. Myself, I would never blame Bill Veeck for trying to draw crowds.

So, knowing Veeck, we all thought it was just a gimmick to show the crowd that he had signed a midget to play on his team. I don't think anyone expected him to actually bat.

That first inning, we went up to bat and St. Louis got our side out. I went out to the mound to start to pitch the bottom half of the first and as I was warming up, Eddie went over and got these little bats. We couldn't understand what was going on. The next thing we know, Eddie's being announced as the batter for Frank Saucier, who was playing center field.

When he came to bat, it was rather embarrassing. He was wearing number 1/8 on his uniform. Ed Hurley, the home plate umpire, at first thought it was a joke—until they officially announced that Eddie Gaedel was batting for Saucier. You could see that Hurley's neck was getting redder all the time. He said, "Let's see a contract."

So he went over to the St. Louis dugout. Zack Taylor, who was managing the Browns, pulled a contract out of his hip pocket and showed it to him. So Hurley came back and just yelled, "Play ball!" At that time, Hurley was the big umpire in the American League. What he said, went.

The crowd thought it was very comical. It got me riled up a little bit, but in a sense it *was* comical. Our catcher, Bob Swift, and I were laughing at first, until Hurley got a little provoked at us and told us to get down to business. As I remember it, we had George Kell at third, Johnny Lipon at shortstop, Jerry Priddy at second, and Dick Kryhoski playing first. They were standing out there on the infield, laughing. Red Rolfe was our manager then. He argued with

"When he came to bat, it was rather embarrassing." Eddie Gaedel, all three feet, seven inches of him, digs in against the Tigers on August 19, 1951. Catcher Bob Swift is on his knees, hoping to give his pitcher a better target. Ed Hurley is the unamused umpire. (Courtesy of the National Baseball Library, Cooperstown, New York.)

Hurley about Eddie batting, but Hurley told him he had a contract. Rolfe didn't give me any instructions. He just watched through the whole thing. Nothing was said, just by Swift. He came out to the mound after Eddie was officially announced. He said, "Let's try to get the ball over to the guy." He said he'd try to give me as low a target as he could.

Swift at first lay down to try and give me a target. Hurley got after him, so he got up on his knees. Eddie spread his feet and squatted down, making an even smaller target. Swift got down as low as he could, but still my pitches were high. I threw four pitches that would've probably been strikes. But on Eddie, of course, they were up around his eyes, and I walked him.

Jim Delsing came in to pinch-run for Gaedel, who gave Delsing a professional pat on the backside as he trotted off the field to cheers. After the game, St. Louis sportswriter Bob Broeg commented to Gaedel that he was what he had always wanted to be— an ex-big leaguer. Gaedel "thrust out his chest and seemed very proud of himself," Broeg recalled. Three weeks later, Gaedel was arrested on a Cincinnati street corner for screaming obscenities. He tried to convince the arresting officer that he was a major-league ball player.

What I was wanting to do was at least get one strike on the kid. I wanted to see if he would swing at a ball. From what we heard later is that Bill Veeck was up on the roof of the stadium with a rifle. He said, "If that little s.o.b. would've swung at a pitch, I would've shot him." As it was, it darn near got me out of the ball game because I turned around and walked another guy, gave up a base hit, and the next thing I knew I was in trouble in the very first inning. But we ended up winning, 6–2.

That midnight, Will Harridge, the American League president, made a ruling that banned midgets. So Bill Veeck said that since they now had a limit on the shortness of a player, he was going out to see if he could find the tallest guy in the world and sign him up. Veeck also mentioned that he wanted Harridge to define exactly what a midget was. He said, "Maybe we can get Phil Rizzuto out of the league."

Bill was a wonderful guy. He never did go find a tall guy. I think he just said that to irritate the commissioner a little more. And the very next season I was pitching for him in St. Louis.

I think one of the reasons I was traded was because I'd had a pretty good record with Detroit in '51 and we had contract trouble. The Tigers only wanted to give me a thousand-dollar raise. I felt I deserved a little better, so I refused to sign the contract they wanted to give me. I just flat refused. It was on Valentine's Day in '52 that four of us from Detroit went for three from St. Louis.

Immediately after that, Bill Veeck called and wanted to know what the trouble was, why I hadn't signed a contract with Detroit. I explained it to him. He asked me what I wanted. I told him and he said over the phone, "Okay, it's yours."

I really don't know how the other owners regarded Veeck, but he treated all the players real good. I thought he was the greatest to play for. If you went out and pitched a good game, he'd send us out and buy us some new shirts or a suit. We won one game against Cleveland, and heavens, the next day we all had a miniature hat with a twenty-five-dollar gift certificate in our lockers. There was another thing Bill did for us boys: every week, each player got a case of beer delivered to his home from Falstaff.

Satchell Paige and I were together down in St. Louis. To me he was one of the greatest guys who ever walked on two feet. A real legend. If he was a day old, he had to be well up in his forties. Regardless of what his age was then, he was still one of the real good pitchers for a few innings. He could still throw the ball right where he wanted. He got in a ball game once in Washington. I think it was in '52. The game wound up going seventeen innings. He pitched eight, nine innings, and even wound up getting a base hit.

Satch mostly pitched relief, so Veeck said he didn't even have to get to the ballpark until about the sixth inning. Satch would be out fishing all day long. There was a few times when we'd come into the clubhouse after a game. We'd undress and go into the shower and there'd be two or three big fish, for heaven's sake, waiting for us. Satch had them laid out in the shower.

Satch had that famous saying, "Don't look back because someone might be gaining on you," and a list of all these other rules. Some of those rules he had, he was the worst offender of the bunch. We used to like him to play hearts with us on train trips. He'd say, "You don't want ol' Satch in your ball game 'cause I'll take all your money." And sure enough, he was lucky in cards. He was either lucky or good or had 'em up his sleeve somewhere.

We had a closeness there with the Browns. We were all trying, but it seemed like sometimes that the harder we tried, the worse we were getting. There just wasn't too much money in St. Louis. Veeck wanted to move the club. The other owners wouldn't let him, but as soon as he sold the club they allowed the new owners to move it to Baltimore. You could tell there was something wrong there. I think Bill was kind of forced out.

After the team moved to Baltimore in '54, I was traded to Philadelphia. I was training down in West Palm Beach, Florida, and that's when I got calcium on my wrist. Right in the wrist joint. I'd pitched five innings against the Brooklyn Dodgers in an exhibition game, pitched very well, and the next day my hand was bent over and I couldn't even straighten out my fingers. They sent me to Toronto to try to work it out, but it never got to the point where I could get my fastball back again.

I finally quit in '56. I'd gone around to Toronto, Birmingham, Memphis, and Oakland. Even when I was ready to quit, Paul Richards, who was managing Baltimore, wanted me to go to Vancouver. I still thought I could come back, but my wife and baby were in Cleveland. I didn't want to go clear across the country to Vancouver, so in the middle of the year I just said, "That's it for baseball," and hung it up completely.

For a long time there, it hurt just to go and sit in the stands and watch baseball. I enjoy baseball, I like watching it on TV or listening to it on the radio, but it still kind of hurts to sit in the stands and watch it—especially with what you see today.

I feel there's pert near half of the fellows playing today who couldn't have played in the major leagues twenty years ago. Some of these players today, if it wasn't for expansion, I don't think they'd ever be up there. There's twenty-six teams, ten more than when I played. At twenty-five players a team, that's 250 big-leaguers who wouldn't have been up there before. I don't blame the players for getting what they can get, but the salaries they're getting are out of this world. I played against some of the greatest players that have ever come along—Williams, DiMaggio, Rizzuto—and they weren't making that kind of money.

It's a big business now. In fact, you can pick up the newspaper just about every day and see what [New York Yankees owner] George Steinbrenner has to say. He's the absolute opposite of Bill Veeck. In fact, there was something this morning about Doyle Alexander. He was making his first start after getting off the disabled list and he got belted around pretty good. Steinbrenner blew his top and told his general manager, "If you can trade him, get rid of him."

I think that's absolutely bush league. I think they've taken a lot of the actual fun out of the game.

For the ten years after his cameo role as baseball's only midget, Eddie Gaedel drifted from job to job, working in promotions for the Buster Brown Shoe Company and Mercury Records and appearing in the Ringling Brothers Circus. Suffering from high blood pressure, an enlarged heart, and injuries brought on by his frequent falls, he died June 18, 1961, in Chicago. Several weeks earlier, Bill Veeck— by then the owner of the Chicago White Sox—had hired him and several other midgets to work as vendors on opening day at Comiskey Park.

I never saw Eddie after I pitched to him, but a few years later we heard that he had died. We went to his funeral. My wife and I both thought, well, since I'd pitched to him, it'd be no more than right to go to Chicago. It really surprised us that no one else from baseball went to the funeral. That's when we became very friendly with his mother, Helen. She told us the whole story about Eddie, about how he'd fallen into the wrong crowd. We didn't know anything about how the whole accident happened.

Eddie had been out drinking and some boys beat him up and robbed him. He came home and foam was coming out of his mouth. They called the family doctor, but he was out of town. They called some other doctor in town and he said, "Oh, he's probably just drunk. Let him sleep." He passed away in his sleep. I think he was just thirty-six.

It really was a pretty sad situation. His mother told us that after Eddie died, someone came over to the house and said he was from the Hall of Fame. She gave him Eddie's little uniform and his bats, but it turned out the guy wasn't really who he said he was. It's a shame. She was real nice. We were in contact with her every Christmas up to about a year ago.

You know, our daughter has the last St. Louis Browns uniform issued. Bill Veeck used to give all the players' babies that were born in St. Louis an authentic uniform, with rubberized pants and cap and a little bat and everything. Our daughter was the last baby born in St. Louis before they moved to Baltimore. Some collectors offered us a thousand dollars for that uniform.

It's really fantastic what some people will offer for some of that stuff. We've had people writing for my baseball hats and gloves and shoes. They used to give us players a thousand packs of bubble gum each year. The wives would chew the bubble gum at the park and just throw the baseball cards away. Today some of those cards are worth twenty-five dollars apiece. You don't think of those things at the time, really.*

There wasn't even too much publicity then about the midget. It seems like I get more questions now when it comes around the anniversary time than I did at the actual time. If it'd happened today I'd be on talk shows and everything. Television is what would really build it up. But back then there wasn't a whole lot of hullabaloo put on about Eddie Gaedel. He was just another one of Bill Veeck's surprises.

—*July 1982*

---

*Baseball cards were first issued in the nineteenth century as premiums by manufacturers of candy and tobacco products. The pairing of gum and baseball cards first became popular in the early 1930s. The giant in the field since the early fifties has been Topps Chewing Gum, Inc., of Brooklyn, New York. Today the value of a 1952 Topps Mickey Mantle baseball card ranges from about seven hundred dollars for one in poor condition to seven thousand dollars for one in mint condition. A Bob Cain card from the same set will fetch between fifteen dollars (poor) and one hundred fifty dollars (mint).

21

George Lerchen

George Edward Lerchen
Born: December 1, 1922, Detroit, Michigan
Major-league career: 1952 Detroit Tigers, 1953 Cincinnati Reds

In a way, George Lerchen embodies the growth of professional baseball in Detroit. His grandfather arrived from Germany in the nineteenth century, when the game was still largely an amateur affair. An uncle played briefly for the Boston Red Sox shortly after the turn of the century, while his father played sandlot games in the shadow of Navin Field. Lerchen's experiences as a vagabond minor-leaguer in the 1940s and 1950s are typical of the marginal ball player stubbornly chasing a dream in baseball's golden age. For a time, Lerchen captured and lived his dream, playing in thirty-six major-league games for the Tigers and Reds in the early fifties.

Lerchen, who became a building contractor after leaving baseball, today lives with his wife and daughter in Garden City, Michigan.

My whole life has been spent around the ballpark. You know the corner where Mexican Village is? Eighteenth and Bagley? Well, that's where I grew up, at 1746 Eighteenth Street.

What today is Cochrane Avenue used to be National. My dad's sister, my Aunt Fanny, lived on National back then, so I used to spend my summers there. The games started at 3:30 in the afternoon back then, and the players would park their cars along National. A whole line of them—Greenberg, Mickey Cochrane, Pete Fox, Gehringer. Home plate was at the corner of Michigan and National, so a lot of foul balls would land on the street. I used to look out for the players' cars, maybe wipe their windshields off, whatever. After the game the players would come out, maybe tip me a quarter, fifty cents. All except Gehringer. He'd just get into his car and drive away.

About twenty years later, when I played my only season with the Tigers, I signed my contract with Charlie. He was the general manager then. I said, "Do you remember that red-headed kid who used to watch your car all the time?"

Charlie said, "Yes, I remember."

I said, "Well, that was me. You never paid me and now I want my money."

I'm being tough on Charlie. Really, if you grew up in my era and were as enthused about baseball as I was, Charlie would have to be your idol. Good player, good hitter, graceful. You never had the good fortune to see him play, but I'm telling you, he made plays at second base you wouldn't believe. You'd say to yourself, "Where'd he come from?" Then you'd go home and try to do the same thing. In fact, I was right-handed, but I learned how to bat lefty because of Charlie. I copied his stance.

Charlie was quiet, meticulous. He shined his own shoes. Nobody touched anything of his. I remember when I was a kid going to the park, the other players would undress and throw their stuff all over the clubhouse. But Charlie was a perfectionist. Everything had to be just so—glove here, shoes there, bat over there. He was polished. He carried himself.

When Gehringer was playing second base, he could almost read in that hitter's eyes where he was going to hit the ball. Honest to God. I worked out once with Charlie when I was in high school. The Tigers had thoughts about making me an infielder. So I stood there and watched ground balls go by in batting practice. Goslin, Coch-

George Lerchen as a Toledo
Mud Hen.

rane, Fox—they could rip that ball. They were going through there
like bullets.

Finally I said, "Charlie, tell me something. I've been noticing
the balls go through there in batting practice. Do they go through
that fast in a game?"

Charlie said, "They go through faster."

I said, "I'll see ya. I'm an outfielder."

And that's what I was, all through school and in the pros. My
first pro team was Jamestown, a Class D team, in 1942. I lost 1943,
'44, and '45 to the service, and then I went to Buffalo in '46. They
sent me to Williamsport in '47. In 1948 I played in Flint. The Tigers
bought my contract in '49, and I played in Toledo from 1949 to
1951. I spent one winter, 1950, in Puerto Rico.

Let's see, then it was the Tigers in '52. Then I went to Tulsa and
Cincinnati, and in '53 Cincinnati sold me to Portland. Portland sold
me to the Cardinals, and the Cardinals sent me to Houston. I played
'54 and '55 in Houston. Then Houston sold me to the Phillies. They
sent me to Miami, and I finally quit in the middle of '56.

Miami released me. They signed a kid by the name of Dave
Mann. I was making good money—seventeen hundred a month—
and Mann was making three hundred a month. They said, "George,

we've got to let you go." Bill Veeck was the general manager. He told me, "George, I've spent a couple hundred dollars on phone calls trying to get you a job. Nobody wants you." I said, "Yeah, nobody wants me because I'm making good money." But that's how it was in my era. You were nothing but a piece of meat.

My grandfather came to Detroit from Essen, Germany, in—I'm guessing now—sometime in the 1870s. The family farm was on Hubbell and Grand River. That's where all the clan got together. My father, George, was born February 11, 1880. My dad tried to play ball, but his younger brother, my Uncle Bert, was the ball player in the family. Good shortstop. He played a little for the Red Sox in 1910. He's in the books: "Dutch" Lerchen. Good field, no hit. He'd laugh about it. He'd come and see me play when I was a kid. He'd say, "If I could just hit like you, George, I'd still be up there. I couldn't hit a balloon with a paddle." When he got finished playing ball, he became a meat inspector for the City of Detroit. Know why? Because of the farm and the cattle.

My dad bought a house on Eighteenth and Bagley a couple years before he got married. The Michigan Central Railroad Depot was behind us. We had a big, long house. One day a couple fellas came up to my dad on the street. They both worked at the railroad and they asked my father if he knew where they could find a room for the night. My mother and dad just got married. Dad said, "Go down to the end of the street. We've got two extra bedrooms. We'll put you up for the night." They stayed thirty-eight years.

See, in those days it wasn't nothing to take on boarders to make ends meet. Scottie was a baggage man. He was from Scotland. Frenchie worked for the railroad express. He was from Montreal. What a pair. Argued like cats and dogs. Scottie would say, "Today's Wednesday," and Frenchie would say, "No, it's Thursday." One would say, "This is black," and the other would say, "No, it's white." You wouldn't believe it. Never got married. Never moved out. They both died in our house.

We were a close-knit crew. I'll say one thing about our family: you had to go to the aunts' and uncles' houses every Saturday and Sunday. That was a ritual. Everybody had a big family. You'd go to someone's house and it looked like Grand Central Station. My Uncle Guy was treasurer of Highland Park, and he had a lot at Elizabeth Lake. We built a picnic table out there that seated thirty-five people. It'd take you half an hour to walk around it.

Detroit was a lot smaller then. West Grand Boulevard was the city limits. A long way off. If you had a house on Grand Boulevard, you were living in style. My Aunt Mabel lived on Woodward and Six Mile. We'd visit her every third Sunday—making the rounds, you know—and I'd say, "Gee, do we really have to go all the way out there?"

We were fortunate. My dad worked all the time, even during the depression, because he worked for the government. He was a United States deputy marshal. So consequently, we weren't one of those families that was destitute during the thirties.

My dad tried to play ball. They'd play at this one empty lot around the corner from our house on Bagley, and he'd play the out-field. He was short and stocky. He would've done better to be a po-liceman. Really. That was his thrill, getting dressed to go to work in the morning—putting the suit coat on, his gun, his badge. He was so proud of that. My dad helped me a lot. He would hit me fly balls by the hour.

My Aunt Mary had a little confectionery store on Bagley and Seventeenth. I used to wash the windows. Instead of a quarter,

A sandlot game in Detroit in 1930: "We collected all the lawn mowers in the neighborhood so we could cut down the weeds and play." (Courtesy of the Burton Historical Collection of the Detroit Public Library.)

she'd give me one of those twenty-five-cent baseballs. You'd hit it three times and the goddamn sawdust would come out and we'd have to wrap it up with tape. The dollar ball was better. It lasted at least three days longer.

So I got an idea. While I washed the windows I'd take the dollar ball and switch it with the quarter ball. When I was finished, she'd say, "Okay, take your ball," and *swoosh*, I grabbed it. Here I think I'm fooling someone. Finally one day Aunt Mary said, "I know what you've been doing, Georgie. It's okay, don't worry." I said, "Yeah, I'm sorry. But those quarter balls, they don't last long, Aunt Mary."

Baseball was easy for me. I was blessed with speed, I could hit, and I loved the game. I remember when I was small, there used to be an old field on Twenty-first and Vernor Highway where the weeds were so bad we'd lose the ball. We collected all the lawn mowers in the neighborhood so we could cut down the weeds and play.

When I was a kid I'd spend my summers at my Aunt Fanny's and Uncle Dick's. They lived on National, right across the street from Navin Field. What made it nice for me was that they always left this one gate open. I got to know Neil Conway, who was the grounds keeper. He was a great friend of my Uncle Dick. So they never stopped me from going in.

Just about every morning I'd shag fly balls for Gehringer, Goslin, Greenberg, whoever. Especially Greenberg. He'd use American Federation pitchers like Ace Lee and Clarence Fuller. He'd pay them a few bucks to come down to the park at ten in the morning and pitch to him. The only thing that got me mad was, that damn Greenberg, he'd hit buckets of balls. He'd say, "Oh, I'm gonna let you hit." Damn it, he'd hit all the balls in the stands, and while you were out getting them, he'd leave and so would the pitcher.

But that Jew, boy . . . I want to tell you something—he was not a good ball player. He made himself a good ball player from practice. He'd be out there in the morning for an hour and a half, two hours. I seen him somedays, honest to God, he'd have blisters like this on his hands from hitting. He'd put them in a bucket of benzoin and then go out that afternoon and rip that ball like a bullet.

I started hanging around the clubhouse and they got to know me. As I got older, I started working out with the Tigers. In high school, I'd come over and they'd let me take early batting practice. In my junior year, the Tigers really got interested in me. I'd come over maybe three times a week and shag ground balls with them. I graduated from Western High, right by the Ambassador Bridge. Wish Egan used to stay at the Book-Cadillac. One day he walked over to our house and said, "Would you like to sign with the Tigers?" I said, "Yeah." I was only eighteen years old. My dad had to sign for me.

I went to an all-veteran team in Class D. Jamestown, New York. They had just won the pennant the year before. We had a guy playing left field, Johnny Newman, who had to weigh 240 pounds if he weighed an ounce. He comes over to me before my first game and says, "Hey rookie. You chew tobacco?" I'd never chewed tobacco in my life. He says, "Here you go." Oh man, I hit a ball to right field, and as I was running around second I turned around to see where the ball was. I tripped over the bag and swallowed that chew. Boy, you talk about a sick dog!

Family and friends gather in an empty lot near the Lerchen home on Bagley for a game of baseball and this informal group shot, circa 1917. George Lerchen, Sr., stands seventh from the left in the back row.

The next day, I bought me a pack of Black Jack gum. Newman came up to me and said, "Hey rook, you got yourself some chew?" And I spit that black juice out and he said, "Okay, rook." I think he would've shot me if he'd known it was Black Jack gum.

I had a good year. Hit .312, played in the All-Star Game, and then I got drafted. Spent the next three years in the navy. I played for Jamestown when I came back, then I went to Buffalo and Williamsport. The low minors, you wouldn't believe it. We used to go from Williamsport to Hartford, Connecticut. It'd take us twelve hours. The bus was so bad, we had to get out and walk alongside it when it went uphill. That's the way it was.

In 1948 I played Class A ball for Flint in the Central League. That was a good ball club, the best I ever played on. I hit .355, we won the pennant. We had a shortstop, Clem Koshorek. Called him "Scooter." Good ball player. He made a demand for more pay one day. They sent his request to Red Rolfe, who was the Tigers' farm director then. It was turned down, so Koshorek quit.

I was in that crazy era where if you quit a team and they didn't want to release you, then you were barred from playing for anyone. If you wanted, you could go on the voluntary retired list, which meant you couldn't play for anyone for five years. The Tigers didn't want Koshorek back in their organization. They finally reinstated him and sent him to Charleston, a Class A team in the Sally League. Later he played a couple seasons with the Pittsburgh Pirates.

I remember one year in Toledo where I sent my contract back twice to the Tigers. I was holding out for more money. I wanted another thousand dollars. I think I was making about eight thousand. I got a telegram back from Billy Evans, who was the general manager. Billy always had the attitude that you should pay *him* for the privilege of playing. It said, "Sorry that you have seen fit to reject your second contract. Rest assured I have no intention of offering third one." How do you like that? Kind of abrupt. I said the hell with it. So I signed what they offered me and sent it back. I did go over and try to renegotiate. I came home and my wife, Anne, said, "How'd you make out?" I said, "I didn't."

You were like a cow. A piece of meat. They did anything they wanted. A couple of times the Tigers had a chance to sell me, and they said no. Pittsburgh—I forget what year—wanted me, and they offered the Tigers a pretty good piece of change. But they said no.

At the time the Tigers had Vic Wertz, Hoot Evers, and Johnny

Groth in the outfield. The ball club would tell me, "George, you're the fourth man." I'd say, "How about Charlie Keller and Pat Mullin?" They'd say, "Oh, we don't care about them."

You had two alternatives and they put them to me. Do you want to sit on the bench in the big leagues, in case one of them gets hurt, in which case you might get into the lineup? Okay, you may sit on the bench for two months and get out of synch. Or do you want to go to Toledo, play every day, with the chance we'll call you up?

So you're much better off going to Toledo, keeping your rhythm. But the bastards never got hurt. Consequently, I kept hanging in there, hanging in there, hanging in there. They wouldn't sell me, they wouldn't release me, so what are you going to do? We didn't have the options like players do now. And by the time you're ready to make a move, they tell you that you're too old. Or they'd come up with the old, "Well, you haven't got enough experience." That's when I finally did get mad.

I told them, "How the hell am I going to get experience if I'm not here? All I hear is that I haven't got any experience and you keep sending me to Toledo." I'm having good years, but they wouldn't even bring me up at the end of the season, when the rosters expanded.

I remember going in to talk to Charlie Gehringer when he was the general manager. I could go into Charlie's office at eight o'clock in the morning and still be talking at ten o'clock and he wouldn't have said a word. I'd be showing him statistics—twenty-six home runs, ninety-eight RBI, .286 average. He'd say, "Well, it wasn't up here." That's when I said, "Well, Charlie, I can't prove it up here if I'm down there." I hate to say it, but Charlie was not the managerial type. Finally, I signed. Charlie said he'd give me an extra two thousand dollars if I made the team out of spring training. And on opening day in '52, I was with the Tigers. Red Rolfe was the manager.

My first game was against St. Louis. I faced Ned Garver. I guessed fastball and I hit it to dead centerfield. If I'd pulled it I would've had a home run. It was full disaster after that. I think I went eleven times without a hit. I know we went to Cleveland and in a three-game series I faced Bob Lemon, Bob Feller, and Mike Garcia. Then we went to New York, and I think I pinch-hit against Allie Reynolds and Vic Raschi. Then we went to Washington and Red says, "You're going to play." The first time up, I hit a home run. Off some Spanish guy. I can't think of his name now. "Man, oh man," I thought, "that's great. First hit." Glad to get that off my chest. Hit it to right field. The shortstop yelled to me, "Whatdya running so hard for? It's over the fence." I said, "I don't care."

In July the Tigers sold me to Buffalo. What were my feelings about that? What could I say? See, I got shafted there. At that time you got three major- and three minor-league options. The Tigers used up all my options sending me back and forth between Buffalo and Williamsport and Flint. Then the Tigers optioned me to Toledo in '49, '50, and '51, so that used up the major-league options. If they hadn't sold me, I would've been claimed on waivers. Paul Richards, who was managing the White Sox, called and said, "George, we're going to claim you." I felt pretty good about that. I thought, "Gee, I'm going to be claimed." But I wound up in Buffalo.

I went to Tulsa in '53. Anne had just gotten to Tulsa when Cincinnati called me up. She had to turn right around and drive back to Detroit. She had just rented a house and we had to move. She was really hot then, boy. I was in Shreveport, Louisiana, when the club called and said, "George, you've got to report to Cincinnati." I said, "No, I've got to go back to Tulsa." They said, "No, you've got to be in Cincinnati tomorrow."

So I flew all night to get to Cincinnati on a Sunday morning. No clothes, and I had three layovers. I went right to the ballpark. Rogers Hornsby was the manager. He said, "Go take batting practice." Ted Kluszewski gave me a bat and I was so tired I couldn't even get it up to my shoulder. In the meantime, Anne's back in Tulsa, packing up and heading back to Detroit with our three-year-old daughter. But that's baseball back then. That's the way they wanted it, so that's the way you did it. In that era, they told you how, when, and what to do. And you did it. If you didn't—well, like Koshorek, we'll suspend you.

I was hitting .294 in Cincinnati and Hornsby wouldn't even talk to me. It seemed Cincinnati was in turmoil all the time. They couldn't make up their minds who they wanted on the ball club. If a guy came up and went oh for three, they'd say, "Get rid of him and find someone else." They used to say, "Two coming, two playing, and two on the way."

Cincinnati sold me to Portland. Portland sold me to the Cardinals and they wanted to send me to Houston. I finally said, "Bullshit. I quit." I came home and told Anne. She said, "Well, that's up to you."

Houston called me up a couple of times, asking if I was going to report. I said, "No, that's it." Then the outfielder they bought from Fort Worth got killed in a car accident on the way to Houston, so they said, "George, we'll give you more money." And I said, what the hell.

I get down there, get all settled, and then I get into a cab to go to the ballpark to sign my contract. The cab driver says, "Mister, you don't want to go there. That club is terrible. They are so far in the cellar it's pitiful." I thought to myself, "Turn around and take me back to the hotel. I'm going back to Detroit. I don't need this." But I reported. That evening I played about five innings. It must've been a hundred degrees. My eyeballs were turning around from the heat.

But you know what? We started off in last place, and we wound up winning the pennant and the Dixie World Series that year. Houston bought Bob Boyd from the White Sox to play first base. Left-handed hitter. He could really rap that ball, boy. He'd tell me when he was going up to bat, "Going over to Miss Mary's house, George. Going over to Miss Mary's."

The next year we played the Atlanta Crackers in the Dixie Series. You know how they beat us? Their pitchers—Don McMahon, Leo Cristante, Glenn Thompson—knocked our colored guys down. They decked Bob Boyd. Willie Brown, our right fielder, liked to bend over the plate. They aimed a few at his head. The players' share for losing was $653.22 each. Here's the pay stub. By the time the government got done with it, I got $536.64. How do you like that? Big deal, huh?

I played a couple more years. I always promised myself that I would quit if I ever got released. So when Miami released me in '56, that was it.

I had to make a living. My dad, being who he was, was bound and determined that I would be a policeman when I grew up. But I hated guns. I think that if I hadn't been a ball player, I would've been a builder. I was always interested in that. When I was small, I'd help my father build a porch. I'd saw the wood. I'd cut some short and I'd cut some crooked. . . . Once, when my dad took a prisoner to Kansas, I tore down the old garage. I was about twelve, thirteen. Just wanted to see how it was built, you know. That's what I did when I got out of baseball. I'm a general contractor now. Remember when the press box at Tiger Stadium burned in 1974? They put in a new one. I was the contractor on that job.

I'd love to be playing today with the kind of money they're making. Are you kidding? But when I played, that was a whole different era. You know, I still play some ball, old-timers games and softball, whatever. I don't know if you know Ray Miller, who still plays, too. I'm sixty-seven, so Ray's two, three years younger than me. He can still sting that ball. He probably was one of the finest hitters around from my era. But his family didn't have any money and he had to go to work. He started off in pro ball, but he wasn't moved quick enough. See, there were certain organizations that moved you quick. They moved you from Class D to B to Double-A ball. Other organizations, you'd stay in D for two years, B for two years. They didn't move you. Gee, my first salary when I went away in 1942 was only $125 a month. My parents had to send me money to live. So consequently, one day Ray Miller finally said, "Gee, I need a job," and that was it for baseball.

I look at it this way. Maybe—maybe—if I'd gotten to the big leagues when I was younger, it might've been different. Let's say I wouldn't have lost three years to the service. . . . But I'm fortunate. Maybe I wasn't that good of a ball player, but I played. And there's only a few that got to the big leagues in that era. I feel that the accomplishment was something. I set out as a kid wanting to play in the big leagues, so whatever I did when I got up there, it satisfied me.

—March 1989

Acknowledgments
and Book List

Although a full chapter of their reminiscences did not make it into this book, I am grateful to former ball players Eldon Auker, Ray Fisher, Ray Hayworth, Charles "Red" House, Art Houtteman, Otis Johnson, Ray Sheppard, Heinie Schuble, Joyner "Jo-Jo" White, and Archie Yelle for sharing memories of their careers with me and providing much background material on baseball life in general. In addition, the recollections of John "Red" Cole, John Glover, Fran Harris, Edgar Hayes, Bill May, Ted Rasberry, Jackie Roggin, Mike Roggin, Stanley "Lefty" Roginski, Nettie Stearnes, Betty Martin Steen, Jeanne Tenge-Shook, and Fred Williams were invaluable in helping me write the narrative portion of this book. Thanks also to Gene Berlin, who explained the background of Mack Stadium to me, and to Dick Clark, a baseball historian who shared his statistical research on the Detroit Stars.

For assistance in photo research, I would like to thank the indefatigable Pat Kelly, photo collections manager at the National Baseball Library in Cooperstown, New York; David Poremba and Noel Van Gordon of the Burton Historical Collection, Detroit Public Library; Charles "Bud" Manning of Manning Brothers Commercial Photographers; the public relations staff of the Detroit Tigers; private collector John A. Conde; and the ever gracious Jeannette Bartz of the *Detroit News*.

Most of my research was conducted at the main branch of the Detroit Public Library and involved heavy use of microfilmed cop-

369

ies of local newspapers, 1920–1952. In addition, I found the following books to be of great help.

Baseball (General)

Asinof, Eliot. *Eight Men Out: The Black Sox and the 1919 World Series.* New York, 1963.
Broeg, Bob. *The Pilot Light and the Gas House Gang.* St. Louis, 1980.
Creamer, Robert W. *Babe.* New York, 1974.
Einstein, Charles, ed. *The Baseball Reader.* New York, 1980. This compilation of classic baseball writing includes Al Stump's fascinating account of Ty Cobb's final days.
Fleming, G. H. *The Dizziest Season.* New York, 1984. Contemporary news accounts of the 1934 St. Louis Cardinals' championship season, including the World Series.
Goldstein, Richard. *Spartan Seasons.* New York, 1980. Baseball during World War II.
Green, Paul. *Forgotten Fields.* Waupaca, Wis., 1984.
Holtzman, Jerome. *No Cheering in the Press Box.* New York, 1973. An earthy, anecdotal collection of interviews with a score of famous sportswriters from the 1920s through 1940s. Unfortunately, no Detroit writers are represented.
Holway, John B. *Blackball Stars.* Westport, Conn., 1988. Contains interviews with former Detroit Stars Ray Dandridge and Turkey Stearnes.
———. *Voices from the Great Negro Baseball Leagues.* New York, 1975.
Honig, Donald. *Baseball between the Lines.* New York, 1976. Includes an insightful oral history of Dick Wakefield.
———. *Baseball When the Grass Was Real.* New York, 1975.
James, Bill. *The Bill James Historical Baseball Abstract.* New York, 1986.
Kirk, Troy. *Collector's Guide to Baseball Cards.* Radnor, Pa., 1990.
Langford, Walter M. *Legends of Baseball.* South Bend, Ind., 1987.
Lieb, Fred. *Baseball as I Have Known It.* New York, 1977.
Lowenfish, Lee, and Tony Lupien. *The Imperfect Diamond.* New York, 1980. A history of baseball labor relations.
Lowry, Philip J. *Green Cathedrals.* Cooperstown, N.Y., 1986.
Mead, William B. *Even the Browns.* Chicago, 1978. A recap of the

1944 American League pennant race between St. Louis and Detroit.

Peterson, Robert. *Only the Ball Was White*. Englewood Cliffs, N.J., 1970.

Reichler, Joseph L., ed. *The Baseball Encyclopedia: The Complete and Official Record of Major League Baseball*. 8th ed. New York, 1990. The title of this 2,781-page record book, first published by Macmillan in 1969, says it all.

Ritter, Lawrence S. *The Glory of Their Times*. New York, 1984. Originally published in 1966, this collection of oral histories is arguably the finest baseball book ever. Of interest to Detroit fans are chapters on Tiger stars Hank Greenberg, Goose Goslin, Davy Jones, and Wahoo Sam Crawford.

Rogosin, Donn. *Invisible Men: Life in Baseball's Negro Leagues*. New York, 1983.

Seymour, Harold. *Baseball: The Early Years*. New York, 1960.

———. *Baseball: The Golden Years*. New York, 1971.

Smith, Curt. *Voices of the Game*. South Bend, Ind., 1986. An exhaustive but uneven overview of baseball broadcasting from 1921 to the present.

Sobol, Ken. *Babe Ruth and the American Dream*. New York, 1974.

Thorn, John, and Pete Palmer, eds. *Total Baseball*. New York, 1989. A 2,294-page record book.

Tygiel, Jules. *Baseball's Great Experiment*. New York, 1983. A well-researched and highly readable account of Jackie Robinson and the desegregation of baseball.

Voigt, David Quentin. *American Baseball*. 3 vols. University Park, Pa., 1983.

Baseball (Detroit)

Alexander, Charles C. *Ty Cobb*. New York, 1984. The best of a rather thin batch of Cobb biographies.

Cobb, Ty, with Al Stump. *My Life in Baseball*. New York, 1961.

Falls, Joe. *Detroit Tigers*. New York, 1975.

Falls, Joe, and Gerald Astor. *The Detroit Tigers: An Illustrated History*. New York, 1989. This book, flawed by shopworn anecdotes and incorrect captions, is redeemed by a color insert that illustrates the evolution of the Tigers' uniform since the nineteenth century.

Greenberg, Hank, with Ira Berkow. *Hank Greenberg: The Story of My Life.* New York, 1989. A candid, revealing look at baseball in the thirties and forties, including the Tigers' four pennant winners. Completed by Berkow after Greenberg's death, it is easily the finest autobiography by a Tiger from any era.

Hawkins, John C. *This Date in Detroit Tigers History.* New York, 1981.

Hill, Art. *I Don't Care If I Never Come Back.* New York, 1980. Hill writes with affection and wit about Tigers past and present, including such favorites as Gee Walker, Harry Heilmann, and Dizzy Trout.

Lieb, Fred. *The Detroit Tigers.* New York, 1946. Though it only goes through the 1945 season and lacks an index, this book remains the best single volume on baseball in Detroit.

McCallum, John D. *Ty Cobb.* New York, 1975.

Sullivan, George. *The Detroit Tigers.* New York, 1985. Career statistics of all Tiger players and year-by-year summaries of every season since 1901.

Tiger Stadium: Where Baseball Belongs. Detroit, 1988. A booklet published by the Tiger Stadium Fan Club.

Detroit History

Angelo, Frank. *On Guard: A History of the Detroit Free Press.* Detroit, 1981.

Astor, Gerald. *". . . And A Credit to His Race."* New York, 1974. One of the better biographies of Joe Louis.

Babson, Steve. *Working Detroit.* New York, 1984.

Bingay, Malcolm. *Detroit Is My Home Town.* New York, 1946.

———. *Of Me I Sing.* New York, 1949.

Clive, Alan. *State of War: Michigan in World War II.* Ann Arbor, Mich., 1979.

Conot, Robert. *American Odyssey.* New York, 1974. The finest single-volume history of Detroit.

Detroit Public Library. *Detroit in Its World Setting.* Detroit, 1953.

Engelmann, Lawrence. *Intemperance.* New York, 1979.

Fine, Sidney. *Frank Murphy: The Detroit Years.* Ann Arbor, Mich., 1975.

———. *Frank Murphy: The New Deal Years.* Chicago, 1979.

Halberstam, David. *The Reckoning.* New York, 1986.

Holli, Melvin, ed. *Detroit*. New York, 1976. A documentary history of the city.

Lacey, Robert. *Ford: the Men and the Machine*. Boston, 1986.

Lewis, David L. *The Public Image of Henry Ford*. Detroit, 1976.

Lochbiler, Don. *Detroit's Coming of Age, 1873–1973*. Detroit, 1973.

Lodge, John C. *I Remember Detroit*. Detroit, 1949.

Lutz, William W. *The News of Detroit*. Boston, 1973.

McGehee, Scott, and Susan Watson, eds. *Blacks in Detroit*. Detroit, 1980.

Osgood, Dick. *Wyxie Wonderland*. Bowling Green, Ohio, 1981. An anecdotal history of radio/TV station WXYZ.

Peterson, Joyce Shaw. *American Automobile Workers 1900–1933*. New York, 1987.

Woodford, Frank B., and Arthur M. Woodford. *All Our Yesterdays*. Detroit, 1969.

Index

Titles in the Great Lakes Books Series

Freshwater Fury: Yarns and Reminiscences of the Greatest Storm in Inland Navigation, by Frank Barcus, 1986 (reprint)

Call It North Country: The Story of Upper Michigan, by John Bartlow Martin, 1986 (reprint)

The Land of the Crooked Tree, by U. P. Hedrick, 1986 (reprint)

Michigan Place Names, by Walter Romig, 1986 (reprint)

Luke Karamazov, by Conrad Hilberry, 1987

The Late, Great Lakes: An Environmental History, by William Ashworth, 1987 (reprint)

Great Pages of Michigan History from the Detroit Free Press, 1987

Waiting for the Morning Train: An American Boyhood, by Bruce Catton, 1987 (reprint)

Michigan Voices: Our State's History in the Words of the People Who Lived it, compiled and edited by Joe Grimm, 1987

Danny and the Boys, Being Some Legends of Hungry Hollow, by Robert Traver, 1987 (reprint)

Hanging On, or How to Get through a Depression and Enjoy Life, by Edmund G. Love, 1987 (reprint)

The Situation in Flushing, by Edmund G. Love, 1987 (reprint)

A Small Bequest, by Edmund G. Love, 1987 (reprint)

The Saginaw Paul Bunyan, by James Stevens, 1987 (reprint)

The Ambassador Bridge: A Monument to Progress, by Philip P. Mason, 1988

Let the Drum Beat: A History of the Detroit Light Guard, by Stanley D. Solvick, 1988

An Afternoon in Waterloo Park, by Gerald Dumas, 1988 (reprint)

Contemporary Michigan Poetry: Poems from the Third Coast, edited by Michael Delp, Conrad Hilberry, and Herbert Scott, 1988

Over the Graves of Horses, by Michael Delp, 1988

Wolf in Sheep's Clothing: The Search for a Child Killer, by Tommy McIntyre, 1988

Copper-Toed Boots, by Marguerite de Angeli, 1989 (reprint)

Detroit Images: Photographs of the Renaissance City, edited by John J. Bukowczyk and Douglas Aikenhead, with Peter Slavcheff, 1989

Hangdog Reef: Poems Sailing the Great Lakes, by Stephen Tudor, 1989

Detroit: City of Race and Class Violence, revised edition, by B. J. Widick, 1989

Deep Woods Frontier: A History of Logging in Northern Michigan, by Theodore J. Karamanski, 1989

Orvie, The Dictator of Dearborn, by David L. Good, 1989

Seasons of Grace: A History of the Catholic Archdiocese of Detroit, by Leslie Woodcock Tentler, 1990

The Pottery of John Foster: Form and Meaning, by Gordon and Elizabeth Orear, 1990

The Diary of Bishop Frederic Baraga: First Bishop of Marquette, Michigan, edited by Regis M. Walling and Rev. N. Daniel Rupp, 1990

Walnut Pickles and Watermelon Cake: A Century of Michigan Cooking, by Larry B. Massie and Priscilla Massie, 1990

The Making of Michigan, 1820–1860: A Pioneer Anthology, edited by Justin L. Kestenbaum, 1990

America's Favorite Homes: A Guide to Popular Early Twentieth-Century Homes, by Robert Schweitzer and Michael W. R. Davis, 1990

Beyond the Model T: The Other Ventures of Henry Ford, by Ford R. Bryan, 1990

Life after the Line, by Josie Kearns, 1990

Michigan Lumbertowns: Lumbermen and Laborers in Saginaw, Bay City, and Muskegon, 1870–1905, by Jeremy W. Kilar, 1990

Detroit Kids Catalog: The Hometown Tourist, by Ellyce Field, 1990

Waiting for the News, by Leo Litwak, 1990 (reprint)

Detroit Perspectives, edited by Wilma Wood Henrickson, 1991

Life on the Great Lakes: A Wheelsman's Story, by Fred W. Dutton, edited by William Donohue Ellis, 1991

Copper Country Journal: The Diary of Schoolmaster Henry Hobart, 1863–1864, by Henry Hobart, edited by Philip P. Mason, 1991

John Jacob Astor: Business and Finance in the Early Republic, by John Denis Haeger, 1991

Survival and Regeneration: Detroit's American Indian Community, by Edmund J. Danziger, Jr., 1991

Steamboats and Sailors of the Great Lakes, by Mark L. Thompson, 1991

Cobb Would Have Caught It: The Golden Years of Baseball in Detroit, by Richard Bak, 1991